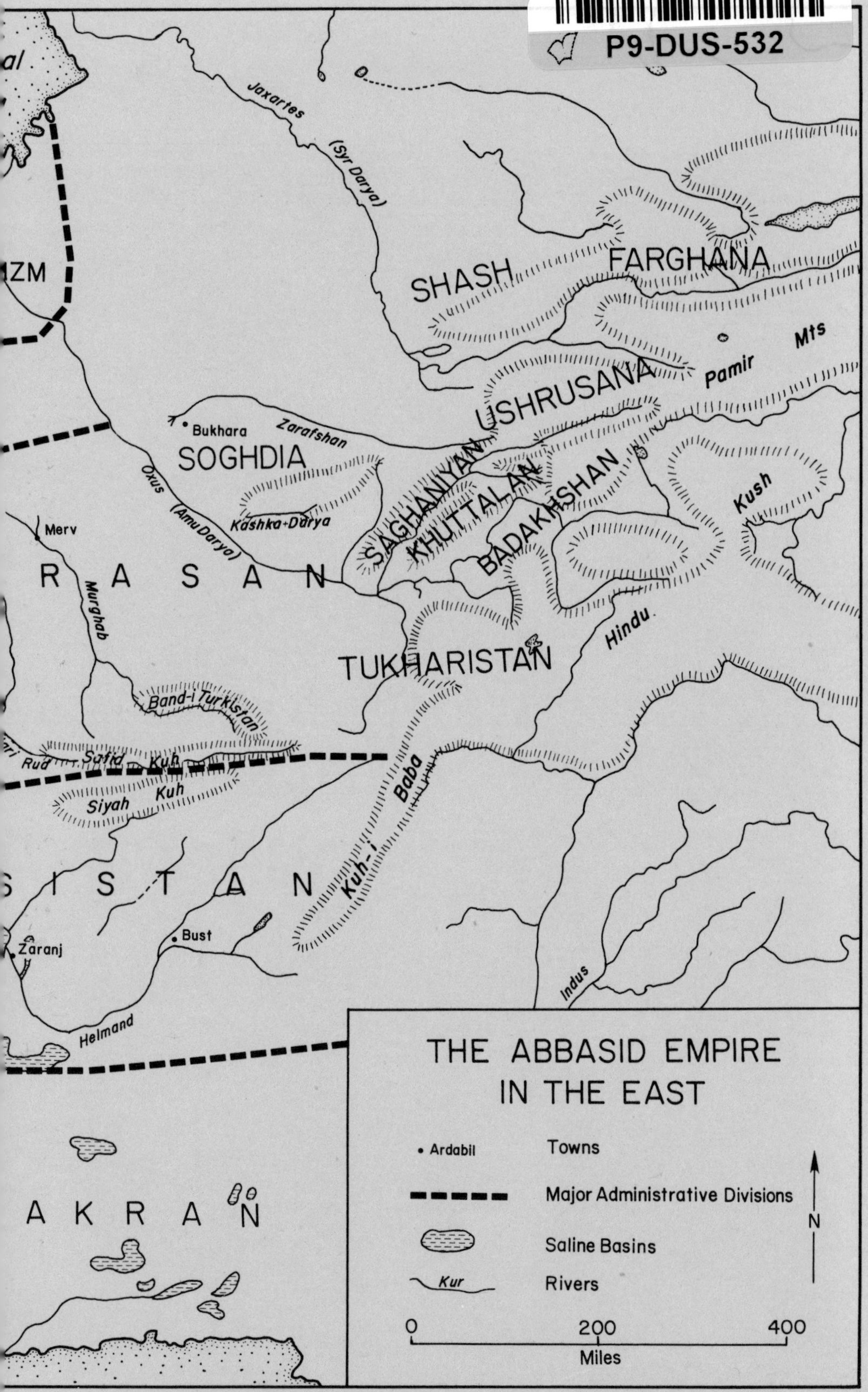
THE ABBASID EMPIRE
IN THE EAST
Ardabil
Towns
Major Administrative Divisions
Saline Basins
Kur
Rivers
N
0
200
400
Miles
al
ZM
Jaxartes
(Syr Darya)
SHASH
FARGHANA
USHRUSANA
Pamir
Mts
Bukhara
Zarafshan
SOGHDIA
SAGHANIYAN
KHUTTALAN
BADAKHSHAN
Kush
Oxus
(Amu Darya)
Kashka-Darya
Merv
R A S A N
Murghab
Hindu
TUKHARISTAN
Band-i Turkistan
Rud
Safid
Kuh
Baba
Siyah
Kuh
Kuh-i
S I S T A N
Bust
Zaranj
Indus
Helmand
A K R A N

KHURASAN UNDER ABBASID RULE 747–820

Front endpaper: *The Abbasid Empire in the East*

Back endpaper: *Greater Khurasan*

A Publication of
THE IRAN-AMERICA FOUNDATION

The Political and Social History of Khurasan under Abbasid Rule 747–820

by
ELTON L. DANIEL

Bibliotheca Islamica
Minneapolis & Chicago
1979

To Ethel, Edward, and Emily

Acknowledgments

A number of people have contributed to the completion of this work, and I owe them all a great debt of appreciation and gratitude. Support for my graduate study and research came from the Center for Middle Eastern Studies of the University of Texas, headed by Dr. Paul English, and from a Fulbright research grant. I wish to express my appreciation for the valuable assistance I received from the staffs of all the libraries at which I worked in the United States, Great Britain, France, Turkey, and Iran, but most particularly to Filiz Öḡütmen of the Topkapisaray Library and Michael Albin, former head of the University of Texas Middle East Collection and now director of the Library of Congress Cairo office. Professors John Williams, Najm Bezirgan, Michael Hillmann, Herbert Bodman, and Richard Frye all carefully read various recensions of the manuscript and offered many valuable suggestions and corrections.

Special thanks go to Professor Hafez Farmayan—teacher, advisor, and friend—who supervised my work on the original doctoral dissertation and patiently guided the manuscript through to its present form.

Of course, I alone am responsible for the book's blemishes and shortcomings.

Preface

For many years, the prevailing wisdom among historians of the Middle East has held that the establishment of the Abbasid caliphate, which lasted from 132/749–656/1258, marked the end of an "Arab Kingdom" and the rise of a cosmopolitan "Islamic Empire." To this, it is frequently added that Persian influence increased under the Abbasids, so that the Abbasid state was Persianized or even "neo-Sassanid."

There is much to be said for this interpretation, but what really does it mean specifically? Does it not give rise to various paradoxes which require explanation? Why did the Islamic empire never include all Muslims? Why did many Iranians oppose a supposedly Persianized dynasty? Why did the Abbasid state soon break up into a number of petty autonomous or semi-autonomous local dynasties? More particularly, why did the process of fragmentation take root in Khurasan, the scene, ironically, of the Abbasid revolt and an ostensible bastion of support for the new regime? What exactly was the relation between Khurasan and the Abbasids?

There are various reasons why such questions as these have not received the attention they deserve. In the case of Khurasan, the most important is undoubtedly that, as R. N. Frye has put it, "the period of Iran's history from the Arab conquest to the Saljuq expansion is very difficult to separate from the general history of the Islamic oecumene."[1] Most of the sources which have come down to us have little or no interest in purely local affairs; when they do mention them it is more often than not with a strong bias in favor of the central

1. R. N. Frye, ed., *The Cambridge History of Iran, volume 4: The Period from the Arab Invasion to the Saljuqs* (Cambridge, 1975), p. xi.

administration. The resultant misleading image of a monolithic empire under the direction of the caliphs has been perpetuated by many modern scholars, who have continued to write about the early Islamic period from an imperial rather than a provincial perspective. Until very recently, few histories of particular regions had been written, and many of those were tainted by strong doses of contemporary national chauvinism. Yet it is only through such specific studies that one can hope eventually to dispel the romantic haze surrounding the history of the caliphate and thus to appreciate the larger processes at work in the history of the Islamic Middle East. The problem is how to go about this.

The present study had its genesis in the belief that by isolating the history of an Iranian province, in this case Khurasan, from that of the Abbasid empire as a whole, one might reconstruct many features of significance from this "lost" period of Iran's history. Several approaches have been employed.

First, a broad range of sources have been consulted, Persian and various non-Muslim as well as Arabic. It is sometimes assumed that the Persian sources have little or nothing to add to the Arabic sources, or that they are too late to be of significance for the history of the early Islamic period. Such an assumption is unfounded. Some Persian sources, along with some relatively late Arabic ones, preserve local traditions or different historiographical viewpoints which are of great value. Many Persian sources are based on older sources which are now lost; an excellent example is Gardīzī's *Zayn al-akhbār*, which, as Barthold has pointed out, must preserve material from the famous, but no longer extant, history of the governors of Khurasan by al-Sallāmī. In other cases, the Persian authorities amplified or corrected material in Arabic sources; Bal'amī's supposed "translation" of Ṭabarī was actually neither a translation nor an abridgment but a work in its own right with much material not found in Ṭabarī at all.

Second, information from these sources has been categorized strictly by geography. In other words, special attention has been given to those events which actually took place in Khurasan rather than in other provinces. This is intended in particular to exclude Iraq, even though it had been for the Sassanids "the heart of Īrānshahr" and was, of course, the location of the Abbasid central government. It is true that many Khurāsānīs were involved in events there, but the issues at stake usually concerned the empire as a whole and tended to obscure uniquely Khurāsānī problems. Naturally, it is sometimes necessary to place events in Khurasan in the context of larger developments, but whenever possible it is preferable to explain local events in the context of local history.

Finally, every effort has been made to identify and analyze revolts and similar manifestations of public discontent. Such incidents are of the utmost value in isolating and explaining issues of popular concern at the local level.

It is hoped that these methods have enabled us to arrive at a coherent history of the province of Khurasan during the century before the Ṭāhirid dynasty was established. We shall attempt to demonstrate that events in Khurasan during that period characterized an important transitional phase in the development of feudalistic society in the area. Specifically, Abbasid agents in Khurasan precipitated a true mass revolt by exploiting the traditional antagonism between the Khurāsānī peasant and feudal classes to the advantage of a new "Muslim" urban and military/land-owning (or controlling) elite. Severe social contradictions within the revolutionary coalition in Khurasan then had to be resolved: Violence resulted from the efforts of the new regime in Khurasan to impose its authority and social system on surrounding peasant communities. There was persistent tension between the new Khurāsānī magnates and the representatives of the central government which they had helped install in Iraq. This produced a century of tremendous social upheaval, culminating in civil war. Against this background, the appearance of the Ṭāhirid dynasty was not the result of some unexplained weakness of the caliphs but of more fundamental changes which undermined the domination of Khurasan by the central government.

Abbreviations

A number of abbreviations and shortened titles for frequently cited sources have been used throughout the footnotes. Most of these can be easily determined by referring to the bibliography. For the convenience of the reader, a list of those forms which might be confusing is provided here:

Akhbār——(Anon.), *Akhbār al-ʻabbās wa wuldih,* ed. ʻAbd al-ʻAzīz Dūrī (Beirut, 1972)

BEO——*Bulletin d'études orientales*

*EI*1——M. T. Houtsma et al., eds., *The Encyclopaedia of Islam,* 4 vols. plus supplement (Leiden 1913–34)

*EI*2——B. Lewis et al., eds., *The Encyclopaedia of Islam,* in progress (Leiden, 1960–)

Fihrist——Ibn al-Nadīm, *The Fihrist of al-Nadīm,* trans. Bayard Dodge, 2 vols. (New York, 1970)

Fragmenta——*Fragmenta Historicorum Arabicorum,* ed. M. J. de Goeje (Leiden, 1968–71); contains (Anon.), *Kitāb al-ʻuyūn wa'l-ḥadā'iq* and Ibn Miskawayh, *Tajārib al-umam* (two volumes with continuous pagination)

IA——Ibn al-Athīr, *al-Kāmil fī l-ta'rīkh,* ed. C. Tornberg, 13 vols. (Leiden, 1851–76; reissued Beirut, 1965–67)

IJMES——*International Journal of Middle Eastern Studies*

GAL——Carl Brockelmann, *Geschichte der Arabischen Literatur,* 2 vols. and 3 supplemental vols. (Leiden, 1934–39)

Ghurar——Ḥusayn b. Muhammad al-Thaʻālibī (?), *Ghurar al-siyar* MS Oxford, Bodleian Library: D'Orville 542

JAOS——*Journal of the American Oriental Society*

JRAS——*Journal of the Royal Asiatic Society*

MMII——*Majallat al-majmaʻ al-ʻilmī al-ʻirāqī*

REI——*Revue des Etudes Islamiques*

RMM——*Revue du Monde Musulman*

RRAL——*Rendiconti della Reale Accademia dei Lincei*

RSO——*Rivista degli Studi Orientale*

Tab.——Ṭabarī, *Ta'rīkh al-rusul wa'l-mulūk,* ed. M. J. de Goeje, 3 "series" (Leiden, 1879–1901)

WZKM——*Wiener Zeitschrift für die Kunde des Morgenlandes*

ZDMG——*Zeitschrift der deutsches Morgenlandischen Gesellschaft*

Contents

Maps

System of Transliteration

Transliterations from the Arabic script conform to the system employed in American periodicals such as the *Journal of Near Eastern Studies* and the *International Journal of Middle East Studies*. To minimize apparent inconsistencies, the Arabic transliteration system is also used for Persian, except that "w" becomes "v." Common geographical names and certain terms which have become accepted in standard English usage are not transliterated.

Introduction

KHURASAN AND KHURASANI SOCIETY

The region known as Khurasan has ill-defined natural boundaries, and its political borders have fluctuated greatly during its long history. As a general rule, Khurasan proper may be understood to refer to a long, narrow swath of territory extending from near the southeastern littoral of the Caspian Sea to the great Pamir and Hindu Kush mountain barriers. At the same time, there has been a persistent notion of a greater Khurasan; for example, the people of medieval Iraq, playing on the meaning of the name, popularly supposed Khurasan to reach from Ḥulwān or Rayy eastwards to "the place where the sun rises." Indeed, Khurasan has at times included the fertile land south of the Aral Sea (Khwārizm), the various regions beyond the Oxus (Transoxiana or *mā warā' al-nahr*), and much of the Iranian plateau.

Theoretically, then, the eastern frontier of Khurasan went as far as China, but in fact it seldom extended very far past Balkh into the district known as Ṭukhāristān (roughly analogous to ancient Bactria). Similarly, it was rare for Khurasan's western border to reach the Zagros, but it did at times encompass Qūmis, Jurjān, Rayy, and parts of Ṭabaristān. Even though Transoxiana was frequently united with Khurasan, the Oxus served as the traditional northern border of Khurasan. At times, the frontier did not even extend that far: the *de facto* limit of Sassanid Khurasan, for example, was probably the Murghāb, and that only in the immediate environs of the Merv oasis. To the south, Khurasan supposedly extended to India, thus including Quhistān, Sīstān, and other areas, but the fringes of the central Iranian desert formed a more practical border.[1]

The geophysical characteristics of this region are surprisingly anomalous and have of course played an important role in shaping the nature of life in Khurasan. A number of intricate mountain chains form the "backbone" of the province, among them the Köpet Dagh, Allah-u Akbar, Hazār Masjid, Chagatā'ī, Shāh Jahān, Surkh, and Bīnālūd ranges, which rise to an elevation of over 11,000 feet near Mashhad (the medieval Ṭūs). East of the Harī Rūd, the terrain becomes even more rugged, as the Band-i Bābā, Fīrūz Kūh, Band-i Turkistān, Safīd Kūh, Siyāh Kūh, and Kūh-i Bābā rise from 11,000 to over 16,000 feet.

Nonetheless, Khurasan is neither as isolated nor as difficult to traverse as one might suspect. Numerous great valleys separate the various ranges, and there are many easy passes through the mountains. Moreover, Khurasan faces the vast open steppes of Central Asia and the tableland of the Iranian plateau. Consequently, Khurasan has tended to serve as a highway between East and West; it has always been vulnerable to invasion.

Khurasan is also relatively arid. The average annual precipitation in most of the province is less than ten inches. A considerable percentage of the land area is composed of inarable highlands and desert wastes. Yet paradoxically, Khurasan can in no way be described as barren. Many streams and rivers bring water and rich alluvial soil from the mountains before losing themselves in the salt deserts or the sea. The most important of these in Khurasan proper are the Atrak, the Harī Rūd, the Murghāb, and the Oxus (Āmū Daryā), beyond which lie the Kashkā Daryā, the Zarafshān, and the Jaxartes (Syr Daryā). These create a number of exceptionally fertile valleys and oases which have been inhabited and intensely cultivated for millenia.

These circumstances have, since antiquity, provided Khurasan with the means for a diverse economy. The exploitable mineral resources included lead, vitriol, arsenic, copper, iron, carnelian, serpentine (for stone jars), materials for millstones and paving stones, silver, gold, and the famous turquoise deposits near Nishapur. Nomads inhabiting the steppes and mountains raised sheep, camels, and the reknowned horses of Ṭukhāristān. They produced butter, cheeses, horns, furs, hides, and felts. Commerce and international trade developed at an early date, but their importance, especially in pre-Islamic Khurasan, has perhaps been exaggerated. Trade was concentrated in a few localities, notably Soghdia (outside Khurasan proper) and Merv. Local industries were highly specialized, primarily in textiles (mostly silk), metalwares, soap, and processed food products.

The chief glory of the Khurāsānī economy has always been agriculture. Khurasan has rightly been called the "granary of Iran"[2] for its ample crops of wheat, barley, and rice. Grain, however, made up only a fraction of Khurasan's agricultural production. Various localities in the province were noted for oranges, apricots, pears, currants, figs, peaches, pomegranates, melons, sugar cane, rhubarb, pistachios, almonds, truffles, sesame, grapes and raisins, medicinal asafetida roots, lilies, firewood, incense, juniper wood, planetree bark (for toothaches), and a curious "edible earth." Medieval Muslim geographers frequently exclaimed about the cheap living made possible by Khurasan's immense agricultural wealth—a reminder to us that the great civilization developed in Khurasan ultimately depended on the labor of the Khurāsānī peasant.

Life in Khurasan, then, was potentially rewarding but precariously balanced. Successful agriculture depended on careful exploitation of the water resources. This typically required an intricate network of canals and dikes requiring constant maintenance. It was equally necessary to provide adequate roads, bridges, mills, and the like. Over both agriculture and trade hung the constant threat of invasion or other disorders which might disrupt or even destroy the province's economic activity.

Of necessity, the Khurāsānīs acquired a reputation of having a warlike character; much of the population were constantly armed. Not surprisingly, they quickly built up an effective and socially significant military institution. This persisted from pre-Islamic into Islamic times: in Khurasan, the Arabs made an exception to their usual practice of allowing only Muslims to bear arms. At the same time, the people of Khurasan came to value greatly the ideal of a stable government which could provide the security and public works conducive to agrarian and commercial development and which would protect local interests from outside interference. These became recurrent themes of Khurāsānī history and helped unite the component parts of the province around common needs and concerns.

The Sassanids considered Khurasan one of the four quarters of their empire, corresponding (as it later did to some extent) to "the East." It was itself divided into four quarters. Traditionally, these were Merv, Nishapur, Herat, and Balkh (which was apparently understood to include Transoxiana and Bactria). This, however, was an idealization of the actual patterns of settlement and administration.

First, by the sixth century much of the region had come under the control of the Hephthalites, a people of uncertain ethnic origin, who were at the very best only nominally subject to the Sassanids.

Second, the administrative centers varied from time to time, and there were probably many more than four. The sites of old cities changed frequently, and the Sassanids founded new cities, notably Nishapur and Marw al-rūdh. Thus a city like Nasā, a Parthian royal city and necropolis, had declined considerably in importance under the Sassanids; and today it is not even known just where another famous Parthian capital, Hecatompylos, was located. The exact situation on the eve of the Arab conquest of Khurasan is debatable, but the chief Pahlavi source (which actually dates from Abbasid times) mentions twelve "capitals" of Khurasan: Samarqand, Navārak, an unnamed city in Khwārizm, Marw al-rūdh, Merv, Herat, Būshanj (or Pūshang), Ṭūs, Nishapur, Qāyin, Jurjān, and Qūmis.[3] Judging from early Arabic records, several other cities could be added to the list.

Finally, the so-called "quarter" constituted a very complex entity. If it is not unreasonably anachronistic to project backwards information obtained from Islamic documents, it may be conjectured that the fundamental unit of settlement in Khurasan was the fortified village (called *dih, rustāq,* or *qarya*). These existed in such profusion as constantly to amaze visitors to the province. A group of such villages made up a rural district (sometimes termed *kūra*), and a number of these in turn formed a canton (*nāḥiyya*).[4] It was not uncommon for the *nāḥiyya* to have an "urban" center, really a large village, from which it would take its name. The "quarter" therefore consisted of several cantons clustered around a large central "city." The city had at least three components: a highly fortified central enclosure, the *quhandiz;* an area of public buildings, perhaps surrounded by a wall; and any number of residential suburbs. Thus the "Nishapur quarter," for example, really referred to the city, surrounded by at least a dozen cantons, each of which might contain hundreds of villages. One must be constantly aware of this structure, since it is not always clear from the sources whether "Nishapur" refers to the city proper, the entire area, or some part of the hinterland.

The social structure in Khurasan in many respects paralleled the geographic-administrative structure. Ibn Khurradādhbih and Gardīzī report that pre-Islamic Khurasan was governed by a "general" (*iṣbahbadh*) and four "marchlords" (*marzbāns*), one for each quarter.[5] Once again, this is most likely an idealization, yet there was certainly a kind of *haute noblesse* of military and religious officials, responsible to the *shāh* but probably holding office by heredity, in the major administrative divisions of Khurasan (typically residing in the *quhandiz*). They bore various titles, such as *marzbān, kanārang, spāhbadh,* or *pādhgūspān,* which varied from place to place. These "Iranian nobles" (*mulūk al-'ajam* or similar descriptions) are frequently mentioned in Islamic sources, and Ibn Khurradādhbih has preserved a fairly comprehensive list of their personal names or titles.[6]

There was also a lesser nobility, living in smaller towns and villages, which included the *kadhagh-khvadhāyān* ("masters of property") and five classes of *dihqān*s (Arabic plural: *dahāqīn;* "masters of villages"). These were generally the hereditary possessors of landed estates, who collected taxes on behalf of the government and performed some military functions. Finally, there was the lowest social stratum, the common people, about whom not much concrete information is available. There were, of course, large numbers of peasants and presumably some artisans, merchants, slaves, and the dispossessed.[7] Of these, the peasants were unquestionably the most important, but their exact social status is not clear. They do seem to have been attached to the land, subjected to corvées, and often obliged to bear arms; in any case, they formed a very significant segment of society.

The combination of frontier location, agrarian economy, landed military institutions, and hierarchical class structure inevitably raises the question of whether Khurasan developed the feudal type of society to which such elements are conducive. The Soviet scholar Nina Pigulevskaya has maintained that Iranian feudalism began during the late Parthian and early Sassanid period (third to fifth centuries A.D.), when a communal slave society gave way to an incipient feudal society characterized by proliferation of cities, subjugation of peasant communities, partial affranchisement of slaves, changes in patterns of land-holding, greater division of labor, and the emergence of a military aristocracy linked by feudal bonds to the *shāh*. The natural accompaniment of this alteration was the great Mazdakite social upheaval. Despite its ostensible populist overtones, the revolt resulted in destruction of the old slave-owning aristocracy, derogation of the

Zoroastrian priestly class, weakening of peasant communities, and the victory of the proprietary-military class, the *shāh,* and the central government.[8] Though many of Pigulevskaya's arguments deal with western Iran, they certainly apply to Khurasan, which seems to have been a critical arena in the conflict between the powerful *āzādhān* (cavalry class) and the peasant interests.

Most Western scholars are not so dogmatic as Pigulevskaya, and in any case they have not yet reached a consensus on endorsing or dismissing the idea of Iranian feudalism.[9] This is partially attributable to deficiencies in the source materials, which simply do not provide the kind of information needed to offer a categorical solution. At the same time, efforts to refine the definition of feudalism through comparative studies have produced only a greater awareness of its complexity and the many guises under which it may appear. Ironically, even the fief (whence the word feudalism) can no longer be claimed as invariably characteristic of feudal society. Finally, there are undeniable differences between the putative feudal society of pre-Islamic (and Islamic) Iran and that found in Europe and elsewhere. In addition to the absence of the manorial system with its complicated juridical status and related institutions, Middle Eastern feudalism was tempered by a certain compatibility with urban life, a money economy, extensive trade and commerce, and important artisan classes.

For our purposes, it is well to be aware of the peculiarities of feudal or proto-feudal society in Khurasan, but this should not be allowed to obscure its fundamental similarity to other feudal systems. The elements of feudalism were most emphatically present in Khurasan (perhaps even more so than in the rest of Iran), and, as we shall see, Khurasan's history is delineated by many of the typical concerns of feudal history: resistance to a centralized state, fragmentation of authority, devotion to local interests, concentration of power in a professional warrior class, legitimization of the possession of land and the power it gave, forging of bonds of servitude and privilege between classes and individuals, and, in the words of Marc Bloch, "the rigorous economic subjugation of a host of humble folk to a few powerful men."[10]

Just as it is clear that there are many varieties of feudalism, so it has become apparent that there are various stages of development within a given feudalistic society. These transformations can be produced by such external or internal forces as alien occupation, technical progress, or changes in population density.[11] In this regard, how did the coming of the Arabs and Islam impact upon Khurasan?

This is not the place to try to untangle the mass of contradictory traditions concerning the Arab conquest of Khurasan. Suffice it to say that the Arabs penetrated Khurasan from the south in the area of Ṭabasayn in the year 30/650 and in very short order established nominal suzerainty over the province. Only the Hephthalites of Quhistān, the cities of Marw al-rūdh and Jūzjān, and such isolated rural districts as Bākharz, Juvayn, or Bīnah seem to have offered significant resistance.[12] There was to be no equivalent of Qādisiyya or Nihāvand in Khurasan.

The "conquest" involved little more than the conclusion of peace agreements with the feudal lords of the various districts of Khurasan. These magnates had remarkably little devotion to the Sassanid cause (in fact, it is more than probable that the *marzbān* of Merv, Māhūyya, was implicated in the murder of Yazdagird III in 651 A.D.). They were chiefly concerned with protecting as much as possible of their personal property and privileges. Thus they found it expedient to agree to pay tribute in exchange for recognition of their traditional position in the province.

The treaties drawn up between the Arab invaders and the Iranian nobles were the source of many future problems. There were disputes over whether a district had capitulated by force (*'anwatan*) or by agreement (*ṣulḥan*). There were disagreements as to whether the terms of an agreement were fair, whether they were in accordance with the requirements of religious law, or whether they were being enforced correctly. Moreover, the treaties varied greatly from locality to locality, thereby increasing suspicions of inequity and impropriety. To make matters even more complicated, several areas subsequently revolted—either out of distaste for the new Arab rule, or because they had made unrealistic agreements with the Arabs which they could not fulfill, or to take advantage of the internal problems convulsing the caliphate—and were retaken. New terms of surrender then had to be imposed. For these reasons, the early Arab administration of Khurasan can only be described as chaotic.

There were, however, some forces which worked to the advantage of the Arabs. They did receive the cooperation of most of the Iranian nobility. The Mazdakite controversy had alienated many of the peasants from their native religious leaders and the feudal aristocracy, so they too gave a tentative welcome to the invaders, in hopeful anticipation of improvement in their condition. Moreover, both the conquerors and the conquered had a common interest in restoring order in Khurasan and in protecting the province from its turbulent and hostile neighbors.

The Arabs were very favorably impressed by the receptive disposition of the Khurāsānī people.[13] They also found the climate acceptable; the province was confortably close to the desert; and, as a frontier province, Khurasan offered many opportunities for the warriors (*muqātila*) to enrich themselves. This created a uniquely congenial atmosphere for further Arab immigration, and successive waves of colonists from Iraq converged on Khurasan. The Arabs were thus able to establish camp cities, small garrisons, and forward military bases throughout the area. In large numbers and at a very early date, they settled in the Merv oasis, the district of Khulm near Balkh, and elsewhere.[14]

The initial policy of the Arabs in Khurasan was to make as few changes as possible in the existing social structure. They sought to minimize contacts between the Iranian and the Arab communities, so that each in isolation might follow its traditional way of life. The tribal *muqātila* would ideally be confined to their camps and fraternization with the indigenous population discouraged. As long as they paid tribute, the Iranians would be left undisturbed. There is, for example, a well-documented letter from the *imām* ʻAlī b. Abī Ṭālib confirming Māhūyya in his capacity as *marzbān* of Merv and recognizing his authority over the affairs (including taxation) of the *dihqān*s, the *asāwira,* and the *dihsālār*s.[15] Thus there was for some time a *modus vivendi* in Khurasan based on the close collaboration of the Iranian and Arab ruling elites. Their alliance, based on good relations and mutual interests, persisted throughout Umayyad times.

Nevertheless, the Arab colonists brought the seed of a profound social crisis as well as the obvious racial, linguistic, cultural, and religious differences. The Arab conception of society could in no way be described as feudal. They respected genealogy and purity of blood so that tribal affiliation was a matter of prestige, but Iranian ideas about hereditary rank, class structure, and other feudalistic notions were alien to them. Islam, too, had a strong egalitarian tendency. There was a Muslim aristocracy of sorts, based at least in theory on piety (the *ṭabaqāt,* arranged according to precedence of conversion to Islam), but there was no recognition of a priestly class as in Iran. Of necessity, the Arabs in Khurasan formed a military class, but this again was quite different from the Iranian. Whereas the Iranian military class derived its wealth from the possession of landed property, the Arab *muqātila* received wages from the state treasury at rates prescribed in a special register (the *dīwān*).

The most important point of difference arose from the ignorance of tribal Arabs, who saw farming as a demeaning occupation, about the requirements of an agrarian society. To be sure, agriculture was known in Arabia, especially in the Yemen, Ṭā'if, Madīna, or the Khaybar oasis. It was, however, centered around date production, which was virtually unknown in Khurasan. Places like Mecca were almost totally dependent on international trade to meet their need for grain and some other foodstuffs. Islam had arisen in an environment which valued nomadic life and city life but had little more than contempt for peasant life.

The evolving legal and fiscal structure of Islam reflected the tribal Arab bias against agriculture. Although it was also influenced by the Sassanid example, what may for lack of a better term be called the Islamic system of taxation in Khurasan unquestionably placed its heaviest burden by far on land and the peasantry.[16] Meanwhile, the burgeoning Arab population of Khurasan flocked to the cities, which also magnetically attracted those Iranians displaced by the changes taking place in their homeland. These people formed the core of a large and highly important artisan/merchant/religious class in Khurasan. They benefited greatly from the "Islamic" economic system, which in effect legitimized the forcible transfer of a large portion of the peasants' surplus production into the hands of the ruling class and thence to the flowering urban civilization. It was inevitable that such a change in the relations between town and countryside be accompanied by profound social repercussions.

At the same time, other developments combined to disturb the *status quo* in Khurasan. The tide of Arab colonists coming to Khurasan rapidly became a flood, and their numbers were no longer limited to the warriors necessary for policing Khurasan and conducting military operations in Transoxiana. Gradually, the ideal of maintaining segregated tribal Arab military colonies in the province collapsed. The resulting process of cultural assimilation and religious conversion has been adequately described by Wellhausen[17] and need not be repeated here, but it is important to note its impact on the social structure. Warriors and officials were no longer content with simply receiving wages; they began to acquire, by whatever means, landed estates. In one famous example, Asad b. 'Abd Allah al-Qasrī obtained an estate, which became known as Asadābādh, in the Bayhaq district of Nishapur, and it remained in his family for generations.[18]

Other Arabs, like the great rebel al-Ḥārith b. Surayj, built up what amounted to private armies with which they could work their will in Khurasan. At a lower level, many common Arab soldiers in Khurasan lost or gave up their military functions, became assimilated with the Khurāsānī peasantry, and were shocked to find that, although Muslims, they had become the vassals of Iranian feudal lords. Yet other Arabs (known as *fulūl* or *suqqāṭ al-'arab*) formed a kind of *Lumpenproletariat* roving about the province and were called "vagabonds" (*ṣa'ālīq, sā'ir al-nās.*)

Thus a situation materialized in Khurasan in which the class interests of various strata of Arab society coincided with those of their Khurāsānī equivalents. There was an upper echelon of Iranian nobles and Arab tribesmen who usually collaborated with each other in ruling the province though they were increasingly troubled by the factious nature of their feudal or tribal politics. Second, there were upper class Arabs, generally outside the ruling elite, who acquired the typically feudal accouterments of landed estates and private armies, and whose interests were virtually identical with those of the Iranian lesser nobility. (It is significant, but not surprising, to find that even though the *dahāqīn* often resented their rulers, they were outspoken in their admiration of men like Asad b. 'Abd Allah.[19]) Finally, there were masses of Arab and Iranian peasants and common people who were united in their acute awareness of oppression and injustice.

It is clear that fundamental social contradictions threatened to disrupt the nature of proto-feudalistic society in Khurasan. The events described here represent the resolution of these contradictions and the consequent transformation of Khurāsānī society.

1. On the geography of Khurasan, see in particular Iṣṭakhrī, *al-Masālik,* pp. 253–54; Ibn Rustah, *al-A'lāq al-nafīsa,* p. 105; Maqdisī, *Aḥsan al-taqāsim,* pp. 213 et seq.; *Ḥudūd al-'ālam,* pp. 102–12 (and notes by Minorsky); and Yāqūt, *Mu'jam al-buldān,* 3:407–8 (based in part on an earlier work by Balādhurī). A late but still useful source is Ḥāfiẓ-i Abrū, *Geography,* Ms. London: British Library, OR 1577, ff. 174a–89b (there is a published edition of the section on Khurasan by Māyil Haravī (Tehran, 1349) which I have not seen). Material from a number of Islamic sources has been collected by Guy LeStrange, *Lands of the Eastern Caliphate* (Cambridge, 1905; reprint London, 1966), pp. 382–432. See also E. Herzfeld, "Khorasan, Denkmalsgeographische Studien zur Kulturgeschichte des Islam in Iran," *Der Islam* 11(1921):107–74; and J. Markwart, *Ērānšahr nach der Geographie des Ps: Moses Xorenac'i* (Berlin, 1901), pp. 47–94.

2. R. Ghirshman, *Iran* (London, 1954), p. 23.

3. J. Markwart, *A Catalogue of the Provincial Capitals of Ērānshahr,* ed. G. Messina (Rome, 1931), pp. 8–13.

4. See R. N. Frye, *The Golden Age of Persia* (London, 1975), pp. 107–9. I have followed the terminology suggested by Yāqūt, but it is not uniformly applied in other sources. The *Fārsnāmah,* for example, implies that the *kūra* was a larger unit, which Frye links with the Persian *ustān.* The theory of the tri-partite division of the city was developed in several works by Barthold (and later criticized by V. L. Voronina). For a recent evaluation, see Otar Tskitishvili, "Two Questions Connected with the Topography of the Oriental City in the Early Middle Ages," *Journal of the Economic and Social History of the Orient* 14(1971):311–20.

5. Ibn Khurradādhbih, *Kitāb al-masālik wa'l-mamālik,* ed. M. J. de Geoje (Leiden, 1889), p. 18; and Gardīzī, *Zayn al-akhbār,* ed. 'A. Ḥabībī (Tehran, 1347/1969), p. 92.

6. Ibn Khurradādhbih, *Masālik,* pp. 39–40.

7. An exposition of the celebrated four-class structure of Sassanid Iran may be found in the *Letter of Tansar,* trans. Mary Boyce (Rome, 1968), p. 38; see also Mas'ūdī, *Murūj al-dhahab,* ed. and trans. Barbier de Meynard and Pavet de Courteille, *Les Praries d'Or* (Paris, 1861–77), 2:240–41. The best secondary study is Arthur Christensen, *L'Iran sous les Sassanides* (Copenhagen, 1944), pp. 97–113; see also R. N. Frye, *The Golden Age of Persia,* pp. 13, 17–19.

8. N. Pigulevskaja, *Les Villes de l'être iranien aux êpoques parthe et sassanide* (Paris, 1963).

9. Christensen does not hesitate to speak of Sassanid feudalism; see also Ann Lambton, *Landlord and Peasant in Persia* (2nd ed.; Oxford, 1969), pp. 10–16. Its existence is questioned by Burr Bundage, "Feudalism in Ancient Mesopotamia and Iran," in R. Coulborn, ed., *Feudalism in History* (Princeton, 1956), pp. 93–119, and R. Coulborn, "The Case of Iran," *ibid.,* pp. 325–43.

10. Marc Bloch, *Feudal Society,* trans. L. A. Manyon (Chicago, 1961), p. 443.

11. An interesting example of this is Rodney Hilton, *Bond Men Made Free* (London, 1973), pp. 14–17. Though his remarks deal with medieval England, they are quite relevant to the medieval history of Khurasan.

12. A concise, accessible, and authoritative account of the conquest is available in al-Balādhurī, *Kitāb futūḥ al-buldān,* ed. M. J. de Geoje (Leiden, 1866), pp. 403–8; trans. F. C. Murgotten, *The Origins of the Islamic State, part II* (New York, 1924), pp. 159–68. See also D. R. Hill, *The Termination of Hostilities in the Early Arab Conquests, A.D. 634–656* (London, 1971), pp. 144–59; Shaban, *'Abbāsid Revolution,* pp. 16–29; and 'A. Zarrīnkūb, "The Arab Conquest of Iran," in *Cambridge History of Iran,* 4:25–29.

13. See, for example, al-Maqdisī, *Aḥsan al-taqāsīm,* ed. M. J. de Goeje (Leiden, 1906), p. 293; Ibn al-Faqīh, *Kitāb al-buldān,* ed. M. J. de Goeje (Leiden, 1885), p. 152; and Mas'ūdī, *Prairies,* 3:128; Yāqūt, *Mu'jam,* 3:409. This opinion, however, was not universal: Ibn Qutayba protested that the people of Khurasan were "arrogant and insubordinate"!

14. See Yāqūt, *Mu'jam,* 3:380, 459, 5:130, 8:33–34; Balādhurī, *Futūḥ,* p. 410; etc. A not altogether satisfactory effort to describe the Arab settlement is Ṣāliḥ al-'Alī, "Istīṭān al-'arab fī khurāsān," *Majallat kulliyat al-adab wa'l-'ulūm fī baghdād* (1958), pp. 36–83.

15. Balādhurī, *Futūḥ,* p. 408; Tab., 1:3249.

16. The vexing problem of the early Islamic system of taxation and its effects is still not settled, though several scholars have made some fine attempts to do so. See M. von Berchem, *La Propriété territoriale et l'impôt foncier sous les premiers califes* (Geneva, 1886); Daniel Dennett, *Conversion and the Poll-tax in Early Islam* (Cambridge, Mass., 1950); and F. Lokkegaard, *Islamic Taxation in the Classic Period* (Copenhagen, 1950). As for the Arab attitude towards agriculture, it is true that some of the early caliphs undertook a number of projects to encourage agricultural production, but, there is also abundant evidence that agriculture in the Middle East steadily declined for several centuries after the Arab conquest and that peasant discontent underlay a number of the conflicts of that period: see E. Ashtor, *A Social and Economic History of the Near East in the Middle Ages* (London, 1976), pp. 36–70; Claude Cahen, "Fiscalité, propriété, antagonismes sociaux en haute Mésopotamie au temps du premiers 'abbāsides d'après Denys de Tell-Mahré," *Arabica* I(1954):136–52. One should not confuse what we have called here the "Islamic" system with the later "Persianized" theories of such statesmen as Niẓām al-Mulk who sought to ameliorate the condition of the peasantry: for example, see the pointed anecdote in Ghazālī, *Counsel for Kings (Naṣīḥāt al-mulūk),* trans. F. R. C. Bagley (London, 1964), p. 81; Niẓām al-mulk, *The Book of Government,* trans. Hubert Darke (London, 1960), pp. 33, 49, 132. Finally, for a general overview of these problems in their Iranian context, see N. Pigulevskaya, *et al., Istoriva Irana s drevneishikh vremen do konsta XVIII veka,* trans. Karīm Kashāvarz, *Tārīkh-i īrān* (Tehran, 1354/1976), pp. 133–168.

17. Wellhausen, *Arab Kingdom,* pp. 493 sqq.

18. Gardīzī, *Zayn,* p. 116; Yāqūt, *Mu'jam,* 1:227; and Barthold, *Turkestan,* p. 188.

19. Tab., 2:1636–37.

CHAPTER ONE

Then (Abū 'Ikrima and Ḥayyān b. 'Aṭṭār) came before the *imām* Muḥammad b. 'Alī in Syria to inform him that they had planted a seedling in Khurasan which they expected would bear fruit in due season.

—Dīnawarī, *al-Akhbār al-ṭiwāl*

The Abbasid Revolt in Khurasan

On the night of 25 Ramaḍān 129 (10 June 747), the inhabitants of Safīdhanj, a village on the outskirts of Merv, witnessed a remarkable spectacle, part religious convocation and part political demonstration. The Khuzā'ī *shaykh* of the village, Sulaymān b. Kathīr, led a group of men dressed completely in black to a place of assemblage near his residence. There they proceeded to raise two large black banners, one which they named "the shadow" on a pole fourteen cubits long and another, called "the clouds," on a pole thirteen cubits long. As they did so, a newcomer in the village known as Abū Muslim chanted a verse from the Koran: "Leave is given to those who fight because they were wronged; surely God is able to help them" (22:39). They then kindled bonfires, and, in response, men from surrounding villages, also robed in black, left their homes to join their comrades in Safīdhanj.

To the initiated, this esoteric display was not without meaning. Just as clouds spread throughout the world, so the message of the Abbasid family would permeate the world; just as the earth was never devoid of shadow, so it would never be without the Abbasid caliphate. The fires were a signal to all the followers of the movement that the time to strike was finally at hand.[1]

The drama performed in the little village that summer night was a declaration of revolt. As unlikely as it might have seemed at the time to a disinterested observer, there had been set in motion a series of events in which armies of these "black devils"[2] would, in a remarkably brief period of time, topple the once mighty Umayyad dynasty and raise in its place a new dynasty which would reign, if not rule, for more than five hundred years.

There has been sustained historiographical interest in this "Abbasid revolution," which is undoubtedly one of the most important events in early Islamic history.[3] Nevertheless, there are as yet no generally satisfactory answers to many of the questions surrounding the revolt. Why did it occur in Khurasan? Who supported it? What did the rebels expect to gain? What really did they accomplish?

One explanation for the widely differing responses to such questions is that studies of the revolt tend to be too broad in scope. In attempting to reveal the roots of the revolt, most of these studies examine Umayyad history in detail from its very beginning, studying the revolt in the context of the history of the Islamic Empire as a whole. The result is that the proximate causes of the revolt are neglected, its consequences receive much less attention than its origins, and the importance of its immediate environment remains unexplained. Accurate appreciation of the significance of the revolt is thus hampered by confusion of its general with its particular features. To reverse these tendencies, we shall concentrate here on those events directly related to the history of revolt in Khurasan, examine closely how it unfolded locally, and study its results as well as its causes.

In this chapter, we will try to show that the Abbasid movement began as a relatively minor and obscure *shīʿī* sect. The Abbasids, however, were able to succeed where many others had failed because they were able to exploit the strength of a united Khurasan at the crucial moment of Umayyad weakness. They recognized the unique revolutionary potential that had developed in Khurasan as a result of the social changes which followed the Arab conquest. They captured a base of power in the province by appealing to two distinct groups there: (1) the bloc of "middling class" Arab colonists, their *mawālī,* and the Iranian *dahāqīn,* all of whom resented the domination of Khurasan by an "alien" Qaysite-Syrian military elite and its aristocratic Iranian collaborators, and (2) the native Iranian peasantry and mostly assimilated lower class Arabs, who wished to overthrow the landholding aristocracy and who dreamed of an egalitarian society based on a mixture of Islamic and neo-Mazdakite concepts. Through shrewd manipulation of these class antagonisms, the Abbasid propagandists managed to bring about a true mass uprising in Khurasan.

THE ABBASID FAMILY AND ITS CLAIM TO THE CALIPHATE

The Abbasids were the descendants of al-ʿAbbās b. ʿAbd al-

Muṭṭalib (d. 652 A.D.), uncle of the Prophet Muḥammad, and thus a branch of the Banū Hāshim, one of the privileged Qurayshī clans of Mecca.[4] It is difficult to determine the exact social status of early members of this family, the nature of their relations with the central government, or when and why they determined to seek the caliphate for themselves. Certainly, once in power, their panegyrists exaggerated their piety and importance out of all proportion to reality.

It is known that al-'Abbās had been one of the wealthier members of the Hāshimī clan, that he was a relatively late convert to Islam, and that his relations with Muḥammad were more correct than warm.[5] Muḥammad did confirm him in his right of *siqāya* (the lucrative privilege of furnishing pilgrims to Mecca with water),[6] but this was a diplomatic gesture, not a token of any special esteem. Most sources depict his son, 'Abd Allah (d. 687), as a great scholar, an authority on traditions, and a close confidant of the Caliph 'Alī b. Abī Ṭālib.[7] Neither he nor his father seem to have had any real political ambitions; indeed, 'Abd Allah was on good terms with both Mu'āwiya and Yazīd I, a fact of some embarassment to later partisans of his family.[8]

The family's fortunes took a different direction in the lifetime of 'Alī b. 'Abd Allah (d. 736). He managed to avoid the political dangers of the troubled reign of 'Abd al-Malik (685–705), but for some reason angered al-Walīd I (705–715), who twice had him flogged and then imprisoned.[9] It is impossible to say whether 'Alī was punished for indulging in suspect political activity or whether he turned to political subversion because of al-Walīd's hostility. At any rate, after his release from prison he settled at Ḥumayma, a village south of the Dead Sea, from whence his son, Muḥammad, directed the conspiracy to overthrow the Umayyad dynasty.

There are three versions of how Muḥammad b. 'Alī first decided to try to win the caliphate for his family. One account asserts that the Prophet Muḥammad promised the office to al-'Abbās and that Muḥammad b. 'Alī was simply working to restore this right. Another account suggests that he was approached by a group of dissatisfied Khurāsānīs looking for a leader. Yet another version claims that he inherited the right of Abū Hāshim 'Abd Allah b. Muḥammad al-Ḥanafiyya to the office.

The first tradition is exceedingly unlikely and may safely be described as a fabrication invented after the movement succeeded, to discredit potential rivals. Nonetheless, it is mentioned in a number of sources.[10] The first Abbasid caliph, Abū'l-'Abbās al-Saffāḥ, emphasized it in his inaugural speech (*khuṭba*),[11] and the Caliph al-Mahdī attempted to make it an official state doctrine.[12]

The story of the Khurāsānī delegation is not easy to prove or to disprove. It states that a group of unnamed Khurāsānīs wanted to form a resistance movement and would only submit to the authority of someone sufficiently noble, pious, and generous. They first approached 'Abd Allah b. al-Ḥasan b. al-Ḥasan b. 'Alī who declined their offer and referred them to Muḥammad b. 'Alī.[13] There is nothing intrinsically implausible about this, and it would certainly help explain the special role of Khurasan in the revolt. However, it does not account for the fact that the movement began its work in Kūfa rather than Khurasan. Perhaps the story resulted from confusion with some of the later meetings of Khurāsānī leaders with Muḥammad b. 'Alī in Mecca; it could as easily have arisen from a propaganda campaign by Abbasid supporters to undercut the 'Alīd cause by showing that 'Abd Allah b. al-Ḥasan had forfeited his claim to the caliphate to the Abbasids.

This leaves the more common, and somewhat more likely, account of Muḥammad b. 'Alī's inheritance of the claims and political organization of Abū Hāshim. The heresiographers tell us that the Kaysāniyya sect believed that the imāmate rightly belonged to the descendants of 'Alī, the Prophet's son-in-law and nephew, but through his Ḥanafī wife and not Fāṭima (Muḥammad's daughter and, of course, the most famous of 'Alī's wives.)[14] The most spectacular manifestation of this sect's existence came with the revolt of al-Mukhtār in Kūfa on behalf of Muḥammad b. al-Ḥanafiyya. As was usually the case with these movements, the sect soon fragmented into various factions which squabbled over who had rightly inherited Muḥammad b. al-Ḥanafiyya's claims to the caliphate. One of these factions maintained that the role of *imām* had been transmitted to Abū Hāshim. This Abū Hāshim and his partisans built up a little political organization in Kūfa, and probably in Khurasan as well. Abū Hāshim seems to have been on friendly terms with both 'Alī b. 'Abd Allah b. al-'Abbās and his son Muḥammad, perhaps as a result of their common persecution at the hands of al-Walīd.

Abū Hāshim was summoned to the Umayyad court, where he either took ill or, like so many of the martyrs of the *shī'a,* was poisoned. He and his band of followers managed to make their way to the residence of Muḥammad b. 'Alī in Ḥumayma, where he died, probably in 98/716. Just before his death, Abū Hāshim supposedly bequeathed his rights to Muḥammad b. 'Alī, intrusted him with certain secrets and instructions, and enjoined his own supporters to work for this new *imām*.[15] Thanks to evidence in a newly discovered source, we even have the names of these supporters, many of whom indeed reappear elsewhere as Abbasid partisans. Their chief was Salama b. Bujayr b. 'Abd Allah al-Muslī, and they included Abū Rabbāḥ Maysara al-Nabbāl (a *mawlā* of Azd), Muḥammad b. Khunays (*mawlā* of Hamdān), Abū Bisṭām Maṣqala at-Ṭaḥḥān (*mawlā* of Ḥārith b. Ka'b), and Ḥayyān al-'Aṭṭār. The same source reports that Ibn Bujayr gave Muḥammad b. 'Alī a list of potential recruits to the cause, among whom were the future leaders Bukayr b. Māhān (whose father was a *mawlā* of the Musliyya) and Abū Salama Ḥafṣ b. Sulaymān (also a *mawlā* of Musliyya.)[16]

Although Wellhausen, foremost historian of the Abbasid revolt, rejected this version of the origin of the Abbasid claim to the caliphate,[17] the evidence strongly suggests that the movement did spring from the extremist Hāshimiyya sect of the Kaysāniyya, but also that this was later obscured by Abbasid partisans, who propagated the theory that the term Hāshimiyya referred to the Prophet Muḥammad's clan of Hāshim rather than to Abū Hāshim's sectarian followers.

THE EARLY HISTORY OF THE *DA'WA*[18]

Roughly thirty years of meticulous preparation were to elapse before the Abbasid cause came to fruition. It is virtually impossible to reconstruct accurately the activities of Muḥammad b. 'Alī and his partisans during this period. Even the best of sources are full of internal inconsistencies and contradictions; discrepancies between the different versions are even more numerous. Events have been altered, dates changed, charaterizations of individuals distorted to suit the writer's bias for or against the conspirators. Still, through this jumble of confused and falsified accounts, one may trace the evolution of the *da'wa* through the several stages of its history.

The Kūfan Period (98/716–102 or 103/722): Like most of the early Shi'ite[19] movements, the Abbasid *da'wa* was centered initially in Kūfa, where it met with as little success as those other movements had. Its director was a man known as Maysara, probably the same

Maysara al-Nabbāl said to have assumed the leadership of the Hāshimiyya upon the death of Ibn Bujayr.[20] The missionaries called for rule by an acceptable member of the family of the Prophet Muḥammad (*al-riḍā min āl Muḥammad*) but were under strict orders not to reveal the name of this person.[21] Except for winning the support of the wealthy *mawlā* Bukayr b. Māhān, the movement in Kūfa made only scant progress. After two years of activity, no more than thirty men had joined the cause.[22] Clearly, it was necessary to abandon Kūfa for a more responsive recruiting ground.

The Organizational Period In Khurasan (103/722–117/735): The important decision to shift the *da'wa* to a new locale is usually attributed to Muḥammad b. 'Alī, though perhaps on the advice of Abū Hāshim, in the appropriately charismatic year 100 A.H. (718–19 A.D.)[23] He reportedly told his followers to abandon Kūfa because its citizens would never support anyone except the 'Alīds. He pointed out that the Syrians were devoted to the Sufyānids; the people of Medina and Mecca still looked back to the days of Abū Bakr and 'Umar; the Baṣrans were invariably 'Uthmānites; and the Jazīra was full of incorrigible Khārijites and other heretics. But the people of Khurasan, he argued, were numerous and strong, free from extremist doctrines, eager to support a member of the family of the Prophet, and most important, not marred by "the Arabs' ambition and love of tribal strife (*'aṣabiyya*)."[24] The most interesting point in the story is the extent to which, even at that early date, factional and sectarian rivalries tended to parallel and to be associated with geographic divisions. The Abbasids aimed at combining their personal interests with those of the province of Khurasan: Here is our first clue about the nature of the Abbasid movement.

Another important aspect of the movement is brought out in a variant tradition, which holds that the move to Khurasan was taken on the advice of Bukayr b. Māhān, who told Muḥammad b. 'Alī:

> I have wandered about the world and have been to Khurasan, [where] I witnessed the conquest of Jurjān with Yazīd b. al-Muhallab. Never have I seen a people more devoted to the family of the Prophet than the people of the East. In Jurjān . . . I chanced to meet one of the Iranians. I heard him say in Persian, 'I have never seen a people more misguided than the Arabs. Their Prophet died and his authority passed to a family other than his own.' Then he cried, and, by God, I could hardly keep myself from weeping with him. I told him, 'May God be merciful to you! How often I have seen deception overwhelm the truth, unbeknownst to the Arabs. . . . But many of them have awakened and have

> seen their errors.' He said, 'Then what keeps you from seeking them [the Prophet's family] and returning authority to them? I guarantee you that my countrymen would stand by you in this.'

Bukayr went on to relate how he had also met Sulaymān b. Kathīr, a prominent citizen of Merv who was on the *dīwān* (pension list) there, while in Rayy on his way to Mecca. He found that he too was warm in his affection for the Prophet's family and would swear to support them just as the Persian had done.[25]

The point, of course, was that there was widespread support among both Arabs and native Iranians in Khurasan for shī'ism, that is, rule by a member of the Prophet Muḥammad's family (though not necessarily an 'Alīd). Unfortunately, it is not stated what more specific issues these sentiments may have represented, though it is clear that the Abbasids could benefit by exploiting them. One possibility is that the drift towards shī'ism reflected a search for an antidote to the rampant factional disturbances in Khurasan. These had become progressively worse, so that the exasperated governor of Khurasan, Jarrāḥ b. 'Abd Allah, reported to the Caliph 'Umar b. 'Abd al-'Azīz that Khurasan could only be governed by "the sword and the whip." There was, however, an alternative to brute force: Balādhurī, for example, states that "the chiefs and nobles of the people of Khurasan wrote to 'Abd al-Malik informing him that Khurasan would not recover from the effects of the civil strife except under a man of Quraysh."[26] In other words, some neutral party was needed to mediate disputes and to provide legitimate solutions to the clash of interests in Khurasan. Some Khurāsānīs may have taken this a step further: Only the charismatic leadership and prestige of a ruler chosen from the *ahl al-bayt* could restore the social order necessary to sustain the area's economy.

Bukayr's report delighted Muḥammad b. 'Alī, who alluded to certain prophecies known to him about black banners advancing from the East to strike down the "Umayyad pharaoh." He immediately sent out his missionaries (*dā'ī,* plural *du'āt*), first to Jurjān and then to Merv.[27] He ordered them to reveal the secrets of the movement not to commoners but only to those whose intelligence and reliability merited it. They were to summon people to the Koran, the tradition (*sunna*) of the Prophet, and rule by a member of the Prophet's family. If asked who *al-riḍā* should be, they were to make use of prudent dissimulation (*taqiyya*) and keep the name secret. They were not to use any threats of violence. They were to befriend the tribes of

Yaman and Rabī'a but to beware of Muḍar (the tribe favored by the Umayyads). Finally, they were to do much for the *'ajam* (non-Arabs, i.e., Iranians), "for they are the people of the *da'wa*."[28]

No doubt much of this information about the beginning of the *da'wa* in Khurasan has been altered with the advantage of hindsight. Nonetheless, the stories point straight to the heart of the matter. The Abbasids had recognized the two strategies that would contribute most to their success: appeal to local interests in Khurasan, and exploit the nascent *shī'ī* tendencies of the population. Khurasan was, in fact, an area ripe for the recruitment of partisan support, among Iranians as well as Arab settlers; it was as yet largely untapped by any religio-political party. The Abbasids saw that the safest way to win this support on a broad scale was to keep the overt message of the *da'wa* as innocuous as possible: vague religious catchphrases, a prudent dose of secrecy, and strict avoidance of the problem of who should replace the Umayyads once they were overthrown.

The early period of the *da'wa* in Khurasan was marked by a constant flow of orders and directions from Muḥammad b. 'Alī in Ḥumayma to his missionaries, and a return flow of information, news, and revenue to him.[29] There were periodic personal meetings between the *imām* and his subordinates, almost invariably in Mecca on pretense of performing the pilgrimage.[30] By pretending to be merchants, the missionaries were usually able to disguise their comings and goings, but they did not escape government surveillance. A number of them were betrayed to local officials, imprisoned, tortured, or executed, especially during the governorship of Asad b. 'Abd Allah (105/723–109/727 and 117/735–120/738.)[31] They also faced intellectual challenges from the rival 'Alīds, notably one Ghālib of Abrashahr (Nishapur).[32] Despite these dangers, the movement as a whole was never seriously jeopardized and continued to prosper. The missionary work was carried on primarily in and near Merv but was soon extended to other areas, especially Jurjān.[33]

The mission in Khurasan was at first not rigidly organized. The head of the partisans—Maysara until his death in 105 or 106 (723 or 724) and then Bukayr—remained in Kūfa except for occasional meetings with the *imām* or with his lieutenants in Khurasan. The missionaries, who were led by Abū 'Ikrima Ziyād al-Hamdānī and the two *mawlā*s Muḥammad b. Khunays and Ḥayyan b. 'Aṭṭār, went about the villages of Khurasan proselytizing and discussing messages from the *imām*, Muḥammad b. 'Alī.[34] Attendence at these meetings was encouraged by distributing food to the people,[35] a circumstance which would suggest that the mission was directed at the lower social strata.

Membership quickly reached the point where it was necessary to create a more formal chain of command. The *imām,* of course, remained the titular head of the movement, but contact with him was normally through his deputy in Kūfa. His identity remained unknown except to the inmost circles of the movement. Following a precedent set by Muḥammad and other prophets,[36] Abū ‘Ikrima (or possibly Bukayr)[37] chose twelve chiefs (*naqīb/nuqabā’*) from among the partisans in Merv. (Interestingly, this method of organization was also used by the later Ismā‘īlīs.[38]) He also designated twelve alternates (called the *nuẓarā’ al-nuqabā’*) to take their place in the event of death or withdrawal. Under these *nuqabā’* were approximately fifty-eight missionaries (the number may be an artificial one designed to produce the total of seventy required by prophetic precedents): forty for Merv, seven for Abīward, six for Nasā, two for Balkh, and one each for Marw al-rūdh, Khwārizm, and Āmul. He also appointed thirty-six *du‘āt al-du‘āt,* whose exact function is unknown.[39]

Some scholars have tried to determine the composition of the groups supporting the Abbasid *da‘wa* on the basis of the names of the twelve *nuqabā’*, given in a number of sources. While these names do constitute one of the few available clues for solving this important problem, generalizations based on them must, for several reasons, be viewed very skeptically.

A name is not always "objective" evidence of an individual's race or status. Obviously, genealogies could be, and often were, forged. Distinguishing between presumed Arabic and Persian names not infrequently involves a subjective judgment: What, for example, should one make of a name like Yāzdān, which appears Persian in form but was actually used by many Arabs? With purely Muslim names (‘Abd Allah and the like), there is of course no way at all to determine the race of the individual unless a source states it explicitly. Nor can a *nisba* be taken as proof of a person's place of origin or residence since Islamic society was highly mobile. It cannot even be accepted as infallible evidence of an individual's occupation: For an excellent example, consider Abū Salama. Because he was styled al-Khallāl, more than one writer has jumped to the conclusion that he was a vinegar-seller; this is sometimes cited as evidence of the bourgeois character of the Abbasid movement. Yet Ibn Khallikān[40] tells us that Abū Salama was a rich Kūfan, who was called al-Khallāl only because he happened to have a house near the street of the vinegar merchants!

There are also many, many discrepancies among the sources concerning the proper form of a name and whether an individual was an Arab, a *mawlā,* or an Iranian. Most sources, for example, describe Sulaymān b. Kathīr as a member by blood of the tribe of Khuzā'a yet Balādhurī, an authority who cannot be disregarded, claims that Sulaymān was their *mawlā.*[41] Consequently, a seemingly straightforward matter such as giving the names of the twelve *nuqabā'* turns out to be fiendishly problematic in light of the extreme variations in the lists as given by different traditionalists.

These difficulties are understandable, if not resolvable, once we recognize that the various lists of names were compiled during the height of the *shu'ūbī* controversy. Far from setting down the names objectively, writers chose to exaggerate or to minimize the roles of the Arabs or the non-Arabs according to their own prejudices. Jāḥiẓ made this point perfectly clear in his essay *Manāqib al-turk.* He cited one list of the *nuqabā'* as given by the anti-*shu'ūbī*s which was, not surprisingly, entirely Arab in composition and then gave a counter-list, as compiled by the *shu'ūbī*s, which consisted almost entirely of *mawālī.*[42] It was quite easy to propagandize in this way. One merely omitted to mention that an "Arab" was a *de jure* member of a tribe (*mawlā*) rather than a member by blood. Conversely, one might not point out that a *mawlā* was a pure Arab who had become the client of another tribe. It was quite tempting to play on the ambiguities inherent in the term *mawlā*[43] to justify a political viewpoint: Since al-Balādhurī wanted to demonstrate the "anti-Arab" nature of the Abbasid movement, he chose to describe Sulaymān b. Kathīr as a *mawlā.* Those who wished to celebrate the Arab role in Islamic affairs no doubt failed to identify various individuals as *mawālī,* while the *shu'ūbī* partisans turned Balādhurī's arguments upside down by identifying pure Arabs, perhaps quite correctly, as *mawālī.* In any event, it is misleading at best, if not plainly ludicrous, when a modern historian like M. A. Shaban purports to prove that Arabs, not non-Arabs, dominated the *da'wa* on the evidence of only one of the many lists of the twelve *nuqabā.*[44] That repeats the very error Jāḥiz warned against.

Finally, even if the name lists could be taken at face value, they would tell us essentially nothing about the movement as a whole. By their very nature, they describe only the *leadership* of the movement, not its complete composition. A true profile of the movement would have to be based on a vertical cross-section of the membership, from the highest ranks to the lowest, not on a horizontal view of the movement's elite. Yet the sources had little interest in the lower strata of the movement; they ignored the faceless multitude in favor of the privileged few. Thus, one should really search for those incidental, but quite revealing, details which indicate the broader make-up of the membership of the *da'wa*.

With these reservations in mind, is it possible to derive any useful insights about the movement on the basis of the name-lists? Perhaps the most reliable, and certainly the most extensive, of these lists is the one preserved in the *Akhbār al-'abbās,* which provides the names of 148 different participants in the early phase of the *da'wa*.[45] An analysis of these names is quite revealing, and may be considered as one piece of evidence about the nature of the *da'wa:* Of the 148 names, 71 either contain the *nisba* of an Arab tribe or it is given elsewhere in the work; 76 names either have no *nisba,* have the *nisba* of place, or are described as belonging to a *mawlā;* one name (al-Sarawī) is of debatable meaning. Interestingly, the 71 "Arab" names refer to some 25 different clans or tribes, representing virtually the entire spectrum of tribal interests in Khurasan. There are 16 instances of Khuzā'ī partisans. That is understandable, since the Khuzā'a have long been considered among the foremost Abbasid partisans: they had been established in Khurasan almost from the time of the Arab conquest, were largely assimilated, and had long had the reputation of being both "poor and numerous."[46] Yet there are also 16 names of partisans from the Banū Tamīm, supposedly the rivals of Khuzā'a and the very backbone of Umayyad tribal support in the province! This is characteristic of the entire list: Representatives of Azd, Ṭayy', Hamdān, Ḥimyar, and 'Akk are side by side with Ṭafāwa, Ḍabba, Asad, and Bāhila. The individuals not included in this "Arab" group represent an equally varied and diverse sampling of Khurāsānī society. Twelve individuals are identified as *mawālī,* six have names which could only be Iranian (Rustam, Mākhanbadh, etc.), eight are associated with a specific town or area; the remaining fifty have no identifiable affiliation at all.

This list of names, like all the others, is naturally open to many objections. Some of the individuals described as Arabs are called *mawālī* in other sources; some of the unaffiliated individuals are described elsewhere as either Arabs, *mawālī,* or *'ajam.* It is nevertheless the most representative sampling available, and the chief conclusion to be drawn from it seems justifiable: No one group, racial or otherwise, dominated the *da'wa.* The movement seems to have appealed to every area and to every social group in the province, save the very highest ruling elite. Of course, it is always possible that this is the view which the author of the *Akhbār* wished to present, but, as we shall see, there is other evidence which leads to the same conclusion.

The Khidāsh Episode (118/736): The career of the heretic missionary Khidāsh is of considerable interest because it anticipated much of what was to occur in the history of the *da'wa* and in Abbasid Iran.

The first mention of Khidāsh in the chronicles comes in the year 109/727, when the governor Asad b. 'Abd Allah captured and executed Abū Muḥammad Ziyād, one of the Abbasid *du'āt.* A Kūfan named Kathīr succeeded Ziyād, proselytizing and instructing converts. A few years later, while he was teaching in the village of Mar'am (?), Khidāsh attended his lessons and soon surpassed him in knowledge.[47] Other sources allege that Khidāsh was a Christian convert to Islam in Kūfa who came to the attention of Bukayr b. Māhān.[48] Whatever the case, Bukayr sent him to Khurasan, apparently in 118/736, as the chief (*wālī*) of the Abbasid partisans there.[49]

With the arrival of Khidāsh, the slow but steady stream of new recruits for the Abbasid cause suddenly became a torrent, for Khidāsh chose to appeal to the esoteric religious and social beliefs of the Khurāsānī masses. According to some sources, he changed his name from 'Ammār or 'Ammāra b. Yazīd to Khidāsh[50]; more hostile accounts state that he was given the nickname because he defamed (*khadasha*) the religion.[51] Far from preaching obedience to the Koran, the *sunna,* and *al-riḍā,* Khidāsh ignored Muḥammad b. 'Alī's directions. He taught that there was no obligation to fast, to pray, or to perform the pilgrimage as required of orthodox Muslims.[52] As proof, he pointed to a verse from the Koran itself: "There is no fault in those who believe and do deeds of righteousness as to what they enjoy, so long as they are Godfearing, and believe, and do good."[53] Like Mazdak[54] before him, Khidāsh allegedly authorized his followers to enjoy each others' wives and to follow the precepts of the so-called Khurramī religion (the name of which is sometimes derived from a Persian word meaning "pleasure").[55] The result was that the people "hastened to him and accepted what he told them; they listened to him and obeyed."[56] Even some of the chiefs of the *da'wa,* including Mālik b. al-Haytham and al-Ḥarīsh b. Sulaym al-A'jamī, joined Khidāsh, perhaps believing that he was following the directives of Muḥammad b. 'Alī.[57]

Not surprisingly, a movement such as this quickly aroused suspicion and suppression. Though some traditions hold that supporters of Muḥammad b. 'Alī surprised and murdered Khidāsh,[58] a more likely account relates that the governor, Asad, heard of his activity and arrested him. Khidāsh spoke impudently to him, so Asad, who was preparing a military expedition to Balkh, had him mutilated and then sent him to the Umayyad agent in Āmul, Yaḥyā b. Nu'aym al-Shaybānī, who crucified him.[59] There are also reports that the corpse was nailed to the city gate of Kābul.[60]

The death of Khidāsh damaged but did not destroy the movement he had initiated. Many of his followers refused to believe that he was dead and claimed that God had concealed him in heaven. A sect devoted to his teachings sprang up and continued to propagate his doctrines right up to the time of Abū Muslim. His followers continued to reject the idea of religious obligations, believed in *tanāsukh* (basically the transmigration of souls), and regarded bloodshed and brigandry as legitimate. To emphasize their alienation from the moderate branch of the *da'wa,* they taught that the imāmate had passed from the family of al-'Abbās to Khidāsh and that Muḥammad b. 'Alī was the devil incarnate.[61]

This intriguing incident illustrates two important trends already present in the Abbasid *da'wa* at an early date. It shows, first of all, that a sizable element within the movement was familiar with and inclined to accept indigenous, popular, Iranian socio-religious beliefs. Second, it reveals a certain amount of tension between local, purely Khurāsānī, interests and the sometimes conflicting ideas and desires of the chiefs of the movement in Kūfa and Ḥumayma. Although temporarily submerged, these two tendencies would reemerge to dominate events in the coming century.

Reassertion of the imām's *Authority (119/737–125/743):* Muḥammad b. 'Alī and his close associates may have been temporarily distracted from events in Khurasan by the death of 'Alī b. 'Abd Allah in the same year as Khidāsh's appearance,[62] but they did not fail to take note of the lesson Khidāsh had given. If their cause was to find the widespread support needed for success, the Abbasids had to exploit popular beliefs and local issues; but to avoid antagonizing their more conservative followers they also had to keep a tight rein over the movement. Consequently, Muḥammed b. ʿAlī remained "estranged"[63] from his partisans in Khurasan for the next two years. This naturally concerned them, so they agreed to send a delegation to the *imān* to solicit his guidance. Sulaymān b. Kathīr emerged as the leader of this group and, in 120/738, he left for Ḥumayma. Muḥammad b. ʿAlī took this opportunity to rebuke all those who had followed Khidāsh: "God curse Khidāsh and whoever follows his religion."[64] Then he sent Sulaymān back to Khurasan bearing a sealed letter containing only the formula "in the name of God, the Compassionate, the Merciful."[65] That cryptic message apparently was insufficient to convince the Khurāsānīs of their error, for later in the same year the *imām* was obliged to send Bukayr b. Māhān to Khurasan with another letter informing his followers that Khidāsh had misled them. This also failed to settle the matter, with the result that Bukayr was despatched again, this time with some staffs, some tipped with iron and the rest with brass.[66] The significance of this gesture is far from clear, but it was enough to discipline the dissidents at last. Thereafter, the partisans were under strict orders not to support anyone who taught doctrines not found in the Koran or the *sunna* of the Prophet.[67]

The importance of this restraint became all too clear with the outbreak of an ʿAlīd rebellion in Kūfa in 122/740 on behalf of Zayd b. ʿAlī.[68] Although the Abbasids may very well have had a hand in provoking this revolt,[69] and although the sympathies of many of their partisans clearly lay with Zayd, Muḥammad b. ʿAlī was too cautious to offer anything more than moral support. He ordered the chiefs of the *daʿwa* to tell the partisans to remain in their houses for the duration of the revolt.[70] As it turned out, this was only a few days before the Syrian troops captured and crucified Zayd.

Far more significant for an understanding of the Abbasid movement is the career of Zayd's son Yaḥyā, who, aided by a *dihqān* of Madā'in, fled towards Khurasan.[71] There could be no clearer example of the discontent with Umayyad rule sweeping the East in the form of proto-Shiʿite sectarianism. As Yaḥyā, pursued by Umayyad generals, made his way through Rayy, Balkh, Sarakhs, and elsewhere, he aroused feelings of sympathy among many segments of the population who expressed their hatred of Umayyad "iniquity" and gave Yaḥyā shelter and assistance. Yaḥyā, however, was young and inexperienced; he lacked the kind of organization necessary to exploit the sentiments he had awakened. Thus he was ultimately hunted down and executed near Jūzjān in 125/743; yet his ill-fated revolt had thrown Khurasan into a turmoil which would not abate until the Umayyads were finally expelled. The experience was so profound and traumatic that one (pro-Shi'ite) source claims that no son was born in Khurasan that year without being named Yaḥyā or Zayd.[72]

All this worked to the advantage of the Abbasids, for there were many similarities between the two movements. Yaḥyā was an 'Alid to be sure, but it is worth noting that his maternal grandfather was none other than Abū Hāshim. Consequently, he as well as the Abbasids could have had affinities with the Hāshimiyya sect. His corpse, left exposed on a gibbet, cried out for vengeance, and this the Abbasids claimed to be seeking. Abū Muslim made vengeance for Yaḥyā one of his slogans; in time, he would kill Salm b. Aḥwāz, the general directly responsible for Yaḥyā's death, and would give the martyr's body a proper burial. The *du'at* were so active in exciting Zaydī sentiments that it was often assumed they were preaching on their behalf rather than for the Abbasids. As always, the Abbasids capitalized on the strength of other movements by assimilating them with their own. Without ever making any real commitment to the Zaydī cause, they used the feelings Yaḥyā had aroused for their own benefit. Their ability to do this was due in large part to the rigid control and discipline Muḥammad b. 'Alī maintained over the inner circles of the *da'wa*.

Bukayr had hurried back to Khurasan shortly before the death of Yaḥyā. After a month in Jurjān, he went on to Merv, where one Abū'l-Ḥajjāj al-Tamīmī informed the governor, Naṣr b. Sayyār, that he was preaching on behalf of Yaḥyā b. Zayd. Naṣr ordered his arrest, but one of his own agents, 'Ubayd Allah b. Bassām, was secretly in league with the conspirators and managed to warn Bukayr. Bukayr immediately ordered the *dā'ī*s to flee to the villages while he himself returned to Iraq.[73] He was not so fortunate there, for, according to the tradition of al-Madā'inī, he was arrested in Kūfa in 124/741-2.[74]

A variant set of traditions relates that late in 124, a group of Khurāsānī leaders—Sulaymān b. Kathīr, Mālik b. al-Haytham, Lāhiz b. Qurayẓ, and Qaḥṭaba b. Shabīb—went to Mecca to meet with the *imām* and to present him with 200,000 *dirham*s and some 30,000 *dirham*s worth of goods collected in his behalf.[75] It was at that meeting that Muḥammad b. 'Alī is supposed to have first heard of Abū

Muslim, prophesized his own imminent death, and designated his son, Ibrāhīm, as his successor.[76] He died on 1 Dhū'l-Qa'da 125 (26 August 743).[77]

Preparation for Revolt (125/743–127/745): The first order of business after Muḥammad b. 'Alī's death was securing recognition of Ibrāhīm's succession from the partisans. Bukayr b. Māhān therefore set out for Khurasan to inform the leaders there of the *imām*'s death and to give them a letter from Ibrāhīm.[78] He stopped first in Jurjān, where he met with Abū 'Awn, 'Āmir b. Ismā'īl, and Khālid b. Barmak.[79] He then went on to Merv and assembled the *nuqabā,* whom he consoled for the death of Muḥammad b. 'Alī. He then solicited and obtained their support for Ibrāhīm.[80] After about two months, he returned to Iraq, accompanied, at his invitation, by a group of Khurāsānī leaders including Sulaymān b. Kathīr, Qaḥṭaba b. Shabīb, and Mālik b. al-Haytham. Abū Salama al-Khallāl joined the delegation in Kūfa. They then proceeded to Mecca, where they presented Ibrāhīm with more funds collected in Khurasan for the movement.[81] The date of these events is problematic: The *Akhbār al-'abbās* claims that the delegation arrived in Kūfa just in time to hear of the death of the Caliph Hishām and the accession of al-Walīd II (125/743),[82] but Ṭabarī states that Ibrāhīm sent Bukayr to Khurasan in 126/743–4 and that the return delegation did not arrive until 127/744–5.[83]

The Khurāsānīs were generally satisfied with Ibrāhīm and gave him their support. Indeed, the only dissenting voice seems to have been that of Yaḥyā, a "feeble-minded" *mawlā* of the late Muḥammad b. 'Alī, who threatened to denounce the partisans to the authorities. A portion of the revenues from Khurasan sufficed to purchase his silence.[84]

Although the main purpose of the delegation was to give the partisans a chance to size up the new *imām* and to pledge their obedience, the Khurāsānīs also took the opportunity to express their impatience with the restraints Muḥammad b. 'Alī had placed on them.[85] For the moment, Ibrāhīm had little choice but to put them off with references to prophecies that the revolt would come in 130 A.H. (that is, approximately one hundred years after the establishment of Umayyad rule).[86]

He did understand their feelings, and it is a mark of his genius that he soon found a way to give them some much-needed moral support. The color black had a special psychological significance for the partisans,[87] so Ibrāhīm ordered Bukayr to go to Khurasan to authorize his followers to wear black garments and to present them with symbolic black banners.[88] Bukayr died before he could carry out his directive, but his son-in-law and designated successor, Abū Salama, perhaps accompanied by Abū Muslim, proceeded to Jurjān, where he presented Abū 'Awn with the first of the banners. He gave a second banner to Sulaymān b. Kathīr in Merv and sent the third to Transoxiana with Mujāshi' b. Harīth al-Anṣarī (or 'Amr b. Sinān al-Murādī).[89] Whether these black banners represented vengeance for Yaḥyā or mourning for the *imām,* or had some eschatological significance, we cannot venture to say, but they provided the eager partisans with a visible sign that the time to strike was near though it was not until much later, when Umayyad rule was already on the verge of collapse, that Ibrāhīm would authorize any overt political subversion.

The Disintegration of Umayyad Authority: It is beyond the scope of this work to describe, let alone to try to account for, the rapid and remarkable deterioration of Umayyad political power in the years immediately after the death of Hishām (reigned 105/724–125/743).[90] It is essential, however, to survey those events in Iran which accompanied the decline of Umayyad power there.

First, the Khārijite revolts which were convulsing Iraq and the Jazīra spilled over into Armenia and Ādharbayjān. According to reports apparently found only in the chronicle of Khalīfa b. Khayyāṭ, Bisṭām b. Layth al-Taghlabī, a member of the Bayhasiyya sect of the Khawārij, revolted in those provinces in 128/746. After several defeats, Bisṭām tried to make his way to Iraq, presumably to join forces with the Khārijite rebel Ḍaḥḥāk b. Qays. However, he and most of his men were annihilated in a battle not far from Shahrazūr.[91]

It is difficult to accept this tradition, since it is based on only one source and must be confused with the much earlier revolt of Shawdhab Bisṭām al-Khārijī (ca. 101 A.H.). Nonetheless, it is certain that a Khārijite revolt began in Ardabīl at about the time reported by Khalīfa. It was led by a butcher-turned-rebel named Musāfir b. Kathīr, who was also reported to have been in league with Ḍaḥḥāk. The Umayyad governor of the area, 'Āṣim b. Yazīd al-Hilālī, attempted to control the revolt by arresting two well-known Khārijites from Baylaqān. Undaunted, Musāfir led a daring night raid on the prison, killing the chief security officer and freeing the prisoners. With that, many people from the Baylaqān area joined the revolt.

'Āṣim, who had been away at the time, prepared to attack Musāfir and encamped near Bardha'a. The Khārijites captured one of his men, whom Musāfir paid to lead the rebels at night to 'Āṣim's position. The Khārijites attacked just before dawn; the government forces were decisively defeated, and 'Āṣim was killed.

When the Caliph Marwān heard of this disaster, he sent 'Abd al-Malik b. Muslim al-'Uqaylī to the province. 'Abd al-Malik, in command of a large force, attacked the Khārijites at Yūnān, a village midway between Baylaqān and Bardha'a. Again, the Umayyad forces were defeated and the commander killed. 'Abd al-Malik's brother, Isḥāq, continued to resist the Khārijites with the remnants of the Umayyad army, but the struggle was not resolved before the dynasty itself had collapsed.[92] Thus it was that Umayyad communications with Khurasan were disrupted at a critical moment by the disturbances in northwest Iran.

At nearly the same time, a profound disturbance of a different nature menaced Umayyad rule in southwest Iran. In Muḥarram 127/October 744, the revolt of 'Abd Allah b. Mu'āwiya broke out in Kūfa.[93] Although usually classed as a Shi'ite revolt, it was 'Alīd only in the broadest sense, for Ibn Mu'āwiya was actually a descendant of 'Alī's brother, Ja'far.[94] The Umayyad general 'Abd Allah, son of the Caliph 'Umar II, rapidly suppressed the insurrection in Kūfa, but Ibn Mu'āwiya showed his mettle by retreating first to Madā'in, then to the Jibāl, and finally to Fārs. He picked up many partisans along the way and actually succeeded in establishing a brief, tenuous rule over large areas of the Jibāl, Aḥwāz, Fārs, and Kirmān. He was even able to mint his own coins to replace those of the Umayyads.[95]

The most remarkable feature of his revolt was the incredible diversity of the groups which supported it. Apparently, anyone who had a grievance against the Umayyads was willing to fight under the banner of Ibn Mu'āwiya; he was able, albeit briefly, to forge a motley coalition which included several shī'ite groups, Khārijites, Iranian *mawālī,* the Umayyad pretender Sulaymān b. Hishām, and a number of Abbasids, including the future Caliph Abū Ja'far al-Manṣūr.[96] A huge Umayyad army commanded by the veteran general Ibn Ḍubāra finally defeated Ibn Mu'āwiya, but by that time the Abbasid revolt had broken out in Khurasan. Ibn Mu'āwiya fled east, anticipating a welcome and assistance from Abū Muslim. As we shall see, the reception he received was not the one he had expected.

The revolt of Ibn Mu'āwiya is not only significant as a symptom of Umayyad weakness. In many ways very similar to the Abbasid *da'wa,* it might almost be considered a dress rehearsal for the revolt in Khurasan. The heresiographer Sa'd al-Qummī pointed out that Ibn Mu'āwiya, like the Abbasids, claimed a close relationship with Abū Hāshim and that his followers believed that Abū Hashim had really bequeathed the imāmate to Ibn Mu'āwiya. Thus, as Sa'd rightly notes, Ibn Mu'āwiya was the chief rival of the Abbasids for control of the Hāshimiyya partisans.[97] The teachings of the Janāḥiyya, the fanatical sect devoted to Ibn Mu'āwiya, closely paralleled many of the ideas propogated by the Abbasid missionaries in Khurasan. Even the coins minted by Ibn Mu'āwiya carried the slogan later used by Abū Muslim for his coinage: "I ask no wage of you save love of my kin."[98]

Because of its popularity and diverse sources of support, the revolt of Ibn Muāwiya, even more than that of Yaḥyā b. Zayd, demonstrated how widespread the various types of anti-Umayyad sentiment had become and that the many disparate factions could be welded into a manageable whole by an astute leader under the vague mantle of proto-shī'ite ideology. This was a lesson the Abbasids had mastered well, much to the eventual discomfort not only of the Umayyads but even of Ibn Mu'āwiya.

While the Western provinces were sliding into anarchy, and to some extent as a result, the Umayyad position also became untenable in Khurasan. The Umayyads faced any number of difficulties in governing there: controversy over tax policies, incompetent governors, the problem of religious conversions (often in less than "orthodox" fashion), reverses in the war with the Turks, famine. Perhaps worse, the Umayyad establishment, in its final years, was divided bitterly against itself; and the competing factions all were increasingly out of touch with the concerns of the subject peoples. In this, the chaotic and vacillating political situation in Khurasan was a small-scale version of the empire as a whole.

The most visible expression of the rivalries between the opposing Umayyad factions was a struggle for control of provincial political offices. In Khurasan, the controversy swirled around three individuals: al-Ḥārith b. Surayj, a perennial rebel and leader of the Arab colonists, who had been established in Khurasan long enough to become somewhat assimilated with the native population and to have close ties with the *dahāqīn;* Juday' b. 'Alī al-Kirmānī, usually known simply as al-Kirmānī, the apparent leader of a new warrior class designed to supplant the old, rather inept, and politically suspect *muqātila*/colonist faction; and the octogenarian governor of the province, Naṣr b. Sayyār.[99]

The roots of the conflict extended deep into the past, and involved a number of social and economic questions, but the immediate source of trouble was Naṣr's appointment as governor. In 120/738, during a reorganization of the provincial administration, Yūsuf b. 'Umar replaced Khālid b. 'Abd Allah al-Qasrī as governor of Iraq. Khurasan was then regarded as a dependency of Iraq, so Yūsuf attempted to install his favorite, Juday' al-Kirmānī, as his deputy in the province. The Caliph Hishām, however, refused to recognize this appointment, despite the objections of many of his advisors as well as Yūsuf. The reasons for his opposition are not altogether clear. It may have been based in part on a desire to bring Khurasan under more direct control by the central government, in the hope of establishing a counterweight to Yūsuf should the need arise, but the primary reason, judging from the confused accounts in the sources, seems to have been Hishām's fear that al-Kirmānī, who was a newcomer to Khurasan and who was openly biased in favor of his own Yamanī tribe of Azd, would further antagonize the older interests in Khurasan, represented by the Muḍarī faction led by al-Ḥārith b. Surayj al-Tamīmī, if it did not lead to outright civil war. Hishām therefore sought a compromise candidate, and finally settled on Naṣr.[100]

In some ways Naṣr was an excellent choice. He had lived in the East for most, if not all, of his long life. He had held several military and adminstrative posts which well qualified him for the governorship. He had distinguished himself in campaigns against the Turks. He spoke what the sources call Persian, was married to the daughter of a powerful Tamīmī tribal leader, and was on excellent terms with the upper echelons of the Iranian aristocracy, particularly those from Transoxiana, like the Bukhār-khudā.[101] He was an exceptionally shrewd politician who was able to implement several reforms during his tenure as governor, most notably of the unpopular system of taxation.[102]

But Naṣr was an unfortunate choice in other ways. He was quite out of touch with the Khurāsānī masses, and his relations with the *dahāqīn,* whom he frequently oppressed, were very strained. The circumstances surrounding his appointment as governor made Naṣr and Yūsuf b. 'Umar bitter enemies, and that frequently worked to the detriment of the central government, as when Yūsuf frustrated the much-needed reform proposed by al-Walīd to separate the administrations of Iraq and Khurasan.[103] For the same reason, Naṣr and al-Kirmānī remained personal rivals, always suspicious of each other. But most of all, Naṣr was notorious for the favoritism he showed his own tribe,[104] and in this he was no better a choice than al-Kirmānī. By blood and by inclination, Naṣr was closer to al-Ḥārith than he could ever be to al-Kirmānī, and this manifested itself in his handling of Khurāsānī affairs.

Matters came to a head in 126/743–4, when al-Kirmānī publicly chided Naṣr for favoring the Muḍar confederation over that of the Yaman. This angered Naṣr and gave him an excuse to throw al-Kirmānī into jail. Al-Kirmānī managed to escape and fled to his home village, where he incited his fellow Azdī tribesmen to revolt. They were soon joined by a confederation of other dissidents whose only common bond was a hatred of Naṣr and his policies.[105]

Naṣr could take temporary comfort in the aid provided him against al-Kirmānī by al-Ḥārith b. Surayj. Naṣr had secured a pardon for the old rebel from Yazīd III, so al-Ḥārith came forward as a spokesman of Arab unity and convinced his followers, mostly Tamīmī tribesmen, to fight al-Kirmānī, who was, after all, their enemy as much as he was Naṣr's.[106] Naṣr and his friend the Bukhār-khudā honored al-Ḥārith for this, but they were quickly disillusioned as to his ultimate intentions. When Marwān seized the caliphate, bringing a different branch of the Umayyad family into power, Naṣr recognized the usurpation in order to hold on to his post. Al-Ḥārith, however, would have nothing to do with that, refused to recognize Marwān, and, joined by many of Naṣr's own former supporters, started a revolt of his own before being killed by his old nemesis, al-Kirmānī.[107]

Thus the great *'aṣabiyya* (tribal strife) was in full swing in Khurasan, and the main beneficiaries were—the Abbasids! It would be difficult to imagine a more ideal environment for their revolt. They inherited some of the support formerly given to al-Ḥārith, had their two chief rivals at each other's throat, and had most of Khurasan excited to a fever pitch of enthusiasm for their cause. They were ready to make the most of this opportunity.

The Revolt (127/744–130/748): This then was the political situation which had made the partisans of Ibrāhīm b. 'Alī increasingly restless. The *imām* was now ready to follow up the psychological gestures he had made to the partisans with concrete actions. He confirmed this by sending his personal representative, Abū Muslim 'Abd al-Raḥman b. Muslim al-Khurāsānī, to lead the partisans.

Abū Muslim's origins, the circumstances surrounding his association with the *da'wa,* and the reasons for choosing him as leader of the Khurāsānī partisans are all shrouded in mystery, and discussion of these problems must be reserved for a separate chapter.

The sources give different dates for the year when Ibrāhīm sent Abū Muslim to Khurasan, varying from as early as 127/744 to as late as 129/747.[108] The confusion may derive from the probability that Abū Muslim had made several trips to Khurasan as a messenger before his appointment as chief of the *da'wa* there.[109] No doubt some confusion also stems from the reluctance of some Khurāsānīs to accept Abū Muslim as their leader. They had hoped that Ibrāhīm would send a member of his own family (although Ibrāhīm seems to have regarded Abū Muslim as his *mawlā* to be in principle a member of the family), and so Ṭabarī reports that Abū Muslim had to return to Ibrāhīm in 128 to inform him that the partisans had refused to obey him.[110]

This angered Ibrāhīm, who flatly refused to appoint another leader. He apparently felt that the appointment of Abū Muslim, whom he had taken great pains to establish in Khurasan, was vital to the success of the mission. Therefore, he arranged a more formal ceremony of investiture of Abū Muslim as his deputy. According to one interesting account, Ibrāhīm made it clear that Abū Muslim was to be the chief authority in Khurasan, Sīstān, Kirmān, Jurjān, Qūmis, Rayy, Isfahan, and Hamadan, while Abū Salama was in charge of Iraq, the Jazīra, and Syria.[111] If so, the missionaries already had a clear idea of the kind of political structure they wished to bring about.

Ibrāhīm also gave Abū Muslim instructions about implementing the *da'wa*. For the most part, these instructions were much like those given to the missionaries on previous occasions. He was to settle among the Yaman, respect the Rabī'a, and beware the Muḍar; he was also told to honor Sulaymān b. Kathīr. There is, however, considerable controversy about one of the directives. It is alleged that Ibrāhīm ordered Abū Muslim not to leave an Arab alive in Khurasan (literally, not to leave anyone who spoke Arabic in Khurasan). Other sources say simply that Ibrāhīm exhorted Abū Muslim to kill anyone he had reason to suspect.[112]

The point is of considerable historiographic interest. Since many of the partisans as well as the Abbasids themselves were Arabs, it is obviously incredible that such an order would have been given, much less carried out. Apparently a copy of Ibrāhīm's directives fell into the hands of his opponents, who then took his remarks out of context or exaggerated and distorted them in an effort to turn Arab tribal sentiments against the Abbasids. This propaganda effort was continued by some later writers, who saw in these remarks proof that the Abbasid revolt represented a Persian plot to overthrow the Arabs. The error was compounded when some national-minded modern historians uncritically accepted the command as evidence of the anti-Arab character of the Abbasid movement. In its proper context, the command, whatever it was precisely, should be considered as nothing more than an encouragement for the rebels to be zealous and ruthless in their struggle. It is also interesting that it is usually phrased so as to be directed against those who "spoke Arabic" in Khurasan. This would tend to indicate, as we have tried to suggest, that the *da'wa* supported assimilationist tendencies in opposition to "foreign" domination of the province.

Abū Muslim's arrival in Merv in 129 A.H. touched off a minor crisis within the leadership of the *da'wa*. The partisans were assembled, and the secretary of the organization, Abū Manṣūr Ṭalḥa b. Zurayq (or Ruzayq), read the communique containing the *imām*'s orders. Sulaymān b. Kathīr was particularly vexed at having to accept Abū Muslim, cursed him, and threw an inkwell at him.[113] We can only speculate about his motives: He may have been jealously protecting his own position; he may have had genuine doubts about Abū Muslim's youth and inexperience; he may have been prejudiced about accepting as his superior a *mawlā* of dubious origin; he may have feared that Abū Muslim, as something of an outsider, would not act in the best interests of the Khurāsānīs; or he may just have been wary about making an error about Abū Muslim as others had about Khidāsh. For his part, Abū Muslim scrupulously obeyed the *imām*'s orders and treated Sulaymān with the greatest dignity and propriety. One by one, the chiefs of the *da'wa* came over to his side, led by Muḥammad b. 'Ulwān al-Marwazī, and voted to accept him.[114] Sulaymān eventually had no choice but to reconcile himself with Abū Muslim, and Abū Muslim continued to keep the ranks of the partisans united by treating Sulaymān with extreme deference and politeness.

After a brief stay in the Kharqān quarter of Merv with his father-in-law, Abū'l-Najm, Abū Muslim and a group of the *nuqabā'* left to hold new consultations with Ibrāhīm in the middle of Jumādā II 129 (early March 747). The account of this trip is of great interest in light of recent suggestions that the *da'wa* had not spread far beyond the confines of the Merv oasis.[115] According to Ṭabarī, the group stopped first in Dāndānqān, where they were questioned closely by a certain Kāmil (or Abū Kamil), whom they told that they were performing the *ḥajj*. Then Abū Muslim exhibited his remarkable powers of persuasion by managing to convert Kāmil to their cause.

After a brief stay in Abīward, where they were joined by 'Uthmān b. Nahīk and a number of the partisans, the group moved on to Nasā. The *da'wa* had clearly been conducted there as well, since the prudent Abū Muslim sent al-Faḍl b. Sulaymān al-Ṭūsī ahead to inform their representative there, Usayd b. 'Abd Allah al-Khuzā'ī, of their arrival. Moreover, al-Faḍl, on the way, recognized another partisan in one of the villages of Nasā. When the group reached Qūmis, they received a letter from the *imām* ordering them to return to Khurasan: The moment to proclaim the revolt was near. On the way back, the party excited the suspicion of Naṣr's agent in Nasā, 'Āṣim b. Qays, who wanted to know why they had not completed their pilgrimage. He finally released them, but sent the chief of his bodyguard, al-Mufaḍḍal b. al-Sharqī, to keep an eye on them. Again, Abū Muslim was able to take the man aside and convert him to the cause.[116]

The accounts of Abū Muslim's return to Merv are full of discrepancies; the most plausible version states that he arrived on 9 Sha'bān 129 (25 April 747) and settled in the village of Fanīn, home of the *naqīb* Abū Da'ūd Khālid b. Ibrāhīm.[117] From there, he sent his deputies to spread the *da'wa:* Abū Da'ūd and 'Umar b. A'yan to Balkh and Ṭukhāristān; al-Naḍr b. Ṣabīḥ al-Tamīmī and Sharīk b. Ghaḍī al-Tamīmī to Marw al-rūdh; Abū 'Āṣim 'Abd al-Rahman b. Salīm to Ṭālaqān; Mūsā b. Ka'b to Abīward and Nasā; and Abū'l-Jahm b. 'Aṭiyya to join al-'Alā' b. Ḥarīth, who was in Khwārizm. Abū 'Awn and Khālid b. Barmak were already at work in Jurjān.[118] Judging from material in one of the manuscripts of Bal'amī's history, as many as ten other towns were also actively involved in the *da'wa*.[119]

Early in Ramaḍān, Abū Muslim moved to Safīdhanj, the Khuzā'ī village which was the home of Sulaymān b. Kathīr.[120] As the fighting between al-Kirmānī and Naṣr had been complicated by the arrival of Shaybān b. Salama, a Khārijite refugee from Iraq, Abū Muslim was able to propagate his doctrine among the citizenry with relative impunity. We are told in a single day he was joined by people from sixty villages who had heard of the arrival of a representative of the Banū Hāshim.[121]

The partisans then convened a consultative assembly to decide where the revolt should begin. Abū'l-Jahm and others urged the selection of Khwārizm, which was far from Naṣr's control. Mūsā b. Ka'b, Lāhiz b. Qurayẓ, Mālik b. al-Haytham, and Ṭalḥa b. Zurayq argued for Marw al-rūdh, where they had found many supporters. Abū Muslim solicited the opinion of Abū Ṣāliḥ Kāmil b. Muẓaffar. He recommended starting the revolt in Merv itself.[122] Abū Muslim approved of this daring suggestion, probably to demonstrate the weakness of the Umayyad faction at the very seat of their power, and the other partisans agreed.

According to the *Akhbār al-'abbās,* the partisans had planned to declare the revolt in Muḥarram 130 (September 747) in accordance with prophecies about the downfall of the Umayyads. Abū Muslim, however, got wind of a plan by Naṣr b. Sayyār to make a pre-emptive strike against them, so the revolt had to be launched prematurely.[123] The black banners were unfurled, and the Abbasid *da'wa* entered its final phase.

Abū Muslim's first task was to summon the partisans to his camp and to organize them into a fighting force. The accounts of this, though often confused and contradictory, are among the best evidence of the movement's sources of support. There is general agreement that the first to join Abū Muslim were "the people of Suqādim."[124] Wellhausen read this as a place name,[125] while Shaban, following a variant spelling given by Ibn al-Athīr, chose to interpret it as meaning the Arab settlers in Merv.[126] However, since Ṭabarī makes several specific references to *rub' al-suqādim,* and even enumerates a few of its villages, it seems more likely, that the name refers simply to a section of Merv, analogous to the Kharqān quarter.[127]

The first contingent of troops, said to have numbered more than 900 men, came from the village of Hurmuzfarrah (the hometown of Bukayr b. Māhān!), led by Abū'l-Waḍḍāḥ 'Īsā b. Shubayl, Sulaymān b. Ḥassān and his brother Yazdān, al-Haytham b. Kaysān, the *mawlā* Buway', and the *naqīb* Muḥammad b. 'Ulwān. They were followed by another group of 1300 infantrymen and 16 horsemen commanded by Abū'l-Qāsim Muḥriz al-Jūbānī and accompanied by the *dā'īs* Abū'l-'Abbās al-Marwazī, Khidhām b. 'Ammār, and Ḥamza b. Zunaym.

The account in the *Akhbār al-'abbās* differs slightly from that given by Ṭabarī. It states that the first to reach Abū Muslim were Khuzā'ī tribesmen, since they lived closest to Safīdhanj. There were some twenty-five of them, followed by twelve Tamīmī tribesmen, six from Ṭayy', and thirty-one others identified simply as partisans (*shī'a*). Then people came from all the various villages around Merv.[128] It would again appear that the movement received support from many diverse sources, without any one tribal or ethnic group being dominant. At the same time, the strong peasant character of the movement is apparent, since so many of the partisans came from small villages.

Abū Muslim's army entered Safīdhanj on 27 Ramaḍān (12 June) and proceeded to repair and strengthen the local citadel. A few days later, during the holiday of the Breaking of the Fast (*yawm al-fiṭr*), Abū Muslim dramatized the partisans' act of revolt by having Sulaymān b. Kathīr lead them in a prayer service which differed in a few respects from standard Umayyad practice.[129]

News of this reached Naṣr. Some of his advisors urged him to raid the Khuzā'ī villages, but Naṣr refused, probably fearing that such action would only aggravate the situation and bring the tribesmen of Rabī'a and Yaman to go to their aid.[130] The first test of strength between Naṣr and Abū Muslim came eighteen days[131] after the proclamation of the revolt, which would have been on 13 Shawwāl (27 June). Naṣr sent Yazīd, a *mawlā,* in command of a substantial cavalry unit to attack Abū Muslim. Abū Muslim sent out about 200 troops under Mālik b. al-Haytham al-Khuzā'ī and Muṣ'ab b. Qays, and the two belligerents clashed in the village of Ālīn. The fighting raged from morning into the afternoon, so Abū Muslim sent reinforcements under Ṣāliḥ b. Sulaymān al-Ḍabbī, Ibrāhīm b. Yazīd, and Ziyād b. 'Īsā to Mālik.

Yazīd should have retreated, but he feared that the rebels would be further strengthened during the night and so resumed the attack. Thirty-four of his troops were killed, and eight were captured. Yazīd himself fell into the hands of 'Abd Allah al-Ṭā'ī. Mālik ordered 'Abd Allah to take Yazīd and the other prisoners to Abū Muslim, while he remained encamped in Ālīn, soon to be joined by Abū Ḥammād al-Marwazī and Abū 'Amr al-A'jamī.[132] Naṣr had made his first blunder: failure, either through miscalculation or ineptitude, to apply sufficient force to check the revolt before it could get out of control.

Abū Muslim had Yazīd's wounds tended, treated him kindly, and made every effort to persuade him to join the rebels. This would suggest that the rebels did try to attract the *mawālī* to their cause, but it also illustrates the problem of placing much faith in the interpretation of the revolt as a *mawālī* uprising inasmuch as Yazīd, like many other *mawālī,* remained loyal to his master. Abū Muslim allowed him to return unharmed to Naṣr, knowing that his reports about the conduct of the rebel's would at least serve to counteract propaganda put about by the Umayyads that the insurgents were not good Muslims.[133]

It is impossible to accept the notion, advanced by Shaban, that the strength of the Abbasid rebels was derived from the Arab colonists in the Merv oasis. We have already seen evidence that people not associated with any Arab grouping participated in both the *da'wa* and the revolt. Ṭabarī states clearly that the Abbasid missionaries circulated throughout *all* of Khurasan.[134] An account preserved in one Bal'amī manuscript states that the partisans collected revenue from forty different towns, each of which had its own *naqīb.*[135] Ibn A'tham confirms that the partisans received support from all of Khurasan, notably the towns of Nishapur, Ṭālaqān, and Marw al-rūdh.[136] Ibn 'Abd Rabbih and a number of other sources also state explicitly that *all* the towns (or villages) of Khurasan responded to Abū Muslim's call.[137]

There is no doubt that there was plenty of activity outside the Merv area. Yāqūt claims that the first battle between the partisans and the Umayyads was at Jundūyah, a village near Ṭālaqān. Dīnawarī is even more emphatic about this, and relates that Abbasid missionaries were sent throughout Khurasan. Their followers, dressed in black and carrying black clubs they called *kāfir kubāt,* came to join Abū Muslim from Marw al-rūdh, Ṭālaqān, Merv, Nasā, Abīward, Ṭūs, Nishapur, Sarakhs, Balkh, Soghdia, Ṭukhāristān, Khuttalān, Kish, and Nasaf.[138] There is other evidence which proves that important action was taking place in Marw al-rūdh, where Khāzim b. Khuzayma incited his fellow Tamīmī tribesmen to revolt. Abū Muslim sent partisans to Khāzim's camp at Kanj Rustāq, and with their assistance, Khāzim was able to engineer a coup at the beginning of Dhū'l-Qa'da (mid-July) in which Naṣr's agent in the town, Bishr al-Sa'dī, was killed. The insurgents proudly informed Abū Muslim that Marw al-rūdh was under their control.[139] Not long after, another of Abū Muslim's colleagues, al-Naḍr b. Nu'aym al-Ḍabbī, was able to expel 'Īsā b. 'Āqil al-Laythī, Naṣr's representative, from Herat.[140] We also know that fighting broke out in Nasā and Ṭālaqān, and that al-'Alā' b. Ḥarīth directed the agitation in Khwārizm, Āmul, Bukhārā, and Soghdia.[141]

Merv, therefore, was *not* the source of the revolt but only its focal point. The evidence is overwhelming that the revolt represented a true mass uprising throughout Khurasan in which both Arabs and Iranians participated. The strength of the movement flowed from the outlying Khurāsānī towns towards Merv, where the contest was to be decided.

After an encampment of forty-two days at Safīdhanj, Abū Muslim's army had reached such proportions that he decided to move to a more suitable location. On or about 9 Dhū'l-Qa'da (22 July),[142] he took his troops to Mākhwān, the home village of Khālid b. 'Uthmān and Abū'l-Jahm b. 'Aṭiyya. There he created a more formal military organization. First he had a protective trench dug around the town. He entrusted one entrance to the trench to Muṣ'ab b. Qays al-Ḥanafī and Bahdal b. Iyās al-Ḍabbī and the other to Abū Sharāḥīl and Abū 'Amr al-A'jamī—thereby demonstrating, perhaps, that equal responsibility was to be given to both Arab and Iranian. A list was taken of the names of the soldiers, who were found to number 7,000.

Abū Muslim appointed Abū Naṣr Mālik b. al-Haytham as chief of the *shurṭa,* which was composed of Abū'l-Waḍḍāḥ and his most trusted followers. He made Khālid b. 'Uthmān head of the *ḥaras,* made up of 83 villagers from Nawshān. Abū Ṣāliḥ Kāmil b. Muẓaffar was in charge of the *dīwān* and paid the troops the three to four dirhams to which they were entitled. Aslam b. Ṣubayḥ (or Ṣabīḥ) acted as chief secretary, and al-Qāsim b. Mujāshi' al-Naqīb al-Tamīmī was chief *qāḍī*.[143] One story has it that al-Qāsim used to lead the prayers for the men in the trench and to tell them stories in the evening about the merits of the Banū Hāshim (apparently not mentioning the Abbasids by name) and the misdeeds of the Umayyads. Abū Muslim took his turn in the trench like any commoner among the *shī'a*.[144]

While at Mākhwān, Abū Muslim ordered Muḥriz b. Ibrāhīm to dig a second trench, staffed by a thousand men, at Jīranj. The names of some of these men have been preserved, and they are more or less evenly divided between Arabs, such as Ziyād al-Azdī, and Iranians, such as Jīlān al-Sughdī and 'Abdawayh al-Jardāmidh, a cattle driver from Herat.[145] The purpose of the trench was to further disrupt communications between Naṣr and his supporters in Marw al-rūdh, Balkh, and the villages of Ṭukhāristān. Some traditions also state that Abū Muslim, fearful that Naṣr might try to cut off his water supply, moved for a while to Ālīn, which was located near a stream in the Kharqān quarter, but these accounts are highly problematic.[146]

An interesting social aspect of this period of the revolt is brought out by reports that the "slaves" (*'abīd*) came over *en masse* to the side of Abū Muslim. This is a matter of considerable historiographical significance, since the extent to which a slave labor system existed in the early Islamic world is controversial. Unfortunately, it is not clear whether *'abīd* is used here in a literal, legalistic sense or whether it was a pejorative term used by the Arabs to denote the Iranian peasants, who were attached to the soil and thus, in a manner of speaking, were like slaves.[147] In any case, Abū Muslim made a special policy of persuading them to defect from the armies of Naṣr and al-Kirmānī, and he used Muṣ'ab b. Qays as a *dā'ī* for that particular purpose. The *Akhbār al-'abbās* gives the example of a slave belonging to 'Āsim b. 'Amr al-Samarqandī who approached Abū Muslim about defecting. Abū Muslim inquired only about whether the slave was a Muslim, and, being answered affirmatively, took the new recruit to the camp, where he informed the partisans that anyone, slave or free, who joined the *da'wa* would be accepted and would have the same privileges and responsibilities as anyone else.

The accounts of Ṭabarī, however, give a very different picture. They confirm that many slaves joined the rebels, but suggest that their presence was not altogether welcome. Abū Muslim would not permit them to congregate in the Mākhwān trench, and finally had to segregate them in a special trench provided for them in the village of Shawwāl, which he placed under the command of Da'ūd b. Karrāz. As their numbers multiplied rapidly, he had to send others off to help Mūsā b. Ka'b in Abīward.[148] That their presence was a source of embarassment is confirmed by Umayyad propaganda, which chided Abū Muslim for having an army composed of slaves stolen from their masters.[149] In other words, the Abbasids deliberately incited the slaves to revolt, probably through vague appeals to Muslim egalitarianism and the kind of teachings propagated by Khidāsh, and were quite willing to use them against the Umayyads, but it is doubtful that they ever had any real intentions of improving the slaves' condition. This internal contradiction in the implementation of the *da'wa* would contribute to some of the Abbasids' future difficulties.

According to one tradition, Abū Muslim made a serious mistake during this period. A group of young ascetics from Merv went to Abū Muslim's camp, ostensibly to ask him about his lineage and some matters of jurisprudence (*fiqh*). Then they baited him by saying that he would have been killed already were it not for the conflict between al-Kirmānī and Shaybān the Khārijite. Abū Muslim shot back, "God willing, I shall rather kill the two of them." The youths hurried back to Naṣr with this information, which he used to persuade al-Kirmānī and Shaybān to join with him in a coalition against Abū Muslim.[150]

Whether literally true or not, the story contains a germ of truth, for Naṣr was working diligently to put together an alliance. He and his rivals had been alarmed by Abū Muslim's rapidly increasing power and were willing to set aside their differences with Naṣr for a while. There ensued a round of complicated diplomatic maneuvering and propaganda activity by the various factions, each trying to find allies but never daring to trust them completely.[151]

Thanks to new evidence preserved in the *Akhbār al-'abbās,* it is possible to reconstruct some of the Umayyad propaganda used against Abū Muslim and his followers. This was based, in essence, on an effort to turn the Abbasids' use of populism and *shī'ī* doctrines against them. Naṣr had his legists condemn the rebels as 'cat worshippers" (i.e., idolators?) made up of slaves, *mawālī,* and the very dregs of Arab society.[152] He kept up a correspondence with Abū Muslim and sent messengers to chide him.[153] They raised several issues which Abū Muslim felt compelled to rebut.

The first of these, mentioned previously, was his practice of accepting slaves into the movement. Abū Muslim argued that the partisans had nothing against slaves, and it was up to their masters to get them to come back. The messengers also wanted to know why he showed a preference for Yaman and Rabī'a, when the Prophet Muḥammad had been a Muḍarī. Abū Muslim replied that his *imām* had ordered him to settle with Yaman and to gather the *'ajam* around him because of their loyalty, but that he was perfectly willing to accept any Muḍarī who would join his cause—and, in fact, many did so. The third, and really the most interesting, charge related to excesses perpetrated by his followers in Nasā, Ṭālaqān, Marw al-rūdh, and Āmul.[154] Abū Muslim disavowed these, saying that they were committed not by true partisans but by people who wanted only to do evil and to shed blood.

Very little is known about the violence, which must have occurred since both sides in the conflict acknowledged them. There are rumors of massacres and suggestions of a mass uprising of the Iranian peasantry in a number of sources, especially the non-Muslim chronicles, which were deeply impressed by the apocalyptic implications of the event; but it is impossible to find enough detailed, explicit information to permit a reconstruction of the history of the insurrection. Perhaps later Abbasid authorities suppressed information relating to this unsavory side of the *da'wa*. In any case, it is one more piece of evidence that the movement, as in the days of Khidāsh, hit a responsive chord among the native peasantry and lower class population of Khurasan. We shall have occasion to see how these extremist tendencies, which the Abbasids were willing to exploit but not to recognize, would continue to assert themselves later.

For their part, the Abbasids endeavored to refute the charges made against them and initiated a special effort to dispel the notion that Abū Muslim was leading an unorthodox religious movement. Abū Muslim sent 'Īsā b. A'yan to explain their teachings to Naṣr b. Sayyār.[155] 'Īsā insisted that the rebels were good Muslims: Muḥammad was their prophet, the Kaaba was their *qibla,* and they called for obedience to Koran and *sunna*. But this, of course, was not what distinguished the rebels from the Umayyads, and 'Īsā's argument was damaged by his refusal to identify the *imām* for whom he was working. This, however, was unavoidable, since it was one of the cardinal principles formulated by Muḥammad b. 'Alī: If the *imām*'s identity were revealed, he could be persecuted, or factionalism might split the ranks of the movement.

Neither did these professions of orthodoxy prevent Abū Muslim and other leaders of the *da'wa* from exploiting Shi'ite and extremist sectarian sentiments, the most obvious example being their fanning of the embers of resentment over the fate of Yaḥyā b. Zayd. As a precaution against misinterpretation by the inner circles of the movement, Abū Muslim summoned the partisans, told them that Naṣr's allegations were just a device to demoralize them, and had them all reaffirm their allegiance to the cause.[156]

Meanwhile, Naṣr made a stupendous blunder, which insured his ultimate downfall by breaking up the coalition against Abū Muslim. Juday' al-Kirmānī was murdered while visiting Naṣr's camp. The assassin was a son of al-Ḥārith b. Surayj, who claimed revenge for his father's murder. It must have appeared unlikely that this could have happened without Naṣr's knowledge or approval. Moreover, tradition holds that, as a final insult, al-Kirmānī's body was crucified next to a fish (symbol of the tribe of Azd).[157] Certainly, Naṣr's empathy for al-Ḥārith was well known, since it was he who had secured al-Ḥārith's pardon. One must also note that al-Ḥārith's son continued to play a prominent role with the pro-Naṣr forces. Still, it seems incredible that a politician as wily as Naṣr could have committed a deed so certain to alienate al-Kirmānī's followers. Wellhausen saw the hand of Abū Muslim behind the murder,[158] and it was certainly he who gained the most from it. One can only speculate about this mysterious event.

Many of al-Kirmānī's outraged followers went over immediately to Abū Muslim; the rest united behind his son 'Alī. Naṣr wooed 'Alī assiduously by appealing to his Arab pride,[159] but this could not compete with the charms Abū Muslim used to seduce 'Alī to his side. He sent Sulaymān b. Kathīr to 'Alī to remind him that he was *mawtūr,* i.e., someone who has not fulfilled the duty of revenge for a slain relative. How, Sulaymān asked, could 'Alī even pray in the same mosque with a man who had just killed and crucified his father?[160] Abū Muslim played on 'Alī's ambition by arranging a meeting at which he rejected a peace offer from Naṣr and swore to follow 'Alī; he went out to meet 'Alī in his camp, called him governor of Khurasan, followed him in prayer, and otherwise feigned deference to him.[161] It should come as no surprise that 'Alī disassociated himself from Naṣr and used his good offices to persuade Shaybān the Khārijite to do likewise.

Shaybān probably realized that he, as an outsider, had no substantial or lasting base of power in Khurasan, that he could never trust a dedicated Umayyad agent like Naṣr, and that he would receive no sympathy from Abū Muslim. It would be far better, therefore, to let the other rivals fight it out until he could intervene at an opportune moment. In Rabī' II 130 (December 747) he withdrew to Sarakhs, hoping to wait out the storm.[162]

Naṣr also managed to alienate the few local inhabitants who were not already up in arms against him. In Dhū'l-Ḥijja 129 (August 747), he sent out columns of troops to look for Abū Muslim: 'Āṣim b. 'Amr to Balāshjird, Abū'l-Dhayyāl to Ṭūṣān, and Bishr b. Anīf al-Yarbū'ī to Julfar. Abū'l-Dhayyāl forced the people of Ṭūsān to quarter his troops, butchered their livestock, expected them to provide food and fodder, and otherwise tyrannized them. Abū Muslim's spies informed him of this, so he sent out some of his own troops, who defeated Abū'l-Dhayyāl, and captured one of his lieutenants, al-A'sar al-Khwārizmī, and several of his soldiers.[163] It should not be difficult to imagine the effect of this action in inducing the peasants to support Abū Muslim.

The situation confronting Naṣr was very bleak. The coalition had evaporated, his troops had been defeated, most of Khurasan was under rebel control, the populace was alienated, and Abū Muslim grew stronger day by day. It is reported that parts of Khurasan began to deliver the *khuṭba* in the name of Abū Muslim, recognized his authority, and paid taxes to him.[164] Naṣr wrote letter after letter to Ibn Hubayra, the governor of Iraq, and to the Caliph Marwān pleading for aid, but to no avail.[165] The former seemed to take a perverse pleasure in Naṣr's discomfiture, and the latter had too many problems of his own in the Arab heartland. Though troops could be spared for the annual summer raid into Anatolia,[166] none were available for Naṣr until it was too late.

The path was open for Abū Muslim to occupy Merv itself, the capital of all Khurasan. Unfortunately, the accounts of how he did this are vague and conflicting, with some portraying Abū Muslim entering the city as a conquering warrior and others claiming that he entered in the role of a peacemaker. The *Akhbār al-'abbās* states that Abū Muslim first sent Shibl b. Ṭahmān and a group of theologians into the city to propagandize for their cause, and that many of the citizens joined them.[167] He soon heard from 'Alī b. al-Kirmānī that fighting had broken out between factions loyal to Naṣr and those who had joined Shibl. He then began his successful advance on the city on 7 Rabī' II 130 (15 December 747).[168] Some of this is confirmed by the account of al-Madā'inī, as preserved in Ṭabarī. He relates that Abū Muslim stayed three months at Mākhwān before making a night march to link up with Ibn al-Kirmānī. This threw Naṣr into a panic, and he offered to surrender the city to Abū Muslim. Ibn al-Kirmānī's cavalry and Abū Muslim's army, however, launched a joint attack on Merv, took the city by force, and thus enabled Abū Muslim to make his triumphal entry into the city on 7 or 9 Rabī' II (15 or 17 December).[169]

Abū'l-Khuṭṭāb gives a very different version. He claims that Abū Muslim persuaded Ibn al-Kirmānī to enter Merv so that factional strife would break out between his supporters and those of Naṣr. Then, playing the part of peacemaker, Abū Muslim brought his army into the fray in order to separate the combatants. He entered Merv quoting an appropriate verse from the Koran: "He entered the city at a time when its people were negligent; he found two men fighting there, one of his party, the other one of his enemies." This took place on 9 Jumādā I 130 (15 January 748).[170]

While it is impossible to be certain about these details, it does appear that Abū Muslim made use of a fifth column inside the city and then occupied it at a propitious moment, pretending to be a friend of Ibn al-Kirmānī while simultaneously conducting negotiations with Naṣr. He carefully insured the loyalty of his own troops by ordering Abū Manṣūr Ṭalḥa b. Zurayq to have the Hāshimiyya *jund* formally reaffirm their oaths of allegiance.[171] Naṣr, who was not so blind to reality as 'Alī b. al-Kirmānī, fled the city almost immediately (10 Jumādā I/16 January) towards Sarakhs, accompanied by 3,000 Muḍarī supporters. Abū Muslim and Ibn al-Kirmānī set out in pursuit, but turned back after finding that Naṣr had abandoned his wife Marzubāna (whom Abū Muslim later married) in the village of Naṣrāniyya and made good his escape.[172] The story goes that Naṣr had been forewarned of Abū Muslim's intention to kill him by Lāhiz b. Qurayẓ, Abū Muslim's envoy in the negotiations with Naṣr. For this act of mercy to the aged Naṣr, Abū Muslim executed Lāhiz, one of the original *nuqabā'*, as a traitor.[173] The chagrined Abū Muslim exclaimed of his wily opponent, "Naṣr claimed I was a magician, but, by God, *he* is the magician!"[174]

Abū Muslim set up his headquarters in the former Umayyad governmental palace (*dār al-imāra*) in Merv.[175] He initiated plans for a provisional government and prepared to deal with his opponents and his former allies in Khurasan.

We have attempted to show that the best description of the Abbasid rebels is the one given to them by the sources themselves: Khurāsānīs. Naṣr received support only from loyalist Syrian troops, some die-hard Arab tribalists and their *mawālī,* and segments of the *haute aristocracie* of Khurasan and, to an even greater extent, Transoxiana. By contrast, the Abbasids won the support of Arabs from an assortment of different tribes, a number of *mawālī,* Iranian freemen, and the Khurāsānī masses, both Iranian and Arab, peasant and urban. It was truly a mass uprising which involved virtually every group and area of the province.

Unfortunately, there is little explicit evidence about the specific issues which motivated the uprising. Perhaps as far as the Abbasids were concerned, there was no issue beyond the change of dynasty; they certainly acted as if that were the case in later years. However, it is clear that they had been able to forge and to maintain the revolutionary coalition only by appealing to feelings of Khurāsānī particularism and a vague form of shī'ism.

From the very beginning, Khurasan was considered the natural seed-bed of the movement. The *du'āt* were ordered to address themselves to all Khurāsānīs, Arab and Iranian; they were so successful that the people of Khurasan were generally recognized as having a special relationship with the Abbasid dynasty, becoming known as *abnā' al-dawla*. If the movement did not efface the old racial and tribal identity, it at least transcended it with a new sense of loyalty and allegiance based on a shared sense of community.[176] It may be that the Abbasids were more successful in this than they had intended, for they not only created the environment for bitter political rancor against and resentment of the Khurāsānīs; they brought into being a vital sentiment of Khurāsānī particularism which, of necessity, involved a rethinking and a redefinition of the nature of the relative positions of the province and the central government. This was reflected in the organization of the movement, the role of the *nuqabā'* as local leaders, the manner in which the *imām* was selected and allegiance pledged to him, and the division of authority between Abū Salama and Abū Muslim. This political dimension of the revolt was probably the greatest concern of those Arabs outside the Umayyad establishment and those Iranians of moderate social standing who made up the leadership and inner circles of the movement.

Shī'ism, in the early stage of its development, was a vague concept and a potentially dangerous one. The missionaries called for Koran, the *sunna,* and *al-riḍā*. Despite efforts to distinguish themselves from the Umayyads in the matter of prayer ritual, and later the deliverance of the *khuṭba,* it was really only the latter point which differentiated the two opponents.

The moderates in the movement no doubt felt that this was quite compatible with their political goals: A legitimate *imām* chosen from the family of Muḥammad, but subject to the approval and confirmation of the (Khurāsānī) partisans, would remain comfortably in the distance tending to the religious welfare of the community while his political deputies dealt with secular affairs. But all the people in the movement who considered themselves *shī'a* were by no means enthusiastic Abbasid supporters; there were any number of candidates for the imāmate, and each had his own faction. Moreover, shī'ism attracted a mass following of social discontents and visionaries who were prone to express the most extravagant and revolutionary socio-religious beliefs. The undeniable strength of this *ghulāt,* extremist, form of shī'ism was amply demonstrated by the Khidāsh incident.

At the time of the revolt, then, the Abbasids were walking a tightrope. They had built a movement around political notions of Khurāsānī particularism, but they would have to govern an empire of which Khurasan was but one part. They had collaborated with factions dedicated to rule by some other family, yet they intended to found their own dynasty. They had tapped the power of a kind of *Lumpenproletariat* made up of vagabonds, social outcasts, oppressed peasants, and the like, but they were fundamentally opposed to the radical and violent goals of these groups.

What would happen when the time came to proclaim an Abbasid caliphate? How could the Abbasids transform a provincial uprising into the foundations of an empire? How would other areas react to the prospect of Khurāsānī dominance? In short, how could the Abbasids resolve the tangled maze of internal tensions and contradictions the success of the *da'wa* would bring into the open? These were questions the coming years would answer.

1. This is the story of the proclamation of the *da'wa* as related in Tab., 2:1954; IA, 5:358; *Fragmenta,* p. 187; see also Ibn Kathīr, 10:30; *Ghurar,* f. 126b; Faṣīḥ, *Mujmal-i faṣīḥī,* 1:199; *Mujmal al-tavārīkh,* p. 317; Mīrkhwānd, 3:365; Bar Hebraeus, *Mukhtaṣar,* p. 119; Sibṭ/Add. 23277, f. 232a. The village of Safīdhanj, also called Sīqadhanj, was located some 3 *farsakh*s from Merv: see Sam'ānī, *Ansāb,* ff. 322b–323a; Qazvīnī/LeStrange, *Nuzhat,* p. 154. Yāqūt, *Mu'jam,* 5:198, gives the distance as 4 *farsakh*s.

2. This is the highly appropriate description of the rebels given by Continuator Isidori: see J. Wellhausen, *The Arab Kingdom and Its Fall,* trans. Margaret Weir (Calcutta, 1927; reprint Beirut, 1963), p. 533.

3. The modern historiography of the Abbasid revolution properly begins with two works by G. van Vloten, *De Opkomst des Abbasiden in Chorasan* (Leiden, 1890) and *Recherches sur la domination arabe, le chi'isme et les croyances messianiques sous les Omayyades* (Amsterdam, 1894). These works refined the racial interpretation of early Islamic history then popular in Europe by advancing the idea that the revolt was an uprising of the Iranian population against their Arab oppressors based on a fusion of Iranian national pride and Shī'ite religious concepts. This interpretation was discredited, but not completely replaced, after the publication of J. Wellhausen's *Das arabische Reich und sein Sturz* (Berlin, 1902). Wellhausen demonstrated that Shī'ism arose quite independently of any Iranian reaction to Arab rule and added an important social dimension to Van Vloten's ideas: The revolt was not simply a rising of the Iranians but more particularly of the *mawālī,* converts to Islam and clients of Arab tribes who had not received the full benefits of being either Muslim or Arabicized. The idea of the overthrow of the "Arab kingdom" in favor of a cosmopolitan Islamic state became the standard interpretation of early Islamic history and dominated the secondary literature for more than fifty years. Gradually, it became clear that Wellhausen's work was not so solid as its hold on the secondary literature would suggest. Many sources not used by Wellhausen became available; old sources were re-examined. D. C. Dennett, *Conversion and the Poll-Tax in Early Islam* (Cambridge, Mass., 1950), sharply criticized Wellhausen's methodological

inconsistency (disguised as textual criticism). R. N. Frye, "The Role of Abū Muslim in the 'Abbāsid Revolt," *Muslim World* 37(1947):28–38, and "The Abbasid Conspiracy and Modern Revolutionary Theory," *Indo-Iranica* 5(1952–3):9–14, found an unjustifiable residue of the Arab vs. Iranian racial interpretation in Wellhausen and went on to suggest that the *mawālī,* many of whom were loyal to the Umayyads, were not the discontented social bloc implied by Wellhausen. Claude Cahen, "Points de vue sur la 'Revolution abbaside,' " *Revue Historique* (1963), pp. 295–335, found that the religious dimension of the revolt had also been misinterpreted. Finally, in two independent (?) works, Farouq Omar, *The 'Abbāsid Caliphate 132/750–170/786* (Baghdad, 1969), and M. A. Shaban, *The 'Abbāsid Revolution* (Cambridge, 1970), offered new, but essentially similar, interpretations. They turned the old racial interpretation upside down and viewed the revolt as the extension of a political dispute between Arab factions. The greatest point of difference with Wellhausen was that Shaban and Omar considered the participation of Iranians/*mawālī* in the revolt to be inconsequential.

4. On the genealogy of this family and its relation to other elements of Meccan society, cf. E. de Zambaur, *Manuel de Genealogie et de Chronologie pour l'Histoire de l'Islam* (Hanover, 1927), Table G; and B. Lewis, " 'Abbāsids," *EI*2, 1:15, 22.

5. On al-'Abbās, see *Akhbār,* pp. 21–24; Ibn Ishāq, *The Life of Muhammad,* trans. A. Guillaume (Oxford, 1970), pp. 202, 301, 309–10, 312; Ya'qūbī, *Historiae,* 2:47; Ibn Sa'd, *Kitāb al- ṭabaqāt al-kabīr,* ed. M. Ḥamīd Allah (Cairo, 1969), 4:5–33 and index; Balādhurī, *Ansāb,* ff. 263b–268b; W. M. Watt, "al-'Abbās," *EI*2, 1:8–9; and Farouq Omar, *The 'Abbāsid Caliphate 132/750–170/786* (Baghdad, 1969), pp. 59–60.

6. Ibn Ishāq, *Life,* p. 96; Ibn Qutayba, *al-Ma'ārif,* p. 121; Ibn Sa'd, *Ṭabaqāt,* 4:15 ff.; and Watt, "al-'Abbās."

7. For examples, see Dīnawarī, *Akhbār,* p. 147; Ya'qūbī, *Historiae,* 1:138; Ibn Ḥazm, *Jamharat,* p. 18; *Akhbār,* p. 41; and Ibn Isfandiyār/Browne, *Ṭabaristān,* p. 111; cf. also L. Veccia Vaglieri, " 'Abd Allah b. al-'Abbās," *EI*2, 1:40–41.

8. The apologists tried to excuse this by claiming that he did so in order to defend 'Alī and his descendants; see comments in Omar, *'Abbāsid Caliphate,* p. 60.

9. The reason usually given for this is that 'Alī married the "Ḥārithī woman" against the caliph's wishes; see Azdī, *Akhbār al-duwal,* ff. 99b–100a; *Akhbār,* pp. 138–40, 149–50; *Ghurar,* f. 121b; Balādhurī, *Ansāb,* f. 283b and IVb:76; Ibn Khallikān, 2:216–221; pseudo-Ibn Qutayba, *Imāma,* 2:110; and K. V. Zettersteen, " 'Alī b. 'Abd Allah," *EI*2, 1:38.

10. See Balādhurī, *Ansāb,* f. 283a; *Fragmenta,* p. 180; Maqdisī, *Bad'*, 6:56; Ibn 'Abd Rabbih, *'Iqd,* 4:475; Tab., 3:24; Ibn Taghrībirdī, *Nujūm,* 1:319; Azdī, *Akhbār al-duwal,* ff. 97b–98a; Jūzjānī, *Ṭabaqāt,* 1:103; Shahrastānī, *Milal,* 1:151; *Fakhrī,* p. 136; and 'Awfī/Ramaḍānī, *Javāmi',* p. 332. It is used as an example of Muhammad's gift of prophecy by 'Alī al-Ṭabarī, *The Book of Religion and Empire,* trans. A. Mingana (Manchester, 1922), p. 45.

11. Tab., 3:30.

12. *Akhbār,* p. 165. The Abbasids were always sensitive about the merit of their claim to the caliphate compared to that of the 'Alīds: Since they themselves had claimed a better right to the office than the Umayyads primarily on the basis of their closer relation to Muḥammad, it was of course extremely inconvenient for them that the 'Alīds could claim an even closer blood relationship with the Prophet. Consequently, the Abbasids tried various forms of propaganda, none of them very con-

vincing, to undercut the 'Alīd claim. See Mas'ūdī, *Prairies,* 6:55; Sa'd al-Qummī, *Maqālāt,* p. 65; C. Pellat, *Life and Works of Jahiz,* p. 17; and W. M. Watt, *The Formative Period of Islamic Thought* (Edinburgh, 1973), p. 155.

13. *Akhbār,* p. 170; *Fragmenta,* pp. 179–180; cf. Dīnawarī, *Akhbār,* p. 332; and Azdī, *Mawṣil,* p. 49. See above, n. 12.

14. On this sect, see Baghdādī, *Farq,* pp. 38–52; Ash'arī, *Maqālāt,* pp. 93–94; Mas'ūdī, *Prairies,* 5:180 sqq.; Khwārizmī, *Mafātīḥ,* p. 29; Nawbakhtī, "Les sectes," pp. 209–210; Shahrastānī, *Milal,* 1:147–50; Tab., 2:598 sqq.; C. van Arendonk, "Kaisānīya," *EI*1, 3:658–59; C. Cahen, "Points de vue sur la 'Révolution abbaside,' " *Revue Historique* (1963), pp. 350 ff.; Muhsen Azizi, *La Domination arabe et l'épanouissement du sentiment national en Iran* (Paris, 1938), pp. 92–93; G. van Vloten, *Recherches sur la domination arabe* (Amsterdam, 1894), pp. 41 ff.; and Henri Laoust, *Les Schismes dans l'Islam* (Paris, 1965), pp. 30–32. It is interesting that there was a connection between the Abbasid family and the *imām* of this sect from an early date; for example, several sources point out that it was Muḥammad b. al-Ḥanafiyya who led the funeral prayers for the pious 'Alī al-Sajjād (Azdī, *Akhbār al-duwal,* ff. 99a–100b; Ibn Ḥazm, *Jamharat,* p. 18, etc.).

15. This story, or versions of it, occur in *Akhbār,* pp. 165, 173; *Fragmenta,* p. 181; Maqdisī, *Bad',* 6:58; Ibn 'Abd Rabbih, *'Iqd,* 4:475–76; Tab., 3:24; Ya'qūbī, *Historiae,* 2:356–58; Anbārī, *Uṣūl,* ff. 16b, 20b; IA, 5:53; Balādhurī, *Ansāb,* f. 283a; Mas'ūdī, *Prairies,* 6:58; Abū Ḥātim, *Zīna,* p. 298; Ibn Khaldūn, *'Ibar,* 3:214; pseudo-Ibn Qutayba, *Imāma,* 2:109; *Fakhrī,* p. 137; Ash'arī, *Maqālāt,* pp. 94–95; Nawbakhtī, "Les sectes," pp. 83–84; Ibn Ḥazm/Friedlaender, p. 28; Shahrastānī, *Milal,* 1:151; Ibn Ḥabīb, *Asmā',* pp. 179–80; Ṣafadī, *al-Wāfī,* 4:103; Ibn Khallikān, 2:593; and Ibn Taghrībirdī, *Nujūm,* 1:319. Iṣfahānī, *Maqātil,* p. 126, notes that this is what the people of Khurasan "allege;" Sa'd al-Qummī, *Maqālāt,* pp. 39–40, and Sibṭ/Add. 23277, f. 118b, point out that the Abbasids competed with the Zaydīs for control of this sect. The account of Abū Hāshim's instructions to Muḥammad b. 'Alī is found in *Akhbār,* pp. 184–85. See also the critical studies of this matter in Cahen, "Points de vue," pp. 92–93; van Vloten, *Recherches,* p. 45; Azizi, *Domination,* pp. 92–93; B. Lewis, "Hāshimiyya," *EI*2, 3:265; A. Rifā'ī, *'Asr al-ma'mūn* (Cairo, 1347/1928), 1:82; and S. Moscati, "Il Testament di Abū Hāshim," *RSO* 28(1952):29–46.

16. *Akhbār,* pp. 183, 191–92; *Ghurar,* f. 122b, gives a few different names; see also Jūzjānī, *Ṭabaqāt,* 1:104. It should be noted that Ḥayyan was also a *mawlā* (of Nakh'); thus *mawālī* may well have dominated the movement in its early phase. The prominent role of the Banū Musliyya, a tribe closely associated with Kūfa (Sam'ānī, *Ansāb,* f. 530a) is also worth noting.

17. Wellhausen, *Arab Kingdom,* p. 503, based this on the undeniable fact that there were other claimants, but a more balanced appraisal may be found in Lewis, " 'Abbāsids," *EI*2, 1:15–16.

18. The word *da'wa* is difficult to translate precisely, and is therefore most often simply transliterated here. It comes from an Arabic root meaning to summon, to invite, to appeal for, or in a sense to propagandize. It might thus be taken to mean "mission" in a religious or political sense, but Professor 'A. Dūrī has suggested that in early Arabic usage it was actually synonymous with *dawla* (itself a vague term meaning a turn or a change, hence "state," "dynasty," or "empire"): see the introduction to *Akhbār,* p. 18.

19. Our usage of this term also needs explanation. When written shī'ī or shī'ism it will mean simply partisan or partisanship, usually but not always involving the

notion that the leadership of the Islamic community belonged by right to some member of the family of the Prophet Muḥammad (*ahl al-bayt*). Whenever it is written as Shi'ite with the capital "S") it refers specifically to partisanship for 'Alī b. Abī Ṭālib and his descendants.

20. *Akhbār,* pp. 188, 192; Tab., 2:1358; Ya'qūbī, *Historiae,* 2:358; Maqdisī, *Bad',* 6:59.

21. *Akhbār,* p. 194.

22. *Ibid.* A legacy of distrust towards Kūfa remained; see *Akhbār,* pp. 193–196, 206.

23. See Tab., 2:1358; Balādhurī, *Ansāb,* f. 292a; *Ghurar,* f. 122b; Mas'ūdī, *Tanbīh,* p. 338; Ibn Khaldūn, *'Ibar,* 3:214; Ṣibṭ/Add. 23277, f. 121a; and Ibn Kathīr, 9:189. There is good reason to be suspicious of this date: see Wellhausen, *Arab Kingdom,* p. 506; Azizi, *Domination,* p. 107. A variant tradition in Tab., 2:1988, gives a more likely date of 103 or 104; Jūzjānī, *Ṭabaqāt,* 1:185, accepts the date 104; IA, 5:143 dates it "in the governorship of Asad b. 'Abd Allah," which could not be before 105; Elias, *Chronographie,* p. 102, gives the date as 111, while Bal'amī/Add. 23497 makes the date as late as 113. It is best, therefore, to dodge the issue by agreeing with Ya'qūbī, *Les pays,* trans. G. Wiet (Cairo, 1937), p. 127, that the *da'wa* probably began before the reign of Hishām or shortly thereafter. The year 100, incidentally, was also the time of the controversial marriage of the "Ḥārithī woman."

24. This follows the version of *Akhbār,* pp. 206–7; see also Sibṭ/Add. 23277, ff. 202b–203a; *Ghurar,* ff. 122b–123a; Maqdisī, Bad', 6:59; Ibn al-Jawzī/Add. 7320, f. 64a (see Amedroz, "Unidentified Manuscript," p. 872); Ibn al-Faqīh, *Buldān,* p. 315; Balādhurī, *Ansāb,* f. 283a; *Fakhrī,* pp. 137–38; Jāhiz, *Tria Opuscula,* p. 8; Maqdisī, *Aḥsan al-taqāsim,* pp. 293–94; and Yāqūt, *Mu'jam,* 3:410–11.

25. *Akhbār,* pp. 198–99.

26. See Tab., 2:1355; Balādhurī, *Futūḥ,* pp. 416, 426 (the translation is that of Murgotten, p. 181).

27. *Akhbār,* pp. 199–200, 201. Such prophecies were apparently quite common; any number of them may be found in Khuzā'ī, *Kitāb al-fitan.*

28. *Ibid.,* pp. 203, 206–7; cf. Tab., 2:1358, 1501, 1988–89; IA, 5:143; Balādhurī, *Ansāb,* f. 283b; Ya'qūbī, *Historiae,* 2:358; and Ibn Taghrībirdī, *Nujūm,* 1:320; see also Rifā'ī, *'Asr al-ma'mūn,* 1:83.

29. Tab., 2:1488, 1492, 1501, 1560; Dīnawarī, *Akhbār,* pp. 332–34; pseudo-Ibn Qutayba, *Imāma,* 2:113–14; *Akhbār,* pp. 233, 237, 225, 223; IA, 5:114, 125, 136: Balādhurī, *Ansāb,* f. 283b; and Ya'qūbī, *Historiae,* 2:374.

30. This was the *imām*'s preferred method of contact: see *Akhbār,* p. 208.

31. Tab., 2:1434, 1488, 1492, 1502, 1560, 1586; *Ghurar,* f. 123b; IA, 5:100, 136, 190; Sibṭ/Add. 23277, ff. 142b, 162b, 173a, 178a; Balādhurī, *Ansāb,* f. 292b; and *Akhbār,* pp. 208, 253. It is interesting that the heaviest punishments fell on the Tamīmī partisans; probably their fellow tribesmen in power regarded them as traitors.

32. Tab., 2:1501; IA, 5:143, *Akhbār,* p. 204.

33. The importance of Jurjān is perhaps over-emphasized in the *Akhbār:* see pp. 201 (Bukayr finds converts there); 203 (*du'āt* ordered to go there before going to Merv); 223 (money contributed there); 232 (Bukayr spends a month there). One is tempted to speculate that the author of the *Akhbār* was a Jurjānī.

34. *Akhbār,* p. 213.

35. Tab., 2:1501.

36. *Akhbār,* p. 215, refers to Koran 7:154 and 5:15; cf. Ibn ʻAbd Rabbih, *ʻIqd,* 4:476.

37. *Akhbār,* p. 215, has Bukayr; others have Abū ʻIkrima (also known as Abū Muḥammad al-Ṣādiq): see Tab., 2:1358; IA, 5:125; Balādhurī, *Ansāb,* f. 292a; Maqdisī, *Bad',* 6:60; Jāḥiẓ, *Tria Opuscula,* pp. 8–9; Balʻamī/Zotenberg, 4:248; and Gardīzī, *Zayn,* pp. 116–17.

38. For example, see ʻAllāmah Ṭabāṭabā'ī, *Shiʻite Islam,* trans. Hossein Nasr (London, 1975), p. 79.

39. A complete list of these appointees may be found in *Akhbār,* pp. 213–223.

40. Ibn Khallikān, 1:468.

41. Balādhurī, *Ansāb,* f. 292a.

42. Jāḥiẓ, *Tria Opuscula,* pp. 12–14.

43. On the different usages of the term, see Watt, *Formative Period,* pp. 45–47. The whole question of who the *mawālī* were and what they represented needs to be re-investigated.

44. Shaban, *ʻAbbāsid Revolution,* pp. 151–52.

45. *Akhbār,* pp. 216–23.

46. See Ibn Isḥāq, *Life,* p. 547; Shaban, *ʻAbbāsid Revolution,* p. 157; and Wellhausen, *Arab Kingdom,* pp. 514–15.

47. Tab., 2:1502–3; IA, 5:144.

48. Balādhurī, *Ansāb,* f. 292a; IA, 5:144; Ibn Khaldūn, *ʻIbar,* 3:216. Perhaps Khidāsh was considered a Kūfan, since he had been sent there for further instruction?

49. Tab., 2:1588; *Ghurar,* f. 123b; IA, 5:196; Maqdisī, *Bad',* 6:60–61; Ibn al-Jawzī, *Excerpta,* f. 102a; and Ibn Khaldūn, *ʻIbar,* 3:216. Modern critics question this date: see Wellhausen, *Arab Kingdom,* p. 514; and Azizi, *Domination,* pp. 96–97.

50. Tab., 2:1588; IA, 5:196; Maqdisī, *Bad',* 6:60; and Ibn al-Jawzī, *Excerpta,* f. 102a.

51. Balādhurī, *Ansāb,* f. 292b.

52. IA, 5:196; Ibn Khaldūn, *ʻIbar,* 3:216; and Ibn Kathīr, 9:326.

53. Koran, 5:93.

54. On Mazdak (fl. ca. 487–531), the famous Sasanid heretic, see A. Christensen, *Le Regne du Roi Kawadh I et le communisme mazdakite* (Copenhagen, 1925); O. Klima, *Mazdak. Geschichte einer sozialen Bewegung im sassanidischen Persien* (Prague, 1957); S. ʻAlī Nagavī, *ʻAqā'id-i mazdak* (Tehran, n. d.); and G. H. Sadighi, *Les Mouvements religieux iraniens* (Paris, 1938), pp. 5–7. The essential source material may be found in T. Nöldeke, *Geschichte der Perser und der Araber zur Zeit der Sasaniden* (Leyden, 1879), pp. 455–467, which translates passages from Ṭabarī, and in the classic exposition by Niẓām al-mulk/Darke, *Book of Government,* pp. 195–211. The idea that later heterodox movements in Islam sprang from Mazdakism is deeply rooted in the sources and persists in modern literature as well. A view widely held by Iranian scholars is that the Mazdakites betrayed Iran to the Arab invaders by turning against the native aristocracy; for example, see the interesting novel by Ṣanʻatzādah Kirmānī, *Dām-gustarān ya intiqām-khāhān-i mazdak* (Tehran, 1921).

55. See Tab., 2:1588; Ibn Khaldūn, *'Ibar,* 3:216; Ibn Kathīr, 9:326; Maqdisī, *Bad',* 6:61; Ibn al-Jawzī, *Excerpta,* f. 102b; *Ghurar,* f. 123b; and Ibn Ḥazm/Friedlaender, p. 36. The charge of communality of woman has been made about almost every heterodox movement in Iran from Mazdak to the Bābīs, and even about some sects outside Iran—see the text taken from the *Sīrat al-hādī* in C. van Arenkonk, *Les Débuts de l'Imamate Zaidite,* trans. J. Ryckmans (Leyden, 1960), p. 330. The practice in Khurasan may have had roots in antiquity; see Narshakhī-Frye, *Bukhara,* p. 147, n. 265; and Procopius, *History of the Wars,* trans. H. Dewing (Cambridge, Mass., 1954), 1. 5. 1–2. It should be noted that Sadighi, *Mouvements,* pp. 187–228, gives a detailed description of the movement in which he argues that Khidāsh was not a true Khurramī (p. 224); cf. Cahen, "Points de vue," pp. 324–25; Wellhausen, *Arab Kingdom,* pp. 515–16; Van Vloten, *Recherches,* p. 49; Azizi, *Domination,* pp. 97–99; and 'Abd al-Rafī' Ḥaqīqat, *Tārīkh-i nahḍathā-yi millī-yi īrān* (Tehran, 1348/1969), pp. 207–8.

56. Tab., 2:1588; IA, 5:196.

57. IA, 5:196.

58. Balādhurī, *Ansāb,* f. 292a; *Akhbār,* p. 212.

59. Tab., 2:1588–89; IA, 5:197; Ibn al-Jawzī, *Excerpta,* f. 102a–b; Anbārī, *Uṣūl,* f. 23a; Balādhurī, *Ansāb,* f. 292a; Maqdisī, Bad', 6:61; and Ibn Ḥazm/Friedlaender, p. 65; Ibn Khaldūn, *'Ibar,* 3:216. Apparently only Ibn Kathīr, 9:326, claims that Khālid al-Qaṣrī executed Khidāsh. See also Van Vloten, *Recherches,* p. 49. Tab., 2:1599, and IA, 5:197, refer to the simultaneous execution of a certain Ḥazawwar, *mawlā* of Ḍabba, but do not make clear whether this was related to the Khidāsh incident or not.

60. Anbārī, *Uṣūl,* f. 23a.

61. Information about this sect is part of the new evidence brought to light thanks to the *Akhbār,* pp. 403–4, and especially Anbārī, *Uṣūl,* f. 21a–23a.

62. Tab., 2:1592; *Akhbār,* p. 159.

63. Tab., 2:1640; cf. IA, 5:218; *Fragmenta,* p. 182.

64. Tab., 2:1640; Sibṭ/Add. 23277, f. 186b.

65. Tab., 2:1640; IA, 5:218; Ibn Kathīr, 9:326.

66. Tab., 2:1640; IA, 5:218–29; cf. Balādhurī, *Ansāb,* f. 292b; and Ibn Kathīr, 9:326. Maqdisī, *Bad',* 6:61, says that this was a sign among the partisans dating back to the time of Maysara al-Nabbāl.

67. *Akhbār,* p. 212; cf. Balādhurī, *Ansāb,* f. 292b; *Fragmenta,* p. 182.

68. On this revolt, see Tab., 2:1667–88, 1698–1716; *Ghurar,* f. 93a; Sibṭ/Add. 23277, f. 190b sqq.; Ibn Khaldūn, *'Ibar,* 3:208–213; Isfahānī, *Maqātil,* pp. 133–51; Ya'qubi, *Historiae,* 2:350 sqq.; Mas'ūdī, *Prairies,* 6:482; Ash'arī, *Maqālāt,* pp. 136–37; *Fakhrī,* pp. 127–28; Ibn Khallikān, 3:275–76; Ibn 'Abd Rabbih, *'Iqd,* 4:482; and Kūfī, *Futūḥ,* ff. 206a–211b. Other sources are cited in the full bibliography given by R. Strothman, "Zaid b. 'Alī," *EI*1, 4:1193–94. See also Wellhausen, *Arab Kingdom,* pp. 337–38; *idem, The Religio-Political Factions in Early Islam,* trans. S. M. Walzer (Amsterdam, 1975), pp. 162–63; M. Abū Zahra, *al-Imām zayd* (Cairo, 1965), pp. 51–66; Ḥaqīqat, *Nahḍathā,* pp. 211–13; Arendonk, *Debuts,* pp. 26–29; Van Vloten, *Recherches,* p. 54; and Laoust, *Schismes,* pp. 34–35.

69. On the question of Abbasid provocation, see Tab., 2:1668 (citing Haytham); and Arendonk, *Debuts,* p. 33.

70. *Akhbār,* p. 231.

71. On Yaḥyā, see *Akhbār,* pp. 232, 242–44; Isfahānī, *Maqātil,* pp. 152–58; Kūfī, *Futūḥ,* ff. 211b–212b; *Ghurar,* f. 110b; Anbārī, *Uṣūl,* f. 64b; Tab., 2:1770–74; Ya'qūbī, *Historiae,* 2:297 sqq., 392; Ibn Qutayba, *Ma'ārif,* p. 216; Gardīzī, *Zayn,* pp. 116–18; Ash'arī, *Maqālāt,* pp. 137–138; Sa'd al-Qummī, *Maqālāt,* p. 74; Sibṭ/Add. 23277, ff. 193b, 196a; Ibn Funduq, *Tārīkh-i bayhaq,* ed. A. Bahmanyār (Tehran, 1317/1939), p. 46; and other sources cited in C. van Arendonk, "Yaḥyā b. Zaid al-Ḥusainī," *EI*1, 4:1151–52. See further, G. van Vloten, *Die Optkomst der Abbasiden in Chorasan* (Leiden, 1890), pp. 60–62; Wellhausen, *Arab Kingdom,* pp. 338–39, 359, 499–500; *idem, Factions,* pp. 163–64; Arendonk, *Debuts,* p. 33; and Ḥaqīqat, *Nahḍathā,* pp. 214–16.

72. Mas'ūdī, *Prairies,* 6:3. Ya'qūbī, *Historiae,* 2:392, records how Zaydī missionaries agitated Khurasan by reporting visions and quoting from books of prophecies. For examples of how the Abbasids exploited this, see Mas'ūdī, *Prairies,* 6:2–3; Tab., 3:506; Bal'amī/Zotenberg, 4:213; Ya'qūbī/Wiet, *Pays,* p. 128; Faṣīḥ, *Mujmal-i faṣīḥī,* 1:196; Iṣfahānī, *Maqātil,* p. 158; and Ibn Ḥabīb, *Muḥabbir,* p. 484.

73. *Akhbār,* p. 233.

74. Tab., 2:1726.

75. Tab., 2:1727, 1769; Azdī, *Mawṣil,* pp. 49–50; Ya'qūbī, *Historiae,* 2:398; Dīnawarī, *Akhbār,* pp. 337–38; Balādhurī, *Ansāb,* f. 292b; Maqdisī, *Bad',* 6:62; *Fragmenta,* p. 182; and IA, 5:254–55.

76. Azdī, *Mawṣil,* p. 53; Ya'qūbī, *Historiae,* 2:398; and Balādhurī, *Ansāb,* f. 292b. *Akhbār,* p. 237, indicates that Bukayr attended this meeting.

77. *Akhbār,* p. 239; cf. Balādhurī, *Ansāb,* f. 283a; Tab., 2:1769; *Fragmenta,* p. 183; and Ibn Kathīr, 10:5.

78. Tab., 2:1869; IA, 5:308; *Fragmenta,* p. 183.

79. *Akhbār,* p. 240.

80. Tab., 2:1869; IA, 5:308; *Fragmenta,* p. 183.

81. *Akhbār,* pp. 240, 241.

82. *Ibid.*

83. Tab., 2:1916; IA, 5:339; cf. *Fragmenta,* p. 183; pseudo-Ibn Qutayba, *Imāma,* 2:113; and Ibn Kathīr, 10:25.

84. *Akhbār,* p. 241; pseudo-Ibn Qutayba, *Imāma,* 2:184.

85. This point is brought out clearly in *Akhbār,* p. 241: The partisans ask Ibrāhīm, "How long will birds eat the flesh of the members of your house and their blood be shed? We left Zayd crucified in the garbage heap and his son pursued through the country. Fear has overcome you, and the domination of the evil dynasty (*ahl bayt al-sū'*) over you has been prolonged." (The word *kunāsa* has been translated as "garbage heap" but it is properly the name of a place in Kūfa where refuse was thrown; see Ibn Khallikān, 3:277 n. 7).

86. *Akhbār,* p. 241; cf. Bal'amī/Zotenberg, 4:323–24. Many such prophecies were current; see Khuzā'ī, *Fitan,* f. 49a etc.; Tha'ālibī/Bosworth, *Laṭā'if,* p. 6; and Azizi, *Domination,* pp. 109–21.

87. There was apparently no single dimension to this brilliant gesture by the *imām* since the sources give many different explanations of the significance of the color black for the partisans. It was supposedly the color used by David in his battle with Goliath, the color of the Prophet Muḥammad's standards (Abū Yūsuf/Fagnan, *Impot foncier,* p. 297), the color of 'Alī at Ṣiffīn, and the color favored by Muḥam-

mad b. ʻAlī (*Akhbār,* pp. 245–46). According to some Persian sources, pre-Islamic Iranian epic heroes wore or used black (ʻAwfī, *Javāmiʻ*, f. 127b); it was also the color employed by al-Ḥārith b. Surayj in Khurasan (Tab., 2:1889, 1919.) It was variously considered the color of dignity and power (Samarqandī, *Aghrāḍ,* f. 184a), the color of revenge among the Arabs (Wellhausen, *Arab Kingdom,* p. 533, citing the *Aghānī*), a sign of mourning either for Muḥammad b. ʻAlī (Dīnawarī, *Akhbār,* p. 339) or Zayd and Yaḥyā (Kūfī, *Futūḥ,* f. 222b; Jūzjānī, *Ṭabaqāt,* 1:105); and it had some eschatological significance, especially in connection with the eastern provinces (Khuzāʻī, *Fitan,* ff. 50a–57b). Mīrkhwānd, 3:403, quotes Abū Muslim as saying that black was chosen because if was worn by Muhammad the day he took Mecca. Ibn Ḥawqal, *Configuration,* p. 422, tells how the black uniforms were dyed at the home of Abū'l-Najm. *Fragmenta,* p. 166, claims that the first to wear black were the people of Abīward, while Dīnawarī, *Akhbār,* p. 339, claims that honor for the partisan Ḥuraysh, a *mawlā* of Khuzāʻa and nobleman from Nasā. Obviously, it would be foolhardy to single out one of these stories as "correct;" they should all be considered examples of how the symbols chosen by the Abbasid propagandists could appeal to many groups and exploit many ideologies.

88. *Akhbār,* p. 245; cf. Dīnawarī, *Akhbār,* p. 360; Masʻūdī, *Prairies,* 6:60. Though very interesting, the story may of course be apocryphal. The use of black had a long history, and the date the Abbasids introduced it in Khurasan is far from certain. Certainly, many Persian sources assert that black had a long tradition of significance for Iranians; see ʻAwfī, *Javāmiʻ*, f. 127b; *Mujmal,* pp. 315, 317; and Balʻamī/Zotenberg, 4:324.

89. *Akhbār,* pp. 245, 247–48.

90. The best accounts of the final phase of Umayyad rule are to be found in Wellhausen, *Arab Kingdom,* pp. 312–96; Shaban, *ʻAbbāsid Revolution,* pp. 114–37; and *idem, Islamic History A.D. 600–750* (Cambridge, 1971), pp. 138–64.

91. Khalīfa, *Ta'rīkh,* p. 402.

92. On Isḥāq, see Kūfi, *Futūḥ,* ff. 216b–217b; Khalīfa, *Ta'rīkh,* p. 432; Balʻamī/Zotenberg, 4:314–16, 347–48; and Balādhurī, *Futūḥ,* p. 209 (Hitti, p. 328). This is probably the revolt discussed also in Yaʻqūbī, *Historiae,* 2:404, 429.

93. See Tab., 2:1879–87, 1976–81; Balādhurī, *Ansāb,* 2:62–67; IA, 5:324–27, 370–73; Masʻūdī, *Prairies,* 6:41; Ibn Khaldūn, *ʻIbar,* 3:246–48; Sibṭ/Add. 23277, ff. 223a, 233a; *Ghurar,* f. 117a; Ibn Ḥabīb, *Asmā',* p. 189; Khalīfa, *Ta'rīkh,* p. 409; Azdī, *Mawṣil,* p. 107; Ibn Qutayba, *Maʻārif,* p. 418; *Fakhrī,* pp. 131–132; the very detailed account in Isfahānī, *Aghānī,* 11:67–79; *idem, Maqātil,* pp. 161–69; Anbārī, *Uṣūl,* f. 25a; Saʻd al-Qummī, *Maqālat,* pp. 39–40; Abū Ḥatim, *Zīna,* p. 298; Ashʻarī, *Maqālat,* p. 164; and Ṣāḥib b. ʻAbbād, *ʻAnwān al-maʻārif* in M. Āl Yāsīn, *Nafā'is al-makhṭūṭāt* (Baghdad, 1964), 1:51. The secondary literature includes Ḥaqīqat, *Nahḍathā,* p. 221; Wellhausen, *Religio-Political Factions,* pp. 164–65; *idem, Arab Kingdom,* pp. 384–386; Shaban, *ʻAbbāsid Revolution,* pp. 148–149; K. V. Zetersteen, " ʻAbd Allah b. Muʻāwiya," *EI2,* 1:48–49; and Laoust, *Schismes,* pp. 35–36.

94. The heresiographers include the Janāḥiyya, the sect which grew up around Ibn Muʻāwiya, among the Shīʻa, but give conflicting accounts of his claim to the caliphate. See Baghdādī, *Farq,* pp. 245–46 (Halkin, pp. 59–61); Isfarāyīnī, *Tabṣir,* p. 110; Ibn Ḥazm/Friedlaender, 45 (and note, pt. 2, p. 44); and Ash'arī, *Maqālāt,* pp. 67–68; Nawbakhtī, "Sectes," pp. 213–14.

95. Ibn Ḥabīb, *Asmā',* p. 189; Balādhurī, *Ansāb,* 2:63; see also Miles, "Numismatics," p. 369.

96. Tab., 2:1976–77 mentions the support of *ʻabīd ahl al-kūfa,* Sulaymān b.

Hishām, Shaybān al-Khārijī, and the Abbasids Abū Ja'far, 'Abd Allah, and 'Īsā. The presence of these groups is confirmed by a subsequent account (2:1980–81); cf. IA, 5:370–72; Sibṭ/Add. 23277, f. 233a. *Akhbār,* p. 306, is quiet about initial Abbasid support for the revolt.

97. Sa'd al-Qummī, *Maqālāt,* pp. 39–40.

98. See above, n. 95.

99. For more detailed information on the situation in Khurasan, cf. Shaban, *'Abbāsid Revolution,* pp. 134–137, etc.; Wellhausen, *Arab Kingdom,* pp. 482–91 etc.; and Barthold, *Turkestan,* pp. 187–94.

100. Tab., 2:1659, 1718–21; IA, 5:226–27; and Shaban, *'Abbāsid Revolution,* p. 131.

101. Kūfī, *Futūḥ,* f. 223b; Ibn Ḥabīb, *Muḥabbir,* p. 450; and Narshakhī/Frye, *Bukhara,* pp. 61–62.

102. On the tax and other reforms, see Tab., 2:1688–89; Shaban, *'Abbāsid Revolution,* pp. 129–31; Anne Lambton, "Īrān," *EI2,* 4:15; Van Vloten, *Recherches,* pp. 71–72; Barthold, *Turkestan,* pp. 192–93; Dennett, *Poll-Tax,* pp. 124–28; and 'Abd al-'Azīz Dūrī, "Niẓām al-ḍarā'ib fī khurāsān fī ṣadr al-islām," *MMII*(1964):87.

103. Tab., 2:1765–67; IA, 5:269; and Wellhausen, *Arab Kingdom,* pp. 257–358.

104. For examples of Nasr's partiality, see Kūfī, *Futūh,* f. 217b; Tab., 2:1473, 1498, 1530, 1661, 1663, 1847; and Bal'amī/Zotenberg, 4:316.

105. On al-Kirmānī and his supporters, see Tab., 2:1859–60, 1862; IA, 5:304; Dīnawarī, *Akhbār,* p. 351; Gardīzī, *Zayn,* p. 118; Khalīfa, *Ta'rīkh,* p. 410; and Shaban, *'Abbāsid Revolution,* pp. 136–37.

106. Tab., 2:1888–90.

107. *Ibid.,* 1917–18; IA, 5:342–43; and *Akhbār,* p. 250. For one statement of how the Abbasids took advantage of this, see Azdī, *Akhbār al-duwal,* ff. 100a–b.

108. The earlier date is given by Azdī, *Mawṣil,* p. 65, Ibn Kathīr, 10:25; and *Fragmenta,* p. 184; the latter is cited by Khalīfa, *Ta'rīkh,* p. 409 and Ibn al-Jawzī/Amedroz, p. 876, Mas'ūdī, Ya'qūbī, and Balādhurī are all vague about the date, and Tab. gives the compromise date of 128, 2:1937; Sibṭ/Add. 23277, f. 228a; IA, 5:347; Maqdisī, *Bad',* 6:62; and *Mujmal,* pp. 314–15.

109. *Akhbār,* pp. 225, 262, 267.

110. Tab., 2:1937; IA, 5:347–48; Sibṭ/Add. 23277, f. 228a; cf. variant tradition in Tab., 2:1960, which attributes leadership of the pro-Abū Muslim faction to Abū Da'ūd.

111. *Akhbār,* p. 270.

112. See Tab., 2:1937; IA, 5:348; *Fragmenta,* p. 184; pseudo-Ibn Qutayba, *Imāma,* 2:144; Maqrīzī, *Nizā',* pp. 66–67; Ibn 'Abd Rabbih, *'Iqd,* 4:479; cf. Azdī, *Mawṣil,* p. 65 and Bal'amī/Add. 23497, f. 235b (which says Abū Muslim was ordered to kill anyone, Arab or *'ajam,* who was not a *shī'a*); *Annales,* f. 5a. Mas'ūdī, *Prairies,* 6:69 and Ibn Taghrībirdī, *Nujūm,* 1:320 mention the letter falling into the hands of Marwān.

113. *Akhbār,* pp. 270–71; the friction between Abū Muslim and Sulaymān is also mentioned in Tab., 2:1937, 1960; Sibṭ/Add. 23277, f. 213b; IA, 5:348; Sam'ānī, *Ansāb,* f. 323a; and Balādhurī, *Ansāb,* f. 293a, where it is suggested that the Khurāsānīs indicated a preference for Sulaymān as their leader in lieu of a member of *ahl al-bayt.* See also Wellhausen, *Arab Kingdom,* pp. 519–22.

114. Tab., 2:1949–51, variant tradition, 1962–63; IA, 5:356–57; Maqdisī, *Bad'*, 6:63; *Fragmenta,* p. 186; Mīrkhwānd, 3:365; and Wellhausen, *Arab Kingdom,* pp. 520–22.

115. This theory has been advanced by Shaban, *'Abbāsid Revolution,* pp. xv, 157–58.

116. Tab., 2:1963–64.

117. Tab., 2:1953; IA, 5:357; cf. Ibn Kathīr, 10:36; and Azdī, *Akhbār al-duwal,* f. 100b.

118. Tab., 2:1953, 1964; IA, 5:357–58; *Akhbār,* p. 272; Bal'amī/Add. 23497, f. 236a. There are minor discrepancies among the lists, and the vocalization of some of the names is uncertain.

119. Bal'amī/Add. 23497, f. 236a.

120. Tab., 2:1953 (but see conflicting account, 1952); IA, 5:358.

121. Tab., 2:1952, a variant tradition (1962); and IA, 5:363 confirm that missionaries circulated throughout Khurasan, and that the people came over in droves to the side of Abū Muslim. Yet another tradition, Tab. 2:1965, states that Abū Muslim preached unhindered by either Naṣr or Kirmānī, so the people flocked to hear him. Ya'qūbī/Wiet, *Pays,* p. 128, states explicitly that the strife between Naṣr and Kirmānī contributed directly to the increase in the number of partisans.

122. *Akhbār,* pp. 273–74.

123. *Ibid.*

124. Tab., 2:1955; IA, 5:358–59. Among variant spellings, *Akhbār,* p. 274, has Yaqāzim.

125. Wellhausen, *Arab Kingdom,* pp. 523–24.

126. Shaban, *'Abbāsid Revolution,* p. 158.

127. Tab., 2:1957, in naming men present in the trench (*khandaq*) of Muḥriz, refers to villages in the Kharqān quarter and to others in the Suqādim quarter. Even though the name, at least in this spelling, does not occur in the various geographies, we are left with the fact that Ṭabarī consistently uses it in this sense. It could easily be a corrupt spelling of the name of the quarter, which in turn could easily be related to the name Safīdhanj or Siqādanj, and which need not have been recorded by the geographers. The only way to accept Shaban's thesis would be to show that all the Arab colonists (*ahl al-taqādum*) lived in one quarter, which is manifestly impossible. On Hurmuzfarrah, see Yāqūt, *Mu'jam,* 8:460; and Sam'ānī, *Ansāb,* f. 589a–b.

128. *Akhbār,* p. 274.

129. Tab., 2:1955–56; IA, 5:359; Sibṭ/Add. 23277, f. 231b; Ibn al-Jawzī/Add. 7320, ff. 88b–89a; *Ghurar,* f. 126b; *Fragmenta,* pp. 187–88; Mīrkhwānd, 3:366; Ibn Kathīr, 10:30; and *Akhbār,* p. 277.

130. *Akhbār,* p. 275.

131. The text (Tab., 2:1957 and IA, 5:360) has "months," but this is obviously implausible; see Wellhausen, *Arab Kingdom,* p. 523.

132. This account of the battle is found in Tab., 2:1957–59; IA, 5:360; Ibn Kathīr, 10:31; and cf. *Akhbār,* p. 277.

133. Tab., 2:1959; IA, 5:360–61; *Akhbār,* p. 282; Mīrkhwānd, 3:366–67; and Bal'amī/Add. 23497, f. 237a.

134. Tab., 2:1962.

135. Bal'amī/Add. 23497, f. 235b.

136. Kūfī, *Futūḥ,* f. 222b.

137. Ibn 'Abd Rabbih, *'Iqd,* 6:477, 479; Bal'amī/Add. 23497, ff. 236a–237a; and 'Imrānī, *Inbā',* p. 59.

138. Dīnawarī, *Akhbār,* p. 361; and Yāqūt, *Mu'jam,* 3:149.

139. Tab., 2:1959; IA, 5:361; and Ibn Kathīr, 10:31.

140. Tab., 2:1966; IA, 5:368; and Ibn Kathīr, 10:31.

141. *Akhbār,* p. 378; cf. Tab., 2:1964; and Azdī, *Akhbār al-duwal,* f. 100b.

142. Tab., 2:1968; IA, 5:366–67; *Akhbār,* p. 278, gives the date as 8 Dhū'l-Qa'da. Wellhausen, *Arab Kingdom,* p. 256, raises the usual tedious chronological objections, but if one takes the forty-two days to refer to the time from the proclamation of the revolt rather than from Abū Muslim's first arrival in the village, the date corresponds exactly. On Mākhwān, see Yāqūt, *Mu'jam,* 7:352.

143. Tab., 2:1968–69; IA, 5:369; and *Akhbār,* pp. 279–80.

144. *Akhbār,* p. 280; Tab. 2:1968.

145. Tab. 2:1956; IA, 5:370; cf. *Akhbār,* p. 279. It is interesting that although Abū Muslim sent 1,000 men to the trench, Humayd only counted 800: Were the other of such ignoble origin that the Abbasids, rather like the Umayyads, did not include them in the *dīwān*?

146. Tab. 2:1969; IA, 5:369; *Akhbār,* p. 299. On the various problems presented by these accounts see Wellhausen, *Arab Kingdom,* pp. 526–28. On Ālīn, see Yāqūt, *Mu'jam,* 1:61 which confirms that it was located near a stream and thus had a safe water supply.

147. On the applicability of the term "slave" to the feudalized peasantry, see I. P. Petrushevskii, "K istorii rabstva v khalifate, VII-X vekov," *Narodii Azii i Afriki* (1971₃), pp. 60–71.

148. *Akhbār,* pp. 280–81; Tab., 2:1968–69; and IA, 5:369.

149. *Akhbār,* p. 284.

150. Tab., 2:1965; IA, 5:367.

151. For information on these alliances and intrigues, see Omar, *'Abbāsid Caliphate,* pp. 100–3; Shaban, *'Abbāsid Revolution,* pp. 159–60 (a rather weak analysis); and Wellhausen, *Arab Kingdom,* pp. 488–491. In Tab., 2:1965 al-Madā'inī is quoted as saying that some of the Arab tribesmen swore to kill Abū Muslim "when his followers had multiplied and his authority increased." Cf. IA, 5:366–67; Khalīfa, *Ta'rīkh,* pp. 410–412.

152. *Akhbār,* pp. 282, 287, 290. They are called *'ulūj* and *suqqāṭ al-'arab,* while Naṣr's supporters are "Arabs, and the sons of Arabs." IA, 5:360, notes that they were suspected of idolatry, murdering infants, and practicing community of women. Dīnawarī, *Akhbār,* pp. 360–61, quotes Naṣr's famous poem in which he condemns the rebels as *mawālī* of no account, with no religion save slaughtering Arabs.

153. The account which follows is based on *Akhbār,* pp. 284–85. Tab., 2:1956, notes the correspondence between the two men and says that Abū Muslim used to needle Naṣr by putting his own name first in his letters.

154. *Akhbār,* p. 284; the charge is repeated, p. 289. This doubtless gave credence to the allegation that Ibrāhīm had ordered Abū Muslim not to leave an Arab alive in Khurasan. It may also well be the source of the incident referred to by Theophanes, *Chronographia,* p. 654 (see Wellhausen, *Arab Kingdom,* p. 534 and Azizi, *Domination,* p. 126). Ibn 'Asākir, 2:131, alleges that Abū Muslim instigated the slaves to murder their masters, while Khalīfa, *Ta'rīkh,* p. 413, reports that "the

people of Khurasan and Jurjān killed the Arabs and Muslims (people of the mosques) there." It is therefore at least plausible that there was a mass uprising of the Iranian peasantry which caused many later writers to interpret the revolt as an anti-Arab movement.

155. *Akhbār,* p. 287. Abū Muslim also refused to identify the *imām* (*Akhbār,* p. 283).

156. *Akhbār,* pp. 291–92.

157. See Tab., 2:1975–76; IA, 5:363–65; Ibn Kathīr, 10:33; Dīnawarī, *Akhbār,* p. 362; Balādhurī, *Ansāb,* f. 295b; pseudo-Ibn Qutayba, *Imāma,* 2:116; *Fragmenta,* p. 188; Kūfī, *Futūḥ,* ff. 223a–b; Ya'qūbī, *Historiae,* 2:407–8; Ibn Ḥabīb, *Muḥabbir,* p. 484; Bal'amī/Zotenberg, 4:328; Mīrkhwānd, 3:367–69; and Faṣīḥ, *Mujmal-i faṣīḥī,* 1:199.

158. Wellhausen, *Arab Kingdom,* p. 490; Shaban, *'Abbāsid Revolution,* p. 159, states flatly that Abū Muslim had Juday' killed, but offers no proof of this.

159. *Akhbār,* p. 289.

160. Tab., 2:1966, 1985: IA, 5:367.

161. Tab., 2:1967, 1985–86, 1993: *Akhbār,* p. 316; Ya'qūbī, *Historiae,* 2:399; Maqdisī, *Bad',* 6:65; and Azdī, *Akhbār al-duwal,* f. 101b.

162. Tab., 2:1996; *Akhbār,* pp. 299, 309–10.

163. Tab., 2:1970; IA, 5:320; *Akhbār,* p. 300.

164. Bal'amī/Zotenberg, 4:328.

165. Because of its eloquence and poetry, much of this correspondence has been preserved: see Tab., 2:1973; Mas'ūdī, *Prairies,* 6:61; Balādhurī, *Ansāb,* f. 296a; *Akhbār,* pp. 304–5, 310–11; *Mujmal,* p. 317; pseudo-Ibn Qutayba, *Imāma,* 2:116; *Aghānī,* 6:128; Mīrkhwānd, 3:369; Ya'qūbī, *Historiae,* 2:408; Ibn 'Abd Rabbih, 'Iqd, 4:479; *Fakhrī,* p. 138; Rifā'ī, *'Aṣr al-ma'mūm,* 1:85–86; and A. Z. Ṣafwat, *Jamharat rasā'il al-'arab* (Cairo, 1937), 2:561–68.

166. Tab., 2:2016.

167. *Akhbār,* p. 310.

168. *Ibid.,* p. 315.

169. Tab., 2:1989–90; cf. Balādhurī, *Ansāb,* f. 295b; and Ya'qūbī/Wiet, *Pays,* p. 128. By contrast, Ḥamza al-Isfahānī, *Ta'rīkh,* p. 161, gives a much earlier date (mid-Rabī' I 130).

170. Tab., 2:1987; cf. IA, 5:379; Mīrkhwānd, 3:373–74; Khalīfa, *Ta'rīkh, pp. 411*–12; and Ibn al-Jawzī/Amedroz, p. 877. The verse from the Koran is 28:15.

171. Tab., 2:1987, 1988–89, gives the text of the oath; cf. *Akhbār,* p. 316.

172. Tab., 2:1995; cf. *Akhbār,* pp. 317–18; Khalīfa, *Ta'rīkh,* p. 412; pseudo-Ibn Qutayba, *Imāma,* 2:116; and IA, 5:372. The information about Naṣr's wife is taken from Ibn Ḥabīb, *Muḥabbir,* p. 450. She later married 'Abd al-Jabbār al-Azdī!

173. Tab., 2:1990, 1994–95; IA, 5:371; Kūfī, *Futūḥ,* f. 224b; Bal'amī/Zotenberg, 4:329; Ibn al-Kalbī, *Jamharat,* f. 85b; Ya'qūbī, *Historiae,* 2:409–10; and Maqrīzī, *Nizā',* p. 68. Khalīfa, *Ta'rīkh,* p. 413, gives a different version of events.

174. Tab., 2:1992.

175. Tab., 2:1984, 1987; *Akhbār,* p. 316.

176. Certainly, the spirit of Khurāsānī solidarity was perceived by a number of sources: see Bīrūnī/Sachau, p. 197; Elias, *Chronographie,* p. 102; *Annales,* f. 3b;

Dionysius, *Chronique,* p. 43; and Severus as cited in J. Walker, ''New Coin Evidence From Sīstān,'' *JRAS* (1935), p. 116. The ramifications of this new concept of self-identity are discussed in relation to the *shu'ūbī* controversy in Roy Mottahedeh, ''The Shu'ūbiyya Controversy and the Social History of Early Islamic Iran,'' *IJMES* 7(1976):161–82.

CHAPTER TWO

The Consolidation of Abbasid Power

In occupying Merv, Abū Muslim had scored a significant victory, but the ultimate objective of establishing and legitimizing a new Abbasid regime was yet to be attained. Before Abū Muslim could secure Abbasid rule—and his own—he and his followers had to resolve a number of problems. First, they pressed the attack against the Umayyads until that dynasty was overthrown. Second, they assured the dominance of the pro-Abbasid faction within the revolutionary coalition by defeating a number of rivals and opponents, real and imagined, from within as well as from without the revolutionary ranks. Third, they asserted the pre-eminence of Khurasan in the east by establishing Khurāsānī-Abbasid domination of the surrounding areas of Iran and Central Asia. Finally, they took the first steps towards controlling the radical, "unorthodox," popular, and peasant forces they had unleashed in Khurasan. How were these goals achieved? What trouble did they portend for the future?

THE CAMPAIGN OF QAḤṬABA B. SHABĪB

The most important task, obviously, was to maintain the momentum the partisans had gained in their struggle with the Umayyad forces. Since Abū Muslim was engaged in setting up a provisional government in Khurasan, Qaḥṭaba b. Shabīb al-Ṭā'ī, one of the original twelve *nuqabā'*, took command of the military operations against Naṣr and his supporters. Interestingly, the sources do not agree as to whether it was Abū Muslim or the *imām* Ibrahim who entrusted this position to Qaḥṭaba.[1] Although this might seem a minor point, it is actually of some importance as it would indicate the extent to which the movement was controlled by either the local leadership or the central organization. The very fact that there is this confusion in the sources would suggest that the respective roles of Abū Muslim as *amīr* and Ibrāhīm as *imām* had not been clearly defined and that the seeds of conflict between the provincial leaders and the central administration were present. In any case, the matter did not present any immediate problem, as we know that Abū Muslim confirmed Qaḥṭaba's command, ordered the partisans to obey him, and supplied him with arms and fresh troops.[2]

Qaḥṭaba entrenched his army near Abīward, where they remained until the end of winter.[3] In the spring, Qaḥṭaba proceeded against Naṣr, who had retreated to Nishapur to await the reinforcements under Nubāta b. Hanẓala which had at last been sent to his aid. The Umayyad agent in Ṭūs, al-Nābī al-'Ijlī, wrote Naṣr about Qaḥṭaba's advance, whereupon Naṣr sent out a detachment of troops, led by his son Tamīm and 'Āṣim b. 'Amir al-Sughdī, to defend the city.[4] Strengthened by new arrivals, Qaḥṭaba sent messengers to invite Tamīm and his army to join the cause of "the Koran, the *sunna* of the Prophet, and *al-riḍā*." They were met with curses and called "louts and Magians."[5] In the ensuing battle, the Umayyads were routed, and the heads of Tamīm and al-Nābī carried in triumph to Qaḥṭaba. This forced Naṣr to evacuate Nishapur and begin a retreat towards Qūmis. He encamped at the village of Mūrūshak with a force of 10,000 Qaysites and pro-Umayyad partisans from Nishapur.[6]

Qaḥṭaba left 'Abd al-Jabbār al-Azdī in charge of Ṭūs and entered Nishapur on the last day of Sha'bān 130 (3 May 748).[7] He pardoned all of its citizens save one, who had been involved in the murder of Yaḥyā b. Zayd.[8] He remained there through Ramaḍān and Shawwāl (May and June), accepting obeisance from the people, while his envoys went around the villages soliciting *bay'a* from their inhabitants.[9]

Meanwhile, a new danger was developing on Qaḥṭaba's flank. The relief forces for Naṣr, commanded by Nubāta and now swollen by the addition of dissident Khurāsānī Arabs,[10] had finally reached Jurjān after a long march via Isfahan and Rayy. Probably in Dhū'l-Qa'da (July), Qaḥṭaba advanced against this new force, joined on the way by many local "wearers of black."[11] Abū Muslim sent orders that no quarter should be given in the coming battle.[12] Qaḥṭaba further encouraged the troops with speeches denouncing such Umayyad atrocities as the burning of the Kaaba, and recalling past Iranian grandeur.[13]

The battle took place on the first of Dhū'l-Ḥijja. Both Nubāta and his son were killed in the melee, along with some 10,000 Syrians.[14] Qaḥṭaba reportedly sent news of the victory to Abū Muslim, praising the gallantry of the Jurjānīs and the common people there who had responded to the *da'wa*.[15] If so, his enthusiasm was premature, for some of the Jurjānīs plotted against him, and he had to execute 30,000 of them.[16]

Naṣr heard of Nubāta's defeat from a tribesman who managed to get through the Abbasid lines to Qūmis by pretending to be a Magian.[17] Naṣr sent a delegation of Khurāsānī notables to Ibn Hubayra to plead for more aid, but Ibn Hubayra imprisoned the messengers and would not send any more troops until forced to do so by Marwān.[18] Naṣr, therefore, had no alternative but to evacuate Qūmis and fall back to al-Khuwār, a village 20 *farsakh*s from Rayy.[19]

Qaḥṭaba stayed in Jurjān from Dhū'l-Ḥijja 130 through Muḥarram 131 (August–September 748).[20] Though this may have been for fear of overextending himself after the abortive revolt of the Jurjānīs, the reason given was to collect taxes to pay his soldiers.[21] On 1 Muḥarram 131 (31 August 748), he sent his son, al-Ḥasan, along with Muḥriz b. Ibrāhīm, Abū Kāmil, and Abū'l-'Abbās al-Marwazī, to Qūmis in pursuit of Naṣr.[22] Pressing the attack against Naṣr, al-Ḥasan sent a detachment under Abū Kāmil to the town of Simnān, located between Rayy and Dāmghān. An Umayyad army surprised and surrounded Abū Kāmil, who avoided certain death by defecting to the enemy.[23] Al-Ḥasan dispatched another force to try to reverse this loss.

Meanwhile, Abū Muslim and Qaḥṭaba initiated an effort to bring other areas of Iran under Abbasid control. Qaḥṭaba sent Khālid b. Barmak to Ṭabaristān, where he was able to persuade the local ruler, the Iṣbahbadh, to join the *da'wa*.[24] Abū Muslim wrote the Maṣmughān of Damāvand to request him to pledge his allegiance, but that prince refused to recognize the new regime, probably because it was affiliated with his rival the Iṣbahbadh.[25]

The date is uncertain, but it may also have been at this time that Abū Muslim took control of Yazd. That city had been governed for some time by an Umayyad agent named Abū'l-'Alā, who had reportedly made himself unpopular by offending the Shi'ite sensibilities of the populace and by building many gardens and palaces for his personal use. After a fairly fierce struggle, the Abbasid forces sent by Abū Muslim and commanded by Aḥmad b. Muḥammad Zamchī (?)

captured Yazd, which promptly began paying taxes to the Abbasids. Zamchī ingratiated himself with the citizens by financing the construction of many mosques for the city.[26]

Finally, Qaḥṭaba felt ready to leave Jurjān and resume the offensive against Naṣr. He left Usayd b. ʿAbd Allah al-Khuzāʿī as his representative in Jurjān, but Abū Muslim, ever jealous of his prerogatives and anxious to exert his authority, immediately appointed his own agent and ordered Usayd back to Qaḥṭaba.[27]

Qaḥṭaba advanced rapidly towards Rayy, which the Abbasid forces occupied in Ṣafar 131 (October 748).[28] The exact sequence of events surrounding the fall of Rayy is obscure. Apparently, Naṣr had despaired of ever receiving assistance from Ibn Hubayra and began a general retreat from al-Khuwār. He either occupied Rayy for two days before falling ill and withdrawing, or attempted immediately to retreat to Hamadan. The disheartened old man died in Sāwah (Saveh) on the way to Hamadan on 12 Rabīʿ I (9 December) at the age of 85.[29] Some of his followers dispersed to Baṣra; others joined his son Sayyār and Mālik b. Adham in Hamadan; still others linked up with the army of Ibn Ḍubāra, which, having defeated ʿAbd Allah b. Muʿāwiya, was moving from Kirmān towards the rebel forces.[30]

It was this latter force which most worried Abū Muslim. He feared, and rightly so, that Ibn Ḍubāra and his army of 50,000 men, undefeated in battle, would try to attack Khurasan through Sīstān. As a precaution, he temporarily moved his capital from Merv to Nishapur, which he proceeded to fortify. Much to his relief, Ibn Ḍubāra decided instead to attack the main Abbasid force commanded by Qaḥṭaba and thus advanced towards Isfahan.[31]

Qaḥṭaba remained in Rayy for five months,[32] probably waiting for the end of winter. He had also heard that a group of "Khārijites and vagabonds" was gathering in Dastbī, and he sent Abū ʿAwn and a force of Jurjānīs to summon them to obey the Koran, the *sunna,* and *al-riḍā*. They refused and were defeated after a fierce battle.[33] Qaḥṭaba also sent his son, al-Ḥasan, with an army of troops from Marw al-rūdh to invest Hamadan. Its defender, Mālik b. Adham, promptly fell back to Nahāwand (Nihavand) to await help from Ibn Ḍubāra. Al-Ḥasan, reinforced by Abū'l-Jahm and 700 men, besieged him there.[34]

Qaḥṭaba now made elaborate preparations for dealing with Ibn Ḍubāra. He got reinforcements from Abū Muslim, sent out small detachments of troops to Qumm and villages near Isfahan to act as scouts, carefully guarded his communications with Qūmis and Rayy, and gave his soldiers their pay.[35] We are told that he commanded a force of 30,000 men from Nasā, Abīward, Jurjān, and Marw al-rūdh, plus an undisclosed number of troops from Rayy and elsewhere.[36]

In Rajab 131 (late February or early March 749), he marched out to confront Ibn Ḍubāra. The battle was to be one of the most important of the entire campaign, for the people of Iraq, as yet uncommitted, awaited its result as a sign of which side would prevail.[37] The two armies confronted each other for several days, with the decisive battle taking place on 23 Rajab (18 March 749) near the village of Jābalq.[38]

After the usual emotional pre-battle harangues, Qaḥṭaba had his soldiers lift up pages from the Koran on their lances (a deliberately mocking reminder of Umayyad behavior at Ṣiffīn?); they were promptly cursed by Ibn Ḍubāra's troops, and the two sides joined battle. For a moment, victory seemed to be within the reach of the Umayyads, as Muḥammad b. Nubāta shattered the left wing of the rebel army, shouting, "Oh sons of free men! They are only barbarians and Arab scum."[39] But then the Abbasid center and right wing closed in, Ibn Ḍubāra was slain, and the remnants of his army fled to Jayy, a suburb of Isfahan.

Tradition has it that the Abbasids seized as much spoil from Ibn Ḍubāra's camp as if they had captured a city. Khālid b. Barmak divided this among the soldiers.[40] It is also alleged that they freed some 10,000 women the Syrians had taken from the towns they passed through.[41] Although probably exaggerated, these stories nevertheless reflect the immense importance of this victory to the Abbasid cause.

Qaḥṭaba stayed in Isfahan for twenty days, soliciting obeisance from its citizens.[42] Towards the end of Sha'bān (March), he recalled the troops he had left with Usayd in Rayy and received some 15,000 fresh troops Abū Muslim had recruited from the villages of Khurasan.[43] He then turned his attention to the siege of Nahāwand.

For forty days, Qaḥṭaba secretely offered to pardon the Khurāsānīs there, mostly aristocrats who had remained loyal to the Umayyads, if they would surrender, but they refused. He then offered the same terms to the Syrians, who accepted with almost indecent haste.[44] Qaḥṭaba took possession of the city, probably on 5 Dhū'l-Qa'da (26 June).[45] The Syrians were allowed to leave unmolested, but some 3,000 Khurāsānī defenders—including the surviving sons of Naṣr b. Sayyār and the traitor Abū Kāmil—were executed on the spot,[46] a clear sign that their conduct was considered an unforgivable affront to the newly aroused sense of Khurāsānī particularism. Apparently unknown to the defenders of Nahāwand, Ibn Hubayra had sent a relief force of 20,000 men under 'Abd Allah al-Kindī; hearing of the fall of the city, they turned back.[47]

With the fall of Nahāwand, the Abbasid conquest of Iran was virtually complete and the theatre of armed conflict with the Umayyad forces shifted to Iraq. While the events there were crucial for the success of the *da'wa* and the proclamation of an Abbasid caliphate, they are outside the scope of this study. It is necessary to concentrate on the way in which the Abbasids consolidated the gains they had made in the eastern provinces, beginning with the bitter power struggle in Khurasan from which Abū Muslim emerged victorious.

PURGING THE REVOLUTIONARY FORCES

The first to feel the weight of Abū Muslim's repression was Shaybān b. Salama al-Ḥarūrī al-Khārijī. It will be remembered that Shaybān had been a participant in the outbreak of Khārijite revolts in Iraq led by Ḍaḥḥāk b. Qays. As these insurrections were crushed, he fled to Fārs, where he probably joined the forces of 'Abd Allah b. Mu'āwiya until the latter was defeated by Ibn Ḍubāra. He next made his way via Kirmān and Sīstān to Khurasan, where he was courted by both Juday' al-Kirmānī and Abū Muslim as an ally against Naṣr b. Sayyār.[48] For a while, he was an active participant in Khurāsānī politics but finally withdrew to Sarakhs to await a resolution of the conflict. After Abū Muslim came to power, he arrested Shaybān for a brief period, but Shaybān was able to escape. As soon as Abū Muslim felt secure enough to do so, he demanded an oath of obeisance from Shaybān, who refused. Seeing the proverbial handwriting on the wall, Shaybān made his way back to Sarakhs, where he gathered to his side his supporters, about 3000 tribesmen of Bakr b. Wā'il. Abū Muslim sent a delegation of nine prominent Azdī leaders to persuade him to desist. Shaybān instead seized and imprisoned the ambassadors. Abū Muslim then ordered Bassām b. Ibrāhīm to bring up a detachment of troops from Abīward to attack Shaybān. The decisive battle occurred in the middle of Sha'bān 130 (April 748); Shaybān was killed and his followers dispersed.[49]

There is little doubt that Shaybān's revolt was sectarian, at least in form; at the same time, it was clearly marked by traditional tribal divisions. He and his followers are described as a Khārijite sect which broke away from the Tha'āliba (itself a subdivision of the 'Ajārida).[50] The heresiographers tell us that other Khārijite factions ostracized Shaybān for aiding Abū Muslim,[51] although it is not apparent from the historical sources that he really gave much material support to the Abbasid cause (as distinct from his support of al-Kirmānī). At any rate, Shaybān was survived by a group of sectarians who tried in vain to rehabilitate his image by claiming that his martyrdom absolved him from the sin of helping Abū Muslim, and who expressed a number of heretical anthropomorphic doctrines.[52]

The next to fall were Abū Muslim's ostensible allies, 'Alī and 'Uthmān, sons of Juday' al-Kirmānī. Their support had been important, perhaps even crucial, to the success of the revolt. For that reason, Abū Muslim had used all his wiles to detach them from Naṣr's coalition. Once Merv had fallen, and Qaḥṭaba's army was safely on its way, the Azdī leaders became a liability and a potential danger rather than an asset. Abū Muslim therefore conferred with Abū Da'ūd Khālid b. Ibrāhīm on ways to eliminate them. First, the two brothers were separated; Abū Muslim appointed 'Uthmān as his agent in Balkh, probably guessing that 'Uthmān's governorship of that troubled area would be a disaster. The Muḍarī faction in Tirmidh, led by Muslim b. 'Abd al-Raḥman al-Bāhilī, launched a revolt, defeated 'Uthmān's troops, and occupied Balkh.

'Uthmān was in Marw al-rūdh when he got word of the defeat and, impetuously launched a counterattack. His lieutenant, al-Naḍr b. Ṣubayḥ, was apparently a party to the conspiracy between Abū Muslim and Abū Da'ūd, for he deliberately delayed his advance so that 'Uthmān had to face the Muḍarī forces alone. Not surprisingly, he was defeated. This gave Abū Da'ūd a pretext for marching from Merv towards Balkh; he and Abū Muslim had made a secret agreement to murder 'Alī and 'Uthmān on the same day. Abū Da'ūd therefore sent 'Uthmān off as prefect of the Khuttal, where the Abbasids had prepared an ambush. 'Uthmān and his companions were captured and summarily executed. Though the sources do not explicitly state it, this was apparently done so that it would appear 'Uthmān had died in combat.

Abū Muslim, meanwhile, had marched to Nishapur accompanied by 'Alī b. al-Kirmānī. There he arranged a special audience with 'Alī and his associates on the pretense of awarding them various honors and governmental posts. Instead, they were all assassinated; Abū Muslim then seated himself on the chair of state and was saluted as governor of Khurasan. This event has been variously dated as Shawwāl 131 (May–June 749) or 28 Muḥarram 132 (September 749).[53]

As noted previously, 'Abd Allah b. Mu'āwiya also fled to Khurasan after being defeated by Ibn Ḍubāra. He had heard that Abū Muslim was fighting on behalf of the Prophet's family and thus hoped to find in him a protector and a champion for his cause. After an unsuccessful effort to drum up support in Sīstān,[54] he moved on to Herat, where Abū Naṣr Mālik b. al-Haytham, Abū Muslim's representative, heard about his arrival and asked about its purpose. 'Abd Allah told Mālik, "I heard that you were calling for *al-riḍā min āl muḥammad,* and so I came to you." Mālik then inquired about his genealogy, expressing some ironic surprise over an 'Alīd being named after Mu'āwiya. Despite a bribe of 100,000 *dirhams,* he refused to recognize the legitimacy of 'Abd Allah's claims. He informed Abū Muslim of developments, and the latter ordered him to arrest 'Abd Allah and his companions.

'Abd Allah's presence in Khurasan was extremely inconvenient for the Abbasid cause, especially since several members of the Abbasid family had taken up arms in his behalf, but Abū Muslim handled the problem with his usual finesse. Despite an eloquent appeal for clemency by 'Abd Allah,[55] he sent orders to Mālik to release 'Abd Allah's brothers, al-Ḥasan and Yazīd, but to kill 'Abd Allah. Mālik then ordered 'Abd Allah to be smothered (so that it would appear he died of natural causes?) and gave him a proper burial in Herat.[56] There are variant traditions about this, including some, probably not to be taken seriously, which claim that Abū Muslim sent an army against 'Abd Allah, who was either killed or died fighting in Fārs.[57]

Ibn Ḥazm described 'Abd Allah's religious opinions as "detestable," and those of his followers, the Janāḥiyya, were little better. Many of them refused to admit that 'Abd Allah was dead and claimed that he was hidden in one of the mountains near Isfahan awaiting the proper time for his reappearance. They denied the existence of heaven and hell, and preached that there was no obligation to perform the ritual prayers, to fast, to go on the pilgrimage, or to give alms. They supposedly authorized "the use of wine, the eating of corpses (i.e., animals not ritually slaughtered), adultery, sodomy, and the other prohibitions'' of Islam. They also believed in *tanāsukh,* the transmigration of souls.[58]

This immediately brings to mind the accusations made against Khidāsh and other extremists in the Abbasid movement. It strongly suggests that there were ideological, and therefore probably political and social, affinities between the Janāḥiyya and elements of the Abbasid *shīʿa*. We have already seen that ʿAbd Allah's coins carried the same slogan as that used by Abū Muslim and have noted that the heresiographers considered him the main rival of the Abbasids for control of the Hāshimiyya. Moreover, Balādhurī reports one tradition which claims that ʿAbd Allah tried to warn the Khurāsānīs not to trust Abū Muslim and the Abbasids and that Abū Muslim was worried that his statements would alienate the Khurāsānī villages.[59] In a sense, then, ʿAbd Allah was one of the Abbasids' most dangerous rivals, for he could easily have become the leader of the *ghulāt* elements in Abū Muslim's camp. His murder eliminated this possibility, but, as we shall see, it did not put an end to this current of feeling in Iran or its explosive potentialities.

Thus far, action against dissidents had been limited to leaders of non-Abbasid factions on the fringes of the revolutionary movement in Khurasan. It was not long, however, before the repression spread to the innermost circles of the *daʿwa*. Though the evidence is fragmentary and inconclusive, one may speculate that this was somehow connected with the death in mysterious circumstances of the *imām* Ibrāhīm and subsequent bitter disputes over the succession of Abū'l-ʿAbbās al-Saffāḥ.[60] It is curious, if not suspicious, that the Umayyads ''discovered'' Ibrāhīm's identity after years of secrecy and at the height of the Abbasid success; this was followed in rapid succession by the disappearance of Qaḥṭaba b. Shabīb en route to Kūfa, the installation of al-Saffāḥ as caliph on the heels of a military coup, and the assassination of Abū Salama, the ''minister of the family of Muḥammad.''

About the same time as this apparent purge in Iraq, Abū Muslim, perhaps on his own initiative, did away with his old rival, Sulaymān b. Kathīr. Accounts of this are quite contradictory, and it is thus impossible to prove whether it was simply a matter of personal revenge for Sulaymān's outspoken opposition to Abū Muslim's appointment as chief of the *daʿwa* or whether it reflected deeper political divisions between the partisans. One set of traditions claims that

Sulaymān, like Abū Salama, conspired to bring an 'Alīd to the caliphate. According to these traditions, Abū Ja'far (al-Manṣūr) visited Khurasan in 132/749–50 to solicit Abū Muslim's acquiescence in the murder of Abū Salama. Among his entourage was an 'Alīd named 'Ubayd Allah b. al-Ḥusayn al-A'raj. Sulaymān allegedly confided in 'Ubayd Allah that he had hoped to see the 'Alīd cause brought to fruition and offered his support for that purpose. 'Ubayd Allah immediately suspected that Sulaymān was a spy sent by Abū Muslim to entrap him, so he went to Abū Muslim immediately to tell him what Sulaymān had done. Abū Muslim summoned Sulaymān, denounced him as a traitor, and executed him, using as his authority the *imām* Ibrāhīm's directive to kill anyone he had reason to suspect.[61]

In other accounts, this story is given a different, but plausible, twist: Sulaymān approached Abū Ja'far, not an 'Alīd, and offered to help him overthrow Abū Muslim.[62] This would at least make more comprehensible the charge later made against Abū Muslim at his arraignment by Abū Ja'far that he had arbitrarily murdered the veteran *naqīb*. In yet another account, Ibn Khaldūn argued that Sulaymān was killed because he refused to sanction the death of Abū Salama.[63] Still other sources point simply to Sulaymān's longstanding opposition to Abū Muslim. He had been known to utter such remarks as "May God make Abū Muslim's face as black as a bunch of grapes" or "We dug a canal, but someone else (i.e., Abū Muslim) let the water in."[64] Abū Muslim had a decided propensity for killing off his personal enemies,[65] and Sulaymān might have been just one more example.

There is a unique account of Sulaymān's execution, however, which indicates a dimension to this conflict that went beyond mere personal rivalry or dubious acts of treachery. According to Maqrīzī, both Sulaymān and his son Muḥammad were executed because of their connection with radical elements of the revolutionary movement. Muḥammad b. Sulaymān was reportedly a devoted partisan of Khidāsh and for that reason bitterly opposed his father's submission to Abū Muslim. Once in power, Abū Muslim killed Muḥammad, so Sulaymān went to the Kaffiyya (?), described as ascetics who had renounced all worldly possessions in hope of attaining paradise, to incite them against Abū Muslim. Abū Turāb, Muḥammad b. 'Ulwān, and others informed Abū Muslim of Sulaymān's intrigues against him. They described him as a Khidāshite and claimed that he had urinated on a letter from the *imām*. Abū Muslim exclaimed, "Take him to Khwārizm," a circumlocution by which he meant to execute him.[66]

There are obviously some problems with this tradition, most notably the mention in many other sources of Sulaymān's leadership of the anti-Khidāsh forces which sought a reconciliation with Muḥammad b. 'Alī. On the other hand, it demonstrates, more than the other traditions, that Sulaymān's murder was part of some larger, dimly understood, controversy; that the Abbasid partisans were divided among themselves. It was not an isolated event: Lāhiz b. Qurayẓ, the *naqīb* executed by Abū Muslim for supposedly warning Naṣr b. Sayyār, was Sulaymān's son-in-law; conversely, Muḥammad b. 'Ulwān was the leader who had first sided with Abū Muslim against Sulaymān.

But what was at stake in this controversy? While it is clear that there were two competing factions, there is no provable answer to the question. Since many of the explanations hinge on the succession to the caliphate and the relative degrees of authority possessed by the caliph, Abū Muslim, and Sulaymān, we may speculate that the problem was essentially political and that it probably pitted local, Khurāsānī interests against those of the movement as a whole. Unfortunately, the discrepancies in the sources make it impossible to be sure who was on which side of the question at this early date.

If the partisans were experiencing difficulties from the political tensions within the movement, there is also evidence that their exploitation of social issues was also beginning to give them trouble. It would appear that partisans loyal to Khidāsh and his ideas continued their agitation in Khurasan well into the time of Abū Muslim's governorship. These Khidāshite sympathizers believed that the right to the imāmate had returned to the family of 'Alī b. Abī Ṭālib after the death of Ibrāhīm. They were called Khālidiyya after their leader, a certain Abū Khālid, who revolted in Nishapur.

Abū Muslim attacked the rebels and drove them across Khurasan into Transoxiana. Thereafter, he used female spies to root out the heretics. These women pretended to believe in the Khālidiyya doctrines; if they met anyone who agreed with them, they would betray him to Abū Muslim. On one occasion, however, Abū Khālid discovered and killed one of these spies, along with sixty soldiers sent to follow her.

Abū Khālid also employed women to spread his teachings. One of them was betrayed to Abū Muslim's agent, who had her lashed six hundred times. Another was Umm al-Fawāris, Abū Muslim's own housekeeper, who had the temerity to rebuke him for his conduct! Abū Muslim ordered her to be beaten with sticks and then stoned. Abū Khālid remained in hiding until the time of 'Abd al-Jabbār al-Azdī's deposition (141 A.H.), when he and five hundred of his followers revolted. His partisans were easily defeated and killed; Abū Khālid himself was taken prisoner and executed by being thrown into a kettle and boiled to pieces.[67]

THE SUBJUGATION OF SĪSTĀN AND SIND

As Qaḥṭaba's army moved westwards, and as the purge of dissident elements in Khurasan proceeded, Abū Muslim took steps to eradicate the last vestiges of Umayyad power in the provinces south of Khurasan. Somehow, Marwān had managed to send into that area a force of a thousand cavalrymen under the command of Haytham b. 'Abd Allah.[68] Abū Muslim consequently appointed Mālik b. al-Haytham al-Khuzā'ī, backed by 30,000 troops, as governor of Sīstān. Mālik trapped the Umayyad army in the citadel of Zaranj and demanded that the populace hand them over to him for execution. The Sīstānīs, however, found this so repugnant that they offered instead to pay a ransom of 1,000,000 *dirham*s on behalf of the Syrians. Mālik accepted this compromise, and the Syrians made good their escape.[69]

Without doubt, the most significant aspect of this incident is that it demonstrates clearly that the widespread support the Abbasids had found in Khurasan did not materialize in other provinces. Not all Iranians hated the Umayyads, nor did they all particularly welcome the prospect of either Abbasid rule or Khurāsānī domination. Subsequent events in Sīstān and elsewhere would confirm the unpopularity of the new regime outside Khurasan.

Thanks to the detailed information preserved in the *Tārīkh-i Sīstān,* it is possible to get some idea of the turbulence of events in Sīstān following the Abbasid coup. Abū Muslim appointed his trusted agent 'Umar b. al-'Abbās b. 'Umayr b. 'Uṭārid b. Ḥājib b. Zurāra to replace Mālik as governor of Sīstān. 'Umar attempted to extend Abbasid control over Sind by appointing his brother Ibrāhīm as its prefect and raising an army to accompany him. This adventure provided an excuse for a general revolt during which Yazīd b. Bisṭām, who had been ordered to conscript the Sīstānīs, was killed by the insurgents. 'Umar himself was compelled to flee, and, if the account of Ya'qūbī is correct, his brother Ibrāhīm was murdered.

There is little doubt that native Sīstānīs participated willingly in this revolt, but it was directed and perpetuated by segments of the Banū Tamīm who were probably sympathetic to the Umayyads, more than a little tainted by Khārijism, and opposed to any outside interference in their affairs. As more and more Tamīmī tribesmen joined the revolt, the situation in Sīstān became so dangerous that Abū Muslim was obliged to send his father-in-law, Abū'l-Najm 'Imrān b. Ismā'il, to aid 'Umar. As it happened, 'Umar died in a pitched battle with the rebel Maṭar b. Maysara (Jumādā I 133/December 750), and Abū'l-Najm had to take on the task of governing Sīstān himself.[70] He was able to do this at least long enough to mint his own coins,[71] but was eventually killed by another Tamīmī rebel, Abū 'Āṣim, who became the true ruler of Sīstān.

Despite these setbacks at the hands of the persistently hostile Sīstānīs, the Abbasids did manage to gain control of Sind. Manṣūr b. Jumhūr al-Kalbī, the same opportunist whom Yazīd had appointed to replace Yūsuf b. 'Umar and who later fought on behalf of 'Abd Allah b. Mu'āwiya, had fled to Sind after the collapse of Ibn Mu'āwiya's revolt. Since the governor of Sind was apparently related to Manṣūr, he may have expected to find a welcome there; as it happened, he took control of the province only after a violent struggle.[72] Stranger still, Abū'l-'Abbās al-Saffāḥ recognized this former Umayyad governor-turned-rebel as the legitimate amīr of Sind,[73] perhaps as part of an effort to establish his authority in the East over that of Abū Muslim, who had hitherto been responsible for administering the area.

In any case, accounts of subsequent events are hopelessly confused. Some sources state that Abū Muslim sent a native of Sīstān named Mughallis to combat Manṣūr, but they disagree as to whether Mughallis or Manṣūr was the eventual victor. Other sources insist that it was the Caliph al-Saffāḥ who took the initiative in deposing Manṣūr, sending an army of 9,000 Baṣran Arabs and 1,000 Tamīmī tribesmen under Mūsā b. Ka'b al-Tamīmī to Sind. Mūsā defeated Manṣūr, who fled into the desert where he died of thirst.[74] It may be, as one scholar has suggested in an effort to reconcile these accounts,[75] that Manṣūr was a pawn in a larger conflict between Abū

Muslim and the caliph. If so, Abū Muslim could have attacked Manṣūr in order to challenge the caliph's right to appoint him to the office. Later, when Manṣūr's counterattack against Abū Muslim's agents proved too successful and threatened to make Manṣūr virtually an autonomous ruler, the caliph felt obliged to intervene to put an end to the affair. Whatever the truth about these events, they were clearly symptomatic of the increasing tension between Khurasan and the other provinces and between the Khurāsānī leadership and the central administration.

THE PACIFICATION OF CENTRAL ASIA

Of all the Iranian provinces, it is unlikely that any was more openly and actively pro-Umayyad than Transoxiana. It would be a mistake to believe that Umayyad strength there was derived solely from the many troops they had, of necessity, to garrison along the Iranian marchlands. Umayyad support went much deeper than that. The Umayyad leadership and the native aristocracy of Transoxiana, the Syrian *muqātila* and the Iranian marchlords and warriors, had a common interest in resisting Turkish encroachments on the area and in preserving Transoxian security and integrity. This coincidence of interests was cemented by many genuine friendships, of which those of Qutayba b. Muslim and Naṣr b. Sayyār with the Bukhār-khudā Ṭughshāda and his family are the most famous. Thus many of the Iranians who fought the Abbasid forces in Khurasan came from the principalities of Transoxiana. It was only with the greatest difficulty that the Abbasids asserted control over these frontier areas.

In 130/747–8, Abū Muslim sent his most trusted lieutenant, Abū Da'ūd Khālid b. Ibrāhīm, to Balkh, just on the Khurāsānī side of the Oxus, to dislodge Ziyād b. 'Abd al-Raḥman al-Qushayrī, the prefect appointed by Naṣr b. Sayyār. Ziyād prepared to resist, and received support from the people of Balkh, Tirmidh, and various villages in Ṭukhāristān. Abū Da'ūd routed this army, which fled back to Tirmidh, and went on to occupy Balkh. Shortly thereafter, Abū Muslim recalled him and sent Abū'l-Maylā' Yaḥyā b. Nu'aym to take his place. This appointment is rather surprising, since Yaḥyā was a leader of Rabī'a who had actively supported al-Kirmānī and might not prove reliable.

The anti-Abbasid elements promptly seized this golden opportunity for intrigue. Ziyād, supported by another of Naṣr's appointees (Muslim b. 'Abd al-Raḥman al-Bāhili), the people of Balkh and Tirmidh, and the princes of Ṭukhāristān and areas of Transoxiana proper, arranged a parlay with Yaḥyā. The results of this convocation was that "they agreed—Muḍar, Rabī'a, Yaman, and the Iranians with them—to fight the wearers of black." Upon hearing this, Abū Muslim ordered Abū Da'ud to return to Balkh to suppress the revolt. Ziyād prepared a strategem to deal with Abū Da'ūd, but it backfired: He had secretly sent some troops to surprise Abū Da'ūd from the rear, but, when they attacked, his own men thought they had fallen into an ambush prepared by Abū Da'ūd. Frightened, they broke and fled, only to be pursued by Abū Da'ūd and slaughtered on the banks of the Sarjanān.[76] Yet even this did not put an end to the trouble: It will be recalled that it was a subsequent revolt by Muslim b. 'Abd al-Raḥman and the people of Tirmidh that Abū Muslim and Abū Da'ūd exploited in their plot to destroy 'Uthmān b. Juday' al-Kirmānī.

Even more serious was the revolt of Sharīk (or Shurayk) b. Shaykh al-Mahrī in Bukhārā in 133/750–1, an event which epitomized the intensifying dissatisfaction with Abbasid rule. Sharīk's origin is obscure. From his name, one would expect that he was one of the Umayyad soldiers stationed in Bukhārā, but it may be inferred from some sources that he was a disillusioned participant in the Abbasid revolt: He repudiated the Abbasids, or more particularly Abū Muslim, saying pointedly, "We did not swear fealty to the family of Muḥammad in order to shed blood and act unjustly."[77] Some sources describe Sharīk as an 'Alīd sympathizer who propagandized the people on their behalf. According to Narshakhī, he said, "We are now free from the affliction of the Marwānids. The plague of the house of 'Abbās is not necessary for us. The children of the Prophet must be the successors of the Prophet."[78] Sharīk evidently benefitted, whatever the case, from the general anti-Abbasid sentiments of the populace, as his followers are said to have numbered as many as 30,000.[79] These seem to have come from a broad social spectrum, for Maqdisī characterizes them as little more than vagabonds (*fulūl al-'arab wa sā'ir al-nās*);[80] but Narshakhī states that Sharīk received support from personages no less prestigious than the amirs of Bukhārā, Khwārizm, and Brzm (?).[81]

The early Arabic sources tell us only that Abū Muslim routinely dispatched Ziyād b. Ṣāliḥ al-Khuzā'ī to Bukhārā, and that Ziyad defeated and killed Sharīk.[82] According to Narshakhī's more detailed account, Ziyād accomplished this only with great difficulty. He claims that Sharīk and Ziyād fought for thirty-seven days, and on each day Sharīk defeated Ziyād, killing or capturing many of his troops. At that point, Qutayba b. Ṭughshāda the Bukhār-khudā intervened on behalf of Ziyād. He ordered the "people of the villages and castles" of Bukhārā (described as exclusively Iranian) to raise the black banners of the Abbasids and forbade them to give food or supplies to Sharīk. This put Sharīk's army in dire straits, but Sharīk hoped to manoeuvre his men between the city and Ziyād so that they could receive sustenance from his supporters inside the city proper (who were apparently Arabs for the most part). Ziyād and the Bukhār-khudā attempted to block this move, but were defeated.

On the advice of the Bukhār-khudā, Ziyād then successfully surprised Sharīk's rear guard and put the rebels to flight. Sharīk fell from his horse and was killed; many of his partisans were slaughtered in the village of Nawkanda, where they had stopped for food. Ziyād then set fire to Bukhārā and allowed the city to burn for three days. He promised to give an amnesty to anyone in the city who would defect, but when Sharīk's son and one of his officers did so, he had them hanged. Since the population inside the city remained hostile, Ziyād finally ordered his soldiers into the city, which they took by storm, killing many of its citizens.[83]

Sharīk's revolt was thus a multi-faceted, and somewhat baffling, event. It was "religious" in the sense that it had the character of a Shi'ite movement and typified the growing hostility between the Abbasids and those who felt the 'Alīds had been cheated out of the caliphate, but it is not obvious that it had any theological or doctrinal content. At the same time, the revolt may have had certain racial overtones. Sharīk found his strongest support inside Bukhārā, most likely from the Arab colony there, while Ziyād was supported by the Bukhār-khudā and his purely Iranian subjects. It is even more probable that the revolt reflected social divisions between the city-dwellers and the rural population, the upper aristocracy and the "vagabonds." This latter interpretation would at least help explain the role of the Bukhār-khudā. Previously loyal to the Umayyads, he felt compelled to support Ziyād in order to suppress a popular insurrection which threatened his own aristocratic interests.

While the Bukhār-khudā may have come to some sort of understanding with Ziyād, it should not be imagined that this constituted a genuine rapprochement with the Abbasids. He received no reward for his assistance and, indeed, it was not long before he was murdered on orders from Abū Muslim.[84] The complexities surrounding this revolt, then, present a problem which will probably continue to tantalize historians seeking to explain it simply.[85]

The Abbasids also attempted to assert their control over the various minor principalities of Central Asia, expelling those rulers who had cooperated with the Umayyads and installing new ones presumably more amenable to the Abbasid regime. Thus Abū Muslim followed up his victory over Sharīk by sending Abū Da'ūd to Khuttal. Abū Da'ūd besieged its king, Ḥanash, who was joined by a number of the local *dahāqīn*. Ultimately, Ḥanash fled with his supporters through Farghāna and Ṭukhāristān to China, where he begged the emperor for assistance.[86] It is also reported that hostility erupted between the Ikhshīd of Farghāna and the King of Shāsh.

The Ikhshīd is supposed to have also requested aid from the Chinese emperor, who sent 100,000 men to attack Shāsh and had its ruler executed.[87] In any event, it is certain that the Abbasid intervention in Central Asian affairs brought the Chinese into the conflict. The Abbasid forces, commanded by Ziyād b. Ṣāliḥ, attacked the Chinese in a terrific battle near the Ṭarāz river in Dhū'l-Ḥijja 133 (June 751). The Abbasids won a great victory, killing 50,000 men and taking 20,000 prisoners.[88] This was one of the most significant Abbasid accomplishments in Central Asia, as it marked the permanent supremacy of Islamic over Chinese influence there. It also provided the Abbasids with considerable booty, including some fabulous jewels and the secret of manufacturing paper.[89] Its most important immediate effect, however, was that it enabled Abū Muslim to continue to assert his authority in the area. Thus Abū Da'ūd attacked Kish, killed its ruler, executed a number of its *dihqān*s, and sent the spoils to Abū Muslim. The dead king's brother, Ṭarān, was installed as the new titular ruler. Abū Muslim also ordered the walls of Samarqand to be fortified and made Ziyād b. Ṣāliḥ his deputy over Samarqand and Bukhārā. He then went back to Merv, and Abū Da'ūd returned to Balkh.[90]

Thus the Abbasids mastered the situation in Transoxīana. They had pacified the area, conclusively ended the Chinese threat, installed their own puppet rulers, and made some concessions to the local inhabitants. Yet their hold over the area remained quite tenuous and would be challenged again and again by particularly virulent outbreaks of violent dissent.

BIHĀFARĪD

The movement led by Bihāfarīd, son of Māhfarwardīn,[91] apparently never constituted a true revolt, but it could easily have become one, and Abū Muslim was obliged to suppress it by force. It is not mentioned in any of the early or more reliable Arabic chronicles, and the information about it which is still extant is fragmentary, contradictory, and often more suitable for legends than for history. Nevertheless, the appearance of the Bihāfarīdiyya was one of the most interesting developments in the wake of the Abbasid revolt, illustrating the varied and esoteric nature of the forces aroused at that time and presaging many of the subsequent "religious" movements in Iran.

Bihāfarīd lived in the village of Sirāwand in the canton of Zūzan, which was part of the district of Khwāf in the environs of Nishapur (Abrashahr).[92] Nothing is known about his origins, character, or early career, though one may deduce, as pointed out by G. H. Sadighi,[93] that he was a man of modest means and some learning. He is supposed to have journeyed to China, almost certainly to engage in trade,[94] and to have remained there for seven years. Although this doubtless has a grain of truth, it should not be taken too literally; the use of the mystic number seven and the parallel with doctrines about the occultation and reappearance of an *imām* are all too obvious.

Upon his return, Bihāfarīd began an active religious mission. One account has it that he pretended to die and had his wife entomb him in a special temple. He remained there for a year, secretly receiving nourishment from pouches of sugar and almonds he had hidden for that purpose and from the moisture provided by rainwater and the ritual ablutions of his wife. When he left the temple, he told people, "I am Bihāfarīd, sent by God to you."[95]

Slightly less fantastic is the story that he brought back from China several curiosities, including a green shirt of such supple material that it could be folded in the palm of his hand. He used these to dupe people into following him. Thus we are told that he went up to a remote temple during the night. The next morning he came down and found a peasant ploughing in the fields, whom he told that he had gone up to heaven where God had robed him in the green shirt and sent him back to earth as a prophet. An interesting variant of this story has it that Bihāfarīd's first convert was not a peasant, but a *dihqān* named Khudādād.[96] Whatever his methods, Bihāfarīd succeeded in winning a considerable following among the people of the Khwāf area. He is variously said to have had from 1,000 to 30,000 adherents.[97]

Contrary to Barthold's assertion that Bihāfarīd attempted to restore "pure" Zoroastrianism,[98] the ideological content of Bihāfarīd's teachings indicates that he had two objectives: the symbiosis or reconciliation of Zoroastrianism with Islam, and social reform. In imitation of the Koran, he composed a "book in Persian" for his followers. Instead of the five prayers of Islam, he imposed seven prayers on his followers, one praising the unity of God and the others dealing with the creation of heaven and earth, the creation of animals, death, the Resurrection and Last Judgment, and the nature of heaven and hell, and finally one in praise of the inhabitants of paradise. He established a *qibla,* or direction of prayer, but towards the sun, not Mecca. He also established an elaborate code of behavior which forbade his followers to drink wine, to eat the flesh of animals which had not been ritually slaughtered, to sacrifice cattle, to mumble prayers (*zamzama*) at dinner, or to marry their mothers, daughters, sisters, or nieces. This effectively removed the features of Zoroastrianism which would have been most objectionable to a devout Muslim. As part of his social legislation, he ordered his followers to contribute a seventh of their property to maintain good roads and bridges and forbade them to give dowries of more than 400 *dirhams*.[99]

Precisely how Bihāfarīd met his death is not clear. According to the *Fihrist,* he was a Magian priest who had absorbed enough of Islam to require the five prayers of his devotees but who would not observe the *qibla*. When Abū Muslim sent the *dā'īs* Shabīb b. Wāj (or Rawāḥ) and 'Abd Allah b. Sa'īd to Nishapur, Bihāfarīd accepted Islam. Later, it was discovered that he was a Magian priest and so he was executed.[100] Other sources state, more credibly, that when Abū Muslim came to Nishapur in 131/748–9, the *mūbadhs* and *hirbadhs*, as representatives of official Zoroastrianism, complained to him that Bihāfarīd was corrupting their religion and Islam as well. Probably anxious not to alienate this important segment of Iranian society at a crucial moment of the Abbasid revolt and not to lend credence to rumors about the less than orthodox beliefs of the Abbasid revolutionaries, Abū Muslim sent 'Abd Allah b. Shu'ba with 10,000 troops to seize Bihāfarīd. 'Abd Allah captured the heretic in the mountains near Bādhghīs and brought him before Abū Muslim, who quickly "sent him to hell."[101]

The death of Bihāfarīd did nothing to stop the spread of the doctrines he had propagated. His attempt to break the power of the Zoroastrian ecclesiastical hierarchy and the wealth they represented by finding a popular religion based on a compromise between Islam and Magianism expressed a deeply-rooted desire among the local populace. Groups of sectarians devoted to Bihāfarīd were active centuries after his death. Sometimes called Sīsāniyya, they remained "the most hostile of God's creatures to the Zamzamī Magians" and believed that their prophet had ascended to heaven on "a common dark-brown horse." They expected that he would soon return to take vengeance on his enemies.[102] Later Muslims maintained a rather charitable attitude towards these groups, refusing to take the poll-tax from them on the chance that they were really misguided Islamic sects.[103]

In reviewing the first few years of Abbasid rule in Iran, it is clear that their policies were ruthless, bloody, cynical—and extremely successful. Elements within the revolutionary forces which might threaten the stability of Abbasid power were identified and liquidated. Other rebels were promptly suppressed. Threats from the Chinese and the petty principalities of Transoxiana were utterly repulsed and their armies crushed. Any popular heterodox movement which might prove troublesome was repressed.

At the same time, several factors, many of them springing from the nature of the *da'wa* itself, had the potential to disturb the equilibrium of Abbasid power in Iran. First, as we have seen, the Abbasid revolt, drawing much of its strength from Khurāsānī particularism, had created a situation especially favorable for the emergence of a semi-autonomous Khurasan and of a Khurāsānī-dominated East. This created a number of potentially dangerous political problems. What would happen if the Abbasid dynasty, as the head of an Islamic empire, attempted to assert its authority over a re-centralized state? How would the areas brought under Khurāsānī control react to that new situation? Would Abū Muslim be permitted the free exercise of his power as the *amīr āl muḥammad?*

In addition to these sources of trouble, there were still many groups discontented with the economic and social policies of the Abbasids whose hopes had been excited by the propaganda of the *da'wa* but whose expectations the Abbasids had no intention of fulfilling. The leaders of these groups—individuals as diverse as Shaybān, Bihāfarīd, Abū Khālid, Ibn Mu'āwiya, and Sharīk b. Shaykh—had been eliminated, but the sources of their discontent remained. Hence, there was always the danger that some new charismatic leader might appear to challenge the Abbasids.

As we shall see in the next chapter, it was the political controversy, an issue at the very heart of the *da'wa*, which first led to conflict. Abū Muslim had become a force to be reckoned with; he was one of the most powerful men in the empire, almost literally a kingmaker—and a potential kingbreaker. Although he was outwardly obedient to the Abbasid family, he was committed to the protection of Khurāsānī interests. As long as he was loyal to Khurasan, he could count on the unswerving support of a formidable army and the unquestioning backing of Khurāsānī society. What would happen if his ideas clashed with those of the caliph? This was the central question in a drama about to unfold in Khurasan.

1. *Akhbār,* p. 321; Tab., 2:2000 (gives a list of the 2001 commanders); IA, 5:385; Balādhurī, *Ansāb,* f. 296b; *Fragmenta,* pp. 190–91; Ibn Khaldūn, *'Ibar,* 3:268. The sources which indicate Abū Muslim appointed Qaḥṭaba include *Mujmal,* p. 370; Bal'amī/Zotenberg, 4:330; Ibn Qutayba, *Ma'ārif,* p. 370; pseudo-Ibn Qutayba, *Imāma,* 2:117; and Ibn Kathīr, 10:35. Later accounts and the Abū Muslim epics carry the point even further, claiming that Abū Muslim personally led the victorious armies to Kūfa to proclaim at-Saffāḥ: see *Fakhrī,* p. 140; 'Imrānī, *Inbā',* p. 59; Irene Melikoff, *Abū Muslim, le "Porte-hache" du Khorassan* (Paris, 1962), pp. 134–40.

2. *Akhbār,* p. 321.

3. *Ibid.;* Tab., 2:2000.

4. This account is pieced together from Tab. 2:2001–2; IA, 5:386; *Akhbār,* p. 323; Dīnawarī, *Akhbār,* p. 364; Khalīfa, *Ta'rīkh,* p. 412; *Fragmenta,* pp. 191–92. The spellings of some of the names vary.

5. *Akhbār,* pp. 323–24.

6. Tab., 2:2003; IA, 5:387; *Akhbār,* p. 325.

7. *Akhbār,* p. 327; Tab., 2:2003.

8. *Akhbār,* p. 327.

9. *Ibid.;* on the date, cf. Ibn Khaldūn, *'Ibar,* 3:268.

10. *Akhbār,* p. 329; cf. Tab., 2:2016.

11. *Akhbār,* p. 328.

12. Tab., 2:2005.

13. Tab. 2:2004–5; IA, 5:387; Bal'amī/Zotenberg, 4:330; Balādhurī, *Ansāb,* f. 296b; *Fragmenta,* p. 192; Kūfī, *Futūḥ,* f. 225a.

14. Accounts of this vary; they also disagree as to the exact date. Tab., 2:2005–6, suggests that Nubāta was killed during the battle; *Akhbār,* pp. 329–30, indicates that he fled to the city and was killed there during the siege. Cf. Khalīfa, *Ta'rīkh,* p. 413; Ya'qūbī, *Historiae,* 2:410; Bal'amī/Zotenberg, 4:330; *Fragmenta,* pp. 192–93; Gardīzī, *Zayn,* p. 119; Ibn Qutayba, *Ma'ārif,* pp. 370, 418; IA, 5:388; Kūfī, *Futūḥ,* f. 225a; Ibn Khaldūn, *'Ibar,* 3:268.

15. *Akhbār,* pp. 330–331.

16. Tab., 2:2016; IA, 5:392–3; *Fragmenta,* p. 193; Faṣīḥ, *Mujmal-i faṣīḥī,* 1:202.

17. *Akhbār,* p. 331.

18. Tab., 2:2016, IA, 5:393; Khalīfa, *Ta'rīkh,* p. 413.

19. *Akhbār,* p. 331; cf. Tab., 3:1; IA, 5:393, 395; on Khuwār, see Yāqūt, *Mu'jam,* 3:473.

20. *Akhbār,* p. 332.

21. *Ibid.;* cf. Bal'amī/Zotenberg, 4:331.

22. Tab., 3:1; *Akhbār,* pp. 331–32; IA, 5:395.

23. Tab., 3:1; IA, 5:395; *Akhbār,* pp. 331–32.

24. *Akhbār,* p. 333; IA, 5:397, says that Abū Muslim (not Qaḥṭaba) wrote the Iṣbahbadh about this; cf. Ibn Khaldūn, *'Ibar,* 3:269. See also W. Madelung, "The Minor Dynasties of Northern Iran," in *Cambridge History of Iran,* 4:199.

25. IA, 5:397.

26. Aḥmad b. Ḥusayn b. 'Alī al-Kātib, *Tārīkh-i jadīd-i yazd* (Yazd, 1317/1939), pp. 59–60; Muḥammad Mufīd Bāfqī, *Jamī'-yi mufīdī,* ed. Iraj Afshār (Tehran, 1342/1964), pp. 37–38. The date for this could have easily come later in Abū Muslim's administration, If it did take place at the time indicated here, it might have served to divert Ibn Ḍubāra's advance towards Khurasan.

27. *Akhbār,* p. 333.

28. *Ibid.,* p. 334; cf. Ibn Khaldūn, *'Ibar,* 3:269.

29. Tab., 3:2; IA, 5:396; *Akhbār,* p. 334; Ibn Kathīr, 10:37; Ibn Qutayba, *Ma'ārif,* p. 363; Ibn Khaldūn, *'Ibar,* 3:269; Khalīfa, *Ta'rīkh,* p. 419 (tells how Naṣr's grave was hidden). Mas'ūdī, *Prairies,* 6:68, notes that he died "of chagrin." On Sāwah, see Yāqūt, *Mu'jam,* 5:21–22.

30. *Akhbār,* p. 334.

31. *Ibid.,* pp. 337–38; Tab., 3:3.

32. *Akhbār,* p. 334.

33. *Ibid.,* p. 335, cf. 342; IA, 5:397; on Dastbī, see Yāqūt, *Mu'jam,* 4:58–59.

34. *Akhbār,* pp. 335–36; Tab., 3:3; IA, 5:397–98; Khalīfa, *Ta'rīkh,* p. 418.

35. *Akhbār,* pp. 336–38; Tab., 3:4–5; IA, 5:397–98.

36. *Akhbār,* p. 339.

37. *Ibid.,* p. 349.

38. On this famous battle, see *Akhbār,* pp. 343–46; Tab., 3:5–6; IA, 5:399; Bal'amī/Zotenberg, 4:331; Balādhurī, *Ansāb,* f. 297a; Khalīfa, *Ta'rīkh,* pp. 418–19; Dīnawarī, *Akhbār,* p. 364; Ya'qūbī, *Historiae,* 2:410-11; Ibn Khaldūn, *'Ibar,* 3:270–71; Ibn Qutayba, *Ma'ārif,* p. 370; Azdī, *Mawṣil,* p. 116; Gardīzī, *Zayn,* p. 119; Yāqūt, *Mu'jam,* 3:32–33.

39. *Akhbār,* p. 345.

40. *Ibid.*, p. 349; cf. Tab., 3:6; IA, 5:399; Ya'qūbī, *Historiae*, 2:410.

41. *Akhbār*, p. 346.

42. *Ibid.*, pp. 350–351; Tab., 3:7; IA, 5:399.

43. *Akhbār*, p. 351.

44. *Ibid.*, pp. 351–53; Tab., 3:7; IA, 5:400; Khalīfa, *Ta'rīkh*, pp. 419–20; Dīnawarī, *Akhbār*, p. 364; Ibn Qutayba, *Ma'ārif*, p. 370; Bal'amī/Zotenberg, 4:331 (claims the Syrians sued for the truce). Cf. Kūfī, *Futūḥ*, ff. 225b–226a.

45. This is the date given in *Akhbār*, p. 354; Khalīfa, *Ta'rīkh*, p. 420, has Shawwāl; Ibn Qutayba, *Ma'ārif*, p. 370, says 1 Dhū'l-Ḥijja.

46. *Akhbār*, p. 353; Tab., 3:7; IA, 5:400; *Annales*, f. 4a; Azdī, *Akhbār al-duwal*, f. 101a; cf. Bal'amī/Zotenberg, 4:332; Ibn Qutayba, *Ma'ārif*, p. 370; *Fragmenta*, p. 194; Kūfī, *Futūḥ*, f. 225a; Ibn Khaldūn, *'Ibar*, 3:271; Ibn Kathīr, 10:37–38.

47. *Akhbār*, p. 354; cf. Khalīfa, *Ta'rīkh*, p. 419, and his report that Marwān sent 10,000 Qaysite Arabs to relieve Nihāwand.

48. The clearest account of this is *Fragmenta*, pp. 165–66; see also Tab., 2:1992–93; IA, 5:368–71; Gardīzī, *Zayn*, p. 118; Khalīfa, *Ta'rīkh*, p. 412. There has been much confusion of this Shaybān with Shaybān al-Yashkarī, a contemporary Khārijite who died in Oman; see Wellhausen, *Arab Kingdom*, pp. 395n, 400; Omar, *'Abbāsid Caliphate*, pp. 99–100.

49. The date is based on *Akhbār*, p. 321 and Faṣīḥ, *Mujmal-i faṣīḥī*, 1:201; other details are found in Tab., 2:1996; IA, 5:372–73; *Annales*, f. 2a; *Fragmenta*, p. 166; Khalīfa, *Ta'rīkh*, p. 412; Ibn Khaldūn, *'Ibar*, 3:356. *Akhbār*, p. 322, gives a detailed account of the battle which claims Bassām used this ruse: He said he was going to Herat and had no hostile intentions against Shaybān. The he turned back to launch a surprise attack on Sarakhs. There is also a very confused account of Shaybān in Ibn Kathīr, 10:34.

50. So in Ash'arī, *Maqālāt*, pp. 180–181; cf. Baghdādī, *Farq*, p. 102 (Seelye, pp. 80–82). Tab., 2:1996, notes that Shaybān's Khārijī beliefs led him to fight Naṣr (as a contrast to Ibn al-Kirmānī, who fought to avenge his father's death). See also S. Moscati, "Studi su Abū Muslim," *RRAL* vol. 8, no. 4(1949): 485–86.

51. In addition to the sources cited above, see Isfarāyīnī, *Tabṣīr*, p. 56; Shahrastānī, *Milal*, 1:132–33.

52. Ash'arī, *Maqālāt*, p. 181; Shahrastānī, *Milal*, 1:132–33, says that his followers believed in predestination and were active in Nasā, Jurjān, and Armenia.

53. See Tab., 2:1999–2000; IA, 5:385; these accounts are generally corroborated, with some minor difference as to the date, etc., by *Fragmenta*, p. 193; Elias, *Chronographie*, p. 105; *Annales*, f. 2a; Balādhurī, *Ansāb*, f. 296a, Ibn Khallikān, 2:105; Ibn Ḥabīb, *Asmā'*, p. 191; Gardīzī, *Zayn*, p. 119; Ibn Khaldūn, *'Ibar*, 3: 266; Ibn Kathīr, 10:34; *Akhbār*, p. 354; Faṣīh, *Mujmal-i faṣīḥī*, 1:201; Ibn Ḥazm, *Jamharat*, pp. 317, 381.

54. This incident is mentioned only in the *Tārīkh-i sīstān*, p. 133, which is generally confused about Shaybān; see the critical remarks of C. E. Bosworth, *Sīstān Under the Arabs* (Rome, 1968), pp. 76–77.

55. The text of 'Abd Allah's letter may be found in Iṣfahānī, *Aghānī*, 11:74–75 and Jāḥiẓ, *Bayān*, 2:89–91; and is reproduced in A. Ṣafwat, *Jamharat rasā'il al-'arab*, 2:572–74.

56. See IA, 5:372–73; Mas'ūdī, *Prairies*, 6:68; Ibn Khaldūn, *'Ibar*, 3:261–62; Sibṭ/Add. 23277, f. 237a; Ibn Khallikān, 1:74; *Fragmenta*, p. 163; Balādhurī, *Ansāb*, 2:66; Khalīfa, *Ta'rīkh*, p. 413: Isfahānī, *Aghānī*, 11:74; *idem*, *Maqātil*,

pp. 168–69; Ibn Qutayba, *Ma'ārif,* p. 207; Ibn Ḥabīb, *Asmā',* p. 189; Anbārī, *Uṣūl,* ff. 25a, 62b–63a; Faṣīḥ, *Mujmal-i faṣīḥī,* 1:207; *Ḥabīb al-siyar,* 2:196–97. 'Abd Allah's tomb in Herat, venerated even today, is mentioned in Tha'ālibī/Bosworth, *Laṭā'if,* p. 134. See also Wellhausen, *Religio-Political Factions,* pp. 164–65.

57. See *Fakhrī,* p. 132; Ash'arī, *Maqālāt,* p. 164; Baghdādī, *Farq,* p. 246 (Halkin, p. 60); Ibn Qutayba, *Ma'ārif,* p. 418; Sa'd al-Qummī, *Maqālāt,* p. 39.

58. The characterization is from Ibn Ḥazm/Friedlaender, p. 45 (see also note in part 2, p. 44); cf. Ibn Ḥazm, *Jamharat,* p. 68. For further information on the group's beliefs, see Baghdādī, *Farq,* pp. 245–47 (and especially the notes to Halkin's translation, pp. 59–61); Nawbakhtī, "Les Sectes," p. 213; Ash'arī, *Maqālāt,* p. 67; Sa'd al-Qummī, *Maqālāt,* pp. 39, 42–44; Abū Ḥātim, *Zīna,* p. 298; Anbārī, *Uṣūl,* ff. 62b–63a; Wellhausen, *Religio-Political Factions,* p. 165; Moscati, "Studi su Abū Muslim," pp. 484–85; Sadighi, *Mouvements,* p. 182; M. Hodgson and M. Canard, "Djanāḥiyya," *EI2,* 2:441.

59. Balādhurī, *Ansāb,* 2:66.

60. *Akhbār,* pp. 403–4, for example, explicitly describes the factionalization of the Abbasid movement following the death of Ibrāhīm.

61. This version is given by Tab., 3:61 and IA, 5:436–437; it is generally substantiated by *Fragmenta,* p. 223, and pseudo-Ibn Qutayba, *Imāma,* 2:125; see also Ibn Ḥabīb, *Asmā,* p. 206; Bal'amī/Add. 23497, ff. 252b–253a; Yāfi'ī, *Mir'āt al-janān,* 1:280; Ibn 'Imād, *Shadharāt,* 1:190; Faṣīḥ, *Mujmal-i faṣīḥī,* 1:208 (which makes the date as late as 136 A.H.).

62. Balādhurī, *Ansāb*/Fonds arabes 6068, f. 800b; Maqrīzī, *Muqaffa' al-kabīr*/Fonds arabes 2144, f. 80b (reproduced in Van Vloten, *Recherches,* pp. 79–80). This story made its way, in a highly distorted version, into the Abū Muslim epic legends: Some of the them claim that Sulaymān, prodded by the caliph, attempted to poison Abū Muslim but was forced to eat the deadly food himself; see Melikoff, *Abū Muslim,* p. 143.

63. Ibn Khaldūm, *'Ibar,* 3:377.

64. Quoted in Maqrīzī, *Nizā',* p. 68.

65. For some examples, see Ibn Sa'd, *Ṭabaqāt,* 7:370; Tab., 2:1628; Faṣīḥ, *Mujmal-i faṣīḥī,* 1:264.

66. Maqrīzī, *Muqaffa' al-kabir*/Fonds arabes 2144, f. 80b; reproduced in Van Vloten, *Recherches,* pp. 79–80. The Kaffiyya are most likely related to or identical with the *ahl al-kaff* mentioned in Tab., 2:1957, which names some of the Arabs associated with them. *Akhbār,* pp. 204–5, says that the Kaffiyya received this name because they were ordered not to use the sword against their enemies and to obey their leaders blindly, in contrast to the partisans who joined the movement in the time of Abū Muslim and were authorized to employ violence against the Umayyads. See also the comments by Van Vloten, *Recherches,* p. 66.

67. *Akhbār,* pp. 403–404.

68. The unique source for this is the *Tārīkh-i sīstān,* pp. 134–35; see the critical examination of it in Bosworth, *Sīstān Under the Arabs,* p. 78.

69. The account in *Tārīkh-i sīstān,* pp. 134–35, is partially confirmed by Ya'qūbī/Wiet, *Pays,* p. 96, and Khalīfa, *Ta'rīkh,* p. 439. Bosworth, *Sīstān Under the Arabs,* p. 78, points out that the figure of 30,000 is based on a scribal error in the manuscript of *sī hazār* instead of *sih hazār.*

70. Again, the only detailed account is *Tārīkh-i sīstān,* pp. 136–37; see Bosworth, *Sīstān Under the Arabs,* p. 78. Ya'qūbī/Wiet, *Pays,* p. 96, says that the Sīstānīs killed 'Umar's brother Ibrāhīm but makes no mention of the motivation; cf. Khalīfa, *Ta'rīkh,* p. 439.

71. J. Walker, "New Coin Evidence from Sīstān," *JRAS* (1935), pp. 118–19.

72. Thus in Ya'qūbī, *Historiae,* 2:407; cf. Khalīfa, *Ta'rīkh,* p. 431.

73. Tab., 3:72; IA, 5:445.

74. Ya'qūbī, *Historiae,* 2:407; Balādhurī, *Futūḥ,* p. 444 (Murgotten, p. 230); Dīnawarī, *Akhbār,* p. 377; and Khalīfa, *Ta'rīkh,* p. 439 all mention Mughallis. Ya'qūbī and Balādhurī, however, state that Mughallis was defeated and killed, while Dīnawarī claims that Mughallis killed Manṣūr. To add to the confusion, Khalīfa says the caliph, not Abū Muslim, sent Mughallis and that Manṣūr captured and executed Mughallis.

The other tradition may be found in Tab., 3:80; IA, 5:453; Sibṭ/Add. 23277, f. 255b; Khalīfa, *Ta'rīkh,* p. 439; Ya'qūbī, *Historiae,* 2:429; *Fragmenta,* p. 211. Balādhurī, *Futūḥ,* p. 444 (Murgotten, p. 230), has it that Abū Muslim, not the caliph, sent Mūsā b. Ka'b against Manṣūr. There is also disagreement as to whether Manṣūr died in the desert or escaped to Khazar territory. Cf. Ibn Ḥabīb, *Asmā',* p. 184; Iṣfahānī, *Aghānī,* 4:96; Ibn Ḥazm, *Jamharat,* p. 458; Ibn Kathīr, 10:57.

75. Omar, *'Abbāsid Caliphate,* p. 162.

76. Tab., 2:1997–98; IA, 5:373–75; the general outline of this is confirmed by 'Abd Allah Balkhī, *Faḍā'il-i balkh,* ed. 'A. Ḥabībī (Tehran, 1350/1972), p. 86.

77. Tab., 3:74; IA, 5:448; *Fragmenta,* p. 211; Ya'qūbī, *Historiae,* 2:425; Balādhurī, *Ansāb,* f. 306a; Maqdisī, *Bad',* 6:74; Sibṭ/Add. 23277, f. 254a; *Ghurar,* f. 157a. There is also a garbled version of this in pseudo-Ibn Qutayba, *Imāma,* 2:139, which gives the name as Sharīk b. 'Awn and dates it during the reign of al-Manṣūr.

78. Gardīzī, *Zayn,* p. 120; quotation from Narshakhī/Frye, *Bukhara,* p. 62.

79. Balādhurī, *Ansāb,* f. 306a; Maqdisī, *Bad',* 6:74; Tab., 3:74; IA, 5:448; *Fragmenta,* p. 211; Ibn Khaldūn, *'Ibar,* 3:379; Sibṭ/Add. 23277, f. 254a.

80. Maqdisī, *Bad',* 6:74.

81. Narshakhī/Frye, *Bukhara,* p. 62. Frye was unable to identify the place the manuscript meant by Brzm.

82. Ya'qūbī, *Historiae,* 2:425; Tab., 3:74; IA, 5:448; *Fragmenta,* p. 211; Maqdisī, *Bad',* 6:74; Balādhurī, *Ansāb,* f. 306a; *Ghurar,* f. 157a.

83. This is based on Narshakhī/Frye, *Bukhara,* pp. 62–65. The intervention of the Bukhār-khudā is confirmed by Gardīzī, *Zayn,* pp. 120–21. If, however, the statements of pseudo-Ibn Qutayba, *Imāma,* 2:139, are worth credence, destruction at Bukhārā was minimal, since Abū Ja'far (*sic*) supposedly refrained from murdering the rebels because their revolt was religious in motivation and a protest of injustice. (It was also, we might add, an embarassment for Abū Muslim!)

84. Thus in Narshakhī/Frye, *Bukhara,* pp. 10, 11; it is accepted as fact by Sadighi, *Mouvements,* p. 43 n. 5, and Barthold, *Turkestan,* p. 195.

85. Omar, *'Abbāsid Caliphate,* pp. 157–58, inclines toward the theory of religious motivation; Moscati, "Studi su Abū Muslim," pp. 487–88, also sees the revolt as proof of the hostility between 'Alīds and Abbasids. Barthold, *Turkestan,* pp. 194–195 and Azizi, *Domination,* pp. 133–34, 136, acknowledge the Shi'ite overtones, but also point to the anti-Arab nature of the revolt. H. A. R. Gibb, *The*

Arab Conquests in Central Asia (London, 1923), p. 95, points out the popular aspects of the movement, a view approved by Soviet scholars; see *Istoriya Narodov Uzbekistan* (Tashkent, 1950), 1:184–86.

86. Tab., 3:74; IA, 5:448–49; Ibn Khaldūn, *'Ibar,* 3:379–80; on this and subsequent developments, see Gibb, *Arab Conquests,* pp. 95–97.

87. IA, 5:449; Ibn Khaldūn, *'Ibar,* 3:380; Barthold, *Turkestan,* p. 195 n. 4 and 196 n. 1, gives reference to the Chinese sources.

88. Maqdisī, *Bad',* 6:75; IA, 5:449; Ibn Khaldūn, *'Ibar,* 3:380.

89. Ibn Abī Ṭāhir Ṭayfūr, *Baghdād,* p. 5; Bayhaqī, *Maḥāsin,* 2:237; Tha'ālibī/Bosworth, *Laṭā'if,* p. 140; see also D. M. Dunlop, "A New Source of Information on the Battle of Talas or Aṭlakh," *Ural-Altaische Jahrbucher* 36(1964):326–330.

90. Maqdisī, *Bad',* 6:74; Tab., 3:79–80; IA, 5:453.

91. There are many variants of the name, this being one of the more common. The sources for the history of Bihāfarīd have been enumerated by Sadighi, *Mouvements,* pp. 113–14; he does not mention Azdī, *Akhbār al duwal,* f. 108b, or, unaccountably, Gardīzī, *Zayn,* pp. 119–20. The best modern accounts of Bihāfarīd include T. Houtsma, "Bihafrid," *WZKM* 3(1889):30–37 (which reproduces a relevant fragment from the *Ghurar al-siyar*); Browne, *Literary History,* 1:308–10; Sadighi, *Mouvements,* pp. 111–131; Azizi, *Domination,* pp. 136–141; Moscati, "Studi su Abū Muslim," pp. 488–94; 'Abd al-Ḥusayn Zarrīnkūb, *Dau Qarn Sukūt* (Tehran, 1344/1966), pp. 141–44; *idem,* "The Arab Conquest of Iran," in *Cambridge History of Iran,* 4:33; Haqīqat, *Nahḍathā,* pp. 226–29; D. Sourdel, "Bih'afrīd," *EI2,* 1:1209; and an interesting, but factually inaccurate, social interpretation by B. S. Amoretti, "Sects and Heresies," in *Cambridge History of Iran,* 4:489–90.

92. This according to Bīrūnī/Sachau, *Chronology,* p. 193; Gardīzī, *Zayn,* p. 119; Houtsma (*Ghurar*), p. 34; Khwārizmī, *Mafātīḥ,* p. 38. *Fihrist,* p. 822, gives the place name as Ruwah (but this could be a misreading of the manuscript); Khwāfī, *Rawḍat-i khuld,* p. 280, has Zāwah. On Khwāf, see Yāqūt, *Mu'jam,* 2:486.

93. Sadighi, *Mouvements,* p. 117.

94. This is the motive cited explicitly in Houtsma, (*Ghurar*), p. 34. Other accounts of the trip to China include Bīrūnī/Sachau, *Chronology,* p. 193; Khwāfī, *Rawḍat-i khuld,* p. 280; 'Awfī/Karīmī, *Javāmi',* 1:227; Azdī, *Akhbār al-duwal,* f. 108b.

95. Houtsma (*Ghurar*), p. 34; Azdī, *Akhbār al-duwal,* f. 108b.

96. Bīrūnī/Sachau, *Chronology,* p. 193; 'Awfī/Karīmī, *Javāmi',* 1:227; Azdī, *Akhbār al-duwal,* f. 108b; the variant is in Khwāfī, *Rawḍat-i khuld,* pp. 280–81. One wonders whether this latter version was an attempt to lend respectability to the movement initiated by a fellow citizen of Khwāf, or to obscure its class motivation?

97. *Ṣuvar-i aqālim,* f. 99b (Salemann, p. 501), gives the number 30,000, which may have symbolic value. According to Sadighi, *Mouvements,* p. 120, n. 3, Khwāfī gives the number 1,000, but the published text (p. 281) has only "many men."

98. Barthold, *Turkestan,* p. 194.

99. For accounts of Bihāfarīd's teachings, see Gardīzī, *Zayn,* p. 120; Houtsma (*Ghurar*), pp. 34–35; Bīrūnī/Sachau, *Chronology,* pp. 193–94; Shahrastānī, *Milal,* 2:43; Azdī, *Akhbār al-duwal,* f. 108b. Sadighi, *Mouvements,* pp. 122–27, puts these in perspective; Amoretti, "Sects and Heresies," p. 490, notes that they expressed typical peasant concerns and interests; see also Haqīqat, *Nahḍathā,* pp. 208–9. The scandalous notion of Magians marrying their relatives in contradic-

tion to Muslim legal practice was well known among the Arabs; see Jāḥiẓ, *Bayān,* 2:291.

100. *Fihrist,* p. 822.

101. Bīrūnī/Sachau, *Chronology,* p. 194; Gardīzī, *Zayn,* p. 120; 'Awfī/Karīmī, *Javāmī,* 1:228; Houtsma (*Ghurar*), p. 35; Azdī, *Akhbār al-duwal,* f. 108b; *Ṣuvar-i aqālim,* f. 99b (Salemann, p. 501); Khwāfī, *Rawḍat-i khuld,* p. 281.

102. The best account of these messianic beliefs is Shahrastānī, *Milal,* 2:44; see also *Fihrist,* p. 822; Houtsma (*Ghurar*), p. 35; Khwārizmī, *Mafātīḥ,* p. 38; Maqdisī, *Bad',* 1:164, 3:8; Mas'ūdī, *Tanbīh,* p. 101; Bīrūnī/Sachau, *Chronology,* p. 194; *Ḥudūd al-'ālam,* p. 105 (and note by Minorsky, p. 328); Baghdādī, *Farq,* pp. 354–55 (Halkin, p. 220–21).

103. Baghdādī, *Farq,* p. 255 (Halkin, p. 221); Baghdādī also suggests a connection between the Bihāfarīdiyya and the Khurramiyya.

CHAPTER THREE

Abū Muslim and the Abbasid Counter Revolution

In the preceding chapters we have noted the important role played by Abū Muslim in engineering and directing the Abbasid revolt in Khurasan and later in the consolidation of Abbasid power in the eastern provinces. We have also noted the potential dangers arising from ambiguities in the conduct of the *da'wa,* especially in regard to the ambivalent conceptions of the political relationship between Khurasan and the central government emerging in Iraq and thus between Abū Muslim and the new Abbasid caliph. In this chapter, we shall examine the serious crisis this situation produced. After studying the problem of Abū Muslim's origins and the nature of his administration of Khurasan, we will survey the mass of evidence which demonstrates that Abū Muslim became increasingly entangled in a struggle to protect his prerogatives and Khurāsānī interests from the encroachments of the imperial factions centered in Iraq. We will also see how the reaction against the revolutionary ambitions of the Khurāsānīs, tantamount to a counter-revolution, led to his destruction.

WHO WAS ABŪ MUSLIM?

Although an occasional unwary scholar may advance gratuitous and unqualified conclusions about Abū Muslim's identity or the way he joined the *da'wa,* the sources themselves emphasize that his origins are shrouded in impenetrable mystery.[1] Was he Iranian, Arab, Kurd or even Turkish? Was he from Isfahan, Merv, Kūfa, Herat or elsewhere? Was he freeman, *mawlā,* servant, or slave? Was he descended from the famous minister Buzurgmihr, the epic hero Gūdarz, an Arab tribesman, the Abbasid family, or a simple villager and a slavegirl? Since there is some evidence for each one of these views, the futility of trying to discover the truth about Abū Muslim becomes obvious. What is important is that he identified himself completely with Khurasan and the Khurāsānīs and, if he had any connections with other places or groups, obliterated any vestige of loyalty to them. With this in mind, let us survey some of the more important traditions concerning Abū Muslim and his social position.

First, some versions of Abū Muslim's origins are found in only one or two sources and have little further evidence to support them. To the Umayyad partisans, he was "nothing but a saddlemaker's slave" who incited the slaves in Khurasan to murder their masters.[2] A descendant of the *imām* Ibrāhīm is quoted by Balādhurī as stating that Abū Muslim was the slave of a man from Herat or Būshanj, in whose company he visited the Abbasid leader. Ibrāhīm was greatly impressed by Abū Muslim's talents, purchased him for about 2,000 *dirhams*, and manumitted him. After living with Ibrāhīm for two years, Abū Muslim went on his mission to Khurasan.[3] There is also a claim that he was a *dihqān* from Isfahan who became a follower of Muḥammad b. 'Alī and served as his messenger to the *nuqabā'* in Khurasan.[4]

A more common story alleges that he was the son of Salīṭ b. 'Abd Allah b. 'Abbās. The evidence for this is circumstantial, based as it is on the accusation made by Abū Ja'far at his arraignment of Abū Muslim that the latter had claimed to be Salīṭ's son. The sources which elaborate on this[5] point out that Salīṭ was the illegitimate child of one of 'Abd Allah b. 'Abbās' slavegirls. After a brief liaison with her, 'Abd Allah abandoned her, and she became pregnant by an unidentified slave. When Salīṭ was born, the girl claimed that 'Abd Allah was his true father. 'Abd Allah disavowed this and thoroughly detested the boy. Under Islamic law, however, Salīṭ certainly had basis for claiming 'Abd Allah as his father. When 'Abd Allah died, he contested the division of the estate. The Umayyads, so the sources claim, were anxious to demean the Abbasid family and prejudiced the courts in favor of Salīṭ. Salīṭ died soon thereafter in suspicious circumstances; the Caliph al-Walīd accused 'Alī b. 'Abd Allah of murdering him, a charge which may have served as the basis for his arrest and exile to Ḥumayma.

These sources, however, give no convincing explanation of why Muḥammad and Ibrāhīm, 'Alī's sons, would have promoted the career of Salīṭ's supposed son in so extraordinary a fashion; nor do they say what Abū Muslim might have hoped to gain by forging so dubious a genealogy. The sordid nature of this story, coupled with its prominent position in several histories of Andalusian and North African origin, suggests that it was part of a pro-Umayyad tradition designed to slander the Abbasids—though it could as easily have been invented by the Abbasids to excuse their treatment of Abū Muslim.

The remaining accounts of Abū Muslim's origins generally fall into two groups, each with many variants. What may be considered the pro-Abū Muslim tradition depicts him as a freeman, often of noble descent. The other, anti-Abū Muslim, tradition describes him as a slave, or at best a menial servant, of ignoble genealogy.

The most coherent account of Abū Muslim as a freeman states that his real name was Ibrāhīm b. 'Uthmān b. Yāsār b. Shadūs b. Jūdirn and that he was descended from Buzurgmihr, son of Bakhtigān, the famous Sassanid minister. His father was a native of Makhwān (where Abū Muslim later made his own home), whose business involved the export of cattle to Kūfa. His taxes fell into arrears, and to escape the government agents, he fled to Ādharbayjān, taking his pregnant slavegirl, Wasīka, with him. He then settled in Fātiq, a canton of Isfahan, where he was befriended by 'Īsā b. Ma'qil b. 'Umayr al-'Ijlī. After his death, the slavegirl gave birth to Abū Muslim, whom 'Īsā raised as if he were his own son.[6]

An interesting variant of this tradition holds that Abū Muslim was descended from Gūdarz; this involves a neat irony, since Gūdarz was the semi-legendary hero who carried the black banners of the Iranians into combat with the Turanian enemy and who, again like Abū Muslim, never laughed except in battle.[7] It is also claimed that Abū Muslim was descended from one of the Sassanid kings,[8] or that he was Zādan, the son of Wasīka and Bandād (Vandād) Hurmuzd, an employee (*wakīl*) of the Banū 'Ijl.[9] Finally, there is a story that he was a saddlemaker apprenticed to a noted Abbasid *'ālim,* Abū Mūsā 'Īsā b. Ibrāhīm, in whose company he travelled through much of Iraq and Iran.[10]

The second group of traditions affirm that Abū Muslim was associated with the Banū 'Ijl, but as a slave or servant rather than a freeman.[11] One such account holds that 'Uthmān b. Yāsār was a *mawlā* of the 'Ijl who sold the slavegirl pregnant with Abū Muslim to

'Īsā b. Ma'qil.[12] Others state that his real name was Ibrāhīm, son of Ḥaykān, a peasant in one of the villages owned by the Banū Ma'qil near Isfahan,[13] that his mother was a slave of the Banū Ma'qil and his father from one of their villages,[14] or simply that Abū Muslim was one of their slaves.[15] Dīnawarī quotes Abū Muslim as saying that his mother was a slavegirl who became pregnant with him by 'Umayr b. Buṭayn al-'Ijlī. 'Umayr then sold her to 'Īsā and Ma'qil (*sic*), at whose home he was born. He described himself as "sort of their slave" (*fa'anā kahay'at al-mamlūk lahumā*).[16] Several other sources point out the ambivalence of Abū Muslim's position, stating that while he claimed to be free, the Banū Ma'qil considered him to be their slave,[17] which is probably as close as one can come to the "truth." Finally, one may mention such varied traditions as the report that Abū Muslim was an emancipated slave from the village of Khuṭarniyya (or Kharṭīna) in the Sawād of Kūfa, who entered the service of Idrīs b. Ibrāhīm al-'Ijlī[18]; the story that he was a slave born in the *mawālī* mosque in Ḥarrān and was purchased by Ibrāhīm the *imām*[19]; or the claim that he was the servant of Yūsuf b. Abī Sufyān al-Bāhilī.[20]

These conflicting accounts of Abū Muslim's origins are reflected in the different versions of how he came to join the *da'wa*. Those accounts which claim he was a freeman usually imply that he joined the mission at an early date, of his own volition.[21] Alternatively, there is a tradition that his employer, Abū Mūsā the saddlemaker, was an active member of the Kūfan *shī'a,* who sent Abū Muslim to take a message to Muḥammad b. 'Alī. The *imām* was greatly impressed by Abū Muslim's abilities and gave him a role in the leadership of the movement.[22]

Most sources, however, claim that he was discovered by some of the *nuqabā'* while he was in the service of some imprisoned 'Ijlī tribesmen. It seems that Idrīs and 'Īsā, sons of Ma'qil, and 'Āṣim b. Yūnis al-'Ijlī were imprisoned in Kūfa (one source says Wāsiṭ) but the reason for their arrest and the visit of the *nuqabā'* is not clear.[23] Some say that they were arrested as Abbasid partisans,[24] while others claim that they were jailed by Khālid b. 'Abd Allah al-Qaṣrī for not paying the *kharāj*[25] or for robbing a trader near Isfahan.[26] These variants disagree as to whether the 'Ijlī tribesmen were Abbasid partisans when they were arrested, or whether they were converted by partisans in the same jail, or whether they had nothing at all to do with the *da'wa*.[27] Possibly the *nuqabā'* visited the jail simply because they regarded it as a logical place to recruit political dissidents. Finally, there is disagreement about whether the 'Ijlīs sold Abū Muslim to the partisans, gave him to them, or just permitted him to join them.[28]

If it is impossible to separate truth from fantasy in these reports about Abū Muslim, it is at least possible to understand the reasons for the confusion. It is likely that many of the traditions were affected by the *shu'ūbī* controversy and were thus altered to suit various historiographic purposes. No doubt other traditions were slanted to slander the Abbasids, to justify their treatment of Abū Muslim or to repudiate it, or to glorify Abū Muslim. The most important point, however, is that different writers were able to take liberties in their description of Abū Muslim because the Abbasid propagandists and Abū Muslim himself *deliberately* obscured his racial, social, and geographic origins to suit their purposes. Secrecy was the watchword of the revolution; it was important that every partisan be able to see in it whatever he wished to see. It was important that Abū Muslim be identifiable only as a Muslim and as a Khurāsānī. Perhaps he had roots in Khurasan, perhaps not. However, the *imām* Ibrāhīm took great pains to see that it appeared that he did: He bestowed upon him the name Abū Muslim 'Abd al-Raḥman b. Muslim al-Khurāsānī, helped arrange his marriage to a daughter of the *dā'ī* Abū'l-Najm, and ordered him to settle in Khurasan.[29]

There was, of course, a danger in this obscurantist tendency. It meant that the moderate partisans could view Abū Muslim as one of their own and his arrival as a concession to Khurāsānī particularism. At the same time, the rumors about Abū Muslim's humble origins and social status would have had great attraction for the lower echelons of the movement; he could easily become the hero of the *ghulāt* elements among the *shī'a*. As we shall see, this is exactly what happened.

ABŪ MUSLIM AND THE ADMINISTRATION OF KHURASAN

If some of the early sources had an undeniable tendency to exaggerate Abū Muslim's importance in Abbasid affairs out of all proportion to reality, some modern historians have gone to the opposite extreme.[30] The available evidence demonstrates that Abū Muslim was a formidable figure during the years he served as *amīr* of Khurasan. He managed to hold together the two main components of the revolutionary coalition, the Khurāsānī particularists and the social reformers, and this was no small task. At the same time, his authority over the political affairs of Khurasan and most of the neighboring provinces was virtually absolute. We will attempt here to survey the extent of his power and its implications for his relation with the resurgent prestige and strength of the caliphate under the Abbasid family.

We may begin by noting the connection between Abū Muslim and the various *ghulāt* elements in Khurasan. There are three types of evidence that Abū Muslim attracted these groups and possibly shared some of their beliefs. First, certain Shi'ite sources claim that Abū Muslim wanted to bring an 'Alīd to the caliphate, especially after the death of the *imām* Ibrāhīm.[31] While that is improbable, given his treatment of Ibn Mu'āwiya, there is no doubt that he fully exploited the sympathies of the Khurāsānī population towards Yaḥyā b. Zayd. Second, there is a tradition that Abū Muslim was originally a member of the *ghulāt* sect founded by Mughīra b. Sa'īd al-'Ijlī.[32] Again, while there is little room to doubt that Abū Muslim wanted to use partisans of such heterodox groups in the revolt, there is no substantial evidence that he was actually a member of so radical a sect as the Mughīriyya. Finally, there is the matter of the unorthodox sects which sprang up after Abū Muslim's death and claimed to be following his teachings. This had led a number of authorities, notably Barthold,[33] to suspect that Abū Muslim really did compromise Islam in order to accommodate various local beliefs, especially the doctrine of the transmigration of souls (*tanāsukh*).

Against all these apparent examples of Abū Muslim's association with heterodox movements must be weighed his unhesitating repression of any faction which flagrantly offended the sense of propriety of the moderates: witness Bihāfarīd, Abū Khālid, and Ibn Mu'āwiya. Similarly, while some sources claim that Abū Muslim never performed the prayers (*namāz*),[34] many others attest to his unusual piety.[35] The evidence is thus far from conclusive or satisfactory, but it seems reasonable to assume that Abū Muslim did not personally share or approve of the *ghulāt* tendencies. He was, rather, anxious to exploit these sects and flexible enough to permit certain vague ideological concessions to them without ever making any practical commitment to their cause. Many of the *ghulāt* perceived Abū Muslim as one of their own and were willing to support him fanatically. As a result, Abū Muslim was able to exercise some control over the radical sects and thereby to prevent an outbreak of social strife in Khurasan which might threaten the new polity created by the success of the revolt.

Abū Muslim's political position was much less equivocal than his position on socio-religious issues. In every sense the ruler of Khurasan, he was deeply commited to protecting the province's interests. The remarkable extent of his power is expressed in a number of anecdotes. To the author of the *Fakhrī,* Abū Muslim was "an awe-inspiring man, politically astute, brave, intelligent, bold in action, sagacious, and learned."[36] Ibn Isfandiyār exclaimed in wonder, "To a villager of humble origin and lowly position, God gave so much power that he took in hand and successfully carried out one of the greatest enterprises ever planned."[37] And no less a personage than the Caliph al-Ma'mūn is reported to have said, "The greatest princes of the earth were three in number: I mean Alexander, Ardashir, and Abū Muslim."[38]

There is ample historical evidence to back up these stories. We have already seen that it may have been Abū Muslim who entrusted command of the revolutionary army to Qaḥṭaba b. Shabīb, and it was certainly he, not the head of the Abbasid family, who appointed the various officials of the provisional government in the East.[39] He minted coins on which he styled himself *amīr āl muḥammad* without acknowledging or even mentioning the authority of the caliph.[40] He liked to hold court and dispense justice in a manner worthy of a prince in his symbolic, four-halled *dār al-imāra.*[41] We hear that he ordered and financed the construction of a number of public works in Khurasan. In Merv, these included a spacious new marketplace and a magnificent congregational mosque, in addition to the new *dār al-imāra*[42]; in Nishapur, he erected a new mosque and laid out public gardens.[43] We have already had occasion to mention traditions which credit his regime with the construction of mosques in Yazd, so it seems plausible that the public works program was implemented throughout the eastern provinces. As if to dramatize his prestige and position, Abū Muslim made it a point to reside at Rāmatīn, the traditional summer home of the Bukhār-khudā, during his visits to Bukhārā.[44]

Of course, Abū Muslim did not acquire all this power without running the grave risk of offending the caliph and his supporters. There are anecdotes which, even if apocryphal, at least reflect his awareness of this danger. "I have extinguished the embers of the

Umayyad dynasty," he is reported as saying,[45] "and kindled the fire of the Abbasids. Now I must avoid being burned by the flames." It was not long before portents of trouble appeared.

ABŪ MUSLIM AND THE EXECUTION OF ABŪ SALAMA

Information about political developments in Iraq after the arrival of the Abbasid armies from Khurasan is frustratingly inadequate. There is every indication that a conflict, centered around the choice of caliph but in fact a struggle to determine the political character of a new government, erupted after the puzzling death of the *imām* Ibrāhīm, but it is difficult to analyze this on the basis of existing evidence. It is clear enough, however, that Abū Salama, for one, was not pleased by the prospect of rule by Abū'l-'Abbās al-Saffāḥ and for that reason delayed his inauguration until compelled by a clique of Khurāsānī officers to recognize al-Saffāḥ as caliph. What is of interest here is the role Abū Muslim played in these events and how this affected his relation with the new dynasty.

A few traditions imply that Abū Muslim discovered Abū Salama's allegedly treacherous behavior and either persuaded the caliph to do away with him or sent some of his cronies to murder him out of jealousy. The most forceful of these traditions claim that al-Saffāḥ was actually a devoted friend of Abū Salama and attempted to prevent his execution, but was overruled by Abū Muslim.[46]

In direct contradiction of this, other sources state that al-Saffāḥ, once installed as caliph, grew increasingly suspicious of Abū Salama, who served as his chief minister, and resolved to kill him. However, he and his advisors were afraid to take this step without Abū Muslim's approval. They therefore sent letters to Abū Muslim informing him of Abū Salama's perfidy, the accusation being that he had tried to persuade an 'Alīd to accept the caliphate. These messages convinced Abū Muslim to send some of his soliders to murder the minister.[47] Some of these sources indicate that the letters to Abū Muslim were carried to Khurasan by Abū Ja'far al-Manṣūr, who took an active role in persuading Abū Muslim to kill Abū Salama, while others insist that Abū Ja'far went to Khurasan only after Abū Salama's death.[48]

Yet another version has it that Abū Ja'far went to Khurasan shortly after al-Saffāḥ's proclamation as caliph in order to solicit Abū Muslim's oath of allegiance and that of his troops, his recognition of Abū Ja'far as heir apparent (*walī 'ahd*), and his consent in the execution of Abū Salama. In Ṭabarī's recension of Madā'inī's account (which was supposedly based on al-Manṣūr's personal testimony), this is the story given: At one of his councils, Abū'l-'Abbās discussed Abū Salama's actions, and one member of the audience wondered if he had been following Abū Muslim's directives. In order to be certain about this, the caliph ordered his brother, Abū Ja'far, to go to Khurasan. Abū Ja'far set out, not without some trepidation, which was relieved only when he reached Merv and was amicably received by Abū Muslim. On the fourth day of his visit, Abū Ja'far brought up the matter of Abū Salama's intrigues. Abū Muslim, somewhat astonished, immediately agreed that Abū Salama would have to be liquidated and dispatched one of his lieutenants, Mirrār b. Anās Al-Ḍabbī to kill him.[49]

Some of the differences between these accounts may be reconciled if we accept the version of events recorded by al-Jahshiyārī. He states that Abū Ja'far went to Khurasan to solicit obeisance from Abū Muslim and returned in Jumādā I 132 (December 749 or January 750). Shortly thereafter, al-Saffāḥ suspected Abū Salama of treachery and, on the advice of Da'ūd b. 'Alī, wrote to Abū Muslim seeking his participation in Abū Salama's execution. Abū Muslim agreed to send Mirrār b. Anās to kill him. Three days before his arrival, the caliph issued a fake proclamation of his intention to bestow honors on Abū Salama. When the assassin was ready, Abū Salama was called to the palace, the doors were locked, and he was murdered. (Rajab 132/ February-March 750). Thereafter the rumor was spread that the Khārijites had killed the minister.[50] The caliph's trick to lull Abū Salama into a false sense of security would explain why some traditions claim that Abū Muslim was responsible for the murder, as their authors obviously took al-Saffāḥ's proclamation at face value. The only remaining difficulty would be the claim that Abū Ja'far visited Khurasan after Abū Salama's murder. It is likely that this is erroneous since, as we shall see, Abū Ja'far was then busy dealing with Ibn Hubayra at Wāsiṭ.

For our purposes, the important thing is that every one of these traditions indicates the existence of friction between Abū Muslim and the Abbasids. Whether he acted on his own, or whether the Abbasids were so initimidated by him they they were afraid to act without his approval, or whether he was persuaded to follow their lead, is immaterial. In each case, it is clear that the relation between Abū Muslim and the caliph was not that between servant and master; his authority acted as a restraint on the caliph's. Moreover, there is general agreement that Abū Ja'far, whenever he made the trip to Khurasan and for whatever purpose, became estranged from Abū Muslim and harbored a bitter resentment of him. The reason given is that he was insulted that Abū Muslim treated him as an equal and did not accord him the deference he expected. As soon as he returned to Iraq, he attempted to turn al-Saffāḥ against Abū Muslim by pointing out that the caliph's authority was not complete so long as he had to worry about his over-powerful subordinate.[51].

THE IBN HUBAYRA AFFAIR

Another example of tension between Abū Muslim and the Abbasids, particularly Abū Ja'far, soon became apparent. Thanks to Abū Ja'far's intercession, Ibn Hubayra, the last Umayyad governor of Iraq, received a pardon from al-Saffāḥ in exchange for surrendering Wāsiṭ to the Abbasid forces. There are admittedly several different versions of what happened after Ibn Hubayra was granted this *aman,* some of which do not mention Abū Muslim at all. But a number of sources make it abundantly clear that Abū Muslim and many Khurāsānīs were outraged by the generous treatment accorded this notorious Qaysī chieftain. Thus we find in Ṭabarī that Abū'l-Jahm, Abū Muslim's chief representative at the Abbasid court,[52] informed Abū Muslim of the negotiations with Ibn Hubayra. Abū Muslim promptly wrote al-Saffāḥ denouncing the pardon and demanding Ibn Hubayra's execution. Al-Saffāḥ was inclined to take this advice—because he was afraid of Abū Muslim or perhaps felt he owed a political debt to him for agreeing to Abū Salama's execution?—but Abū Ja'far resisted the move to execute Ibn Hubayra.[53]

One must accord this report some credibility. It was typical of Abū Muslim to seek vengeance against his Umayyad opponents, and it was equally typical of Abū Ja'far, an outspoken admirer of men like Mu'āwiya, al-Ḥajjāj, and 'Abd al-Malik, to seek reconciliation with talented Umayyad officials.[54] In the end, Abū'l-'Abbās did execute Ibn Hubayra, charging that he had violated the terms of the pardon and being careful to have the execution performed by a Muḍarī partisan rather than a Yamanī in order to avoid exciting tribal sentiments.[55]

FURTHER SIGNS OF TROUBLE

There is an interesting sequel to the Abū Salama affair which gives another indication of the split between Abū Muslim and the central government. Abū Muslim sent Muḥammad b. al-Ash'ath al-Khuzā'ī to the province of Fārs with orders to kill all the agents appointed there by Abū Salama. Meanwhile, al-Saffāḥ, in accordance with his policy of appointing his uncles to provincial offices, sent 'Īsā b. 'Alī to assume control of Fārs. When he arrived, Muḥammad refused to relinquish the office and even threatened to kill 'Īsā. He said that Abū Muslim had ordered him not to recognize anyone appointed by someone else and to kill the pretender if he persisted. The chagrined 'Īsā had little alternative but to go back to Iraq, swearing that he would not take any further part in public affairs except for the *jihād*.[56] It is thus clear that Abū Muslim would not tolerate any intrusion into what he regarded as his sphere of political authority. The curious thing about this incident is that while it could hardly have failed to excite Abbasid suspicions about Abū Muslim, it did not in the least prejudice them towards Muḥammad, who was after all an Arab tribesman and who remained in their service long after Abū Muslim's death.

In 134/751–2, Bassām b. Ibrāhīm and a group of Khurāsānīs revolted near Madā'in.[57] This revolt came to nothing, and there is absolutely no concrete evidence that Abū Muslim was connected with it. But Bassām, one of Naṣr b. Sayyār's generals who had defected to Abū Muslim and served valiantly under him, nevertheless represented the views of at least a segment of the Khurāsānī forces stationed in Iraq. The Abbasids were assiduously courting the Khurāsānī *jund* through flattery and cajolery in an attempt to shift their loyalty away from Abū Muslim to the new dynasty. It is possible that Bassām's revolt indicated that some of the troops saw the danger in this and decided to protest. In any case, it shows that some Khurāsānīs were dissatisfied with the drift of events in Iraq, this would have tended to make Abū Muslim's position vis-a-vis the Abbasids even less tenable than it was before.

One final piece of evidence suggests that the Abbasids, including the caliph himself, were increasingly suspicious of Abū Muslim. According to Jahshiyārī, al-Saffāh approached Abū'l-Jahm and suggested that he invite Abū Muslim to visit the court. When Abū Muslim accepted the invitation, the caliph abruptly changed his tune and refused permission for the visit, claiming that Abū Muslim's services were too badly needed in Khurasan.[58] The exact purpose of this charade is not apparent, but it would seem to have been either a test of Abū Muslim's loyalty or a ruse to entice him out of Khurasan.

THE REVOLT OF ZIYĀD B. ṢĀLIḤ

Whether or not Abū Muslim had previously had reason to suspect that the Abbasid family might be intriguing against him, the revolt of Ziyād b. Ṣāliḥ, governor of Bukhārā, must have left little doubt in his mind that this was indeed the case. In 135/752–3, it came to his attention that Ziyād had been slandering him and preaching sedition. Ziyād is reported to have said, "We swore allegiance to the establishment of justice and the revival of the precedents set by the Prophet (*sunna*); but this infamous despot behaves like a tyrant" and had otherwise stirred up sentiment against Abū Muslim.[59] Obviously, it was intolerable for a subordinate to behave in this fashion, so Abū Muslim left Merv to attack Ziyād. As a precaution, he also had Abū Da'ūd send Naṣr b. Rashīd to Tirmidh to prevent Ziyād from receiving any support from that bastion of anti-Abū Muslim sentiment. However, a group of people from Ṭālaqān, described as Rāwandī sectarians and led by a certain Abū Isḥāq, attacked and killed Naṣr. Abū Da'ūd then sent 'Īsā b. Māhān, a *mawlā* of Khuzā'a, to suppress those rebels.[60]

Meanwhile, Abū Muslim had hurried to Āmul. There he learned that a member of his retinue, Sibā' b. Nu'mān al-Azdī, was actually an intermediary between al-Saffāḥ and Ziyād. Moreover, Ziyād had claimed to have a letter from the caliph conferring the governorship of Khurasan on him. It was clear that the caliph was intriguing with Ziyād and had promised him the governorship of Khurasan and incited him to kill Abū Muslim if he got the chance. Apparently, Abū Muslim could hardly believe this perfidy, since he only had his agent in Āmul imprison Sibā' and marched on to Bukhārā. There he was joined by several officers who had refused to follow Ziyād and who confirmed that Sibā' was an instigator of the treachery. Abū Muslim then gave orders that Sibā' be scourged and executed.[61]

Ziyād probably received some support from the very same dissident forces in Transoxiana which he had helped suppress during the revolt of Sharīk b. Shaykh. If, however, he had expected to win the support of many Khurāsānīs, he was sorely disappointed. Faced with the desertion of his officers, he took refuge with the *dihqān* of Barkath (also spelled Barkad). This also proved a miscalculation, for the *dihqān* murdered Ziyād and sent his head to Abū Muslim.[62] It is said that Abū Muslim, rather impudently if with purpose, sent the head to the caliph.[63]

The affair was not over. After Abū Da'ūd was relieved of the task of fighting the Rāwandites, Ibn al-Najjāḥ was dispatched to besiege the Iṣbahbadh of Shāwaghar. The inhabitants of that area asked for an armistice and this was granted.[64] At the same time, 'Īsā b. Māhān was ordered to fight a certain Bassām (?), but 'Īsā, who was either offended by Ziyād's death or more likely in collusion with the caliph, took no action. He tried to secure Kāmil b. Muẓaffar's support with letters accusing Abū Da'ūd of tribal factionalism (*'aṣabiyya*).[65] He also called on the populace to fight Abū Muslim, claiming that the caliph was angry about Ziyād's murder and that he had ordered him to take over as governor of Khurasan.[66] Abū Muslim obtained the letters to Kāmil and passed them on to Abū Da'ūd, who invited 'Īsā to his camp and, once he arrived, arrested him. The story goes that Abū Da'ūd administered only a beating to 'Īsā and then released him for his fellow soldiers to judge. They, of course, pounced on him and killed him.[67]

The caliph, with what can only be described as incredible brazenness, wrote a letter to Abū Muslim rebuking him for 'Īsā's death and ordering him to kill Abū Da'ūd. Abū Muslim replied that 'Īsā had behaved like Ziyād, i.e., had rebelled against Abū Muslim's authority; he defended Abū Da'ūd.[68]

From these accounts, it is clear that al-Saffāḥ had resorted to two strategems to rid himself of Abū Muslim. He first tried to destroy Abū Muslim by exploiting the anti-Khurāsānī sentiments in Transoxiana against him. That is why he bribed Ziyād with the offer of the governorship, and set Bukhārā as the center of his intrigue. These were not strong enough to seriously challenge Abū Muslim, especially since the Khurāsānī officers remained loyal, and the revolt collapsed.

The caliph's next step was a typical Abbasid policy of playing off one faction against another. By having his puppet 'Īsā write Kāmil about Abū Da'ūd's tribal favoritism, he hoped to stir up discord within the Khurāsānī army and thus weaken Abū Muslim. However, his inability to get at Abū Muslim either from without or within the province only showed that the Khurāsānīs, Arab and Iranian, formed a solid bloc in support of Abū Muslim. The chief result of his intrigues was that relations between al-Saffāḥ and Abū Muslim reached the breaking point, precipitating a crisis.

THE FALL OF ABŪ MUSLIM

In Ramaḍān 136 (February–March 754), Abū Muslim wrote the Caliph al-Saffāḥ requesting permission to perform the ritual pilgrimage to Mecca.[69] Coming as it did immediately after the Ziyād b. Ṣāliḥ scandal, this must be seen either as an effort on Abū Muslim's part to reconcile his differences with the caliph or else an attempt to intimidate him further. The caliph, who was hardly in a position to turn down such a request, gave the permission, but as he was clearly worried about the possibility of a revolt, he authorized Abū Muslim to bring no more than five hundred of his troops with him.

Instead, Abū Muslim prepared for the worst. He stationed 8,000 men on the road from Nishapur to Rayy, moved his treasury to Rayy, left the trusted Abū Da'ūd in charge of Khurasan, and set out for Iraq at the head of a force of 1,000 men. Upon his arrival, mobs of people and army officers came forward to greet him. He then approached the caliph for permission not only to go on the pilgrimage but actually to lead the caravan to Mecca, an honorary function which would have further increased his prestige.

The sources disagree about what happened at this point. According to some traditions, Abū Ja'far, who was of course Abū Muslim's chief nemesis, left his post as governor of the Jazīra and rushed before al-Shaffāḥ to accuse Abū Muslim of plotting some new treachery and to urge the caliph to kill him. After some vacillation, al-Saffāḥ refused, and defended Abū Muslim against Abū Ja'far's charges.[70] Other traditions state that al-Saffāḥ deliberately evaded Abū Muslim's request to lead the pilgrimage by promising that he would permit it if Abū Ja'far did not wish to do so. Meanwhile, he was secretly ordering Abū Ja'far to lead the pilgrimage in order to circumvent Abū Muslim.[71] In any case, Abū Ja'far did lead the pilgrimage that year, accompanied by Abū Muslim.

There is no way of knowing for certain what Abū Muslim's intentions may have been, but events placed him in a position for which he could hardly have been prepared. Towards the end of the pilgrimage season, al-Saffāḥ died in Anbār at the age of thirty-three.[72] The caliph's death left Abū Muslim far from his base of power in Khurasan, isolated from his troops, and at the mercy of his inveterate enemy, the new caliph, Abū Ja'far al-Manṣūr. There are conflicting accounts of what happened during the weeks after al-Saffāḥ's death, but it seems that Abū Muslim tried to make the best of a bad situation by apparently ingratiating himself with Abū Ja'far,[73] while simultaneously encouraging Abū Ja'far's nephew, 'Īsā b. Mūsā, to claim the caliphate.[74] Other reports indicate that Abū Ja'far was further incensed because Abū Muslim did not rush to make obeisance to him, or because he sent a letter in which he put his name ahead of that of the new caliph.[75] There is one report that Abū Ja'far was on the verge of ordering Abū Muslim's murder.[76]

In any event, Abū Muslim escaped immediate death because his services were needed to suppress the revolt of 'Abd Allah b. 'Alī, in command of a large army in Syria, which posed a serious threat to Abū Ja'far's hold on the caliphate. In a shrewd, if somewhat surprising, move, Abū Ja'far placed Abū Muslim in command of the expedition against 'Abd Allah. Abū Muslim accepted this task, despite some misgivings. It appears that he felt certain he would triumph, since most of 'Abd Allah's troops were Khurāsānīs and would obey him implicitly.[77] There is no point in detailing the Syrian campaign here; it was little more than an interlude in the struggle between Abū Muslim and Abū Ja'far. Their quarrel erupted anew as soon as 'Abd Allah was defeated.

When Abū Muslim captured 'Abd Allah's camp, he came into possession of considerable treasure. Both Abū Muslim and Abū Ja'far were proverbially avaricious, so conflict would naturally develop over division of the spoils. But greed was not the only motive, for the conflict involved political questions as well. Abū Ja'far sent his *mawlā* Abū'l-Khaṣīb (or Yaqṭīn b. Mūsā) to make a record of what Abū Muslim had captured, thus asserting his authority over Abū Muslim as well as making sure he got his full share of the loot. Abū Muslim was furious that the caliph would trust him in war but not in the division of the spoils; in his anger, he threatened Abū'l-Khaṣīb's life, but later released him. Abū'l-Khaṣīb hurried back to inform Abū Ja'far of what had transpired.[78]

At this point, Abū Ja'far apparently had second thoughts about provoking a showdown with Abū Muslim, realizing that Abū Muslim was in a position to escape to Khurasan and foment rebellion. He thus attempted to placate Abū Muslim by offering him the governorship of Syria and Egypt. Abū Muslim was no fool; he knew very well that his only base of power was in Khurasan and scornfully rejected the caliph's offer. He determined to return to Khurasan, a move which could only be interpreted as a sign of revolt.[79]

Abū Ja'far used all his considerable cunning to persuade Abū Muslim to abandon his plan to return to Khurasan. He wrote a letter urging Abū Muslim to return to the court; Abū Muslim pointed out that the caliph had no more enemies in the field and that his services were needed more in Khurasan than at court, citing a Sassanid proverb to justify his behavior. Abū Ja'far's second letter disparaged the wisdom of "the deceitful kings" and repeated the summons to the court in blunter language. This also failed to change Abū Muslim's mind.[80] Next, Abū Ja'far had several respected Hāshimite notables, including 'Īsā b. Mūsā, write Abū Muslim and sent the letters through a delegation headed by Abū Ḥumayd al-Marw arūdhī and Jarīr b. Yazīd, the shrewdest diplomats of the time. They were to assure Abū Muslim of the caliph's good intentions in inviting him to court, but also to warn him of the dire consequences of refusal.[81] At the same time, Abū Ja'far attempted to bribe Abū Da'ūd into urging Abū Muslim to obey the caliph by offering him the governorship of Khurasan.[82]

Abū Muslim's advisors, especially Mālik b. al-Haytham, urged Abū Muslim in the strongest terms to reject the caliph's demands and go on to Rayy. They emphasized that the "troops, chiefs, and *dahāqīn* of Khurasan" would rally to his support.[83] Despite this advice, he decided to return to the caliph. The sources give scant evidence to explain why he made such a blunder. The claim that he had seen in his horoscope that he would die only in Rūm (Anatolia) is imaginative, but hardly convincing.[84] Perhaps the best explanation is the story that Abū Muslim had sent Abū Isḥāq to ascertain the caliph's true feelings, but Abū Ja'far, through a judicious bribe, persuaded Abū Isḥāq to lie to Abū Muslim and thus entice him to the court.[85] Whatever the case, it was the most fateful—and fatal—decision Abū Muslim ever made.

When Abū Muslim arrived at Abū Ja'far's encampment—located ominously in a place outside Madā'in called Rūmiyya!—the caliph ordered the people and a number of Hāshimites to great him and assure him that all was well.[86] Abū Muslim's first audience gave little indication of what lay ahead. Then he was prevented from seeing the caliph for some time. Abū Ja'far summoned the head of his bodyguard, 'Uthmān b. Nahīk, and several of his cronies, whom he instructed to hide behind a curtain until he clapped his hands, a signal to leap out and murder Abū Muslim.[87]

Abū Muslim was then called in for a second audience, at which the caliph abruptly berated him for several alleged misdeeds: for claiming to be Salīṭ's son, for wanting to marry Āmana, the daughter of ʿAlī b. ʿAbd Allah, for killing Sulaymān b. Kathīr, for plotting with ʿĪsā b. Mūsā, and for such petty personal grievances as preceding him on the pilgrimage, for calling him by his proper name instead of his *kunya,* and for saluting al-Saffāḥ but ignoring Abū Ja'far.[88] Abū Muslim attempted to defend himself against these charges, but Abū Jaʿfar quickly lost his temper. He clapped his hands; the conspirators pounced on Abū Muslim and stabbed him to death. After Abū Jaʿfar had gloated over the body for a while, it was thrown into the Tigris. Abū Jaʿfar later reckoned this the first day of his reign and ranked it among the three things in his life which had given him the most satisfaction.[89]

The Abbasids had long feared to act against Abū Muslim because of his soldiers' loyalty, and there was still a threat that the Khurāsānīs might try to avenge their master. Abū Jaʿfar had partially defused this through speeches which praised Khurasan and emphasized that the army's personal loyalty should be to the caliph, thus winning the support of many of the troops stationed in Iraq, who had, in effect, become his creatures. After the murder, he ordered money to be given to Abū Muslim's followers until they were satisfied. Some of them were ashamed of this and muttered, "We have sold our master for *dirhams*." However, officers loyal to the caliph, led by Abū Isḥāq, called them dogs and ordered them to disperse.[90] Some traditions relate that Abū Jaʿfar also wrote to Mālik b. al-Haytham, putting Abū Muslim's seal on the letter. Thanks to a prearrangement with Abū Muslim, Mālik realized that the letter was not genuine, guessed what had happened, and set out for Khurasan bent on revenge. Abū Jaʿfar had the governor of Hamadan, Zuhayr al-Turkī, arrest Mālik when he arrived there. He sent orders to Zuhayr to kill Mālik, but Zuhayr had released him the day before the death sentence arrived. Mālik then appeared before Abū Jaʿfar, who forgave him and appointed him to new offices.[91] Other intimates of Abū Muslim, notably Abū'l-Jahm and Naṣr b. ʿAbd al-ʿAzīz were not so fortunate.[92] They paid for their allegiance to Abū Muslim and to Khurasan with their lives. All of these measures by Abū Jaʿfar to pacify the Khurāsānī forces in Iraq helped forestall any outbreaks of discontent against him and his policies, at least until his hold on the caliphate was consolidated.

Abū Muslim's death seemed to clear the way for Abū Ja'far and his associates to dismantle the achievements of the Khurāsānī revolutionaries. The goal of Khurāsānī autonomy was abandoned, and in its place the caliph established a powerful, bureaucratic, and highly centralized government in which his authority was absolute. This reaction had a disruptive effect on the Khurāsānī revolutionary coalition. Some of the Khurāsānīs, for the most part those who had become established in Iraq, accepted the change and remained loyal to the caliph, who praised them as the foundation of the state. Many others refused to abandon their revolutionary goals; they continued to agitate for political concessions at every opportunity. At the same time, Abū Muslim was transformed into a kind of martyr in the eyes of the radical *ghulāt* factions, which displayed their discontent in a number of violent insurrections.

As we shall discover in the following chapters, the struggle for reform in the eastern provinces was far from over; if anything, Abū Muslim's murder only increased its intensity.

1. The most emphatic in this regard is probably Ibn Qutayba, *Ma'ārif,* p. 420; see also Tab., 2:1726; IA, 5:254 (perhaps the best single account of Abū Muslim's origins); *Akhbār,* p. 256; *Fragmenta,* p. 182; Mas'ūdī, *Prairies,* 6:59; Mīrkhwānd, 3:361; Azdī, *Akhbār al-duwal,* f. 109a; Ibn Khaldūn, *'Ibar,* 3:217; Ibn Khallikān, 2:108; Bar Hebraeus, *Mukhtaṣar,* p. 121; Ibn Kathīr, 10:68; Jūzjānī, *Ṭabaqāt,* 1:106. *Fakhrī,* p. 132, exclaims, not without reason, that it is "useless to discuss it at great length." For one modern effort to solve the problem, see A. Yūsufī, "Abū Muslim Kīst?," *Yaghmā* 18(1344/1966):468–474.

2. Ibn 'Asākir, 2:291; my attention was drawn to this by Omar, *'Abbāsid Caliphate,* p. 78.

3. Balādhurī, *Ansāb,* f. 293a; cf. IA, 5:258; Ibn Khaldūn, *'Ibar,* 3:219.

4. *Akhbār,* p. 225.

5. This story, or fragments of it, may be found in *Fragmenta,* p. 183; *Fakhrī,* p. 133; *Akhbār,* p. 256; Ibn Ḥazm, *Jamharat,* p. 20; Ibn Khaldūn, *'Ibar,* 3:218–19; Ibn Qutayba, *Ma'ārif,* p. 420; IA, 5:256–57; Mīrkhwānd, 3:362; Shābushtī, *Diyārāt,* p. 217.

6. The best version is found in Ibn Khallikān, 2:100–1; see also Ibn Khaldūn, *'Ibar,* 3:216; *Fakhrī,* pp. 132–33; *Akhbār,* p. 253; Yāfi'ī, *Mir'āt al-janān,* 1:286; *Mujmal,* p. 305; IA, 5:254; Ya'qūbī, *Historiae,* 2:392 (also gives his father's name as 'Uthmān); Fasīḥ, *Mujmal-i fasīḥī,* 1:210; Maqdisī, *Bad',* 6:92; Sibṭ/Add. 23277, f. 264b; Ibn Taghrībirdī, *Nujūm,* 1:336. Ibn Kathīr, 10:68, gives his name as 'Abd al-Raḥmān b. Shīrwān b. Isfandiyār al-Marwazī. Qazvīnī/LeStrange, *Nuzhat,* p. 154, states that his original home was Safīdhanj.

7. *Mujmal,* p. 315, on the authority of Ḥamza al-Iṣfahānī; see also Mīrkhwānd, 3:362; *Ḥabīb al-siyar,* 2:193; Qazvīnī, *Guzīdah,* p. 282. Māfarrukhī, *Maḥāsin iṣfahān,* ed. J. Tihrānī (Tehran, 1312/1933), p. 24, claims Abū Muslim as a native of Isfahan, giving his descent from Ruhām b. Jūdharz or Shīdhūs b. Jūdharz (obvious variants of Gūdarz); part of this also appears in Abū Nuʿaym, *Dhikr akhbār iṣbahān,* ed. Sven Dedering, *Geschichte Iṣbahāns* (Leiden, 1931–34), 1:27. Gardīzī, *Zayn,* p. 119, also affirms that Abū Muslim was from Isfahan, while Maqdisī, *Aḥsan al-taqāsim,* p. 318, notes that Abū Muslim was the most popular *kunya* of people from Isfahan.

8. Balādhurī, *Ansāb,* f. 293a.

9. *Ibid.*

10. *Ibid.*, f. 284a citing Abū Masʿūd al-Kūfī; cf. *Akhbār,* p. 254; IA, 5:255; Ibn Khaldūn, *ʿIbar,* 3:218. A variant tradition quoted in Balādhurī, *Ansāb,* f. 293a, citing Hishām b. al-Kalbī, says that Abū Muslim's father was a servant of the Banū Maʿqil, but that Abū Muslim attached himself to Abū Mūsā, accepted Islam from him, and accompanied him to Kūfa. Tab., 2:1726, however, states that the *imām* Ibrāhīm sent Abū Muslim to Abū Mūsā for indoctrination; this is substantiated by a report in *Akhbār,* p. 253, that Abū Muslim was seen so often in the company of Abū Mūsā that people thought he was a saddler, too. This tradition has the backing of Abū'l-Khuṭṭāb, one of the best informants regarding the *daʿwa.*

11. For examples, see *Mujmal,* p. 315 (which later challenges the veracity of this allegation); *Fakhrī,* p. 133; Balādhurī, *Ansāb,* f. 293a; IA, 5:257. He is variously described as *ʿabd, mamlūk, qahramān,* etc.

12. *Akhbār,* pp. 257–58.

13. Balādhurī, *Ansāb,* f. 292b; that version of his name is also found in a variant, f. 284a, and in *Akhbār,* p. 255. *Akhbār,* p. 263, states further that he was from *ʿulūj iṣbahān.*

14. Balādhurī, *Ansāb,* f. 293a.

15. *Ibid.*, cf. Dīnawarī, *Akhbār,* p. 337.

16. Dīnawarī, *Akhbār,* p. 338.

17. Azdī, *Mawṣil,* p. 53; Balʿamī/Zotenberg, 4:323; Tab., 2:1769; Dīnawarī, *Akhbār,* pp. 337–38; Maqdisī, *Badʾ*, 6:61–62; Ibn ʿAbd Rabbih, *ʿIqd,* 4:477; Kūfī, *Futūḥ,* f. 220a; Qazvīnī, *Guzīdah,* p. 292.

18. Tab., 2:1960; Masʿūdī, *Prairies,* 6:59.

19. Azdī, *Mawṣil,* p. 121.

20. Jūzjānī, *Ṭabaqāt,* 1:104.

21. *Akhbār,* p. 225, which describes Abū Muslim as a *dihqān,* indicates that he was in the service of Muḥammad b. ʿAlī at an early date; Balādhurī, *Ansāb,* f. 284a, says Abū Mūsā gave Abū a letter to carry to Ibrāhīm, who was so impressed by his talents that he promoted his career. Masʿūdī, *Prairies,* 6:59, says only that he attached himself to Ibrāhīm.

22. Balādhurī, *Ansāb,* f. 284a, cf. 293a; *Akhbār,* p. 253; Balʿamī/Zotenberg, 4:323.

23. There is much disagreement about the particulars of this incident: Maqdisī, *Badʾ*, 6:62; has Yūnus b. ʿĀṣim instead of ʿĀṣim b. Yūnus; Dīnawarī, *Akhbār,* p. 337, says ʿĪsā and Maʿqil; etc. Dīnawarī also says the jail was in Wāsiṭ, while Maqdisī has "in Ibn Hubayra's prison."

24. Tab. 2:1727 implies that they had already accepted the *daʾwa;* Balādhurī, *Ansāb,* f. 292b, describes the ʿIjlīs as *shīʿa.*

25. Balādhurī, *Ansāb,* f. 292b; Ibn Khallikān, 2:101; *Mujmal,* p. 316; Yāfiʿī, *Mir'āt al-janān,* 1:286.

26. *Akhbār,* p. 253.

27. See above, n. 22; Tab. 2:1726; *Akhbār,* p. 253. Ibn Khaldūn, *'Ibar,* 3:219, and IA, 5:257, suggest that they were converted while in jail. Other accounts, such as *Akhbār,* p. 255, are vague about the reason for the visit of the *nuqabā'* but at least imply that they came to the jail looking for recruits or to visit imprisoned partisans.

It is interesting that the 'Ijlī tribe plays such an important part in most of these traditions. Some writers have drawn attention to the supposed Persophile tendencies of the 'Ijl: see I. Goldziher, "Islamisme et Parsisme," *Revue de l'histoire des religions* 43(1901):23; Watt, *Formative Period,* p. 46; Omar, *'Abbāsid Caliphate,* p. 78. This has probably been a bit over-emphasized, and it is worth noting that several members of this tribe are identifiable as Umayyad supporters. Perhaps more significantly, some members of this tribe had a history of religious activism not dissimilar to the Abbasid *ghulāt,* the most visible examples being the founders of the Mughīriyya and the Manṣūriyya.

28. Balādhurī, *Ansāb,* f. 293a, says he was sold for more than 2,000 *dirhams* (but a variant, f. 293a, says 700 *dirhams*); Tab., 2:1726, says 400 *dirhams*; cf. IA, 5:258; Sibṭ/Add. 23277, f. 199b; Ibn Khaldūn, *'Ibar,* 3:219; Maqrīzī, *Nizā',* p. 68; Ibn Kathīr, 10:68. Dīnawarī, *Akhbār,* p. 338, says he was sold but gives no price; Azdī, *Mawṣil,* p. 53, says he was given to the *imām.* Ya'qūbī, *Historiae,* 2:392; Tab., 2:1727; *Mujmal,* p. 316; and Yāfiʿī, *Mir'āt al-janān,* 1:286, imply that he was permitted to join the *da'wa.* Ibn Khallikān, 2:102 says that 'Īsā and Idrīs escaped from prison, and, joined by Abū Muslim, met the *naqībs* in Mecca. *Akhbār,* p. 253, asserts that Abū Muslim was tending to business for the 'Ijlīs and, as a favor, carried messages for the *shī'a* in the same jail. They came to trust him, and he came to accept their teachings, so they sent him with a letter to the *imām,* who, impressed by his abilities, brought him into the movement.

29. Tab., 2:1960; see also Melikoff, *Abū Muslim,* p. 48.

30. Several late sources, such as the *Inbā'* of al-'Imrānī and the anonymous *Ta'rīkh al-dawla al-'abbāsiyya,* greatly exaggerate the role of Abū Muslim by having him lead the revolutionary army into Kūfa to proclaim al-Saffāḥ as caliph. These works seem to be a link between the historical Abū Muslim and the legendary figure in the Turko-Persian Abū Muslim epics described in Melikoff, *Abū Muslim.* His charismatic example has not lost its fascination for modern Muslims: It inspired Jamāl al-Dīn al-Afghānī, who was Abū Muslim's equal in his ability to obscure his background as well as in his revolutionary fervor (see Nikki Keddie, "The Pan-Islamic Appeal," *Middle Eastern Studies* 3(1966):55) and provided material for a popular novel by Jurjī Zaydān, *Abū Muslim al-Khurāsānī* (many editions, including Cairo, 1965) and a short story by S. Nafīsī, "Javānmard-i khurāsān," in *Māh-i nakhshab* (Tehran, 1334/1956), pp. 33–48. This romantic view has been sharply critized by Moscati, "Studi su Abū Muslim," p. 97, *et passim,* and Omar, *'Abbāsid Caliphate,* pp. 17, 23, *et passim.* For other studies of Abū Muslim, see Zarrīnkūb, *Sukūt,* pp. 130–49; R. N. Frye, "The Role of Abū Muslim in the 'Abbāsid Revolt," *Muslim World* 36(1947):28–38; G. H. Yūsufī, *Abū Muslim, sardār-i khurāsān* (Tehran, 1345/1967); A. Ḥabībī, "Kārnāmah-yi abū muslim khurāsānī," *Āryānā* 22(1342/1964):14–39 and 23(1343/1965):9–22, 122–32; M. Mudarrisī, "Abū Muslim Khurāsānī," *Armaghān* 22(1320/1944):458–63; A. Fayyāḍ, "Abū Muslim va khurāsān," *Nashriyyah-yi farhang-i khurāsān* 3(1339–40/1961–2): pt. 1, pp. 7–10; pt. 2, pp. 4–6; pt. 3, pp. 2–3; pt. 5, pp. 3–5; pt. 6, pp. 5–7; pt. 8, pp. 2–3; pt. 10, pp. 2–6; and M. Yinanç, "Ebū Muslim," *Islam Ansiklope-*

desi (Istanbul, 1964), 4:39–41 (which is superior to either Moscati, "Abū Muslim," *EI*2, 1:141 or Barthold, "Abū Muslim," *EI*1, 1:101–2).

31. ʻImrānī, *Inbāʼ*, p. 65; Banākitī, *Rawḍat*, pp. 135–36; Shahrastānī, *Milal*, 1:154; Ibn Kathīr, 10:71; Ibn Ḥazm/Friedlaender, p. 90.

32. Tab. 2:1620–21; see W. F. Tucker, "Al-Mughīra b. Saʻīd and the Mughīriyya," *Arabica* 22(1975):35–47.

33. Barthold, *Turkestan*, p. 194 (based on the description of the Rāwandiyya in Tab., 3:129).

34. *Mujmal*, p. 315.

35. Thaʻālibī/Bosworth, *Laṭāʼif*, p. 43. Maqdisī, *Badʼ*, 6:94–95, notes that Marwān tried to scare the Meccans by telling them that Abū Muslim burned copies of the Koran, but they found him to be extremely pious and correct in his behavior when he visited their city.

36. *Fakhrī*, p. 162.

37. Ibn Isfandiyār/Browne, *Ṭabaristān*, p. 110.

38. Ibn Khallikān, 2:102; cf. *Mujmal*, p. 326.

39. Tab., 2:2001, gives the names of several of his appointees; cf. pseudo-Ibn Qutayba, *Imāma*, 2:116.

40. See R. Guest, "A Coin of Abu Muslim," *JRAS* (1932), pp. 555–56.

41. Ibn Ḥawqal/Kramers and Wiet, *Configuration*, p. 420; Iṣṭakhrī, *Masālik*, p. 259; see also A. U. Pope, *Persian Architecture* (New York, 1965), p. 80, and K. A. C. Creswell, *A Short Account of Early Muslim Architecture* (Baltimore, 1958), p. 161.

42. Gardīzī, *Zayn*, p. 119; Qazvīnī/LeStrange, *Nuzhat*, p. 154; Iṣṭakhrī, *Masālik*, p. 259; Ibn Ḥawqal/Kramers and Wiet, *Configuration*, p. 420; Maqdisī, *Taqāsīm*, p. 321. He is also credited with the construction of public buildings in Samarqand: see ʻUmar b. Muḥammad al-Nasafī, *Kitāb al-qand fī taʼrīkh samarqand* in W. Barthold, *Turkestan v epokhu mongolʼskago nashestviia*, Vol. I: *Teksty* (St. Petersburg, 1900), p. 49.

43. Muḥammad al-Naysābūrī, *Tārīkh-i nīshābūr*, ed. B. Karīmī (Tehran, 1339/1961), pp. 124, 141–142.

44. Narshakhī/Frye, *Bukhara*, p. 16.

45. Bayhaqī, *Maḥāsin*, 1:482.

46. Ibn Khallikān, 1:467 (but cf. his scornful remark after Abū Salama's murder, p. 468); Masʻūdī, *Prairies*, 6:134–36; Dīnawarī, *Akhbār*, p. 370; Azdī, *Mawṣil*, p. 144; Yāfiʻī, *Mirʼāt al-janān*, 1:280; Yaʻqūbī, *Historiae*, 2:422.

47. Tab., 3:60–61; IA, 5:436–37; Ibn Khallikān, 1:467; *Fakhrī*, pp. 148–49; Ibn Khaldūn, *ʻIbar*, 3:376–77; *Fragmenta*, pp. 212–13; pseudo-Ibn Qutayba, *Imāma*, 2:117–18; Ibn Ḥabīb, *Asmāʼ*, pp. 187–88; Ibn Kathīr, 10:53–54.

48. Tab., 3:61, and IA, 5:436–37, both say explicitly that he went after the murder; Dīnawarī, *Akhbār*, p. 376, also says Abū Jaʻfar went to explain the murder and, curiously, to bring Abū Muslim to Iraq; Azdī, *Akhbār al-duwal*, f. 101b, and Maqdisī, *Badʼ*, 6:71, state that Abū Jaʻfar went to apologize for the murder; Ibn Khaldūn, *ʻIbar*, 3:383–84, and pseudo-Ibn Qutayba, *Imāma*, 2:125, mention the trip but give no date; Yaʻqūbī, *Historiae*, 2:420, dates the trip *before* the murder.

49. Tab., 3:59–60; cf. IA, 5:437; Balādhurī, *Ansāb*, f. 301a; Balʻamī/Zotenberg, 4:326–27; Kūfī, *Futūḥ*, f. 234a–b; *Mujmal*, pp. 323–24; Mīrkhwānd, 3:362, 391–92; Faṣīḥ, *Mujmal-i faṣīḥī*, 1:205–6. Ḥamza, *Taʼrīkh*, p. 161, and Jūz-

jānī, *Ṭabaqāt,* 1:109, both confirm that Abū Ja'far went to accept the *bay'a* of Abū Muslim and his troops. Ya'qūbī, *Historiae,* 2:420, confirms the trip; Gardīzī, *Zayn,* p. 120, confirms its purpose; see also Maqrīzī, *Muqaffa' al-kabīr*/Fonds arabes 2144, f. 87b; *Fragmenta,* p. 212 (gives the date as 135 A.H., certainly an error).

50. Jahshiyārī, *Wuzarā',* pp. 89–90; cf. Ya'qūbī, *Historiae,* 2:420, 422.

51. See Ya'qūbī, *Historiae,* 2:420; Bal'amī/Zotenberg, 4:327; pseudo-Ibn Qutayba, *Imāma,* 2:125; *Mujmal,* p. 324; Tab., 3:60; IA, 5:437; Ibn Khaldūn, *'Ibar,* 3:383–84; Dīnawarī, *Akhbār,* p. 376; Balādhurī, *Ansāb,* f. 301a; cf. Ibn Ḥabīb, *Asma',* p. 193. For a monographic treatment of relations between Abū Ja'far and Abū Muslim, see M. Aḥmad, "Dau nābighah" (translated from *al-Muqṭaṭaf*), *Armaghān* 19(1318/1940):53–61, 100–106.

52. Abū'l-Jahm's role is confirmed by Tha'ālibī, *Thimār,* p. 153; Jahshiyārī, *Wuzarā',* p. 93; Ya'qūbī, *Historiae,* 2:433; Maqrīzī, *Nizā',* p. 76.

53. This according to Tab., 3:67. Ibn Khallikān, 4:206, 209–10, quotes Abū Muslim as urging the execution and al-Manṣūr regretting it. Ya'qūbī, *Historiae,* 2:424, also states that Abū Muslim pressed for Ibn Hubayra's execution, but after Ibn Hubayra had violated the terms of the *aman* by conspiring with an 'Alīd. Similar versions may be found in *Fragmenta,* p. 209; Balādhurī, *Ansāb,* f. 299a–b; IA, 5:440–41; Ibn Khaldūn, *'Ibar,* 3:375; Kūfī, *Futūḥ,* f. 234a. Bal'amī/Zotenberg, 4:344–45; Dīnawarī, *Akhbār,* pp. 373–74; and Khalīfa, *Ta'rīkh,* pp. 422–26, make no mention of Abū Muslim in connection with this affair. Ibn 'Abd Rabbih, *'Iqd,* 1:93 indicates that al-Manṣūr *suspected* Abū Muslim of turning al-Saffāḥ against Ibn Hubayra. The date of the execution is sometimes given as 10 Dhū'l-Qa'da 132 (26 June 750).

54. Balādhurī, *Ansāb,* f. 311b; Mas'ūdī, *Prairies,* 6:198; see also T. Noeldeke, "Al-Mansur," in *Sketches From Eastern History,* trans. J. S. Black (Edinburgh, 1892; reprint Beirut, 1963), p. 36.

55. See comments by Omar, *'Abbāsid Caliphate,* p. 131.

56. See Tab., 3:71–72; IA, 5:443; Dīnawarī, *Akhbār,* p. 376; pseudo-Ibn Qutayba, *Imāma,* 2:125; Ṣafadī, *Wāfī,* 2:228; Ibn Kathīr, 10:55; Moscati, "Studi su Abū Muslim," pp. 331–32.

57. Tab., 3:75–77; IA, 5:450–51; Sibṭ/Add. 23277, f. 255a; Balādhurī, *Ansāb,* f. 305b.

58. Jahshiyārī, *Wuzarā',* pp. 93–94.

59. This quote is preserved in Balādhurī, *Ansāb,* f. 305a, and Maqrīzī, *Nizā',* p. 67. See also Tab., 3:81–82 (which states that Ziyād revolted); IA, 5:455–56; Maqdisī, *Bad',* 6:75; Ibn Khaldūn, *'Ibar,* 3:372–73; Moscati, "Studi su Abū Muslim," pp. 332–33.

60. Tab., 3:82; IA, 5:455; Ibn Khaldūn, *'Ibar,* 3:382.

61. In addition to the above sources, see Maqdisī, *Bad',* 6:76; *Ghurar,* f. 157a.

62. Tab., 3:82; IA, 5:455; Ibn Khaldūn, *'Ibar,* 3:382–83; *Ḥabīb al-siyar,* 2:206.

63. Maqdisī, *Bad',* 6:76; *Ghurar,* f. 157a.

64. Tab., 3:82–83; IA, 5:455–56.

65. Tab., 3:83; IA, 5:456; Ibn Khaldūn, *'Ibar,* 3:383; Sibṭ/Add. 23277, f. 256a.

66. Maqrīzī, *Nizā',* p. 68 implies that 'Īsā fabricated this because he was angry that so prominent a figure as Ziyād had been murdered, but Balādhurī, *Ansāb,* f. 305a, indicates that it is true.

67. Tab., 3:83–84; IA, 5:456; Sibṭ/Add. 23277, f. 256a; Ibn Khaldūn, *'Ibar,* 3:373; Balādhurī, *Ansāb,* f. 305b (says Abū Muslim ordered Abū Da'ūd to kill 'Īsā).

68. Balādhurī, *Ansāb,* f. 305b.

69. There are many sources which mention this: Tab., 3:84–87; IA, 5:458–59; Sibṭ/Add. 23277, f. 258a–b; *Ghurar,* f. 160a; Balādhurī, *Ansāb,* f. 305a; Bal'amī/Zotenberg, 4:348–49; Ibn Khaldūn, *'Ibar,* 3:383–84; Gardīzī, *Zayn,* p. 121; *Mujmal,* p. 324; Azdī, *Ta'rīkh,* p. 159; Khalīfa, *Ta'rīkh,* p. 441; Maqdisī, *Bad',* 6:75–76; Dīnawarī, *Akhbār,* p. 377; Faṣīḥ, *Mujmal-i faṣīḥī,* 1:208; Ibn Kathīr, 10:57; Ya'qūbī, *Historiae,* 2:433; *idem*/Wiet, *Pays,* pp. 128–29; Qazvīnī, *Tārīkh-i guzīdah,* pp. 89–95. There are confused accounts in pseudo-Ibn Qutayba, *Imāma,* 2:124, 133; *Tārīkh-i sīstān,* pp. 137–38. See Moscati, "Studi su Abū Muslim," pp. 89–95.

70. Bal'amī/Zotenberg, 4:348–49; Azdī, *Mawṣil,* p. 159; Maqdisī, *Bad',* 6:76; Balādhurī, *Ansāb,* ff. 305a, 309b; Kūfī, *Futūḥ,* f. 236a; Tab., 3:85–86; IA, 5:457–58; *Fragmenta,* p. 213; pseudo-Ibn Qutayba, *Imāma,* 2:132.

71. Tab., 3:85, 99; IA, 5:468; Ibn Khaldūn, *'Ibar,* 3:383; Dīnawarī, *Akhbār,* p. 377; Maqdisī, *Bad',* 6:76; but Ya'qūbī, *Historiae,* 2:433, indicates nothing irregular about this.

72. Tab., 3:87–88; IA, 5:459; Ibn Khallikān, 2:106; *Fragmenta,* p. 214 (gives his age as 32.)

73. Accounts of this are contradictory: Tab., says at 3:89 Abū Ja'far got news of Saffāḥ's death in Mecca and Abū Muslim immediately made obeisance, but says at 3:87 that Abū Ja'far was ahead of Abū Muslim and ordered him to catch up. Yet another variant (3:90) says Abū Muslim was ahead of Abū Ja'far and thus received the news first and so wrote Abū Ja'far to console him for Saffāḥ's death. *Fragmenta,* p. 215, also says that Abū Muslim was ahead but that he turned back to help Manṣūr.

74. Tab., 3:100; Balādhurī, *Ansāb,* f. 309b; Kūfī, *Futūḥ,* f. 236b; Maqrīzī, *Muqaffa' al-kabīr*/Fonds arabes 2144, f. 87b.

75. These claims are usually based on the tradition in Tab., 3:90, 100–101 (and IA, 5:361–62, 368), that Abū Muslim preceded Abū Ja'far on the return from Mecca. Abū Ja'far was upset that Abū Muslim did not wait for him to catch up, put his name first in his letters to Abū Ja'far, and saluted him as *amīr al-mu'minīn* rather than *khalīfa.* Balādhurī, *Ansāb,* f. 309b, says that Abū Muslim wrote Abū Ja'far but did not salute him as caliph because he had not yet heard of his proclamation.

76. Balādhurī, *Ansāb,* f. 309b, cf. 314a; Maqrīzī, *Muqaffa' al-kabīr*/Fonds arabes 2144, f. 88a. There are, of course, many stories about Abū Ja'far soliciting advice about killing Abū Muslim: see, e.g., Ibn 'Abd Rabbih, *'Iqd,* 1:93 (repeated 2:130); Yāfi'ī, *Mir'āt al-janān,* 1:288.

77. Tab., 3:90; *Fragmenta,* p. 216. On the campaign, see Tab., 3:92–99; IA, 5:464–68; Bal'amī/Zotenberg, 4:350–54; Ibn Khaldūn, *'Ibar,* 3:335–38; *Fragmenta,* pp. 217–19; Maqdisī, *Bad',* 6:76–78; Jahshiyārī, *Wuzara',* p. 103; *Mujmal,* p. 325; Ḥamza, *Ta'rīkh,* p. 161; Moscati, "Studi su Abū Muslim," pp. 95–101. Ya'qūbī, *Historiae,* 2:438, indicates that Abū Muslim was not anxious to get involved in this affair, but Dīnawarī, *Akhbār,* pp. 378–79, states that he volunteered to suppress the revolt.

78. Tab., 3:102–4 gives the various traditions; cf. IA, 5:469; Balādhurī, *Ansāb,* f. 314a; Qazvīnī, *Tārīkh-i guzīdah,* p. 293; Dīnawarī, *Akhbār,* p. 379; Ibn Khaldūn, *'Ibar,* 3:388; Bal'amī/Zotenberg, 4:354; *Fakhrī,* p. 162; Ya'qūbī, *Historiae,* 2:439–40; Gardīzī, *Zayn,* pp. 121–22; *Fragmenta,* p. 219; Maqdisī, *Bad',* 6:78; Khalīfa, *Ta'rīkh,* p. 163; Azdī, *Mawṣil,* p. 163; Mas'ūdī, *Prairies,* 6:177–78; Kūfī, *Futūḥ,* f. 238b; *Ghurar,* f. 164a–b; Ibn Qutayba, *'Uyūn,* 1:26.

79. There are reports that Abū Ja'far decided to kill Abū Muslim after this in Quḍā'ī, *Nuzhat,* f. 28a–b; Azdī, *Akhbār al-duwal,* f. 107b; see also Tab., 3:103; IA, 5:469; Ibn Khaldūn, *'Ibar,* 3:388; Bal'amī/Zotenberg, 4:355; Balādhurī, *Ansāb,* f. 314a; Ibn Taghrībirdī, *Nujūm,* 1:333; Kūfī, *Futūḥ,* f. 239a. Ḥamza, *Ta'rīkh,* p. 161 says Abū Muslim set out for Khurasan in Rajab and arrived at Ḥulwān on 13 Sha'bān. In a curious passage, Ibn Isfandiyār/Browne, *Ṭabaristān,* p. 112, says Manṣūr had given Abū Muslim permission to return.

80. Texts of the correspondence may be found in Tab., 3:103–5; IA, 5:469–471; Kūfī, *Futūḥ,* ff. 239b–240a; Bal'amī/Zotenberg, 4:355–56; *Fragmenta,* pp. 219–22; Maqdisī, *Bad',* 6:78–79; Azdī, *Mawṣil,* pp. 163–65; Mas'ūdī, *Prairies,* 6:179; Jahshiyārī, *Wuzarā',* p. 111; Ṣafwat, *Rasā'il,* 3:13–14, 17, 21–23. There is some controversy about the authenticity of these letters, especially one in which Abū Muslim breaks with the caliph completely; see Omar, *'Abbāsid Caliphate,* p. 171; Moscati, "Studi su Abū Muslim," p. 98.

81. Slightly differing versions of this delegation and its mission may be found in Mas'ūdī, *Prairies,* 6:179; Tab., 3:105–7; IA, 5:471–72; Ḥamza, *Ta'rīkh,* p. 162; Balādhurī, *Ansāb,* f. 314b; Maqdisī, *Bad',* 6:78; *Fakhrī,* p. 162; Ibn Khaldūn, *'Ibar,* 3:388–89); Ya'qūbī, *Historiae,* 2:440; *Fragmenta,* p. 220; Dīnawarī, *Akhbār,* pp. 379–80; Gardīzī, *Zayn,* p. 122; Khalīfa, *Ta'rīkh,* p. 441; Bar Hebraeus/Budge, 1:113.

82. Tab., 3:107; IA, 5:472–73; Bal'amī/Zotenberg, 4:358–59; *Fragmenta,* p. 221; Ibn Khaldūn, *'Ibar,* 3:389; Ḥamza, *Ta'rīkh,* p. 162 (implies that Abū Da'ūd was in Ṭabaristān then).

83. Bal'amī/Zotenberg, 4:357–58; *Fakhrī,* p. 163; Ya'qūbī, *Historiae,* 2:440; *Fragmenta,* p. 221; Mas'ūdī, *Prairies,* 6:180; Balādhurī, *Ansāb,* f. 314b; Jāḥiẓ, *Bayān,* 2:102–3; Ibn Qutayba, *'Uyūn,* 1:30; Ibn Isfandiyār/Browne, *Ṭabaristān,* p. 112; 'Imrānī, *Inbā',* p. 65. In many of these the implication is clear that Abū Muslim's authority did not legitimately extend beyond Rayy.

84. Bal'amī/Zotenberg, 4:360; Tab., 3:104; Sibṭ/Add. 23277, f. 266b; Dīnawarī, *Akhbār,* p. 380; Maqdisī, *Bad',* 6:79; Mas'ūdī, *Prairies,* 6:180; Ibn Khallikān, 2:106; pseudo-Ibn Qutayba, *Imāma,* 2:134; Yāfi'ī, *Mir'āt al-janān,* 1:288–89.

85. Tab., 3:107–8; IA, 5:473; *Fragmenta,* p. 222; Ibn Khaldūn, *'Ibar,* 3:389–90.

86. Tab., 3:109 (cf. 112); IA, 5:474; Ya'qūbī, *Historiae,* 2:440; Mas'ūdī, *Prairies,* 6:180; *Fakhrī,* p. 164.

87. Ya'qūbī, *Historiae,* 2:440; IA, 5:474–75; Tab., 3:110–11; Bal'amī/Zotenberg, 4:362; Ibn Khaldūn, *'Ibar,* 3:390; Dīnawarī, *Akhbār,* p. 380 (notes that Abū Ja'far kept Abū Muslim waiting in revenge for his having to wait in Khurasan); Balādhurī, *Ansāb,* f. 315a; Ḥamza, *Ta'rīkh,* p. 162; *Fragmenta,* p. 222; Maqdisī, *Bad',* 6:80; pseudo-Ibn Qutayba, *Imāma,* 2:135.

88. There are many different versions of the assassination, but they present no critical discrepancies: see Dīnawarī, *Akhbār,* pp. 381–82; Kūfī, *Futūḥ,* ff. 240b–241a; *Fakhrī,* pp. 164–65; Ibn Isfandiyār/Browne, *Ṭabaristān,* pp. 112–13; Gardīzī, *Zayn,* p. 122; *Fragmenta,* pp. 222–24; Maqdisī, *Bad',* 6:80–82; Khalīfa, *Ta'rīkh,* p. 442; *Ghurar,* f. 166b; Jāḥiẓ, *Bayān,* 3:323–24; Azdī, *Akhbār al-duwal,* ff. 109b–110a; 'Awfī, *Javāmi',* f. 104a; Ya'qūbī, *Historiae,* 2:440–41; Mas'ūdī, *Prairies,* 6:180–82; Ibn Qutayba, *'Uyūn,* 1:26; Bayhaqī, *Maḥāsin,* 2:231; Yāfi'ī, *Mir'āt al-janān,* 1:289–90; Ibn Khallikān, 2:106–7; Qazvīnī, *Tārīkh-i guzīdah,* pp. 293–95; *Mujmal,* pp. 326–27; Balādhurī, *Ansāb,* ff. 315a–b; Ibn Khaldūn, *'Ibar,* 3:390–92; Tab., 3:112–115; IA, 5:474–475; Bar Hebraeus/Budge, 1:113; Ibn Kathīr, 10:66.

89. For examples, see Ibn Qutayba, *'Uyūn,* 1:26; Ya'qūbī, *Historiae,* 2:441.

90. Tab., 3:117; IA, 5:477; cf. Ya'qūbī, *Historiae,* 2:441; pseudo-Ibn Qutayba, *Imāma,* 2:136–37; Khalīfa, *Ta'rīkh,* p. 442; Azdī, *Mawṣil,* p. 166; Kūfī, *Futūḥ,* f. 241a; *Fragmenta,* p. 224; Qazvīnī, *Tārīkh-i guzīdah,* p. 295; 'Imrānī, *Inbā',* p. 66. Dīnawarī, *Akhbār,* p. 382, says the soldiers were given 1,000 purses each containing 3,000 *dirhams*. Jāḥiẓ, *Bayān,* 3:368, indicates that they accepted only because they realized the futility of resistance when they were cut off from Khurasan.

91. Balādhurī, *Ansāb,* f. 316a–b; Tab., 3:117–18; IA, 5:477–78; Bal'amī/ Zotenberg, 4:366. Azdī, *Mawṣil,* p. 166, says Mālik fled to Hamadan but was persuaded to return by Abū Ja'far.

92. Yāqūt, *Mu'jam,* 8:291, preserves the information about Naṣr's death; Jahshiyārī, *Wuzarā',* pp. 136–37 and Balādhurī, *Ansāb,* f. 311a, relate that Abū Ja'far poisoned Abū'l Jahm. See also Sourdel, *Vizirat,* pp. 71, 75–76.

Rural Discontent and the Ghulāt Revolts

An important factor in the success of the Abbasid movement was the support it received from the peasant and lower class population of Khurasan, attracted by the missionaries' rather unscrupulous exploitation of the esoteric and syncretistic socio-religious doctrines peculiar to the "extremist" (*ghulāt*) sects or groups. Although there was some overlap between the social and political aspects of the revolution, there was always a certain amount of tension between the dissatisfied masses and the more conservative and well-to-do political reformers. These two wings of the *da'wa* gradually bifurcated, and the murder of Abū Muslim greatly exacerbated their relations both with each other and with the central government. Thus there appeared two types of opposition to the Abbasid regime, sometimes complementing each other, but eventually separating and moving in different directions.

Of these two sources of resistence to Abbasid rule in Khurasan and annexed areas, the *ghulāt* revolts are probably the best known. But a real understanding of these revolts has been hampered by a tendency to distort them and overgeneralize about them. Most, but not all, of these insurrections involved the idea of "revenge" for Abū Muslim, or an idealization of him—despite the repressive actions he had taken against earlier manifestations of the *ghulāt* opposition. At the same time, all these revolts had, or were perceived as having, a heterodox religious ideology contrary, or even dangerous, to Islam. Though these two features are clearly exaggerated and stereotyped in the sources, many modern writers have accepted them as the distinguishing characteristics of the *ghulāt* opposition.

In reality, the heterodox aspects of the revolts are far less interesting, or useful for an understanding of the phenomenon, than the examples of class conflict, social reform, and simple religious syncretism which invariably accompanied them. The *ghulāt* revolts typically represented the efforts of peasant communities to resist subjugation by the new "Muslim," Arabo-Iranian, urban elite in Khurasan. They took place in isolated, usually very mountainous, rural areas; the participants were drawn from the peasantry and lower social strata, yet paradoxically, they were often led by upper class, charismatic, Iranians (perhaps the last representatives of the old aristocracy?) whom the sources took great pains to depict as ignoble social outcasts. Unusual religious ideas may have served to give the rebels a sense of communal solidarity, but the accusations of heterodoxy in the sources were most often based on misinterpretation, or even sheer imagination.

SUNBĀDH

Popular resentment over the murder of Abū Muslim, which served as the most convenient focal point for disaffection with the policies of the Abbasid government, first manifested itself in the revolt of Sunbādh the Magian,[1] which broke out two months after Abū Muslim's death.[2] The revolt is of great importance, not only because it was the first, but because it helped close the ranks of popular opposition to the Abbasids, formulate the ideology behind the opposition, and extend the protest beyond the limits of Khurasan proper.

Sunbādh is variously described as a Magian from Nishapur,[3] or a village near there,[4] and as a friend or associate of Abū Muslim.[5] Ya'qūbī maintains that Sunbādh was encouraged to seek revenge for Abū Muslim by a group of the latter's followers who had fled to Khurasan after the assassination,[6] while Maqdisī states that Sunbādh "claimed" he was Abū Muslim's successor (*walī*) and avenger.[7] Bal'amī describes Sunbādh as a rich citizen of a canton of Nishapur, who had been honored by Abū Muslim and who therefore vowed to use his wealth, even his life, to seek revenge for his slain friend.[8] This is partly substaniated by Niẓām al-Mulk, who depicts Sunbādh as the Zoroastrian mayor (*ra'īs*) of Nishapur, on friendly terms with Abū Muslim and a commander in his army.[9]

We noted earlier that some sources allude to a violent mass uprising of the Iranian peasantry in the period of the *da'wa,* during which the native landholders and the Arab elite were massacred. We also noted charges made in the Umayyad propaganda that Abū Muslim co-operated with "the Magians" and that he incited the "slaves" to attack their masters. There is an exceptionally interesting tradition about Sunbādh's origins which perfectly complements this feature of the *da'wa*. According to the *Tārīkh-i alfī*, Sunbādh was a citizen of Nishapur. At the time of the distrubances in Khurasan, he incited the people of Nishapur to revolt and encouraged them to kill "the noble Arabs and the aristocratic Iranians" (*ashrāf-i 'arab va akābir-i 'ajam*). His speeches attracted the attention of Abū Muslim, who was very pleased by them and who decided to cultivate Sunbādh's friendship. Sunbādh and his brother "wore black," provided the Abbasid rebels with supplies, and received assistance in fighting "the Arabs."[10]

It is not clear whether Sunbādh's revolt began in Nishapur or Rayy. Some traditions state or imply that Sunbādh, supported by as many as 100,000 of the Zoroastrian or nominally Muslim mountain dwellers of north-central Iran,[11] seized Nishapur, Qūmis, and finally Rayy. Sunbādh then appropriated the treasury Abū Muslim had left in Rayy and styled himself Fīrūz Iṣbahbadh.[12] Other traditions claim that Sunbādh was an officer in Abū Muslim's army, perhaps the one appointed to guard the treasury in Rayy, and that he rebelled first in the environs of Rayy.[13] The most complete of these traditions (in Balādhurī) relates that Sunbādh was stationed in Ḥulwān when he heard of Abū Muslim's assassination. He then seized a considerable sum of money and set out for Khurasan. Since the governor of Rayy, Abū 'Ubayda, had been ordered not to permit any of Abū Muslim's followers to return to Khurasan, he detained Sunbādh when he reached the city. This annoyed and angered Sunbādh, who escaped by night and raised a revolt. Abū 'Ubayda pursued Sunbādh, who defeated him in battle. Sunbādh then forced Abū 'Ubayda, who had taken refuge in a fort in Rayy, to sue for peace. Abū 'Ubayda asked for and received a pardon, but as soon as he was in Sunbādh's control he was put to death. Sunbādh thus took control of Rayy, returned to Magianism, and commited a number of atrocities and injustices against the Muslim population.[14]

The startling rapidity with which this revolt spread apparently caught the Abbasid government off guard. The local Muslims, led by the governors of Dastbī and Qūmis, attacked Sunbādh, but they were defeated.[15] The Caliph Abū Ja'far then intervened directly, sending

Jahwar b. al-Mirrār al-'Ijlī to combat the rebels.[16] His army, variously numbered at 10,000 or 20,000 men,[17] was composed of soldiers from Khuzistān and Fārs, volunteer auxiliaries from Isfahan and Qumm, and 'Ijlī tribesmen.[18] This essentially alien force was supported by some local elements, notably a few *dahāqīn* and 'Umar b. al-'Alā, a butcher from Rayy who distinguished himself in battle against Sunbādh and was later promoted to the post of governor of Ṭabaristān by the grateful caliph.[19]

Jahwar organized his forces and exhorted his troops to be firm in battle: "You are going to fight a people (*qawm*) who want to eradicate your religion and expel you from your lands."[20]

The opposing forces confronted each other on the fringes of the desert between Hamadan and Rayy at a place called Jurjānbān.[21] The terrific battle which ensued lasted four days before Sunbādh's army was ultimately defeated.[22] Some sources explain Sunbādh's defeat by noting that he made the tactical error of putting captured Muslim women and children on camels in front of his troops. When the animals heard the Muslims' outraged war-shouts, they took fright and charged back, trampling Sunbādh's own forces.[23] In any case, Sunbādh's army was definitely routed, and over 60,000 of his followers were slain.[24] Niẓām al-Mulk claims that Jahwar entered Rayy and slaughtered the Magians there, plundered their property, and took their women and children captive.[25]

Some authorities indicate that Sunbādh himself was killed during the battle,[26] while others indicate that he was killed subsequently as he fled to Ṭabaristān. Ṭabarī, for example, states that Lūzān al-Ṭabarī killed Sunbādh on the road between Qūmis and Ṭabaristān.[27] Balādhurī claims that the Iṣbahbadh of Ṭabaristān killed Sunbādh and his companions and sent their heads to Jahwar.[28] A more detailed tradition asserts that Sunbādh fled to Ṭabaristān to seek refuge with the Iṣbahbadh, to whom he had earlier sent a prudent "present" of six million dirhams. The Iṣbahbadh sent his cousin or agent, a man named Ṭūs, to receive Sunbādh and to provide him with arms and supplies. Sunbādh, however, behaved arrogantly and disrespectfully towards Ṭūs, who vented his anger by murdering Sunbādh. This vexed the Iṣbahbadh, who nevertheless hastened to send Sunbādh's head to the grateful caliph. He refused, however, to hand over Sunbādh's treasury to al-Manṣūr's deputies, an act which subsequently involved him in a number of difficulties.[29] Finally, Bal'amī, in his recension of Ṭabarī's history, states that the Iṣbahbadh of Jurjān,

Zarbar (?) b. Farkhān, killed Sunbādh;[30] this seems plausible in light of the fact that al-Manṣūr is reported to have made the descendants of a certain Hurmuzd b. al-Farkhān the hereditary Iṣbahbadhs of Ṭabaristān.[31]

Although the revolt had lasted for only seventy days, it was more than a minor incident. The rebels controlled a substantial amount of territory and forced the Abbasids to abandon the traditional summer raid against Byzantium.[32]

The ostensible motive for Sunbādh's revolt was revenge for Abū Muslim,[33] but clearly, it also involved a much broader range of sentiments. To Balādhurī, the revolt was both anti-Arab and anti-Islamic. He noted that Sunbādh bragged about this to the ruler of Daylam, whom he persuaded to help him slaughter many Muslims.[34] Other sources assert that Sunbādh appealed to the Zoroastrians of Rayy and Tabaristan for support by predicting the end of the "Arab empire," and by promising to march on Mecca to destroy the Kaaba and thus to make "the sun our *qibla* as it was in olden times."[35] This had led to conjectures that Sunbādh was following in the steps of Bihāfarīd by posing as one of the saviors predicted in Zoroastrian legends,[36] but it is equally possible that these motives were attributed to him in order to bring him into disrepute. However, Sunbādh does seem to have amalgamated Islamic and Zoroastrian beliefs in a manner not uncommon among the various radical sects which participated in the Abbasid *da'wa*. In a mixture of the doctrines of the Kaysāniyya and the Abū Muslim sects, he taught that al-Manṣūr had not killed Abū Muslim, who had really been able to escape by reciting God's greatest name and thus being transformed into a white dove. Abū Muslim was rather concealed in a secret fortress with Mazdak and the Mahdī, all three of whom would soon reappear.[37] It is thus tempting to see Sunbādh as the precursor of the various activist religious sects which later appeared in the Jibāl; but one must be very wary of such a hypothesis, since it is exactly the conclusion most of the sources wished to present.

At the same time, it is important not to lose sight of the social basis of the movement. Although the sources attempt to depict Sunbādh as an unscrupulous opportunist, they also reveal that he gave up his own fortune to finance the revolt,[38] and that he made an equitable distribution of Abū Muslim's treasury among his followers.[39] This crude attempt at redistribution of wealth was accompanied by a policy of plundering the rich and barring traders from access to the area under rebel control.[40] Moreover, the descriptions of the battles with Sunbādh strongly suggest a conflict between the people settled in the area at the foothills of the Elburz and an influx of new colonists. The Abbasid government seems to have adopted a policy of opening up more of northern Iran to colonization, or at least to have encouraged new settlements in the region. This precipitated a conflict with the established population.

We may conclude, then, that historians of the revolt such as Niẓām al-Mulk may have been correct, in a sense, in claiming that the objective of Sunbādh's revolt was the forging of an alliance between the Zoroastrians, the Khurramiyya (meaning neo-Mazdakites), and the extreme shi'ite elements (Rāfiḍiyya).[41] This does not mean, as Niẓam al-Mulk intended, that the revolt was part of a long tradition of heterodox religious sedition in Iran stretching from Mazdak to the Ismā'īlīs; nor was it part of a conspiracy against Islam. It does mean that the revolt had its roots in the Abbasid *da'wa,* that it reflected disappointment with the results of the revolution, that it consolidated several sources of opposition to the new regime through an imaginative use of *ghulāt* ideology and the Abū Muslim issue, and that it opened up new areas to the influence of such movements.

THE ABŪ MUSLIM SECTS, ISḤAQ TURK, AND BARĀZ

Even as Sunbādh carried the *ghulāt* struggle to the western periphery of Khurasan, other groups renewed the agitation in Khurasan proper and extended it into Transoxiana, a traditional refuge for political, social, and religious dissidents. And once again, Abū Muslim provided a focal point for the unrest.

As mentioned earlier, the *ghulāt* were active in Khurasan long before Abū Muslim's murder. Their relations with him were ambivalent; they were tolerated or encouraged as long as they were useful, but they were repressed if they threatened to get out of control. They were present in the revolutionary army and could appear anywhere the Khurāsānī *jund* went.[42] They thus posed a threat to al-Manṣūr even in Iraq, but he thwarted any expression from them of discontent over Abū Muslim's murder, at least until the Rāwandī uprising compelled him to use force against them. However, many of Abū Muslim's more fanatical partisans renewed the *ghulāt* activity in Khurasan. The danger from them was sufficient for al-Manṣūr to declare it lawful to murder these sectarians wherever they were found. Many consequently found it prudent to flee to the frontiers of the empire.[43]

The general term for the Abū Muslim sects is Rāwandiyya, meaning those who believed the imāmate had passed from Ibrāhīm to Abū Muslim. Within this group were three sub-sects which combined the Abū Muslim mythology with various other heterodox doctrines. One of these was called the Rizāmiyya after its founder, Rizām b. Sābiq (almost certainly an Iranian), and taught that Abū Muslim's defeat of the Umayyads was proof that the spirit of divinity was within him. The sectarians believed in *tanāsukh,* i.e., that Abū Muslim's divine spirit had passed on after his death to his various legitimate successors. A more extreme group in Herat and Merv, called the Abū Muslimiyya or Barkūkiyya, asserted that al-Manṣūr had not killed Abū Muslim but rather a devil in his form, and that Abū Muslim was still alive. While awaiting his return, they are supposed to have abandoned all the obligations of Islam and to have permitted every form of license, since they believed that knowledge of the *imām* was the only requirement of religion.[44] It may help in distinguishing between these two sects to cite Sa'd al-Qummī, who notes that whereas the Rizāmiyya could be traced back to the Kaysāniyya (and thus had a very early connection with the Abbasid movement?), the Abū Muslimiyya were originally Magians (whom Abū Muslim had brought into the movement?) and formed the nucleus of what became the Khurramiyya.[45] Much less is known about the third sect, called the Ḥurayriyya. They venerated Abū Muslim, but do not seem to have believed the imāmate passed to him or to have semi-deified him. It is said that they believed al-'Abbās had become the *imām* after the Prophet Muḥammad and that they exaggerated the special character of his descendants. They are also reported to have been uneasy about the inclusion of "infidel" groups in the movement. They believed in the imāmate of Abū Muslim's close friend, 'Īsā b. Mūsā.[46]

It seems likely from these descriptions that the various Abū Muslim sects originated from the same groups which had supported Khidāsh, Ibn Mu'āwiya, and other radicals, and that they conveniently transferred the center of their cult to Abū Muslim after his "martyrdom," probably in hopes of acquiring a greater degree of respectability. They did not represent any single group or interest, but rather served as a consolidating force for several sources of discontent in Khurasan and the East. Some of them were closely associated with the *da'wa;* others had been co-opted into the Abbasid movement.

Some were genuinely anti-Abbasid, others were simply dissatisfied with Abbasid policies and believed that their problems could be solved if the succession to the caliphate had been different or if it could be altered. And some were more successful than others in translating their discontent into action. It is thus necessary to describe further the exodus of Abū Muslim's partisans to the eastern frontiers and to examine the career of the individual credited with spreading the new *ghulāt* ideology in Transoxiana, Isḥāq Turk.

One tradition claims that Isḥāq was the son of Yaḥyā b. Zayd, who had gone into hiding with the Turks to seek refuge after the death of his father. A rather more credible story describes Isḥāq as an illiterate commoner living in Transoxiana.[47] At any rate, Isḥāq was not a Turk but more probably a Jew or an Arab[48] who was called Isḥāq Turk only because he propagated the doctrines of the Abū Muslimiyya among the Turks of Transoxiana after fleeing with other partisans from al-Manṣūr's persecution.[49]

The doctrinal content of Isḥāq's propaganda was remarkably similar to that of Sunbādh, probably because both saw religious syncretism as the most useful tool for welding together some of the disparate anti-Abbasid factions. Isḥāq taught that Abū Muslim was not dead but was concealed in the mountains near Rayy awaiting the time for his reappearance.[50] At the same time, he attracted the Magian factions by claiming that Zoroaster was still alive and by predicting that he (Zoroaster) would soon come forward to revivify the true religion.[51] Although the only extant source categorizes Isḥāq as a Khurramite, he seems to have been responsible for precipitating a movement, quite widespread in Central Asia, known as the "wearers of white" (*mubayyiḍa* in Arabic, *safīd-jamagān* in Persian). Their white banners could be interpreted as a repudiation of the black of the Abbasids, an endorsement of the Umayyads, or a call for the return of the "white" religion of Zoroastrianism to supplant Islam, the "black" religion.[52]

While there is no evidence that Isḥāq himself led a revolt against the Abbasids, the *mubayyiḍa* did find partisans among segments of the Khurāsānī *jund*. These dissidents, already disturbed by the murder of Abū Muslim may have created the agitation in Merv in 140/757–8 which led to the death of Abū Da'ūd, Abū Muslim's successor as *amīr* of Khurasan.[53]

The man who emerged as the leader of the activists among the *safīd-jamagān* was a certain Barāz, who pretended to be Ibrāhīm b.

'Abd Allah al-Hāshimī and who carried on a *da'wa* in his own behalf. It is claimed that 'Abd al-Jabbār, the renegade governor of Khurasan, chose to join forces with this Barāz and became a "wearer of white."[54] Evidently, the rebels failed to win any widespread support in Khurasan, as they were easily suppressed. Although the movement was temporarily forced "underground," it managed to carry on its mission, which eventually had dramatic results in Transoxiana with the revolt of al-Muqanna'.

USTĀDHSĪS

The revolt of Ustādhsīs[55] is probably the least understood of all the supposedly "heretical" movements during this period of Khurāsānī history. Contrary to the assumptions of many authorities, there is no proof that Ustādhsīs connected himself in any way with the memory of Abū Muslim,[56] and only the most fragmentary evidence that he envisaged himself as a sectarian leader.[57] However, the revolt does resemble the *ghulāt* movements in its social composition, its rural setting, and its opposition to the post-Abū Muslim government in Khurasan and Iraq.

There are at least four different, but not necessarily contradictory, accounts of how the revolt began. Ya'qūbī implies that Ustādhsīs revolted to protest the nomination of al-Mahdī as *walī al-'ahd*. After noting that a clique of Khurāsānī army officers had pressured al-Manṣūr to transfer the right of succession from his nephew 'Īsā b. Mūsā b. Muḥammad b. 'Alī to his son Muḥammad al-Mahdī, Ya'qūbī pointed out that all the regions of Khurasan recognized al-Mahdī as *walī al-'ahd* and swore fealty to him, except for Bādhghīs. It was there that Ustādhsīs instigated a revolt.[58]

Ya'qūbī's political explanation is echoed by al-Dhahabī and Suyūṭī.[59] They describe Ustādhsīs as the ruler (*amīr* or *malik*) of the Herat area. Ustādhsīs and his followers had apparently supported the Abbasids at one time and had cooperated with their forces. Then, for some unexplained reason, they decided to break with the Abbasids and launched a revolt.

This is not incompatible with a story related by Gardīzī. According to the *Zayn al-akhbār,* a number of the members of the Bihāfarīdiyya sect in Bādhghīs offered to accept Islam from al-Mahdī. In return, they were allowed to participate in a raid on Kābul and to receive a share of the spoils (*fay'*) from that campaign. After receiving their share, they returned to their homes, apostasized from Islam, and revolted, led by Ustādhsīs.[60]

According to Bal'amī, Ustādhsīs was originally a member of one of the Khārijite groups in Sīstān. He emigrated to Bādhghīs and was able to persuade the inhabitants there to join in a revolt with the Khārijites.[61] As we shall see, there is little doubt that there was an alliance between the Khārijites in Sīstān and the rebels from Bādhghīs, but there is no corroborating evidence that Ustādhsīs was himself a native Sīstānī.

As many as 300,000 men supposedly came forward to join Ustādhsīs in the revolt.[62] Reports that the rebels were armed with hoes, shovels, and axes[63] clearly indicate that peasants made up the main source of support for the insurrection. Some regular infantry and cavalry units from the area, along with Khārijite tribesmen from Sīstān, may have joined the peasants. Some sources also mention that the rebels were assisted by yet another faction, whose precise identity is obscured by orthographical problems in the relevant manuscripts. In one of the clearer indications, Maqdisī refers to this group as "Ghuzziyya," apparently meaning the Turkish tribesmen of the Oğuz confederation.[64] In any case, we may be sure that the revolt had a broad base of support among the peasants, local military elements, and nomads or semi-nomadic peoples of the mountainous Bādhghīs area.

The exact date the revolt began is problematic,[65] but once initiated it spread rapidly. From their bases in Bādhghīs (the Kanj Rustāq area), the insurgents linked up with Khārijites from Sīstān led by an 'Abd Allah al-Sanjawī (?) and jointly took control of Herat and Būshanj.[66] They murdered some 700 tribesmen of 'Abd al-Qays in Būshanj and "practiced sinfulness (*fisq*) and highway robbery."[67] They then began to raid Khurasan proper, where they came into conflict with the people of Marw al-rūdh. The prefect of Marw al-rūdh, al-Ajtham, led the citizens in an attack on Ustādhsīs. However, Ustādhsīs defeated and killed al-Ajtham and many of his people.[68] Most sources insist that the rebels actually took control of the greater portion of Khurasan, but this is obviously an exaggeration. They do not seem to have occupied Marw al-rūdh and certainly did not even threaten al-Mahdī's camp in nearby Nishapur. The rebels were content to raid and plunder some adjacent areas of Khurasan and managed to defeat a number of the Abbasid authorities sent to suppress them.[69]

Finally, al-Manṣūr sent the veteran general Khāzim b. Khuzayma (Bal'amī says Ḥumayd b. Qaḥṭaba) to Nishapur to help al-Mahdī deal with the insurrection.[70] At least one source suggests that the rebels fled immediately upon hearing of the advance of Khāzim's army,[71] but Ṭabarī gives a long, colorful, and probably exaggerated account of Khāzim's campaign.[72]

Khāzim's immediate problem was less Ustādhsīs than the obstructionism of his chief rival at al-Mahdī's court, Mu'āwiya b. 'Ubayd Allah. Even though he was ill at the time, Khāzim left his encampment and went before al-Mahdī in Nishapur to demand complete personal authority over the expedition and an end to Mu'āwiya's interference. Mahdī agreed, so Khāzim returned to his camp and prepared to attack Ustādhsīs. He gave command of the right flank of his army to al-Haytham b. Shu'ba b. Zuhayr, the left flank to Nahār b. al-Ḥusayn al-Sa'dī, the vanguard to Bakkār b. Muslim al-'Uqaylī, and the rear-guard to Turār-khudā, "one of the sons of the kings of Khurasan."

After some manoeuvering, Khāzim found a favorable site for battle and prepared his trenches. Ustādhsīs' forces, commanded by al-Ḥarīsh (or Ḥuraysh) al-Sijistānī (Sīstānī), attacked and were on the verge of overruning Khāzim's fortifications, when Khāzim thought of a strategem. Both he and the rebels knew that Abū 'Awn was approaching with reinforcements from Ṭukhāristān. Khāzim thus ordered al-Haytham to make a sortie to attack the rebels from behind. Meanwhile, he ordered Bakkār to pass the word that Abū 'Awn had arrived, as soon as he saw al-Haytham's banners. The ruse worked, and the frightened rebels were encircled. Khāzim's troops butchered "70,000" of the insurgents; 14,000 prisoners captured during the battle were subsequently executed.[73]

Ustādhsīs and a coterie of his closest companions managed to escape to the mountains nearby, but they were besieged there by Khāzim, who had by that time been joined by Abū 'Awn and Salm b. Qutayba. Realizing that his position was untenable, Ustādhsīs offered to accept the arbitration of Abū 'Awn. Khāzim agreed. Abū 'Awn decided that Ustādhsīs, and perhaps his family, should be put into chains, but he allowed some 30,000 of the surviving rebels to go free. The author of the *Ghurar al-siyar,* states however, that Abū 'Awn also pardoned Ustādhsīs. He explains this and the call for arbitration by pointing out that Ustādhsīs and Abū 'Awn knew each other,[74] a circumstance which lends further credence to the possibility that Ustādhsīs had at one time participated in the Abbasid movement. Only al-Ya'qūbī claims that Ustādhsīs was sent to Baghdad, presumably so that al-Manṣūr could have him executed.[75] The death or capture of Ustādhsīs did not put an end to unrest in the Bādhghīs area. The region remained disturbed until at least 153/770, when al-Mahdī killed some 20,000 of the agitators.[76]

In a curious postscript to the revolt, some sources claim that the daughter of Ustādhsīs, who was apparently taken captive to become a court concubine, was none other than Marājil, mother of the future caliph al-Ma'mūn.[77] It has been suggested that the purpose of this tradition was to provide Ustādhsīs with a noble background,[78] but it seems more probable that it was circulated during the *shu'ūbī* controversy as part of a campaign to cast aspersions on al-Ma'mūn and his pronounced philo-Iranian tendencies.

Ustādhsīs' revolt really does not make much sense when interpreted as a heterodox religious movement. Certainly, there are reports that Ustādhsīs pretended to be a prophet, that he encouraged infidelity (*kufr*), and, most explicitly, that he "took the way (or *madhhab*) of Bihāfarīd" (meaning religious syncretism?).[79] Ustādhsīs may also have posed as one of the saviors predicted by Zoroastrian legend, and may have been connected with a very obscure sect called the Sīsāniyya.[80]

There are two important objections to this point of view. First, support for the revolt cut across religious lines just as surely as across racial lines. We have already had occasion to note that the Khārijites collaborated with the so-called Bihāfarīdiyya of Bādhghīs. In what seems to have been the Sīstānī phase of the revolt, one finds that the Khārijite Muḥammad b. Shaddād joined forces with Ādharūya al-Majūsī and Marzbān al-Majūsī.[81] It is extremely difficult to understand why these Khārijites, even allowing for their tolerance of *dhimmī*s, would have co-operated with Zoroastrians, even if less than orthodox ones, in any revolt which had a confessional basis or in which religious issues were of any real importance. Second, the earlier sources, such as Ṭabarī, simply refer to Ustādhsīs as *al-'ilj* without elaborating on the precise meaning of the term or giving it much significance. It is only the later sources which emphasize the religious dimension of the revolt, for it was not until the fifth/eleventh century, when Islamic scholars were deeply concerned with the problem of the existence and strength of various heterodox and schismatic movements, that the issue received much attention.

By contrast, the secular aspects of the revolt are much more coherent. It must be remembered that Bādhghīs was an isolated, essentially semi-autonomous, region right up to Abbasid times. For many years, it had its own local ruler and was only indirectly involved in events taking place in metropolitan Khurasan. With more than three hundred villages, and no cities worth the name, Bādhghīs was still overwhelmingly rural. There is no solid information about what ethnic, linguistic, or cultural differences may have complemented the social differences between Bādhghīs and Khurasan proper, but these were probably appreciable inasmuch as Bādhghīs had been the center of Hephthalite power. (In view of the disputed origin of the Hephthalites, it is interesting to note again the indications that Turks were involved in Ustādhsīs' revolt.) In any event, there were fundamental differences between the peasant society in Bādhghīs and the new social order in Khurasan. The sudden expansion of Khurāsānī power posed a direct threat to Bādhghīs' traditional position—especially since the central government saw Bādhghīs as an attractive source of silver bullion.[82]

It was inevitable that the people of Bādhghīs would resist subjection to Khurasan, and consequently they struck out at the two cities through which they were exploited, Herat and Marw al-rūdh. In this sense, it is not surprising that the rebels received help from Sīstān, for both areas were equally menaced by Abbasid domination. Nor is it surprising that the urban "Muslim" class in Khurasan might have employed charges of religious heresy to legitimize the subjugation of Bādhghīs. Thus, the revolt of Ustādhsīs accompanied the fall of one of the last traditional peasant communities remaining in Khurasan.

AL-MUQANNA'

Very similar to the revolt of Ustādhsīs, but not directly connected with it, was perhaps the most famous of all the *ghulāt* revolts, that of al-Muqanna'. The materials for the study of his revolt are particularly rich and detailed, although openly hostile and sometimes contradictory.[83] However, the secondary literature about the revolt is full of misconceptions and inaccuracies, so that much of it is little better than the nonsense familiar to English readers of Moore's tale of the "veiled prophet of Khorasan."[84] In its proper perspective, the revolt constitutes a clear example of how popular insurrectionary movements developed out of the Abbasid *da'wa,* were held together by a charismatic individual and a radical "religious" ideology, and spread from the Khurāsānī heartland to outlying rural areas, where they incorporated and transformed existing sources of unrest. It is thus important to see the revolt of al-Muqanna' as both a consequence of general disillusionment with Abbasid rule and a uniquely Central Asian event.

Al-Muqanna' was a native of Balkh who later moved to a village outside Merv, probably Kāzah.[85] His given name was either 'Aṭā',[86] Ḥakīm,[87] or Hāshim b. Ḥakīm[88]; the name of al-Muqanna' is of course a sobriquet accorded him because of his custom of always concealing his face, either with a green silk veil[89] or a golden mask.[90] His followers believed that this habit was designed to shield them from his divine radiance; the less charitable attributed it to his desire to conceal his personal deformities—he was said to be short, bald, badly formed, one-eyed, and a stutterer.[91] He originally occupied the lowly profession of fuller,[92] but he was nonetheless able to acquire considerable knowledge of magic, incantations, engineering, and mechanics,[93] all skills which he used to considerable effect in his efforts to recruit followers.

Al-Muqanna' apparently played an active and important role in the Abbasid *da'wa*. He served for a while as an officer in Abū Muslim's army,[94] or perhaps as a secretary in his *dīwān*,[95] and subsequently became chief secretary to 'Abd al-Jabbār al-Azdī, the renegade governor of Khurasan.[96] If so, he was clearly associated with the *ghulāt* wing of the revolution, for he called for vengeance for Yaḥyā b. Zayd,[97] taught that Abū Muslim was greater than Muḥammad,[98] and joined the Rizāmiyya sectarians.[99]

The first, shortlived, phase of al-Muqanna''s career as a religio-political rebel came when he declared himself a prophet. The date of this momentous event is unknown, though one authority argues that the most likely time was during 'Abd al-Jabbār's revolt in 141/759.[100] Shortly thereafter, one of al-Manṣūr's agents arrested al-Muqanna' and sent him to Baghdad, where he was imprisoned for a few years.[101] Upon his release, he returned to Merv where, no longer content to be a mere prophet, he claimed to be a god who had the power to take his followers to Paradise and to raise the dead.[102] He commenced a propaganda mission of his own modeled after the Abbasid *da'wa*. He sent missionaries throughout Khurasan to recruit partisans,[103] circulated letters urging people to accept his doctrines,[104] and may have corresponded with other heretic agitators.[105]

One of his missionaries was an Arab from Merv named ‘Abd Allah b. ‘Amr, who, after giving al-Muqanna‘ his daughter in marriage, carried the *da‘wa* into Transoxiana.[106] The people of Sūbakh, a village near Kish, were the first to raise a revolt in the name of the new faith, killing the Arab prefect in the village.[107] Almost all the villages of Soghdia and Bukhara joined the movement; equally important in augmenting the strength of the rebels was the favorable response of many Turks.[108] Transoxiana was soon devastated by new uprisings, attacks on caravans, and plundering of villages.[109]

There are several reasons why this area of Central Asia provided an ideal environment for the nurture of the sect founded by al-Muqanna‘. The activities of Isḥāq Turk had quite likely prepared the ground for just such a movement. Central Asia abounded in a variety of religious sects and doctrines; the presence of Christians, Jews, Buddhists, and Zoroastrians as well as orthodox and heterodox Muslims there is well attested, and no doubt there were also shamanists and other pagan representatives. This profusion of religions in one area necessitated a measure of religious tolerance and contributed to much syncretism among the different groups. Thus Central Asia had a traditional role as a refuge for religious non-conformists of all persuasions.

It is also possible that al-Muqanna‘ had personal connections with the area. We have mentioned that he came from Balkh, a bastion of anti-Abbasid sentiment, and thus might have been familiar with the people and interests of Ṭukhāristān (Bactria). In this respect, it is interesting that the mosque in Balkh was called the mosque of al-Muqanna‘ because someone by that name helped raise its walls[110]; this of course may have nothing to do with the Muqanna‘ in question but it is a curious coincidence. Several Persian sources also refer to al-Muqanna‘ as "king of Farghāna and the Turks."[111] He may have been an important local leader in Central Asia; in any case such statements clearly define the main sources of his support. The point that must be made is this: Many of the things reported about al-Muqanna‘ which appeared strange or offensive to the Muslim chroniclers can become perfectly comprehensible to us once they are related to the Central Asian environment in which they developed.

In light of ‘Abd Allah b. ‘Amr's success in proselytizing the Turks and Iranians, and spurred on by Ḥumayd b. Qaḥṭaba's decision to arrest him, al-Muqanna‘ decided to leave Merv and establish himself in Transoxiana.[112] He had earlier fled from his village and remained in hiding until he had news of events in Transoxiana. Aided by thirty-six followers, he evaded Ḥumayd's patrols, built a raft, and escaped across the Oxus.[113] After reaching Kish, where his partisans were especially numerous, he took refuge in a chain of mountain fortresses concentrated along the Zarafshān and Kashkā Daryā valleys. The most famous of these was Sanām, large enough to contain running water and cultivated fields. It consisted of an inner citadel, situated on a hill, surrounded by a much larger walled area.

The fortress provided a romantic subject for the fantasies of various Muslim writers. The citadel was supposedly strictly forbidden to any but al-Muqanna' and his women and servants, with whom he spent every day drinking wine and carousing. The outer fortress, which contained a spring of water and gardens, was occupied by his generals, associates, and partisans.[114] In reality, Sanām was merely a typical Central Asian settlement: These almost always were built around the palace-fortress of the local lord, with a much larger perimeter wall to protect the cultivated lands from the encroachments of the desert and the threats of invaders.[115] The only question is whether al-Muqanna' was one of the native hereditary lords or whether he somehow usurped control of these fortresses.

The partisans of al-Muqanna', whose professed antipathy to Abbasid rule caused them to be called *safīd-jamagān,*[116] wreaked so much havoc in the provinces that many fugitives fled to al-Mahdī and persuaded him "that there was a danger that Islam would be lost and the religion of Muqanna' would spread throughout the entire world."[117] A good example of their activity is the raid on Numijkat, a village near Bukhārā. Led by a certain Ḥakīm b. Aḥmad and his captains (described as vagrants and thieves), the rebels entered the village by night, killed the muezzin and fifteen people in the mosque, and then butchered all the people in the village.[118]

In Rajab 159 (April 776), the prefect of Bukhārā, Ḥusayn b. Mu'ādh, and its *qāḍī,* 'Āmir b. 'Imrān, led a number of troops and volunteers to Narshakh, a notorious rebel stronghold. The rebels refused to accept the summons of the *qāḍī* to return to the true faith, and battle was joined. Thanks to the heroic efforts of men like the Arab warrior Nu'aym b. Sahl, the *safīd-jamagān* were defeated; seven hundred were slain. The next day the rebels sent a message stating that they had become Muslims and requesting an amnesty. This was granted on condition that they return to their villages, obey the government officials, and refrain from brigandry and the murder of Muslims. Not surprisingly, as soon as the government forces were withdrawn, the rebels resumed their highway robbery, killed, plundered, and carried off the unripened grains of the Muslims to Narshakh.[119]

The local authorities having failed, al-Mahdī took direct action himself, sending a number of commanders to fight al-Muqanna'. These included Abū'l-Nu'mān and two sons of Naṣr b. Sayyār, al-Junayd and Layth. Although they attacked al-Muqanna' time and time again, they failed to vanquish him. Ḥassān b. Tamīm b. Naṣr and Muḥammad b. Naṣr lost their lives in the effort.[120]

After these initial setbacks, leadership of the campaign against the "wearers of white" passed to Jibra'īl b. Yaḥyā, the veteran officer who had participated in the war against Ustādhsīs. Jibra'īl was apparently responding to an appeal from Ḥusayn b. Mu'ādh for help in expelling the rebels from Bukhārā.[121] However, Bal'amī reports that the people of Bukhārā, and Soghdia in general, were divided among themselves, some siding with Jibra'īl and others sympathizing with the rebels.[122] Jibra'īl's strategy was to dig a trench around the insurgents' stronghold in the Bukhārā area (either Narshakh or the village of Būnjikath),[123] thereby preventing them from launching any of their infamous night raids.

After four months of indecisive combat, Jibra'īl adopted a ruse suggested by Mālik b. Fārim to tunnel under and set fire to the walls of the rebels' fortress. His sappers accomplished this, the walls were breached, and the town fell to Jibra'īl. The survivors of the battle agreed to a truce on the same terms as those previously granted by Ḥusayn b. Mu'ādh. However, Jibra'īl had detained Ḥakīm, the rebel leader, with the intention of putting him to death in secret. Unfortunately for Jibra'īl, his son 'Abbās inadvertently informed his father that he had killed Ḥakīm in the presence of Khshwī (?), one of Ḥakīm's lieutenants. Jibra'īl ordered that Khshwī be executed forthwith, but the "wearers of white" realized what was happening and started a second attack. They were again defeated and many of them were slain.[124]

An interesting postscript to this notes that the leader of Narshakh was a woman whose husband had been killed by Abū Muslim. Jibra'īl executed her for cursing Abū Muslim.[125] If this is true, it would suggest that not all the rebels were responding to *mubayyiḍa* propaganda but were rather following in the tradition of anti-Abbasid sentiment which had permeated Transoxiana during the original period of the Abbasid *da'wa*.

After the fall of Narshakh, the surviving rebels fled to al-

Muqanna' in Kish; Jibra'īl took the heads of the slain to Soghdia in order to intimidate the partisans and sympathizers there. His ploy failed, and al-Muqanna''s lieutenant there, Ṣughdiyān, led the rebel forces in several battles with Jibra'īl. Finally, one of the Bukhārīs killed Ṣughdiyān, so his followers dispersed.

From Soghdia, Jibra'īl proceeded to Samarqand, where he attacked the local *safīd-jamagān* and their Turkish allies and took possession of the city. Al-Muqanna' sent 10,000 men under a general named Khārija to retake the city, but the invaders were repulsed by 'Uqba b. Muslim. The defeated rebels then sent a fake letter to 'Uqba, informing him that the *safīd-jamagān* had killed Jibra'īl. 'Uqba, deceived, immediately withdrew to Merv. Thereafter, Khārija beseiged Jibra'īl in Samarqand, while another of al-Muqanna''s generals, Sarḥamah (?), blocked any further attempt by 'Uqba and his men to advance from Tirmidh to reinforce Jibra'īl. At the same time, al-Muqanna' sent a third force to attack Nakhshab, but it was routed by the villagers and their *dihqān*. In revenge, al-Muqanna' lured a detachment of troops away from Jibra'īl's main army and ambushed them. Jibra'īl's brother, Yazīd, died of wounds sustained in the attack. Al-Muqanna' next solicited the assistance of the Turkish Khāqān for an assault on Samarqand. After a number of skirmishes, Layth b. Naṣr killed Fīl, the Khāqān's brother, in single combat; the rest of the rebels then slipped away during the night.[126]

Mu'ādh b. Muslim arrived in Merv in Jumādā I 161 (February 778) to replace Abū 'Awn 'Abd al-Malik b. Yazīd as governor of Khurasan.[127] After putting the affairs of Khurasan in order,[128] he took personal charge of the campaign against al-Muqanna'. Crossing the desert, he reached Bukhārā on his way to link up with the forces of Sa'īd al-Ḥarashī, the *amīr* of Herat. Kayāl-i Ghūrī, a Turkish commander who supported al-Muqanna', briefly threatened Mu'ādh's lines of communication between Bukhārā and Merv, but Mu'ādh was able to attack and disperse the Turks.[129] He then returned to Bukhārā, where the *dahāqīn* had levied 570,000 peasants and soldiers to assist him in the war with al-Muqanna'.[130] Mu'ādh ordered the manufacture of axes, shovels, swords, spears, catapults, ballistae and other implements of war. Thus prepared, he moved into Soghdia, where the resurgent "wearers of white" had been joined by more Turkish troops.[131] He was joined by Sa'īd al-Ḥarashī and 'Uqba b. Muslim at Ṭawāwīs, a rich agricultural village inside the walls of Bukhara.[132]

They made a joint attack on al-Muqanna''s partisans, but final victory proved just as elusive for Mu'ādh as it had for his predecessors. There were two reasons for this. First, the rebels simply withdrew to the fortress at Sanām, which was well prepared for any siege. Second, there was considerable tension between Mu'ādh and Sa'īd; the latter wrote letters to al-Mahdī disparaging Mu'ādh's ability.[133] According to Narshakhī, Mu'ādh requested retirement after two years of inconclusive warfare,[134] but other sources state that Sa'īd's intrigues led al-Mahdī to recall Mu'ādh and to entrust the supreme command of the army to Sa'īd.[135]

Ultimately Sa'īd was able to bottle up al-Muqanna' and his partisans at Sanām. As the siege became increasingly severe, it appeared Sa'īd would be able to take the outer fortress by storm. Some of the rebels then sought an armistice from Sa'īd, which he granted. About 30,000 of the partisans defected to Sa'īd, but some 2,000 others remained loyal and sought refuge in the inner citadel. Sa'īd then took possession of the outer fortress.[136]

Al-Muqanna' realized that his position in the inner citadel was untenable. There being no escape, he chose to commit suicide. According to one set of traditions, he prepared a great bonfire and declared that anyone who wanted to go to heaven with him should throw himself into the flames. His family, wives, and close associates plunged into the fire, followed by al-Muqanna' himself. When Sa'īd's troops took the castle, they found it empty.[137] Other traditions state that al-Muqanna' and his women all drank poison. The Abbasid army entered the castle, found his body, and sent the head to al-Mahdī in Aleppo in 163/779–80.[138] Yet another version, combining elements of these two and supposedly handed down on the authority of the only one of al-Muqanna''s wives to survive him to her grandson the *dihqān* of Kish, has it that al-Muqanna' poisoned his women but threw himself into a heated oven so that his followers would believe that he had gone to heaven to bring down angels to restore his faith.[139] A variant adds that he was thwarted in this, as his body was found in the oven and sent to al-Mahdī.[140]

Al-Muqanna' was nevertheless survived by a group of dedicated partisans in the districts of Kish, Nakhshab, and Bukhārā who preserved his doctrines and customs. Like the followers of Khidāsh and other *ghulāt,* they did not pray or fast and were exceedingly permissive in their sexual habits.[141] Rather like the Bihāfarīdiyya, they believed that al-Muqanna' would someday return to earth, riding on a grey horse, to restore his rule.[142]

While it is difficult to be certain about what is fact and what legend in the accounts of al-Muqanna''s teachings and customs, they seem to illustrate the way in which a kind of popular religious ideology evolved out of the Abbasid *da'wa* and to be generally explicable in relation to similar notions current in Central Asian society at that time. There is general agreement that al-Muqanna' first declared that he was a prophet and later called himself a god, so that his followers would pray to him and call on him for assistance in battle.[143] This was the most horrendous of heresies in the eyes of any devout Muslim, but it is probably based on a common misinterpretation of the Iranian concept of the divine right of kings. As recently as the seventeenth century, the Ṣafavid monarch was regarded by his followers just as those of al-Muqanna' had viewed him.[144]

At the same time, this idea had affinities with those expressed by various groups during the time of the Abbasid *da'wa*. At the heart of al-Muqanna''s claim to divinity was the doctrine of *tanāsukh,* a belief which can be traced back through the Rizāmiyya (to which al-Muqanna' had belonged) all the way back to the Kaysāniyya and beyond. Supposedly the divine spirit had entered Adam and then had passed from him to Seth to Noah to Abraham to Moses to Jesus to Muḥammad to 'Alī to Muḥammad b. al-Ḥanafiyya to Abū Hāshim to Muḥammad b. 'Alī to al-Saffāḥ to Abū Muslim, and finally to al-Muqanna'.[145] Whether or not al-Muqanna' really taught the doctrine of *tanāsukh* in this form, it demonstrates eloquently the ideological ancestry of his movement, its acceptance of and subsequent alienation from the Abbasid imāmate, and its probable links with non-Islamic elements in Central Asia (in this case, with Hinduism or Buddhism).

There are several famous stories about how al-Muqanna' used his knowledge of the occult and the mechanical sciences to convince people of the truth of his claim to divinity. On one occasion, some 50,000 of his followers—citizens of Transoxiana and Turks—gathered outside his fortress and would not leave until they obtained a view of their lord (cf. the Rāwandiyya riots!). He put them off, saying that they would not be able to stand the sight of his splendor. Finally, he gave mirrors to his women and stationed him on the roof of his castle. When he appeared on the battlements, they reflected sunlight onto his body and thus overawed the crowd.[146]

His greatest illusion, however, was the creation of a false moon, much celebrated in poetry, which would rise and set at his command. This was supposedly accomplished by putting a bowl of quicksilver at the bottom of a well, but it greatly impressed the common people, who flocked to Nakhshab to see the miracle.[147] One suspects, however, that they were attracted as much by his encouraging them to seize the possessions of his enemies[148] as by his miracles. It hardly need be said that there is probably little truth in these stories; both Mazdak and Bihāfarīd were accused, in much the same manner, of employing tricks to deceive people into following them.

Finally, there is the matter of the social customs authorized by al-Muqanna', which bear a striking resemblance to those alledgedly encouraged by the Khurramiyya, Khidāsh, and Mazdak. Since knowledge of the *imām* was the only requirement for salvation,[149] virtually any type of conduct would be tolerated. Al-Muqanna''s personal conduct is depicted as loathsome. Shut up in his castle, he whiled away the time drinking wine with his hundred wives, who were chosen from the daughters of the *dahāqīn* of Soghdia, Kish, and Nakhshab, and any other beautiful woman who happened to catch his eye.[150] He abolished the requirements of prayer, fasting, and other acts of faith and allowed his followers to commit any of the practices prohibited by Islam.[151] This apparently included eating pork and the flesh of animals not ritually slaughtered, and the freedom to have intercourse with the wives of other men. We make no pretense that these customs were actually practiced; but if they were, they were most likely compromises with existing traditional practices in Central Asia and not the scandalous conspiracy against Islam depicted in the sources.

There are thus many parallels between the revolt of al-Muqanna' and the other *ghulāt* revolts, though not in the sense the heresiographers would have intended. It represented a complex, doubled-edged movement, partly a response to local issues and partly an expression of disaffection with the new, and powerful, social order in Khurasan.

First, the revolt of al-Muqanna' had a very distinct geographic setting, the upper Kashkā Daryā/Zarafshān valley, where the rebels maintained their strongholds near Kish and the Sanām mountains. As with other *ghulāt* revolts, this was a rugged, remote area which was essentially rural, had its own local ruler, and had preserved its own cultural identity.[152] From accounts of the revolt, it may be inferred that the region had closer affinities with Farghāna and Turkish Central Asia than with its Soghdian or Khurāsānī neighbors. Once again, the autonomy of a traditional rural society was threatened with absorption, and once again the inhabitants struck out at the cities to which they would be subjected.

Naturally, the strong regional basis of the revolt affected its social composition. Most of the rebels were peasants or from the poorer classes. At the same time, there is no doubt that they were joined by large numbers of Turks (presumably nomads though they could have been sedentary people) and that they were led by members of their native aristocracy who were perhaps willing to make some social concessions in order to consolidate popular support (al-Muqanna', "King of Farghāna," may have been a Central Asian nobleman himself). Yet it should be noted that the people of Kish had some interests in common with segments of the adjacent population equally threatened by the advent of Abbasid power. Consequently, the rebels received support from some fellow peasants, *dahāqīn,* and the Bukhār-khudā Bunyāt b. Ṭughshādā.[153] Other peasants and *dahāqīn* refused to support al-Muqanna', and the rebels did not hesitate to fight them when necessary. However, the chief adversaries of the insurgents were the townsmen; that is, the representatives of the urban Arabo-Iranian elite which the Abbasid revolt had brought to power in Khurasan and subsequently in the great cities of Transoxiana. It is thus that one witnesses the spectacle of the sons of Naṣr b. Sayyar fighting gladly alongside the very generals who had overthrown and humiliated their father.

The much celebrated "religious" aspect of the revolt must be seen in its proper social and geographic setting. The movement was doubtless influenced in its sectarian nature by the *ghulāt* dissidents who propagated their ideas, formulated during the *da'wa,* in Transoxiana, but their doctrines came to represent a somewhat different set of interests. If the example of the woman from Narshakh is any indication, the doctrinal aspects of the movement were not universally understood or respected among the partisans. Even for those who did profess the teachings of the *mubayyiḍa,* most of their beliefs were only abstractions of *ghulāt* thought amalgamated with contemporary concepts and customs in the traditionally syncretistic environment of Central Asia. They simply provided a kind of ideology which bound together the various components of the rebel forces by creating a strong sense of group feeling, just as the "orthodox" Islamic beliefs of the urban elite in Khurasan and Bukhara reflected and enhanced their spirit of solidarity. It is hardly surprising that the sources depicted the revolt as an example of conflict between Islam and heretics or infidels. Our perception of the revolt, however, need not be limited by theirs. The revolt of al-Muqanna' was the product of a social conflict between a beleaguered Central Asian peasant community and the emerging Islamic social order in Transoxiana.

THE MUḤAMMIRA IN JURJĀN

Information about one further example of the *ghulāt* opposition in eastern Iran is unfortunately very limited. The *muḥammira*, a term which apparently means "wearers of red," are variously described as either the original Khurramiyya (followers of Mazdak who were scattered throughout Ādharbayjān, Armenia, Daylam, Hamadan, Dīnawar, Isfahan, and al-Ahwāz),[154] or as "allies" of the Khurramiyya.[155] In 162/778–79, a group of these sectarians revolted in Jurjān under the leadership of an 'Abd al-Qahhār (also given as 'Abd al-Qāhir or 'Abd al-Wahhāb).[156] They took control of the area after killing many people. Their slogan was "Abū Muslim is alive! Let us seize the kingdom and give it back to him." There is even a report that their leader was Abū Muslim's son.[157] They also considered lawful the things which Islam had prohibited, including the holding of wives in common.[158]

The revolt was suppressed easily by an army from Ṭabaristān commanded by 'Umar b. al-'Alā, the butcher from Rayy who had volunteered to fight Sunbādh. Nevertheless, the *muḥammira* revolted again in 179/795–6. They were reportedly incited to do so by 'Amr b. Muḥammad al-'Amrakī, who was then branded a *zindīq* and executed in Merv on orders of Hārūn al-Rashīd.[159] Two years later, the *muḥammira* were still strong enough to take temporary control of Jurjān.[160] It would thus seem that the *muḥammira* constituted a popular faction which reflected both feelings of Jurjānī particularism and the *ghulāt* social philosophy.

The *ghulāt* opposition in the east reached a peak in the time of al-Muqanna' and gradually faded away as a major source of resistance to Abbasid rule. It never constituted the anti-Islamic conspiracy depicted in most sources, but was rather a remarkably flexible and adaptive ideology. It took its inspiration from the Abbasid *da'wa*, but typically expressed localized interests and problems, serving as a guise for any number of anti-Abbasid sentiments shared by the rural population of greater Khurasan.

1. The main sources for the history of Sunbadh's revolt are listed in Sadighi, *Mouvements,* pp. 132–33, but there are, a number of sources to which Sadighi did not have access or did not cite. The most important of these are Balādhurī, *Ansāb,* f. 326a–b; *Ghurar,* ff. 170b–171a; *Fragmenta,* p. 224; Khalīfa, *Ta'rīkh,* pp. 442–43; Ibn Khaldūn, *'Ibar,* 3:393; Mīrkhwānd, 3:404–6; a very detailed account in *Tārīkh-i alfī,* ff. 247b–248b; Ḥāfiẓ-i Abrū, *Zubdat,* s. v. Sunbādh (partially reproduced in Zarrīnkūb, *Sukūt,* pp. 153–55, 158); Elias, *Chronographie,* p. 107; Faṣīḥ, *Mujmal-i faṣīḥī,* 1:211–12; *Ḥabīb al-siyar,* 2:210; Sibṭ/Add. 23277, f. 264a; Ibn Kathīr, 10:73; and Mar'ashī, *Ṭabaristān,* p. 33.

Secondary studies include Browne, *Literary History,* 1:313–14; Azizi, *Domination,* pp. 143–46; Sadighi, *Mouvements,* pp. 132–49; Ḥaqīqat, *Nahḍathā,* pp. 250–253; J. Mashkūr, "Sunbādh," *Pashūtan* vol. 1 no. 6:15–17 and no. 7:31–34; Dh. Ṣafā, "Sunbād: Iṣpahbad Fīrūz," *Artish* 7:28–35; Zarrīnkūb, *Sukūt,* pp. 152–59; and E. Blochet, *Le Messianisme dans l'heterodoxie musulmane* (Paris, 1903), pp. 44–46.

2. Bal'amī/Zotenberg, 4:367. This would have been in Shawwāl 137 (March–April 755).

3. Ya'qūbī, *Historiae,* 2:441; Maqdisī, *Bad',* 6:82; and *Fakhrī,* p. 165. *Fragmenta,* p. 224, says only that he revolted in Khurasan; Mas'ūdī, *Prairies,* 6:188, calls him a Khurramī rather than a Magian.

4. Tab., 3:119, has Ahan; IA, 5:481 has Ahrawāna.

5. Niẓām al-Mulk/Darke, p. 212; Bal'amī/Zotenberg, 4:366; Tab., 3:119; IA, 5:481; *Fakhrī,* p. 165; Ibn Khaldūn, *'Ibar,* 3:393; Sibṭ/Add. 23277, f. 264a; and *Ḥabīb al-siyar,* 2:210.

6. Ya'qūbī, *Historiae,* 2:441–42.

7. Maqdisī, *Bad',* 6:82.

8. Bal'amī/Zotenberg, 4:366–67; cf. Sibṭ/Add. 23277, f. 264a.

9. Niẓām al-Mulk/Darke, p. 212.

10. *Tārīkh-i alfī,* ff. 247b–248a; cf. Ḥāfiẓ-i Abrū, *Zubdat,* s. v. Sunbādh.

11. Niẓām al-Mulk/Darke, p. 213, has 100,000; Maqdisī, *Bad',* 6:83, has 90,000; Bal'amī/Zotenberg, 4:367, has 60,000. *Tārīkh-i alfī,* f. 248a, says he called on the Zoroastrians of Rayy and Ṭabaristān to avenge Abū Muslim; his followers are described as inhabitants of the Jibāl by IA, 5:481; *Fakhrī,* p. 165; and Mas'ūdī, *Prairies,* 6:188. Elias, *Chronographie,* p. 107, says that the army of Banū Sāpūr, 50,000 strong, sought revenge for Abū Muslim.

12. See Tab., 3:119; IA, 5:481; Bal'amī/Zotenberg, 4:367; Niẓām al-Mulk/Darke, p. 212; Maqdisī, *Bad',* 6:82–83; Ibn Khaldūn, *'Ibar,* 3:393; Mas'ūdī, *Prairies,* 6:188; *Ghurar,* f. 171a; Sibṭ/Add. 23277, f. 264a; Ibn Kathīr, 10:73; and *Fragmenta,* p. 224. Azizi, *Domination,* p. 145, suggests that the title was an allusion to the son of Yazdigard III, the last Sassanid king; it may have meant nothing more than the honorific "victorious general": see Sadighi, *Mouvements,* p. 135.

13. Balādhurī, *Ansāb,* f. 326a; and Ibn Isfandiyār/Browne, *Ṭabaristān,* p. 112. Khalīfa, *Ta'rīkh,* p. 442, also states that Sunbādh incited the people of Rayy to revolt. Browne, Azizi, Sadighi, and most other authorities have rejected this view, but the fact that both Balādhurī and Khalīfa, two of the earliest authorities, tend to confirm Ibn Isfandiyār casts a different light on the problem. It would appear that the arguments of Browne, *et al.,* need revision.

14. This is a summary of Balādhurī, *Ansāb,* f. 326a; cf. *Tārīkh-i alfī,* f. 248a and Ḥāfiẓ-i Abrū, *Zubdat.* Niẓām al-Mulk/Darke, p. 212, confirms the death of Abū 'Ubayda; cf. Mīrkhwānd, 3:404–5.

15. Balādhurī, *Ansāb,* f. 326b.

16. Ya'qūbī, *Historiae,* 2:442; *idem, Pays,* p. 129; *Fragmenta,* p. 224; Maqdisī, *Bad',* 6:83; Tab., 3:119; IA, 5:481; Mas'ūdī, *Prairies,* 5:481; Ibn Khaldūn, *'Ibar,* 3:393; Balādhurī, *Ansāb,* f. 326b; and Ibn Isfandiyār/Browne, *Ṭabaristān,* p. 117. There are various forms of the name given in the sources, but the numismatic evidence proves that the correct form is the one given here: see G. Miles, *The Numismatic History of Rayy* (New York, 1938), pp. 22–23. Khalīfa, *Ta'rīkh,* p. 443, gives the commander's name as Ibn Muḥammad b. al-Ash'ath.

17. Mas'ūdī, *Prairies,* 6:188; *Fakhrī,* p. 165; Tab., 3:119; IA, 5:481; Maqdisī, *Bad',* 6:83; and Bal'amī/Zotenberg, 4:367, all give the number as 10,000. *Fragmenta,* p. 224, has 20,000.

18. Niẓām al-Mulk/Darke, p. 213.

19. Balādhurī, *Futūḥ,* p. 339 (Murgotten, p. 46); *idem, Ansāb,* f. 326; and Ibn al-Faqīh, *Buldān,* p. 309.

20. Balādhurī, *Ansāb,* f. 326b.

21. Ibn Khaldūn, *'Ibar,* 3:393; Bal'amī/Zotenberg, 4:367; IA, 5:481; *Fragmenta,* p. 224; Maqdisī, *Bad',* 6:83; Tab., 3:119–20; and Mas'ūdī, *Prairies,* 6:188. Only Ibn Isfandiyār/Browne, *Ṭabaristān,* p. 117, specifies the place as Jurjānbān.

22. Niẓām al-Mulk/Darke, p. 213; cf. Mas'ūdī, *Prairies,* 6:188.

23. *Fakhrī,* p. 165; IA, 5:481.

24. Maqdisī, *Bad',* 6:83; *Fragmenta,* p. 224; Tab., 3:120; *Fakhrī,* p. 165; Mas'ūdī, *Prairies,* 6:188; IA, 5:481; and Ibn Khaldūn, *'Ibar,* 3:393.

25. Niẓām al-Mulk/Darke, p. 213.

26. Ya'qūbī, *Historiae,* 2:442; Niẓām al-Mulk/Darke, p. 213; Maqdisī, *Bad',* 6:83; and Mas'ūdī, *Prairies,* 6:188. Ya'qūbī/Wiet, *Pays,* p. 129, says Jahwar executed Sunbādh.

27. Tab., 3:120; cf. *Fragmenta,* p. 224; Sibṭ/Add. 23277, f. 264a; and Ibn Kathīr, 10:73.

28. Balādhurī, *Ansāb,* f. 326b.

29. Ibn Isfandiyār/Browne, *Ṭabaristān,* pp. 117–18; Ibn Khaldūn, *'Ibar,* 3:393; IA, 5:482; and *Tarīkh-i alfī,* f. 248a.

30. Bal'amī/Zotenberg, 4:367.

31. Tab., 3:120.

32. Tab., 3:121; IA, 5:483.

33. Ya'qūbī, *Historiae,* 2:441–42; *idem, Pays,* p. 129; Maqdisī, *Bad',* 6:82; *Fragmenta,* p. 224; Tab., 3:119; *Fakhrī,* p. 165; Mas'ūdī, *Prairies,* 6:188; Ibn Khaldūn, *'Ibar,* 3:393; IA, 5:481; and Bal'amī/Zotenberg, 4:366–67.

34. Balādhurī, *Ansāb,* f. 326a–b.

35. Niẓām al-Mulk/Darke, p. 213; cf. *Tārīkh-i alfī,* f. 248a; IA, 5:481; Ibn Khaldūn, *'Ibar,* 3:393; and *Fakhrī,* p. 165.

36. See Azizi, *Domination,* p. 145, and Sadighi, *Mouvements,* pp. 142–43, 149.

37. Niẓām al-Mulk/Darke, pp. 212–13; Mīrkhwānd, 3:405. On the sectarian aspects of the movement, see Murtaḍa, *Tabṣirat,* pp. 180–81. Browne, *Literary History,* 1:314, n. 2, pointed out the similarity of these teachings with those of groups mentioned in other sources such as Ya'qūbī, *Historiae,* 2:313.

38. Bal'amī/Zotenberg, 4:366–67.

39. Maqdisī, *Bad',* 6:82–83.

40. IA, 5:481–82; Ibn Khaldūn, *'Ibar,* 3:393.

41. Niẓām al-Mulk/Darke, p. 212; cf. Mīrkhwānd, 3:405.

42. Consider the case of a Rāwandī named Ablaq in Tab., 3:418–19. There are reported incidents similar to this, with the fanatics trying to fly like birds, in places as unlikely as Aleppo.

43. *Mujmal,* p. 329; cf. Mas'ūdī, *Prairies,* 6:186; *Fihrist,* pp. 822–23.

44. On these two sects and their doctrines, see Anbārī, *Uṣūl,* ff. 20b–21a; Shahrastānī, *Milal,* 1:153–54; Baghdādī, *Farq,* pp. 256–57 (Halkin, pp. 75, 93); Nawbakhtī, "Les sectes," pp. 78–79; Ibn Ḥazm/Friedlaender, p. 70 (and notes, pp. 118–19); Isfarāyīnī, *Tabṣīr,* p. 114; Ash'arī, *Maqālāt,* p. 96; Murtaḍa, *Tabṣirat,* p. 114; and Abū Ḥātim, *Zīna,* pp. 298–300. See also Sadighi, *Mouvements,* pp. 216–17; Blochet, *Messianisme,* pp. 43–47.

45. Sa'd al-Qummī, *Maqālāt,* p. 64.

46. Sa'd al-Qummī, *Maqālāt,* p. 65; Abū Ḥātim, *Zīna,* pp. 298–300; Nawbakhtī, "Les sectes," p. 79.

47. Both of these traditions are found in *Fihrist,* p. 823 (the unique source for information about Isḥāq). See also Sadighi, *Mouvements,* pp. 150–54; Browne, *Literary History,* 1:314–15; Ḥaqīqat, *Nahḍathā,* pp. 253–54.

48. This is a conjecture by Sadighi, *Mouvements,* p. 152, and Amoretti, "Sects and Heresies," p. 496.

49. *Fihrist,* p. 823.

50. *Ibid.*

51. *Ibid.*

52. See Amoretti, "Sects and Heresies," p. 513; but Sam'ānī, *Ansāb,* f. 506, gives preference to the anti-Abbasid theory.

53. This according to Sadighi, *Mouvements,* pp. 153–54, citing the Cambridge manuscript of Gardīzī, *Zayn,* f. 73a. The published text does attribute the agitation to the *safīd-jamagān* but mentions not Isḥāq but a certain Sa'īd Jūlāh (?); see below, p. 000.

54. Gardīzī, *Zayn,* p. 123. Laoust, *Schismes,* p. 63, suggests that 'Abd al-Jabbār encouraged the teachings of Isḥāq in order to defuse the Shi'ite threat.

55. The sources for the history of this revolt have been classified in Sadighi, *Mouvements,* pp. 155–56; he neglects to mention some very important accounts in Fasawī, *Ta'rīkh,* f. 8a–b; *Ghurar,* ff. 192b–93a, as well as Ḥāfiẓ-i Abrū, *Geography,* f. 199b; *Annales,* f. 15b; Khalīfa, *Ta'rīkh,* p. 453; Ibn Taghrībirdī, *Nujūm,* 2:12; Dhahabī, *Islām,* 6:32; *idem, Duwal,* p. 73; Faṣīh, *Mujmal-i faṣīḥī,* 1:231–32, 234: Elias, *Chronographie,* p. 110; Michael the Syrian, 2:522–23; Ibn Kathīr, 10:106; and *Tārīkh-i alfī,* f. 253a. The best secondary accounts are Browne, *Literary History,* 1:317–18; Sadighi, *Mouvements,* pp. 155–62; Azizi, *Domination,* pp. 147–48; Zarrīnkūb, *Sukūt,* pp. 159–62; Ḥaqīqat, *Nahḍathā,* pp. 156–61; Amoretti, "Sects and Heresies," pp. 497–98; and J. Kramers, "Ostādsīs," *EI*1, 3:1004.

Note that this revolt is identical with that of "Ashnās" mentioned by Barthold, *Turkestan,* p. 198. Barthold was following the variant spelling given in Gardīzī, *Zayn,* p. 124, which, incidentally, is similar to the form given by Khalīfa, *Ta'rīkh,* p. 453 (Ashnāshīsh). Azizi, *Domination,* p. 149, and F. Omar, *al-'Abbāsiyun al-awā'il* (Baghdad, 1390/1970), p. 285, both mistakenly considered this to be a separate revolt.

56. Amoretti, "Sects and Heresies," p. 489; Sadighi, *Mouvements,* p. 157; and

A. Lambton, "Īrān," *EI*2, 4:16 all imply a connection between Ustādhsīs and Abū Muslim. This writer, however, must concur with Zarrinkub, *Sukūt*, p. 159, that there was no direct relationship between this revolt and those seeking revenge for Abū Muslim.

57. *Ghurar*, f. 192b, says explicitly that he took "the way of Bihāfarīd." Sadighi, *Mouvements*, pp. 160–62, concluded that Ustādhsīs was Bihāfarīd's successor; Kramers, "Ostādsīs," *EI*1, 3:1004, speculated that he might have portrayed himself as one of the saviors predicted in Zoroastrian legend.

58. Ya'qūbī, *Historiae*, 2:457. On 'Īsā's deposition, see below, p. 162.

59. Dhahabī, *Duwal*, p. 73: Suyūṭī, *Khulafā'*, p. 262. They describe his followers as "some of the Khurāsānī troops."

60. Gardīzī, *Zayn*, p. 125.

61. Bal'amī/Add. 7622, f. 418b; cf. *Mujmal*, p. 332.

62. Fasawī, *Ta'rīkh*, f. 8a; Maqdisī, *Bad'*, 6:86; Ibn al-Jawzī, *Muntaẓam*, 8:58a; Rashīd al-Dīn, *Jāmi'*, f. 154b; Ibn Kathīr, 10:106; Dhahabī, *Islām*, 6:32a; Ḥāfiẓ-i Abrū, *Zubdat*, s. v. 150 A.H.; Kutubī, *'Uyūn*, 6:33b; and Ibn Taghrībirdī, *Nujūm*, 2:12. However, *Ghurar*, f. 192b has the number as 100,000; Ya'qūbī, *Historiae*, 2:457, simply has *khalq kathīr*.

63. Tab., 3:356; Maqdisī, *Bad'*, 6:86; IA, 5:592; *Fragmenta*, p. 262; and Ibn Khaldūn, *'Ibar*, 3:421. It might be that these implements were required to breach Khāzim's trenches, but it is interesting that the source thought this so remarkable as to make special mention of it.

64. Maqdisī, *Bad'*, 6:86. *Ghurar*, f. 192b, has what appears to be *al-l-gh-riyya*. This latter form is similar to the *al-l-ghāriyya* given by Ḥamza, *Ta'rīkh*, p. 153, along with a note that they revolted against Khāzim in 151 A.H. It also resembles the *l-gh-?-r-yān* (?) mentioned in *Tārīkh-i sīstān*, p. 142. Sadighi, *Mouvements*, p. 158, n. 4, discusses the problem; he favors identifying this group with a sect known as *al-ghayyariyya* mentioned in a commentary on Ijī's *Mawāqif*. In any case, he doubts the presence of Oğuz tribesmen in Khurasan at so early a date. That question, however, is still open: see R. N. Frye and Aydin Sayili, "Turks in the Middle East Before the Saljuqs," *JAOS* 63(1943):194–207. Another tempting reading would be to connect the term with Ghūr, but the vowel indications make this improbable.

65. Khalīfa, *Ta'rīkh*, p. 453, says the revolt began in 149 and that Ustādhsīs was beaten in 150; Tab., 3:358, says Ustādhsīs was defeated in 151 (this in a variant tradition); Ya'qūbī, *Historiae*, 2:457, implies that the revolt began soon after 148. The traditional date is 150/767.

66. *Ghurar*, f. 192b.

67. *Ibid.*

68. Tab., 3:354; IA, 5:591; Ibn Khaldūn, *'Ibar*, 3:421; Dhahabī, *Islām*, 6:32 a (*Duwal*, p. 73); Ḥāfiẓ-i Abrū, *Zubdat*, s. v. 150 A.H.; Ibn Taghrībirdī, *Nujūm*, 2:12; and Suyūṭī, *Khulafā'*, p. 262.

69. Tab., 3:354, and most of the other sources. These commanders included Mu'ādh b. Muslim, Jibrā'il b. Yaḥyā, Ḥammād b. 'Amr, Abū'l-Najm al-Sijistānī (Abū Muslim's father-in-law!), and Da'ūd b. Karrāz.

70. Tab., 3:354; Ya'qūbī, *Historiae*, 2:457; *Fragmenta*, p. 262; Maqdisī, *Bad'*, 6:87; Gardīzī, *Zayn*, p. 125; etc. But cf. Bal'amī/Add. 7622, f. 418b; *Mujmal*, p. 332.

71. Gardīzī, *Zayn*, p. 125.

72. Tab., 3:355–58, and the sources which copy him.

73. Naturally, these figures are not to be taken literally. Maqdisī, *Bad'*, has 90,000 killed; *Ghurar*, f. 193a, has 30,000 killed and 10,000 captured.

74. *Ghurar*, f. 193a.

75. Ya'qūbī, *Historiae*, 2:458.

76. Elias, *Chronographie*, p. 110.

77. The story is found in Gardīzī, *Zayn*, p. 125; IA, 5:593; and Ibn Khaldūn, *'Ibar*, 3:422. Gardizi also suggests that the Ghālib who murdered al-Faḍl b. Sahl at Sarakhs was Ustādhsīs' son (Qazvīnī, *Guzīdah*, p. 312, claims Ghālib was the son of al-Muqanna').

78. Kramers, *EI*1, 3:1004. Sadighi, *Mouvements*, p. 164, corrected Muir's statement (*Caliphate*, p. 465) that Ustādhsīs' daughter was Khayzurān, mother of al-Hādī and Hārūn al-Rashīd. But the error persists: See Amoretti, "Sects and Heresies," p. 498.

79. As a prophet: Ya'qūbī, *Historiae*, 2:457; IA, 5:593; and Ibn Khaldūn, *'Ibar*, 3:421. The charge of *kufr:* Jahshiyārī, *Wuzarā'*, p. 378; cf. Tab., 3:773. The connection with Bihāfarīd: *Ghurar*, f. 192b; and Gardīzī, *Zayn*, p. 125. One might also wonder if Ustādhsīs' revolt may be identified with the "Magian" revolts of that period mentioned by Michael the Syrian, *Chronique*, 2:522–23, and Bar Hebraeus/Budge, *Chronography*, 1:114.

80. Shahrastānī, *Milal*, 2:43; see Sadighi, *Mouvements*, p. 162; Kramers, *EI*1, 3:1004.

81. *Tārīkh-i sīstān*, pp. 142–43. On the connection between the distrubance in Sīstān and Ustādhsīs, see the note by Bahār and Bosworth, *Sīstān Under the Arabs*, pp. 81–82; also, cf. above, n. 61.

82. See Yāqūt, *Mu'jam*, 2:31; Iṣṭakhrī, *Masālik*, pp. 268–69; Ibn Hawqal, *Configuration*, p. 425; *Ḥudud*, p. 104; Sam'anī, *Ansāb*, f. 43a; and LeStrange, *Lands*, pp. 412–15. Ibn Khurradādhbih, *Masālik*, p. 40, calls the "king" of Herat, Būshanj, and Bādhghīs Barāzan; Bādhghīs was the home of the famous Hephthalite general Nīzak, on whom refer to E. Esin, "Tarkhān Nīzak or Tarkhān Tīrek?" *JAOS* 97(1977): 323–31. According to material appended to the ms. of Khalīfa's *Ta'rīkh*, the revenue from Khurasan in the time of Hārūn included 1000 *raṭls* of silver from Bādhghīs: see Ṣ. al-'Alī, "A New Version of Ibn al-Muṭarrif's List of Revenues," *Journal of the Economic and Social History of the Orient* 14(1971):303–10 (which includes a facsimile of the manuscript test).

83. A work devoted exclusively to the subject, *Akhbār al-muqanna'*, has unfortunately been lost, but parts of it seem to have been preserved in works by Narshakhī, Bal'amī, Ḥāfiẓ-i Abrū, and the Tārīkh-i alfī. Sadighi, *Mouvements*, pp. 164–76, gives a fairly complete bibliographical survey; it is supplemented by Moscati, "al-Mahdī," p. 333. Among works they do not cite are *Tārīkh-i alfī*, ff. 257a–259a; Ḥāfiẓ-i Abrū, *Geography*, f. 199b; *idem, Zubdat*, s. v. al-Muqanna'; Gardīzī, *Zayn*, pp. 66, 125–28; Azdī, *Mawṣil*, p. 244; Ḥamza, *Ta'rīkh*, p. 163; Mīrkhwānd, 3:314–15; *Annales*, f. 31b; Dhahabī, *Islām*, 6:79a–81b, 144a; Banākitī, *Rauḍat*, p. 143; Faṣīḥ, *Mujmal-i faṣīḥī*, 1:231–34; *Ḥabib al-siyar*, 2:220; Juzjānī, *Ṭabaqāt*, 1:110, Diyarbakrī, *Ta'rīkh al-khamīs* (Cairo, 1283), 2:330; and a possible reference in Bayḍavī, *Niẓām*, p. 52.

84. The best study is A. Y. Yakubovskii, "Vosstanie Mukanny-Drizhenie hyudei v belyka odezhdakh," *Sovetskoe Vostokovedenie* 5(1948):35–54; other works, of greatly varying quality and insight, include Ḥaqīqat, *Nahḍathā*, pp. 261–65; Zarrīnkūb, *Sukūt*, pp. 179–86; Sadighi, *Mouvements*, pp. 163–86; Moscati, "al-Mahdī," pp. 333–44; Amoretti, "Sects and Heresies," pp. 498–503;

Browne, *Literary History,* 1:318–23; and Dh. Ṣafā, "Naqābdār-i khurāsān: al-muqanna' hāshim b. ḥakīm," *Mihr* 4(1315–16/1927–28):1217–1226 and 5(1316–17/1928–9):49–57.

85. Maqdisī, *Bad',* 6:97, has Kārah; Narshakhī/Frye, Bukhara, p. 65, has Kāzah (on which see Yāqūt, *Mu'jam,* 7:207); cf. Baghdādī, *Farq,* p. 257 (Halkin, p. 75); and Bīrūnī/Sachau, p. 194. Qazvīnī/LeStrange, *Nuzhat,* p. 151, has Kāriz, a town in Bādhghīs—one of the few bits of evidence to suggest a connection between al-Muqanna' and Ustādhsīs.

86. Jāḥiẓ, *Bayān,* 3:104; Ibn Khallikān, 2:205; Yāfi'ī, *Mir'āt al-janān,* 1:341; Ibn Taghrībirdī, *Nujūm,* 2:38; *Tārīkh-i alfī,* f. 258a; Ibn Kathīr, 10:146; and Dhahabī, *Islām,* 6:79a.

87. Gardīzī, *Zayn,* p. 125; Ya'qūbī/Wiet, *Pays,* p. 131; Banākitī, *Rauḍat,* p. 143; Maqdisī, *Bad',* 6:97; *Fragmenta,* p. 273; IA, 6:38; Ibn Kathīr, 10:146; Faṣīḥ, *Mujmal-i faṣīḥī,* 1:231; and Tab., 3:484. *Ḥabīb al-siyar,* 2:220 has Ḥakīm b. 'Atā'.

88. Bīrūnī/Sachau, p. 194; 'Awfī/Banū Muṣaffā, *Javāmi',* p. 299; *Mujmal,* p. 334; Narshakhī/Frye, *Bukhara,* p. 65; Khwārizmī, *Mafātīḥ,* p. 28; Baghdādī, *Farq,* p. 257 (Halkin, p. 77), Qazvīnī, *Guzīdah,* p. 299; Maqrīzī, *Khiṭaṭ,* 2:354; Murtaḍā, *Tabṣirat,* p. 185; Ibn Khaldūn, *'Ibar,* 3:439; Isfarāyīnī, *Tabṣīr,* p. 114; and IA, 6:39. Ibn Taghrībirdī, *Nujūm,* 2:38, says either 'Aṭā' or Ḥakīm; *Fakhrī,* p. 174, has only Hāshim. Niẓām al-Mulk/Darke, p. 237, gives no name, but just calls him "a dog!"

89. Murtaḍā, *Tabṣirat,* p. 184; Narshakhi/Frye, *Bukhara,* pp. 63, 73; Baghdādī, *Farq,* p. 257 (Halkin, p. 75); Maqdisī, *Bad',* 6:97; Bīrūnī/Sachau, p. 194; and *Mujmal,* p. 335.

90. Ibn Khallikān, 2:205; IA, 6:38; *Fakhrī,* p. 174; Ibn Khaldūn, *Ibar,* 3:439; Gardīzī, *Zayn,* p. 125; Yāfi'i, *Mir'āt al-janān,* 1:350–51; Dhahabī, *Duwal,* p. 78; and Ibn Kathīr, 10:146.

91. Descriptions of al-Muqanna' may be found in Narshakhī/Frye, *Bukhara,* p. 66; IA, 6:38; Ibn Khallikān, 2:205; Ibn Khaldūn, *'Ibar,* 3:439; Bīrūnī/Sachau, p. 194; Mīrkhwānd, 3:415; Isfarāyīnī, *Tabṣīr,* p. 114; Murtaḍā, *Tabṣirat,* p. 185; Jāḥiẓ, *Bayān,* 4:103; and Bar Hebraeus, *Mukhtaṣar,* p. 126. Qazvīnī, *Guzīdah,* p. 299 says al-Muqanna' lost his eye in a battle. The description in *Mujmal,* p. 335, suggests he may also have had epilepsy or a similar physical disorder.

92. Ibn Khallikān, 2:205; Baghdādī, *Farq,*, p. 257 (Halkin, p. 75); Narshakhī/Frye, *Bukhara,* p. 65; and Gardīzī, *Zayn,* p. 125 (which uses the term *gāzur*).

93. Baghdādī, *Farq,* p. 257 (Halkin, p. 75); Maqdisī, *Bad',* 6:97; Mīrkhwānd, 3:416; Narshakhī/Frye, *Bukhara,* p. 65; Bar Hebraeus, *Mukhtaṣar,* p. 126; and Isfarāyīnī, *Tabṣīr,* p. 114.

94. Narshakhī/Frye, *Bukhara,* p. 66; Murtaḍā, *Tabṣirat,* p. 184 says he was a "follower" of Abū Muslim.

95. Qazvīnī, *Guzīdah,* p. 299.

96. Narshakhī/Frye, *Bukhara,* p. 66.

97. Ibn Khaldūn, *'Ibar,* 3:439; Mīrkhwānd, 3:416; and IA, 6:39.

98. Tab., 3:773; and Jahshiyārī, *Wuzarā',* p. 277.

99. Baghdādī, *Farq,* p. 257 (Halkin, p. 75); Maqrīzī, *Khiṭaṭ,* 2:353–54; Murtaḍā, *Tabṣirat,* p. 184; and Isfarāyīnī, *Tabṣir,* p. 114.

100. Narshakhī/Frye, *Bukhara,* p. 66; and Sadighi, *Mouvements,* p. 168.

101. Narshakhī/Frye, *Bukhara,* p. 66.

102. Maqdisī, *Bad'*, 6:97.

103. Narshakhī/Frye, *Bukhara*, pp. 66–67; and Maqdisī, *Bad'*, 6:97.

104. Narshakhī/Frye, *Bukhara*, p. 66.

105. Niẓām al-Mulk/Darke, p. 237, makes this claim, but the men with whom he says al-Muqanna' corresponded were not his contemporaries. Cf. Narshakhī/Frye, *Bukhara*, p. 67.

106. Narshakhī/Frye, *Bukhara*, p. 67.

107. *Ibid.*

108. *Ibid.;* cf. Bīrūnī/Sachau, p. 194; IA, 6:39; Gardīzī, *Zayn*, p. 126; Baghdādī, *Farq*, p. 258 (Halkin, p. 76); and Bal'amī/Add. 26174, f. 294a (Cawnpore, p. 541).

109. Narshakhī/Frye, *Bukhara*, p. 67.

110. *Faḍā'il-i balkh*, p. 207.

111. Bal'amī/Add. 26174, f. 294a; cf. *Tārīkh-i alfī*, f. 257a.

112. Narshakhī/Frye, *Bukhara*, p. 67; cf. *Fragmenta*, p. 273; Ibn Khaldūn, *'Ibar*, 3:439; Maqdisī, *Bad'*, 6:97; Bīrūnī/Sachau, p. 194; and 'Awfī/Banū Muṣaffā, *Javāmi'*, p. 229.

113. Narshakhī/Frye, *Bukhara*, p. 67.

114. *Ibid.;* cf. Ibn Khaldūn, *'Ibar*, 3:439; IA, 6:39; Tab., 3:484; Gardīzī, *Zayn*, p. 126; *Tārīkh-i alfī*, f. 258b; Baghdādī, *Farq*, pp. 258–59 (Halkin, pp. 77–78); and Ibn al-Faqīh, *Buldān*, p. 322. There are several spellings of the name.

115. See Barthold, *Turkestan*, p. xxix; Frye, *Golden Age*, p. 40; and Aleksandr Belenitsky, *Central Asia* (Geneva, 1968), pp. 113–14.

116. Khwārizmī, *Mafātīḥ*, p. 28; cf. Shahrastānī, *Milal*, 1:154; Narshakhī/Frye, *Bukhara*, p. 68; Gardīzī, *Zayn*, p. 127; *Tārīkh-i alfī*, f. 258b; Maqdisī, *Bad'*, 6:98; *Ḥabīb al-siyar*, 2:220; Bal'amī/Add. 26174, f. 294a; and Sam'ānī, *Ansāb*, f. 506a.

117. Narshakhī/Frye, *Bukhara*, p. 68.

118. *Ibid.*

119. *Ibid.*, pp. 68–69; this is suspiciously similar to a story told by Gardīzī, *Zayn*, p. 126, about Jibra'īl.

120. Tab., 3:484; Ibn Khaldūn, *'Ibar*, 3:439; IA, 6:39; and Gardīzī, *Zayn*, p. 126.

121. IA, 6:39; Gardīzī, *Zayn*, p. 126; and Narshakhī/Frye, *Bukhara*, p. 69.

122. Bal'amī/Cawnpore, p. 541.

123. IA, 6:39, has Būnjikath, but if it is near Bukhara it cannot refer to the city in Ushrūsana nor the one near Samarqand (Panjikath) and must mean Numijkat, the village near Bukhara attacked by the rebels; Narshakhī/Frye, *Bukhara*, p. 69, says Narshakh (Nasaf).

124. Narshakhī/Frye, *Bukhara*, pp. 69–70.

125. *Ibid.*, p. 71. Her husband, Sharaf, was in Abū Muslim's army before he was killed.

126. See Narshakhī/Frye, *Bukhara*, p. 71; Gardīzī, *Zayn*, p. 126; Bal'amī/Add. 26174, f. 294a (Cawnpore, p. 541, 542–43); and *Tārīkh-i alfī*, f. 257a–b.

127. Ḥamza, *Ta'rīkh*, p. 163; Narshakhī/Frye, *Bukhara*, p. 71; Gardīzī, *Zayn*, p. 127; IA, 6:39; Baghdādī, *Farq*, p. 258; and *Tārīkh-i alfī*, f. 257b.

128. Gardīzī, *Zayn*, p. 127.

129. Bal'amī/Cawnpore, p. 543.

130. Narshakhī/Frye, *Bukhara*, p. 71. Baghdādī, *Farq*, p. 258, says Mu'ādh

had 70,000 men. Bal'amī/Add. 26174, f. 294a–b, confirms the opposition of some of the *dahāqīn* to al-Muqanna'.

131. Narshakhī/Frye, *Bukhara*, p. 71.

132. IA, 6:51; cf. Gardīzī, *Zayn*, p. 127. On Ṭawāwīs, see Yāqūt, *Mu'jam*, 6:66.

133. IA, 6:51; Narshakhī/Frye, *Bukhara*, p. 72, gives an example of their discord; cf. *Tārīkh-i alfī*, ff. 257b–258a.

134. Narshakhī/Frye, *Bukhara*, p. 72.

135. IA, 6:51; Ibn Khaldūn, *'Ibar*, 3:439; cf. Baghdādī, *Farq*, p. 258 (Halkin, p. 77).

136. Narshakhī/Frye, *Bukhara*, pp. 73–74; cf. Baghdādī, *Farq*, pp. 258–59 (Halkin, pp. 77–78).

137. IA, 6:51–52, says they were given poison first and dates the event as 166. See also Qazvīnī, *Guzīdah*, p. 299; *Fakhrī*, p. 175; Gardīzī, *Zayn*, p. 128; Baghdādī, *Farq*, p. 259; Isfarāyīnī, *Tabṣīr*, p. 115; Diyarbakrī, *Ta'rīkh*, 2:336; and Bar Hebraeus, *Mukhtaṣar*, p. 126.

138. See Tab., 3:494; Maqdisī, *Bad'*, 6:97; *Fragmenta*, p. 273; Gardīzī, *Zayn*, p. 66; IA, 6:52; Ibn Khallikān, 2:206; Ya'qūbī/Wiet, *Pays*, p. 132; Yāfi'ī, *Mir'āt al-janān*, 1:350; Ibn Taghrībirdī, *Nujūm*, 2:44; and Dhahabī, *Duwal*, p. 78. Azdī, *Mawṣil*, p. 244, confirms the data as 163, but Ibn Khaldūn, *'Ibar*, 3:439, says 173, almost certainly too late.

139. Narshakhī/Frye, *Bukhara*, pp. 74–75; cf. *Mujmal*, p. 355; and 'Awfī/Banū Muṣaffā, *Javāmi'*, p. 230.

140. Bīrūnī/Sachau, p. 194.

141. Narshakhī/Frye, *Bukhara*, p. 75; cf. Baghdādī, *Farq*, p. 259 (Halkin, p. 78); Isfarāyīnī, *Tabṣīr*, p. 115; Bīrūnī/Sachau, p. 194; and 'Awfī/Banū Muṣaffā, *Javāmi'*, p. 231; *Ḥudūd*, p. 117.

142. Maqdisī, *Bad'*, 6:97; and Bar Hebraeus, *Mukhtaṣar*, p. 126 (translated in Browne, *Literary History*, 1:323).

143. See Narshakhī/Frye, *Bukhara*, p. 66; Shahrastānī, *Milal*, 1:154; 'Awfī/Banū Muṣaffā, *Javāmi'*, p. 229; IA, 6:39; Jāḥiẓ, *Bayān*, 3:103; Ibn Taghrībirdī, *Nujūm*, 2:38; Mīrkhwānd, 3:415; Baghdādī, *Farq*, p. 257 (Halkin, p. 75); Isfarāyīnī, *Tabṣīr*, p. 114; Yāfi'ī, *Mir'āt al-janān*, 1:341; *Fakhrī*, pp. 74–75; Gardīzī, *Zayn*, p. 125; Murtaḍā, *Tabṣirat*, p. 184; *Mujmal*, p. 335; Qazvīnī, *Guzīdah*, p. 299; Maqrīzī, *Khiṭaṭ*, 2:354; Maqdisī, *Bad'*, 6:97; Niẓām al-Mulk/Darke, p. 237; Diyarbakrī, *Ta'rīkh*, 2:330; and Dhahabī, *Duwal*, p. 78.

144. For several examples, see V. Minorsky, trans., *Tadhkirat al-Mulūk: A Manual of Safavid Administration* (London, 1943), pp. 12–13.

145. Different accounts of al-Muqanna''s use of this doctrine are preserved in Tab., 3:484; IA, 6:38–39; *Fakhrī*, p. 175; Maqdisī, *Bad'*, 6:97; *Fragmenta*, p. 273; Narshakhī/Frye, *Bukhara*, p. 66; Ibn Khaldūn, *'Ibar*, 3:439; Gardīzī, *Zayn*, pp. 66, 125; Yāfi'ī, *Mir'āt al-janān*, 1:350; Ibn Khallikān, 2:205; Juzjānī, *Ṭabaqāt*, 1:110; Ibn Kathīr, 10:145–46; Jāḥiẓ, *Bayān*, 3:103; Dhahabī, *Duwal*, p. 78; Diyarbakrī, *Ta'rīkh*, 2:330; Mīrkhwānd, 3:416; Ibn Taghrībirdī, *Nujūm*, 2:38; Baghdādī, *Farq*, p. 258 (Halkin, p. 76); and Isfarāyīnī, *Tabṣīr*, p. 114. Maqrīzī, *Khiṭaṭ*, 2:354, curiously includes Abū Salama in the list of al-Muqanna''s spiritual genealogy.

146. Narshakhī/Frye, *Bukhara*, p. 73; Isfarāyīnī, *Tabṣīr*, p. 115; Maqrīzī, *Khiṭaṭ*, 2:354; and Murtaḍā, *Tabṣirat*, pp. 184–85.

147. Ibn Khallikān, 2:206; *Mujmal*, p. 335; 'Awfī/Banū Muṣaffā, *Javāmi'*,

p. 229; Yāfi'ī, *Mir'āt al-janān,* 1:341; Qazvīnī, *Guzīdah,* p. 299; *idem, Nuzhat,* p. 151; *idem, Āthār al-bilād* are translated in Browne, Literary History, 1:319–20; Faṣīḥ, *Mujmal-i faṣīḥī,* 1:232; Ibn Kathīr, 10:145; and *Ḥabīb al-siyar,* 2:220. See also H. Hālah, "Avvalīn mukhtara'-yi māh-i maṣnū'ī," *Adab* 5(1336/1958 n. p.) and the novelette by S. Nafīsī, *Māk-i nakhshab* (Tehran, 1334/1956), pp. 9–32. Nakhshab is another name for Nasaf, or modern Qarchi.

148. Narshakhī/Frye, *Bukhara,* p. 73; and Bīrūnī/Sachu, p. 194.

149. Shahrastānī, *Milal,* 1:154.

150. Narshakhī/Frye, *Bukhara,* p. 73.

151. See Bīrūnī/Sachau, p. 194; Isfarāyīnī, *Tabṣīr,* pp. 114–15; Niẓām al-Mulk/Darke, p. 237; Baghdādī, *Farq,* pp. 258–59 (Halkin, pp. 76, 78); Shahrastānī, *Milal,* 1:154; and Narshakhī/Frye, *Bukhara,* p. 75.

152. Ibn Khurradādhbih, *Masālik,* p. 40, mentions a ruler of Kish named Nīdūn (?); on the geography of the region, see Barthold, *Turkestan,* pp. 135–42. It is noteworthy that Kish suffered a steady decline in Abbasid times and was in ruins by the tenth century.

153. Narshakhī/Frye, *Bukhara,* p. 10. He was later murdered by the caliph's men.

154. *Fihrist,* p. 817; cf. Sam'ānī, *Ansāb,* f. 512b.

155. Niẓām al-Mulk/Darke, p. 238.

156. On this revolt, see Tab., 3:493; IA, 6:58; Dīnawarī, *Akhbār,* p. 386; Ibn Taghrībirdī, *Nujūm,* 2:42; Ya'qūbī, *Historiae,* 2:479; Niẓām al-Mulk/Darke, pp. 238–39; *Annales,* f. 32a; Ibn Kathīr, 10:135; Khalīfa, *Ta'rīkh,* p. 468; and Maqdisī, *Bad',* 6:98. This is probably the event referred to in the *Mujmal,* pp. 336–37, even though it describes the rebels as Khārijites.

157. Niẓām al-Mulk/Darke, p. 238.

158. *Ibid.,* pp. 238–39.

159. Tab., 3:645; IA, 6:158; and Ibn Kathīr, 10:175.

160. Tab., 3:646; and IA, 6:159.

CHAPTER FIVE

Khurasan and the Central Government

Because the Abbasid revolt began in Khurasan, and because many of the government's functionaries and supporters were people from Khurasan, historians often assume a special relationship between the Abbasids and the province. Khurasan is seen as a bastion of support for the Abbasid dynasty and as a prime source of manpower and material for the central government. Consequently, the appearance of the Ṭāhirid dynasty in Khurasan is considered something of a historical accident, or in any case an event of minimal significance. Is this an accurate assessment? How cordial were relations between the Abbasids and Khurasan? Why should a semi-autonomous dynasty have appeared in Khurasan at so early a date?

In reality, there was a tremendous amount of opposition to the Abbasid government in Khurasan. This does not refer simply to the instances of Shi'ite and Khārijite movements in Khurasan, nor to Khurasan's troubled relations with Sīstān and other adjacent regions. It means instead that there was considerable resistance to the supposed Abbasid-Khurāsānī axis of power in Khurasan itself, from the very groups which had supported the revolution. As the years progressed, the Khurāsānī rebels, at least those who had remained in Khurasan, were chagrined to realize that the dynasty they had helped place in power had little sympathy for their political ideals.

Indeed, a reactionary trend had established itself which was diametrically opposed to the wishes of many of the Khurāsānīs and which manifested itself all too clearly in the murder of Abū Muslim, and the persecution and execution of men like Abū'l-Jahm or Ibn al-Muqaffa'; it culminated in the striking revival of caliphal power under Abū Ja'far al-Manṣūr. This resulted in the factionalization of the moderate forces in the revolutionary coalition in Khurasan and precipitated a conflict between those who elected to support the new regime and those who sought to change its political policies, if not the dynasty itself.

In this chapter, we shall survey the symptoms of the political struggle in Khurasan after the death of Abū Muslim. The events are difficult to follow and are often obscured by the biases and inadequacies of the source material; they are further confused by the still overlapping political and social aspects of the revolutionary movement. After the suppression of the *ghulāt* opposition (ca. 160/776–7), however, the divisions between Khurasan and the central government deepened and focused on more specific issues: taxation, the responsibility of provincial officials, and the central question of Khurāsānī autonomy. These tensions, brought to a climax by the policies of 'Alī b. 'Īsā b. Māhān, were finally resolved only through the trauma of a civil war which might be called the second Abbasid revolution.

THE DEATH OF ABŪ DA'ŪD[1]

When he left Khurasan on his ill-fated journey to Iraq, Abū Muslim had designated his own deputy there, as if to emphasize the political independence of the province from caliphal control. The man he chose was Abū Da'ūd Khālid b. Ibrāhīm al-Dhuhlī, one of the original twelve *nuqabā'*, who had rendered many services to the cause of the *da'wa,* who had proved himself a capable general, and who had remained loyal to Abū Muslim during the Ziyād b. Ṣāliḥ affair.

Abū Da'ūd must have found this new position rather precarious, however, during the crisis which developed between al-Manṣūr and Abū Muslim. He had to steer a dangerous middle course between fidelity to his old commander, who could—and almost did—return to Khurasan, and compliance with the rising power of the caliph. Thus, he was afraid to give formal allegiance to al-Manṣūr upon his accession without specific authorization to do so from Abū Muslim[2]; on the other hand, he did not come to Abū Muslim's aid and may have responded favorably to al-Manṣūr's offer of the governorship of Khurasan in return for his neutrality.[3] Although the sources do not provide enough information to know precisely which course Abū Da'ūd followed, his policies must have been prudent, for al-Manṣūr did recognize him as governor of Khurasan. This could, of course, have been as much from fear of further antagonizing the Khurāsānīs as from gratitude that Abū Da'ūd had not actively supported Abū Muslim.

Subsequent events are even more confused. According to one set of traditions, al-Manṣūr suspected Abū Da'ūd of "treachery," presumably meaning loyalty to Abū Muslim. After ordering him to raid Transoxiana, he abruptly sent a summons to appear at court. Abū Da'ūd immediately suspected that the caliph planned to interrogate him about Abū Muslim and then put him to death; he also recognized that obedience to the summons would constitute a tacit acknowledgment of his political subservice to al-Manṣūr. The caliph's spies reported Abū Da'ūd's equivocation to al-Manṣūr, who then gave orders for his murder.[4]

A second set of traditions gives a rather different account. According to Ṭabarī and some other sources, elements of the troops in Khurasan revolted against Abū Da'ūd and began clamoring around his residence in Merv. As Abū Da'ūd came out to see what the disturbance was about, the parapet on which he was standing collapsed, so that he plunged to his death.[5] A variant of this notes that Abū Da'ūd was not in Merv, but on campaign against the Turks, or preparing the campaign, when the revolt occurred.[6] Finally, Gardīzī reports that Abū Da'ūd was murdered by members of the *ghulāt* faction in Khurasan, which he calls the "wearers of white" (*safīd-jāmagān*), drawn from the clan of a Sa'īd Jūlāh.[7]

Because of these many discrepancies, it is impossible to know how Abū Da'ūd died. It is enough for us, however, to see that the murder of Abū Muslim had inflamed, rather than extinguished, the political struggle in Khurasan. Whether or not Abū Da'ūd's death was accidental, whether he died for opposing al-Manṣūr or for supporting him, it is clear that two rival factions were at work in Khurasan, either of which could have been capable of murder to advance its political goals. Abū Da'ūd's death or murder was a symptom of this struggle and helped plunge Khurasan into a period of chaos and revolt.

THE REVOLT OF 'ABD AL-JABBĀR AL-AZDĪ

In the confusion following Abū Da'ūd's death, authority in Khurasan passed temporarily to the chief of his bodyguard, Abū 'Aṣṣām 'Abd al-Raḥman b. Salīm, who may have ruled for as long as a year.[8] Then a new governor, selected and approved by al-Manṣūr, arrived in Merv. He was ʿAbd al-Jabbār al-Azdī,[9] a prominent figure in the struggle against the Umayyads and head of the *shurṭa* for both al-Saffāḥ and al-Manṣūr. If al-Manṣūr had intended to install a reliable crony as governor of Khurasan and thereby manifest his complete sovereignty over the province, he was badly fooled. Within months of his arrival, ʿAbd al-Jabbār was caught up in the internal Khurāsānī political conflict and ultimately rebelled against the caliph.

The sources give a number of reasons for ʿAbd al-Jabbār's breach with the caliph. Some of these are inconsistent and may reflect the political biases of their authors. They may be grouped into four categories:

(1) ʿAbd al-Jabbār was over-zealous in his execution of an order from al-Manṣūr to suppress pro-ʿAlīd activity in Khurasan. He used it as a pretext to launch a reign of terror which numbered among its victims such Khurāsānī notables as Mujāshiʿ b. Ḥarīth al-Anṣārī, prefect of Bukhārā; Abū'l-Mughīra, a *mawlā* of Banū Tamīm; Khālid b. Kathīr, prefect of Qūhistān; and al-Ḥarīsh b. Muḥammad al-Dhuhlī. A number of other Khurāsānī military, political, and religious leaders were arrested. The caliph was angered by these excesses, all the more so because he had explicitly ordered ʿAbd al-Jabbār to send any suspects to him rather than dealing with them on the spot.[10]

(2) ʿAbd al-Jabbār actively and persistently harassed the noble Abbasid partisans in Khurasan, both civilian and military.[11]

(3) ʿAbd al-Jabbār was guilty of gross misconduct in office, especially nepotism. He became over-proud of his position, and, having duped al-Manṣūr into permitting his family to join him in Khurasan, decided to revolt. To finance this, he raised the taxes of Merv, Balkh, and other cities, and allowed his nephew to rule oppressively at Nishapur. When the caliph ordered the nephew dismissed and sent to him for punishment, ʿAbd al-Jabbār proclaimed his revolt.[12]

(4) ʿAbd al-Jabbār was really a crypto-shīʾite. One account claims that he called for an ʿAlīd ruler[13]; another that he accepted the radical doctrines of the *safīd-jāmagān* as taught by Barāz and Ibrāhīm al-Hāshimī and carried on a *daʿwa* in their behalf, thus offending many of the army officers and Khurāsānī notables who refused to collaborate with him.[14] This, incidentally, would not be incompatible with his alleged persecution of the nobles (*ruʾasāʾ* or *ʿaẓāʾim*).

Though there is no way of knowing which of these diverse traditions may be accurate, all of these reports have in common the idea that ʿAbd al-Jabbār refused to recognize the caliph's sovereignty, either by outright opposition or by acting on his own initiative in a way contrary to the caliph's directives.

The point is illustrated by an anecdote preserved in a number of sources. Al-Manṣūr feared that ʿAbd al-Jabbār was plotting to revolt and sought the counsel of his minister Abū Ayyūb. Acting on Abū Ayyūb's advice, the caliph ordered ʿAbd al-Jabbār to send troops from Khurasan for a raid against Byzantium. ʿAbd al-Jabbār evaded this by claiming that he needed the troops to ward off Turkish invasions. The caliph then offered to send his own troops to Khurasan, ostensibly to help but hoping, of course, to use them against ʿAbd al-Jabbār. Once again, ʿAbd al-Jabbār, perceiving the caliph's intent, refused to comply, arguing that a recent famine in Khurasan would make it a burden for the people to quarter more troops. With that, the caliph sent a large army, nominally commanded by his son Muḥammad al-Madhī, to Rayy with orders to recall ʿAbd al-Jabbār.[15] It is significant that ʿAbd al-Jabbār refused either to give up his office or to obey the summons to appear before the caliph.[16] To do so would have exemplified the final capitulation of Khurāsānī autonomy. The caliph would have to wrest control of the province by force of arms.

Al-Mahdī encamped at Nishapur and sent Khāzim b. Khuzayma to attack ʿAbd al-Jabbār at Merv. Meanwhile, several local revolts broke out against ʿAbd al-Jabbār, many of them by army officers who felt they should remain loyal to the caliph. Many local aristocrats, whom ʿAbd al-Jabbār had persecuted, perhaps as part of the price of an alliance with the *safīd-jāmagān,* also took the opportunity to exact their revenge; the people of Marw al-rūdh were particularly vigorous in opposing ʿAbd al-Jabbār.[17] ʿAbd al-Jabbār's reported heavy-handedness in raising taxes, as well as his unpopularity with the higher social classes, may have turned much of the local population against him. In any event, his army was routed, and his mentor Ibrāhīm al-Hāshimī was killed. ʿAbd al-Jabbār fled, but his enemies hunted him down and took him to Khāzim. Abbasid troops liquidated the remnants of his supporters in the Ṭālaqān and Balkh districts.[18]

Khāzim dressed ʿAbd al-Jabbār in a woolen cloak and sent him to al-Manṣūr riding backwards on a camel. Once in the caliph's hands, he was beaten and dismembered, his property confiscated, and his family exiled to the Yaman.[19] The date for this is uncertain—some time between 141/758 and 143/761—but it marks the establishment of caliphal control over Khurasan.

The revolt of ʻAbd al-Jabbār is, of course, important as an example of the political friction between the Khurāsānī administration and the central government. It also illustrates the forces which were disrupting the revolutionary coalition in Khurasan. It is clear from all the accounts that many Khurāsānīs elected not to support ʻAbd al-Jabbār and helped suppress his revolt. Some of them may have been genuinely loyal to al-Manṣūr; others may have harbored some personal resentment against ʻAbd al-Jabbār. However, the key factor seems to be that his affection for the *ghulāt* alienated the moderates. We do not know if ʻAbd al-Jabbār did this simply to drum up support for his cause, or if he actually sympathized with the radicals. What is certain is that he translated their social dreams into reality by openly attacking the Khurāsānī elite. The moderates' fears of this program of social reform, remarkably close to class warfare, provided the Abbasids with the tool they needed to assert their authority over the province. Caliphal power was established in Khurasan and maintained there by playing off the moderates against the *ghulāt*.

THE DEPOSITION OF ʻĪSĀ B. MŪSĀ

After the execution of ʻAbd al-Jabbār, Khurāsānī attitudes toward the caliph and the central government remained bitterly divided. For the moment, the conflict no longer manifested itself in open revolt but rather in smouldering discontent, reflected in one of the most pressing political questions of the time: the deposition of ʻĪsā b. Mūsā b. Muḥammad b. ʻAlī as heir apparent.[20]

When al-Saffāḥ designated Abū Ja'far al-Manṣūr as his heir, he stipulated that their nephew ʻĪsa b. Mūsā should succeed Abū Jaʻfar. While one can only speculate as to his motives, it does not seem unreasonable to assume that al-Saffāḥ, who had witnessed Abū Jaʻfar's fanatical hatred of Abū Muslim and the threat to caliphal supremacy which he represented, was acutely aware of Abū Jaʻfar's authoritarian character and thus deliberately chose ʻĪsā b. Mūsā to counterbalance his brother's excesses and to help appease the Khurāsānīs.

There is some extenuating evidence to suggest that ʻĪsā enjoyed a special relationship with the progressive wing of the *shīʻa*. He never tried to interfere in Khurāsānī affairs and judiciously limited his political influence to lower Iraq. Unlike other Abbasid caliph-designates, he never took a pompous regnal title like al-Manṣūr, al-Mahdī, or al-Hādī. It could hardly be coincidental that it was 'Īsā whom Abū Muslim was accused of plotting to make caliph, or that it was 'Īsā who was chosen as special emissary to Abū Muslim and who played the role of honest broker in the conflict between al-Manṣūr and Abū Muslim, or that it was he, by most accounts, who was most shocked by the murder and its possible effects on the Khurāsānī *jund*.

There is also explicit evidence that one faction among the Abbasid partisans felt so strongly about 'Īsā's right to the caliphate that they broke completely with al-Manṣūr and al-Mahdī. Abū Ḥātim al-Rāzī calls them the Ḥurayriyya, a group known from other sources to have had close affinities with Abū Muslim and the sects which sprang up after his death.[21] There is no way of knowing whether 'Īsā sympathized with Abū Muslim's partisans or not, but it does seem that they envisaged him, rightly or wrongly, as the champion of their cause. It might very well be that Bal 'amī was expressing the considered opinion of the Khurāsānī moderates when he said that 'Īsā was "the bravest and wisest of all the Banū 'Abbās and the head of the family."[22]

In complete contrast was 'Īsā's rival for the caliphate, al-Manṣūr's son, Muḥammad al-Mahdī. He, too, was reportedly popular in Khurasan, but with factions quite different from those of 'Īsā b. Mūsā. He was the darling of the anti-radicals among the Khurāsānī civilians and *jund,* those who were more worried about the photo-socialism of an 'Abd al-Jabbār or the *ghulāt* than the political power of the central government. To these groups, al-Mahdī was, at least in name, the commander who had defeated 'Abd al-Jabbār, the conqueror of the rebellious infidels in Ṭabaristān, the stern governor of the Jibāl, and the vanquisher of heretical movements.

Perhaps, then, the question involved in the deposition was not so much support for 'Īsā as it was opposition to al-Mahdī; conversely, al-Mahdī's supporters may not have feared 'Īsā as much as they disliked his partisans. As a bonus, the deposition of 'Īsā would give the conservatives at least the illusion that (some) Khurāsānīs had influence on the decisions made by the Iraqi regime.

For some time after his investiture, Abū Ja'far had shown 'Īsā a proper degree of respect and allowed him to take precedence over al-Mahdī on official occasions. In 147/764, however, he decreed that his successor would be his son Muḥammad and not his nephew 'Īsā. The sources give several different explanations for this flagrant violation of al-Saffāḥ's testament. If Bal'amī is to be believed, al-Manṣūr had always secretly plotted ʿĪsā's deposition and deliberately sent him on dangerous missions in the hope that he would be killed. That al-Manṣūr gave ʿĪsā the onerous task of suppressing the ʿAlīd revolt led by al-Nafs al-Zakiyya would tend to corroborate this. Manṣūr is also said to have ordered ʿĪsā to kill ʿAbd Allah b. ʿAlī, although he had been granted an official pardon for his abortive revolt. He then had al-Mahdī incite other members of the Abbasid family to clamor for ʿĪsā's death in revenge for ʿAbd Allah. ʿĪsā, who on this occasion, at least, was al-Manṣūr's equal in cunning, had not really obeyed the order to kill ʿAbd Allah, and produced him once al-Manṣūr had denied ordering the execution, much to the caliph's embarrassment.

All his ruses having failed, al-Manṣūr tried to cajole ʿĪsā into voluntarily giving up his right to the caliphate and, when that failed, attempted to poison him. In the end, al-Manṣūr, with the help of Khālid b. Barmak and veiled threats against ʿĪsā's person, forced ʿĪsā to give up his claims in exchange for a guarantee that ʿĪsā would succeed al-Mahdī.[23] It is worth noting that al-Manṣūr could not take overt action against ʿĪsā until 147. It was not until then—with Abū Muslim dead, the ʿAlīd threat obliterated, the Rāwandī uprising suppressed, and the eastern provinces quieted—that it was politically safe to move against ʿĪsā, who, as we have suggested, would have been likely to receive support from just such sources (the ʿAlids excepted).

Other sources claim that al-Manṣūr did not depose ʿĪsā willingly but in response to pressure from "the Khurāsānīs." Yaʿqūbī is most explicit in this regard, stating that a delegation of Khurāsānī leaders approached al-Manṣūr praising al-Mahdī and urging that he be named *walī ʿahd*. When ʿĪsā was reticent about relinquishing his claim to the succession, the *jund* stationed in Baghdad and Kūfa clamored around his residences and intimidated him into accepting his deposition.[24] Ṭabarī also preserves a tradition that Abū ʿUbayd Allah, al-Mahdī's secretary, and a group of Khurāsānīs took the lead in forcing ʿĪsā to give up his place as heir apparent, but he does add that this was supported by the troops only because they knew it to be the wish of al-Manṣūr himself.[25]

At first glance, these traditions appear to contradict the notion that ʿĪsā had the backing of Khurāsānī opinion, but this is not the case. We have already suggested that the Khurāsānī moderates were divided against themselves, some supporting al-Manṣūr and others opposed. Moreover, it is quite possible that the use of the term "Khurāsānī'' in the sources is misleading. It really refers to a clique of army officers, troops, and bureaucrats whose ancestral home was Khurasan but *who no longer lived there*. They were residents of Iraq and had become sycophants attached to al-Manṣūr and al-Mahdī, dependent on them for their livelihood and social position. Whenever the term is used in a source, it is well to keep in mind this distinction between true Khurāsānīs and the Khurāsānī *abnā' al-dawla*, some of whom had never seen Khurasan.

In any case, it is the reaction to the deposition in Khurasan which is of most interest to us, and the evidence on this point clearly demonstrates that the decision to depose 'Īsā was not welcomed in all quarters of the province. The people of Bādhghīs, led by Ustādhsīs, revolted and refused to make obeisance to al-Mahdī.[26] Elias of Nisibis reports that the ''Magians'' remained in revolt from then until 151–52/768–79.[27] Gardīzī notes that a faction among the troops revolted and murdered Ḥasan b. Ḥamrān and his brother,[28] although this might have been a consequence of 'Abd al-Jabbār's execution rather than a reaction to the deposition. Ya'qūbī reports a revolt in Ṭālaqān ca. 155/771–72, but is not explicit about which town of that name he means or what might have been the reason for the revolt.[29]

The most concrete evidence of opposition is a report in Ṭabarī that in 153/770 the *mawlā* 'Abbād, Yūsuf b. 'Ulwān, and Harthama b. A'yan had to be brought from Khurasan in chains because of their outspoken partisanship (*ta'aṣṣub*) for 'Īsā b. Mūsā.[30] Yūsuf, let it be noted, was the brother of the *dā'ī* who had led the faction supporting Abū Muslim against Sulaymān b. Kathīr; Harthama's brother had been one of the twelve *nuqabā'*, and, as we shall see, he himself would play a leading role in Khurāsānī opposition to al-Amīn and support for al-Ma'mūn.

Thus it is fairly certain that the years following 'Īsā's deposition marked a period of unrest in Khurasan. While there is little conclusive proof that this unrest was connected with the deposition, or what questions were at issue, some sort of conflict was certainly brewing. Mansūr's death and the accession of al-Mahdī aggravated the situation rather than easing it. In 159/775–76, ''the Hāshimites and their Khurāsānī partisans'' began agitating for a second deposition of 'Īsā b. Mūsā, and either encouraged or forced al-Mahdī to abrogate the agreement over the succession hammered out by Khālid and al-Manṣūr by naming Mūsā al-Hādī as *walī 'ahd* instead of 'Īsā. As before, the violent outcry of the Khurāsānī *jund* stationed in southern

Iraq—coupled with judicious bribes—sufficed to insure 'Īsā's compliance with the caliph's wishes.[31]

By that time, the succession of 'Īsā could in itself have been of scant importance to most Khurāsānīs; perhaps it was never more than a symbolic issue. Yet once again there were signs that some Khurāsānīs could not tolerate al-Mahdī, his son al-Hādī, or the policies they had come to represent. Before, there had been rumblings of dissatisfaction; now there was an explosion.[32]

YŪSUF AL-BARM[33]

The revolt of Yūsuf b. Ibrāhīm, called al-Barm, in 160/776–7, is often considered one of the "religious" revolts in Iran, similar to that of al-Muqanna', with which it was roughly contemporary. It seems more satisfactory to regard it, however, as a final outburst of protest against the authoritarian drift of Abbasid policies which had been symbolized in the successive depositions of 'Īsā b. Mūsā.

The history of the revolt is somewhat confused. Most sources say only that Yūsuf revolted in Khurasan. Moscati,[34] following Ya'qūbī, suggested that the revolt began in Bukhārā; actually the text says only that Yūsuf was a *mawlā* of the Thaqīf in Bukhārā and adds that both Soghdia and Farghāna were agitated at the time of his appearance.[35] Other sources state that the revolt began in Būshanj when Yūsuf expelled its prefect, Muṣ'ab b. Zurayq (grandfather of Ṭāhir and al-Ḥusayn, the Ṭāhirids), and spread rapidly to Marw al-rūdh, Ṭālaqān, and Jūzjān.[36]

Yūsuf quickly found a number of supporters, described by one source as "rabble,"[37] and turned down an offer of pardon from the caliph.[38] Al-Mahdī sent one contingent of troops, commanded by either Aḥmad b. Asad or Sa'īd b. Salm, to Farghāna; there the royal city, Kāsān, fell easily. He also ordered Yazīd b. Mazyad to break off a campaign against Yaḥyā al-Shārī in order to deal with Yūsuf's main army. After several skirmishes, Yūsuf was defeated, and Yazīd offered a pardon of any of Yūsuf's followers who would join him under his standard. Most of Yūsuf's partisans defected, and Yazīd captured Yūsuf and his most important lieutenant, Abū Mu'ādh al-Faryābī.[39]

Like 'Abd al-Jabbār before him, Yūsuf was sent to the caliph riding backwards on a camel. When he appeared in Ruṣāfa, al-Mahdī rebuked and cursed him. He was beheaded and his corpse hung up on a bridge over the Tigris overlooking al-Mahdī's encampment. Interestingly, it was Harthama b. A'yan whom the caliph ordered to deliver the *coup de grace* to Yūsuf. The ostensible reason was that the rebels had killed Harthama's brother in Khurasan, so he was permitted to exact blood revenge.[40] Yet we have seen that Harthama was a leading supporter of 'Īsā b. Mūsā and had opposed al-Mahdī's nomination as *walī 'ahd.* Thus his choice as executioner, coupled with the display of Yaḥyā's corpse to the army, could have been designed as a symbolic gesture of his political repentance and as a formal acknowledgement of al-Mahdī's position as caliph and the choice of al-Hādī as his successor.

Was Yūsuf a representative of the *ghulāt* and his revolt in essence a sectarian movement? While the revolt was apparently more Central Asian than Khurāsānī in composition, and Yūsuf seems to have espoused some heterodox doctrines, the evidence on this point is inconclusive and contradictory. Some sources describe Yūsuf as a Ḥarūrī,[41] that is a Khārijite, yet that description is vague and could mean simply a rebel. Certainly his name does not figure in the heresiographer's categories of Khārijī sects; in fact, Jahshiyārī called Yūsuf an infidel.[42] Neither is Maqdisī's unique assertion that Yūsuf claimed prophetic gifts in order to incite the "rabble" completely convincing.[43]

It is more likely that Yūsuf's revolt was primarily political but with a slight "religious" dimension. Thus the sources tell us that while Yūsuf used a vague slogan calling for the establishment of good and the repression of evil (*al-amr bi'l-ma'rūf*), what he actually did was to attack the state (*fa-ḥāraba al-sulṭān*).[44] Moreover, Ṭabarī and a number of other authorities explicitly state that Yūsuf revolted because he was strongly opposed to al-Mahdī and his policies.[45] The ideological content of the revolt, its timing, and the way its leader was punished strongly suggest that the revolt was political, and that it was directed against al-Mahdī.

PRELUDE TO REVOLUTION

The years in which al-Mahdī, al-Hādī, and Hārūn al-Rashīd reigned are most often remembered as marking the golden age of the Abbasid caliphate and the Islamic Empire. Yet while one ponders the wealth and power of Baghdad during the last half of the second Islamic century, it is well to recall that there was a darker side to the facade of glory. These were the same years which witnessed the tragic fall of the Barmakī family, the relentless persecution of the *zanādiqa,* the beginnings of the *shu'ūbī* controversy, and unsurpassed examples of corruption and misgovernment. Though a study of these complicated and inter-related events is outside the scope of this work, they should be remembered as the background for the drama unfolding in the east.

With the collapse of Yūsuf's revolt, organized resistance to the Abbasid caliphs and their policies declined in Khurasan and the surrounding area; but a residue of dislike and suspicion smoldered, ready to flame up again, especially if fueled by some specific grievance against the central government and its representatives. At the same time, the political issues became more distinct as they were disentangled from the social issues which had contributed to the defeat of 'Abd al-Jabbār and Yūsuf al-Barm, and as the *ghulāt* threat evaporated.

As we shall see, Abbasid policies toward Khurasan began to fluctuate between two extremes. One governor would attempt to extract as much wealth as he could from the province for the benefit of Iraq, the central government, and, not infrequently, himself. When the people protested loudly enough, such governors would be temporarily replaced by ones who would attend to local interests. This finally brought the problem of the relationship between the province and the central government to a test which was resolved only after serious revolts and civil war.

In Jumādā II 163 (February 780), al-Musayyib b. Zuhayr al-Ḍabbī assumed the governorship of Khurasan. He proved to be as oppressive as any Umayyad official had ever been. He increased existing taxes and levied new and illegal taxes on the population. The province was thrown into an uproar until the complaints of the people forced al-Mahdī to recall at-Musayyib in Muḥarram 166 (August 782).[46]

Musayyib's replacement was al-Faḍl b. Sulaymān al-Ṭūsī, whose name would suggest that he might have had a greater understanding of Khurāsānī concerns than his predecessor. His actions confirm this impression. He rectified all the unjust taxes imposed by al-Musayyib, rebuilt the desolated areas near the Oxus, and erected walls to protect Soghdia and Bukhārā from Turkish incursions.[47]

Ya'qūbī reports that al-Hādī, after successfully resisting al-

Mahdī's attempt to depose him in favor of Hārūn, assumed the caliphate while campaigning in Jurjān. He appointed his maternal uncle, al-Ghiṭrīf b. ʻAṭā', as governor of Khurasan. The province at the time of the latter's arrival was tranquil and the various subject princes obedient. Al-Ghiṭrīf proceeded to undo all this by a number of oppressive actions, which Yaʻqūbī does not enumerate, so that the province was soon agitated. Though the text is somewhat ambiguous, it seems to imply that Ghiṭrīf's actions led to a resurgence of ʻAlid activity, with various members of that family encouraging the local notables to reassert their authority.[48]

Yaʻqūbī is almost certainly wrong in saying that al-Hādī appointed Ghiṭrīf, since most other sources indicate that it was Hārūn who sent Ghiṭrīf to Khurasan, probably in 175/791–92, long after al-Hādī's death. He is correct, however, in drawing attention to Ghiṭrīf's misconduct. From Gardīzī, we learn that Ghiṭrīf had trouble with Jabghūyah (A Turkish prince in Farghāna?), while Narshakhī reports that Ghiṭrīf's reform of the coinage placed a heavy and oppressive tax burden on the people of Bukhārā (and probably elsewhere). Some sources indicate, moreover, that disturbances in Khurasan led to the appointment of al-Faḍl b. Yaḥyā al-Barmakī, who had to suppress a revolt in Ṭālaqān while on his way to Khurasan.[49]

At any rate, the sources are virtually unanimous in praising the conduct of al-Faḍl b. Yaḥyā during his tenure as governor of Khurasan (Ṣafar 178/May 794–Rabīʻ I 179/May 795). Much celebrated by poets, al-Faḍl served as a prototype of the ideal governor: one committed to the interests of the people whom he was sent to serve, not to exploit. He built mosques and hospices, raided Transoxiana, brought the king of Ushrūsana into obedience, and thwarted Turkish invasions. Most interesting of all, he created a special, self-governing corps of elite troops, said to number half a million, composed of native Khurāsānīs selected from the *ʻajam,* which he called the *ʻabbāsiyya.*[50] Only twenty thousand of these accompanied him to Baghdad upon his recall. The rest remained behind; it is tempting to speculate that they played an important and active role in the events which followed.

Manṣūr b. Yazīd and Jaʻfar b. Yaḥyā succeeded al-Faḍl in Khurasan. Between the two of them, they governed the province for only a few months. It is not known whether protests resulted from the recall of the popular al-Faḍl or not. Dīnawarī does say that the people of Khurasan seized one of their *ʻāmils* in 180/796–97,[51] and the rapid change of governors further suggests some turbulence in the province which may have favored the spread of Khārijite activity from Sīstān during this period.

In any case, a new governor, who was to rule Khurasan for ten years, arrived in Merv in Jumādā II 180 (August 796). He was ʿAlī b. ʿĪsā b. Māhān,[52] who stands out in the history of the early Abbasid caliphate: He is as classic an example of the tyrannical, corrupt, and incompetent administrator as al-Faḍl was the exemplar of the model governor.

ʿAlī's family came from a village near Merv, but they were examples of those "Khurāsānīs" whose connection with the province was tenuous. They had been associated with the Abbasid cause from the very beginning, but they are usually mentioned in an unsavory or reactionary context. ʿAlī's father had been beaten to death by Abū Da'ūd's soldiers for intriguing against Abū Muslim; ʿAlī himself was instrumental in the murder of the ʿAlīd Yaḥyā b. ʿAbd Allah in order to embarass his rival, al-Faḍl, who had arranged Yaḥyā's pardon. He had opposed ʿĪsā b. Mūsā (supposedly due to his anti-Rāwandī actions). He had also come out as a strong supporter of Hādī's abortive nomination of his son Jaʿfar as *walī ʿahd* instead of Hārūn al-Rashīd. With good reason, Khālid b. Barmak had strongly apposed Hārūn's appointment of ʿAlī as governor of Khurasan, but Hārūn decided to disregard the advice.

There is no question that many of the sources are strongly biased against ʿAlī and attempt to present him in the worst possible light. It is equally clear that he stood for a policy diametrically opposed to that of the Barmakī family. He wanted to exploit the provinces for all they were worth, send the revenue back to Iraq—after skimming off a bit for himself, of course—and give the province as little as possible in return. This is exactly what he did in Khurasan; stories about his avarice and tyranny are legion.[53] The results were disastrous.

Reactions to ʿAlī's oppression were not long in coming. In addition to the outbreak of the *muḥammira* sedition in Jurjān and the activities of Ḥamza the Khārijite in Sīstān, Hārūn heard rumors about ʿAlī's misconduct, along with suggestions that he was plotting to oppose the caliph. These rumors had to be given some credibility because of ʿAlī's well-known partisanship for Jaʿfar, son of al-Hādī. Hārūn thus ordered ʿAlī to appear before him in 183/799. Leaving his son in charge of Khurasan, ʿAlī dutifully appeared before the caliph, being careful to bring with him enough rich and rare gifts for the caliph, extracted at Khurāsānī expense, to insure his return as governor.[54]

Meanwhile, a revolt broke out at Nasā. Taking advantage of 'Alī's absence, the revolt was led by a *mawlā* of Ḥarīsh named Abū'l-Khaṣīb Wuhayb b. 'Abd Allah.[55] Some sources describe Abū'l-Khaṣīb as a Khārijite,[56] but there is no real evidence that his revolt had any sectarian characteristics. Rather more believable is a report in the *Tārīkh-i alfī* that he was the *wālī* of Abīward.[57]

By 184/800, 'Alī had forced or persuaded Abū'l-Khaṣīb to sue for peace. He then granted him a pardon and bestowed honors upon him in Merv. (It is unlikely that a Khārijite would have been treated in this fashion, but an important, if wayward, local prefect might have been.)

If 'Alī had held out the promise of reform to pacify Abū'l-Khaṣīb, it must have remained unfulfilled, for Abū'l-Khaṣīb revolted again the following year and was able to take control of Nasā, Abīward, Ṭūs, Sarakhs, and Nishapur, and finally to threaten Merv itself. All this reflects the extraordinary unpopularity of 'Alī b. 'Īsā in Khurasan. When the seige of Merv failed, Abū'l-Khaṣīb withdrew to Sarakhs to recruit new followers and to reorganize his forces. In 186/802, 'Alī was able to attack Abū'l-Khaṣīb in his stronghold at Nasā. The rebel was killed, his family and property were appropriated, and Khurasan was temporarily pacified.

By 189/804–5, complaints about 'Alī had again reached the point where Hārūn could no longer ignore them. Ṭabarī relates that 'Alī had brought Khurasan to the brink of disaster. He had mistreated the nobles and seized their property; he scorned and abused the common people in equal measure. He had extracted vast sums of money to build a pleasure palace for himself at Balkh which stood as a flagrant symbol of his abuses. The nobles wrote directly to Hārūn about 'Alī; lesser folk pleaded with their relations and friends to bring the matter to the caliph's attention. Finally, Hārūn, compelled by rumors that 'Alī planned to revolt, set out for Rayy with the intention of deposing 'Alī. 'Alī presented himself before Hārūn with great ceremony and new offerings of money and precious gifts such as jewels, a gold and silver mirror, weapons, and riding animals. Satisfied that 'Alī had no intention of revolting, Hārūn honored him and returned him to office.[58]

It would not be much of an exaggeration to say that, by returning 'Alī to Khurasan, Hārūn had made a major revolt inevitable. It was apparent to all that the forces of reaction, duplicity, and corruption were everywhere triumphant: The Barmakīs were in disgrace, al-Amīn had been confirmed as heir apparent, and now 'Alī was rewarded for his misdeeds.

RĀFI' B. LAYTH

The general uprising against 'Alī b. 'Īsā was precipitated in a surprising quarter and for a most unlikely, almost ludicrous, reason. Rāfi' b. Layth was one of the army officers who had accompanied 'Alī to Khurasan and was posted to Samarqand.[59] Since we know that he was the grandson of Naṣr b. Sayyār and that there was a strong, previously pro-Umayyad, faction in Transoxiana, it is possible that Rāfi' either had some personal connection with the area or found the people sympathetic. In any case, he was a popular member of the Samarqand garrison, well known for his fondness for wine and women.[60]

The story goes that one of the women who caught his eye was the wealthy and beautiful wife of Yaḥyā b. al-Ash'ath al-Ṭā'ī. Yaḥyā had left her in Samarqand while he went off to Baghdad, where he stayed for a long time and acquired several concubines. Rāfi' took advantage of this opportunity for intrigue and easily persuaded Yaḥyā's wife to apostasize from Islam, thus ending her marriage to Yaḥyā; he then married her himself after her re-conversion. Yaḥyā complained to Hārūn al-Rashīd, who ordered 'Alī b. 'Īsā to punish Rāfi'. 'Alī publicly humiliated Rāfi' by parading him around Samarqand. As a lesson to others, he forced Rāfi' to divorce the woman and then imprisoned him. Rāfi' escaped from prison one night and, being refused permission to remarry the lady, returned to Samarqand. There he easily raised an army of "adventurers" and declared a revolt, defeating the force sent against him.[61]

Fortunately, we need not really believe that all Transoxiana and then most of Khurasan rebelled on behalf of a rash army officer and his paramour. Some sources suggest that Rāfi' actually was implementing a *da'wa* for himself or for the Umayyads,[62] but this is probably overstating the case. Even if we assume that the story about the immediate cause of the revolt is true, the real conflict was clearly between the popular Rāfi' and the hated 'Alī b. 'Īsā, and thus between the desires of the local inhabitants and the authority of the central government.

This *cause célèbre* provided the people of Khurasan and Transoxiana with just the opportunity to revolt against 'Alī for which they had hoped. Bal'amī[63] explicitly states that Rāfi' was supported by those who were discontented with 'Alī and his agents. Ibn A'tham al-Kūfī[64] attributed the revolt to 'Alī's oppressive behavior and says that Rāfi' had complained about this to Harun. Dīnawarī[65] affirms that Rāfi' revolted because of 'Alī's misconduct, and the *Mujmal al-tavārīkh*[66] notes that the revolt occurred when 'Alī's policies of taxation threatened to ruin Khurasan. This interpretation of the ultimate cause of the revolt is confirmed by other sources[67] and by subsequent events.

The revolt spread rapidly into Khurasan proper. The people of Nasaf swore allegiance to Rāfi' and implored him to help them kill 'Alī's son. Rāfi' sent a detachment of troops commanded by the ruler of Shāsh (which indicates that the dissident Iranian princes of Central Asia also took the opportunity to revolt) to assist the people of Nasaf. 'Īsā b. 'Alī b. 'Īsā was surrounded by the rebels and killed in Dhū'l-Qa'da 191 (September 807).[68] The people of Balkh also revolted, killed 'Alī's agent there, and plundered the palaces 'Alī and his son had built. They reportedly found a cache of thirty million *dirhams* hidden in the garden of the son's palace.[69] Many other Khurāsānīs joined Rafi''s forces, so that there was a danger he would capture control of the entire province.[70]

Hārūn finally realized just how serious the situation in the East had become. His chief of the post in Khurasan, the newly appointed Ḥammawayh (or Ḥamūyah) al-Khādim, informed him that the insurgents were not opposed to him as caliph but to 'Alī b. 'Īsā; at the same time he warned Hārūn that 'Alī was in command of a sizeable army and considerable wealth, so it would be risky to depose him abruptly.[71] It might also be noted that Hārūn also had undeniable evidence of 'Alī's perfidy: He had given up Balkh without a fight and had had the temerity to ask the caliph for more funds when his son had been able to stash a fortune in his garden! He therefore sent Harthama b. A'yan to Khurasan, ostensibly to help 'Alī against Rāfi'. Harthama was thus able to arrest 'Alī before his suspicions were aroused. After a formal dinner, when 'Alī could have no opportunity to resist, Harthama presented him with a letter from the caliph, charging him with abusing his office and ordering his deposition. Harthama subsequently took 'Alī in chains to the congregational mosque, where he was publicly rebuked and forced to indemnify those he had abused. His fortune of eighty million *dirham*s was confiscated, and he was sent to the caliph for punishment.[72]

Hārūn left for Khurasan to direct in person the struggle against Rāfi'. In Jurjān, 'Alī b. 'Īsā was brought before him. Hārūn appropriated the wealth 'Alī had extorted from his subjects and sent him to Baghdad, with orders for Muḥammad al-Amīn to imprison him. He also posted his son al-Ma'mūn to Merv as governor of Khurasan, along with the minister al-Faḍl b. Sahl, and directed Harthama to attack Rāfi' in Samarqand. Hārūn advanced to Ṭūs in Ṣafar 193 (November-December 808). Harthama, meanwhile, had pressed the offensive against Rāfi'. After several battles, Bukhārā fell. Rāfi''s brother was taken prisoner and sent to Hārūn, who reviled him and had him horribly executed. A few days later Hārūn himself died, to be succeeded by al-Amīn as caliph.[73]

With the fall from power of 'Alī b. 'Īsā, the main reason for Khurāsānī support of Rāfi' b. Layth's revolt vanished. As early as 192/807–8, some of his followers, described ambiguously as *shī'a,* defected to Harthama.[74] Ṭāhir b. al-Ḥusayn and 'Abd al-Raḥman al-Naysābūrī came to Harthama's assistance and helped prevent Ḥamza the Khārijite from threatening his army from the south.[75]

Rāfi' was reduced to support from a hard core of Central Asian supporters: Ya'qūbī mentions people from Shāsh, Farghāna, Khujanda, Ushrūsana, Ṣaghāniyān, Bukhārā, Khwārizm, Khuttal, some villages of Balkh and Ṭukhāristān (Bactria), Soghdia, and the Karluk and Dokuz Oğuz Turks.[76] Late in 193/809, Harthama was able to breach the outer wall of Samarqand, thus forcing Rāfi' to take refuge in the inner city. Rāfi' appealed to the Turks for assistance, but once Harthama succeeded in moving his army between Rāfi' and the Turks, the latter simply went away.

Having thus lost the two main sources of its strength—Khurāsānī dissidents and the restive Central Asians—the revolt gradually faded away. There are several contradictory versions of how it terminated. Some sources claim that Harthama stormed Samarqand and killed or captured Rāfi'.[77] Narshakhī reports that al-Ma'mūn solicited the assistance of Asad, son of the Sāmān-khudā, who arbitrated a settlement with Rāfi'.[78] Yet other sources state that once Rāfi' heard reports of al-Ma'mūn's exceptionally just rule in Khurasan, he sought a pardon, which was granted, and went to join al-Ma'mūn.[79]

On this point, the confusion of our sources may be forgiven, for the fate of Rāfi' was overshadowed by a dramatic new conflict over the issues his revolt had helped bring into the open.

AL-AMĪN AND AL-MA'MŪN

The civil war which erupted upon the death of Hārūn al-Rashīd has been the subject of a number of studies, of varying quality, which have depicted it as a conflict over the succession between a rather incompetent, besotted al-Amīn and his shrewdly competent brother al-Ma'mūn; as the product of harem intrigues; as an extension of the personal rivalry between the ministers al-Faḍl b. Rabī' and al-Faḍl b. Sahl; or as a struggle between Arabs and Persians for control of the government.[80] It may have reflected some or all of these factors, but we shall attempt to study it here in the context of the political controversy which had embroiled Khurasan since the days of Abū Muslim and which it finally and definitively resolved.

One is struck forcibly by the frequency of disputes about the succession to the caliphate in the early Abbasid period. Al-Saffāḥ came to power only because of a coup by a faction of Khurāsānī officers; al-Manṣūr had to suppress the revolt of 'Abd Allah b. 'Alī and later deposed 'Īsā b. Mūsā; al-Mahdī deposed 'Īsā a second time in favor of al-Hādī; al-Hādī tried unsuccessfully to prevent the accession of Hārūn al-Rashīd. Khurāsānīs played an important role in each decision; there was, moreover, a remarkable correlation between the succession disputes and the frequency of revolts in Khurasan. While the available evidence does not necessarily *prove* that the two were related, we have tried to suggest that the succession question may have been linked to political considerations regarding the relation of the provinces to the central government and thus the extent of the caliph's powers. In the matter of Hārūn's succession, we are on much firmer ground in showing that this was true.

It will be recalled that Hārūn had nominated al-Amīn as *walī 'ahd* in 175/791–92. Events compelled him to reconsider this, and, in 186/802, after much deliberation and consultation he promulgated a new regulation regarding the succession which was tantamount to a plan for the devolution of the empire. Al-Amīn was confirmed as *walī 'ahd,* to be succeeded by al-Ma'mūn, who subsequently but at his own discretion would be succeeded by a third of Hārūn's sons, al-Qāsim al-Mu'taman. While the institution of the caliphate would thus be retained, its political authority was to be divided among the three sons and would pass to their heirs. Al-Amīn was given Iraq and Syria, al-Qāsim the Jazīra and the marchlands along the Byzantine frontier, and al-Ma'mūn the provinces east of Hamadan. The secular authority of each of the brothers in his own area would be complete and could not be infringed upon by any of the others, whether acting as *amīr* or as caliph.[81]

This arrangement represented an interesting compromise with what seems to have been the aim of the Khurāsānī revolutionaries. It provided for locally responsible officials, but selected them from the royal family rather than setting up unrelated governors whose rule was legitimized by the caliph. It was a reasonable, if idealistic, solution to the problems created by al-Manṣūr's counter-revolution.

It was, alas, unworkable for several reasons. Although al-Amīn had none of al-Manṣūr's abilities, he wanted to be no less of an autocratic caliph. The various beneficiaries of the existing Baghdad regime had no desire to relinquish their control over the rich component parts of the empire. The Khurāsānīs could take little comfort from the promise of future benefits when they were groaning under the burdens imposed by 'Alī b. 'Īsā. The fall of the Barmakīs (who had a leading role in the formulation of this scheme) and the consequent deterioration of the political situation in the east cast further doubt on Hārūn's plans; they were ignored, if not forgotten.

As soon as al-Amīn succeeded to the caliphate, he initiated a series of actions designed to assert his sovereignty over al-Ma'mūn and thus over Khurasan. After hearing that Hārūn, on his death-bed in Ṭūs, had taken steps to confirm al-Ma'mūn's authority in Khurasan, al-Amīn sent an agent, Bakr b. al-Mu'tamir, to keep him informed about his brother's actions. This intrigue was thwarted when Hārūn detected the spy and ordered his execution. With the connivance of al-Faḍl b. Rabī', Bakr's life was spared, and al-Amīn later embarrassed al-Ma'mūn by demanding his release from prison.[82]

The following year (194/809–10), al-Amīn ordered all the prefects of the empire to add the name of his son Mūsā to the Friday prayers, protested the reported pardon of Rāfi' b. Layth, and demanded that al-Ma'mūn's agent in Rayy supply him with choice products from that city. He subsequently demanded tribute, and thus recognition of his sovereignty, from the prefects of Qūmis, Nishapur, and Sarakhs. He then demanded that al-Ma'mūn cede several other Khurāsānī towns to his own dominions, and claimed the right to appoint his own tax agents and an officer of the post (read spy!) in the east. In an act calculated to outrage the Khurāsānīs, he released 'Alī b. 'Īsā from prison and promoted him to high office. We are told that he even went so far as to demand that al-Ma'mūn's wife turn over to him a jewel given her by her husband![83]

The final breach came the next year. Al-Amīn withdrew recognition of al-Ma'mūn's coinage (which no longer bore the caliph's name), dropped his brother's name entirely from the Friday prayers, insisted that his son Mūsā, now styled *al-Nāṭiq bi'l-ḥaqq,* be recognized as *walī 'ahd*—in flagrant violation of Hārūn's will—and finally sent al-Ma'mūn an ultimatum demanding recognition of his authority in all of Khurasan. When al-Ma'mūn refused, al-Amīn ordered the invasion of the province. When the commanding officer of his army refused to obey this violation of Hārūn's instructions, al-Amīn delivered the final insult of naming none other than 'Alī b. 'Īsā as governor of the Jibāl, including Nahāwand, Qumm, Hamadan, and Isfahan, and ordering him to invade Khurasan.[84] If Hārūn had invited a revolt by sending 'Alī to Khurasan, al-Amīn was inviting a full fledged civil war.

While al-Amīn easily brushed aside his father's directives as far as al-Qāsim was concerned, circumstances had placed al-Ma'mūn in a position of formidable strength. He was in Khurasan and in command of the substantial army that had been required to subdue Rāfi' b. Layth and the rebellious Central Asian princes. Coming after 'Alī b. 'Īsā, he was regarded by the Khurāsānīs as a liberator and had their full backing and genuine affection. There is a story that Hārūn, on his deathbed, had summoned the Khurāsānī leaders, including al-Ḥusayn b. Muṣ'ab, the progenitor of the Ṭāhirids, and told them that Amīn's position was weak and that they should be loyal to al-Ma'mūn.[85] In any event, the Khurāsānīs needed little prodding to support al-Ma'mūn; they saw at last the opportunity to achieve the goal of political autonomy for Khurasan, or perhaps even a Khurāsānī-dominated empire, and were not about to give it up. The sources, which are generally partial to al-Ma'mūn, insist that he gave al-Amīn all due respect but, at the instigation of his advisors, resisted all encroachments on his own power and sovereignty in Khurasan.

Following the testimony of al-Faḍl b. Sahl himself,[86] it is possible to point to four steps taken by al-Ma'mūn and his associates to insure that Khurasan would face al-Amīn's challenge united and determined to resist:

(1) Al-Ma'mūn made it clear that 'Alī b. 'Īsā's disastrous taxation policies would be reversed. Not only were his excesses requited; the *kharāj* in future years would be reduced by one quarter and the past year's tax restored. Lest the army fear that this would restrict their income, al-Ma'mūn gave the troops a bonus equivalent to a year's salary.[87]

(2) Steps were taken to restore faith in the competence and justice of the administration. Ma'mūn would hold court in person in the great mosque, surrounded by legists and theologians, to render judgment in disputes brought to his attention. Contacts with the *fuqahā'* were cultivated, and they were assured of the ruler's support for truth, good works, and the *sunna*.[88]

(3) Al-Ma'mūn made a special effort to honor the local leaders and members of the native Iranian aristocracy. Ibn al-Athīr reports that special concessions were made to the rebellious princes, such as "Jīghūyah" (=Jabghūyah/Yabghu?), the Karluk *khāqān,* the king of Kābul, and Atrābanda, thus bringing them into obedience.[89]

(4) Finally, and most interestingly, appeals were made to the various tribal factions in terms designed to recall the principles of the original Abbasid *da'wa:* The Banū Tamīm were reminded of the example of the *naqīb* Mūsā b. Ka'b; the Rab'ī of Abū Da'ūd, the Yaman of Qaḥṭaba, and so on.[90]

The result of all this was that the people of Khurasan were delighted with al-Ma'mūn. They thought of him as their "nephew" and of course a member of the Prophet's family; the sources are filled with praise of his wisdom and judicious behavior.[91]

Thus Khurasan was placated and consolidated. One by one, the notables of Khurasan, led by al-Faḍl b. Sahl, came forward to pledge allegiance to al-Ma'mūn and to plead with him to defend Khurāsānī integrity, often combining their requests with allusions to the time of the *da'wa*. Typical of their position is a remark by Abū 'Alī Hishām that he would swear complete allegiance to al-Ma'mūn, but only for so long as he remained in Khurasan, and that he would expend all his energy, even his life, to prevent al-Ma'mūn from making concessions to al-Amīn.[92]

Consequently, as the conflict between the brothers escalated, al-Ma'mūn dropped al-Amīn's name from the coins he minted, cut communications between Iraq and Khurasan, closed the borders to keep out al-Amīn's spies, and refused to appear in person before the caliph, to give up any of his territory, or to recognize Mūsā as *walī 'ahd*. With the advance of 'Alī b. 'Īsā, the civil war began in earnest.[93]

'Alī b. 'Īsā set out, on or about 15 Jumādā II 195 (3 March 812), at the head of a force of 40,000 to 60,000 men, so confident of victory that he carried a silver chain with which to bring back al-Ma'mūn. Al-Amīn accompanied the army as far as Nahrāwān, where he harangued the men and made some conciliatory gestures to the Khurāsānīs. Three days later, the army marched to Hamadan and thence towards Rayy. For his part, al-Ma'mūn named Ṭāhir b. al-Ḥusayn governor of Qūhistān and ordered him to occupy Rayy in order to block 'Alī's advance. This Ṭāhir did. His army, variously numbered at 3,800 to 20,000, was, to a remarkable degree, Iranian in composition—in its ranks were seven hundred Khwārizmīs and officers like Mikā'il, Sabsal, Da'ūd Shāh, al-Rustamī, and Muhammad b. Muṣ'ab—but it could better be considered essentially Khurāsānī in nature.

After the customary pre-battle speeches and challenges to individual combat, the engagement with 'Alī commenced. Amīn's army was completely routed; the body of 'Alī b. 'Īsā was found on the field of battle, and his head sent off to Khurasan with the announcement of the victory. The news made the people of Khurasan delirious with joy, and they immediately hailed al-Ma'mūn as caliph.[94]

Upon receiving news of the disaster, the unfortunate al-Amīn seized al-Ma'mūn's property in Baghdad, beat back as best he could the revolts which were flaring up all around him, and sent a second army under 'Abd al-Raḥman al-Abnāwī (or al-Anbārī) to Hamadan. Ṭāhir, meanwhile, expelled the prefects appointed by al-Amīn from Qazvīn and the Jibāl before marching out to meet 'Abd al-Raḥman.

The subsequent battle was much more bitterly contested than the one at Rayy; 'Abd al-Raḥman was ultimately compelled to seek refuge inside the city. After a few days of recuperation, he attempted to break out, encouraging his men with haughty remarks about the mere *'ajam* opposing them. Ṭāhir was again victorious, and proceeded to clamp a tight siege around Hamadan. As supplies dwindled, and since he feared the people of Hamadan might rebel, 'Abd al-Raḥman sought and obtained an armistice from Ṭāhir. Shortly thereafter, reinforcements arrived from Baghdad, so 'Abd al-Raḥman treacherously launched a surprise attack on Ṭāhir's forces which inflicted heavy casualties. In the end, Ṭāhir's men recovered the momentun and slaughtered 'Abd al-Raḥman's troops unmercifully. The remnants of his army fled in confusion all the way back to Baghdad. Ṭāhir occupied the heights of Ḥulwān and awaited orders from al-Ma'mūn authorizing him to invade Iraq.[95]

Although al-Amīn would raise yet another army, our story properly ends with the battle of Hamadan. It would be both tedious and unnecessary to attempt to detail all the events, important though they may be, which followed the fall of Hamadan and which occurred for the most part outside Iran: the fierce fighting in Iraq, the march on Baghdad, the siege of the capital, and the murder of al-Amīn (198/813).

Suffice it to say that the complete victory of Ma'mūn, Faḍl b. Sahl, Ṭāhir, and the Khurāsānīs constituted an event of enormous magnitude. It shattered the sacrosanct aura which had surrounded the person of the Abbasid caliphs: For the first time, an Abbasid ruler had been humiliated and put to death by rebellious subjects. It brought some real racial antipathy to the surface of political affairs: The supposed "Persian-ness" of al-Ma'mūn and his followers alarmed the anti-*shu'ūbī* factions. It threatened to turn the existing imperial system topsy-turvy: It appeared that Iraq would suddenly become no more than a province of Khurasan. At the same time, it accelerated separatist tendencies in other provinces: Revolts broke out in Egypt, Syria, the Jazīra, Ādharbayjān, and Ṭabaristān. In short, it challenged the very basis of the Islamic polity and ushered in a turbulent period of innovation and experimentation, which culminated in al-Ma'mūn's startling proclamation of the 'Alid 'Alī b. Mūsā al-Riḍā as heir apparent.[96]

The radical drift of affairs provoked a wave of reaction. Some of al-Ma'mūn's more moderate followers were shocked by the murder of al-Amīn and subsequent events. Harthama b. A'yan broke with Ṭāhir and attempted to "warn" al-Ma'mūn of the turmoil which was brewing; for his trouble, he was executed. Various minor revolts flared up in Iraq and the west, including the unabashedly anti-Persian revolt led by Naṣr b. Shabath. But by far the most virulent center of discontent was in the imperial metropolis, the area most directly harmed by the collapse of the old imperial system and al-Ma'mūn's efforts to make Merv the new capital city. The revolt of the "Volunteers," including people of Khurāsānī descent in the Ḥarbiyya quarter of Baghdad, expressed a militant popular unrest, which continued to smoulder in the form of aggressive Ḥanbalism. The higher social classes, including members of the Abbasid family, posed a more direct challenge to al-Ma'mūn by proclaiming Ibrāhīm b. al-Mahdī as counter-caliph.

These reactionary developments finally compelled al-Ma'mūn to make some concessions. Conveniently, al-Riḍā died from eating a surfeit of grapes (poisoned, according to the Shi'ites). After consulting with the Khurāsānī nobles (*mulūk*),[97] al-Ma'mūn returned to Baghdad to take charge of affairs. Finally, al-Faḍl b. Sahl, that "Magian and son of a Magian" who was anathema to the factions in Iraq, was murdered in his bath at Sarakhs.

It should not be thought, however, that al-Ma'mūn capitulated completely to the desires of the people of Iraq. Shi'ism was abandoned, but Mu'tazilism took its place as a favored state doctrine. Outspoken critics of the new regime such as Aḥmad b. Ḥanbal and his partisans were kept in check through a veritable inquisition (the *miḥna*).[98]

Throughout, one crucial achievement of the revolution remained unchallenged. It had permanently changed the political balance between the caliphs of Baghdad and the province of Khurasan (and thus, ultimately, all the constituent parts of the empire). Once he left Khurasan, al-Ma'mūn inevitably had to choose between his role as political leader of the Khurāsānīs and his duties as caliph. However reluctantly, he delegated power in the province to a governor, Ghassān b. 'Abbād.

This arrangement was not enough to satisfy the Khurāsānīs, despite al-Ma'mūn's undoubted popularity. Signs of trouble appeared at once. The people of Herat murdered one of their prefects.[99] The grandson of Yūsuf al-Barm led a brief insurrection.[100] Local leaders built up and employed private armies for their own purposes; 'Abd al-Raḥman al-Naysābūrī and his "volunteer" army, for example, sought to deal with the Khārijites from Sīstan on their own initiative.[101]

It was against this background that al-Ma'mūn decided, in 205/820–21, to appoint Ṭāhir b. al-Ḥusayn as governor of Khurasan.[102] Even though it is claimed Ṭāhir won this post through various intrigues, al-Ma'mūn had clearly been confronted with the possibility of renewed agitation in Khurasan and must, in any case, have known what the consequences of this extraordinary appointment would be. It was not comparable in any sense to the previous appointment of Ghassān. Ṭāhir, the Abū Muslim and the Qaḥṭaba of the second Abbasid revolution, was a man of unusual ability who had a real base of power in Khurasan. Like Abū Muslim, Ṭāhir did not behave as a "governor" of Khurasan, but as its legitimate ruler. As is well known, he went so far as to mint coins in his own name and to omit mention of the caliph in the *khuṭba*. It is said that this prompted al-Ma'mūn to have Ṭāhir murdered, but this is difficult to believe in view of his continued recognition of Ṭāhirid rule in Khurasan. In any event, it did nothing to disturb the new relationship between Khurasan and the central government, since the province's autonomy and fiscal integrity were maintained.

Thus, the significance of the appearance of the Ṭāhirids should not be underestimated.[103] The first hereditary, autonomous Muslim dynasty in Khurasan had come into being, not because of the momentary weakness of the caliph who legitimized it, but as the result of a century of continuous struggle.

1. On this incident, see Balādhurī, *Ansāb,* f. 320b; Tab., 3:128; IA, 5:498; Bal'amī/Zotenberg, 4:320; Ibn Khaldūn, *'Ibar,* 3:396; Ibn Taghrībirdī, *Nujūm,* 1:339; Sibṭ/Topkapi, 7:183a; Gardīzī, *Zayn,* p. 123; *Ghurar,* f. 173b; Maqdisī, *Bad',* 6:85; Fasawī, *Ta'rīkh,* f. 5a; Ḥamza, *Ta'rīkh,* p. 162; and Maqrīzī, *al-Muqaffa' al-kabīr*/Fonds arabes 2144, f. 99a–b.

2. Balādhurī, *Ansāb,* f. 320b; cf. Maqrīzī, *al-Muqaffa' al-kabīr*/Fonds arabes 2144, f. 99a–b.

3. Tab., 3:107.

4. Balādhurī, *Ansab,* f. 320b. Fasawī, *Ta'rīkh,* f. 5a, also implies that Abū Da'ūd was murdered but does not say by whom; Maqrīzī, *al-Muqaffa' al-kabīr*/ Fonds arabes 2144, f. 99a–b, claims that al-Manṣūr sent Abū 'Aṣṣām to stir up the soldiers against Abū Da'ūd.

5. Tab., 3:128; Bal'amī/Zotenberg, 4:320 is similar but makes no mention of a revolt. The similarity of this incident to the Rāwandī uprising is striking.

6. *Ghurar,* f. 173b; Maqdisī, *Bad',* 6:83.

7. Gardīzī, *Zayn,* p. 123.

8. Tab., 3:128; Ḥamza, *Ta'rīkh,* p. 162.

9. On 'Abd al-Jabbār, see Tab., 3:128, 134–5; IA, 5:505–6, Ibn Kathīr, 10:76–77; Ibn Ḥazm, *Jamharat,* p. 385; Ḥamza, *Ta'rīkh,* p. 162; Balādhurī, *Ansāb,* ff. 320b–321a; Bal'amī/Zotenberg, 4:377–80; Ya'qūbī, *Historiae,* 2:445; *idem, Pays,* p. 129; *Fragmenta,* p. 228; Ibn al-Faqīh, p. 310; *Ghurar,* f. 173b; Ibn Taghrībirdī, *Nujūm,* 1:340; Ibn Khaldūn, *'Ibar,* 3:396–97; *Mujmal,* p. 330; Jāḥiẓ, *Bayān,* 2:111; Sibṭ/Topkapi, 7:183a, 186a–b; Dhahabī, *Islām,* 6:2–3; Faṣīḥ, *Mujmal-i faṣīḥī,* 1:213; Fasawī, *Ta'rīkh,* f. 5a; 'Aynī, *'Iqd,* 7:171a; Ibn al-Jawzī, *Muntaẓam,* 8:13b; Gardīzī, *Zayn,* pp. 123–24; and Ḥāfiẓ-i Abrū, *Geography,* f. 99a. See also S. Moscati, "La Rivolta di 'Abd al-Ġabbār contro il Califfo al-

Manṣūr," *RRAL* vol. 8, no. 2(1947):613–15; and Omar, *'Abbāsid Caliphate,* pp. 204–8.

10. Tab., 3:128; IA, 5:498; and Sibṭ/Topkapi, 7:183a. Bal'amī/Zotenberg, 4:370, adds the name of Ḥarb b. Ziyād, a Persian of Ṭālaqān; Ḥāfiẓ-i Abrū, *Geography,* f. 99a says he killed many noble Arabs; and Ya'qūbī, *Historiae,* 2:445 gives the same names but describes them as Hāshimites.

11. Ya'qūbī, *Historiae,* 2:445; *Fragmenta,* p. 228; *Ghurar,* f. 173b; cf. Balādhurī, *Ansāb,* f. 321a; Dhahabī, *Islām,* 7:2.

12. *Ghurar,* f. 173b; Gardīzī, *Zayn,* p. 123; Balādhuri, *Ansāb,* f. 321a; Ḥamza, *Ta'rīkh,* p. 162.

13. Balādhurī, *Ansāb,* f. 321a–b. This fascinating account claims that 'Abd al-Jabbar, egged on by an astrologer who said he would become a great king, broke with al-Manṣūr, persecuted the Hāshimites, and finally sided with the 'Alīds. It describes how he had a *mawlā* named Yazīd preach against al-Manṣūr and recite tales about the caliph's persecution of the 'Alīds, which moved the people to tears and caused them to join the revolt.

14. Gardīzī, *Zayn,* p. 123, describes the victims as *'ayyār,* a difficult term which currently means scoundrels but apparently refers in early texts to a kind of urban bourgeoisie.

15. Tab., 3:134; Bal'amī/Zotenberg, 4:378–80; Dhahabī, *Islām,* 7:3; and Balādhurī, *Ansāb,* f. 321a.

16. Tab., 3:134; *Fragmenta,* p. 228; and Balādhurī, *Ansāb,* f. 321a.

17. *Ghurar,* f. 173b; Balādhurī, *Ansāb,* f. 321a; and Gardīzī, *Zayn,* pp. 123–24.

18. This account of the campaign represents a brief summary of several sources which disagree about almost every detail: Tab., 3:134–5; Gardīzī, *Zayn,* pp. 123–24; IA, 5: 505–6; Ibn Ḥazm, *Jamharat,* p. 385; Ibn Khaldūn, *Ibar,* 3:397; Bal'amī/Zotenberg, 4:380; and Balādhurī, *Ansāb,* ff. 321a–b. The name of the commander is given as Abū 'Awn, Usayd b. 'Abd Allah, etc.

19. Gardīzī, *Zayn,* p. 124; *Fragmenta,* pp. 228–29; Ya'qūbī, *Historiae,* 2:446; Jāḥiẓ, *Bayan,* 2:111; Ibn al-Jawzī, *Muntaẓam,* 8:14a; and Tab., 3:135 (and sources which follow him).

20. On 'Īsā, see Tab., 3:331–52, 471–76; IA, 5: passim, 6:44–45; Ya'qūbī, *Historiae,* 2:457–58; Azdī, *Mawṣil,* pp. 159, 200–201; *Ghurar,* f. 191a; 'Awfī/Banū Muṣaffā, *Javāmi',* Isfahānī, *Aghānī,* 15:30–34, 17:150; *Fragmenta,* pp. 257–60, 268–71; *Ḥabīb al-siyar,* 2:207, 212–24, 221; Bal'amī/Zotenberg, 4:421–30; and Kūfī, *Futūḥ,* f. 236b.

21. Abū Ḥātim, *Zīna,* p. 299; see also Kūfī, *Futūḥ,* f. 236b; *Ḥabīb al-siyar,* 2:207; and above, Chapter IV.

22. Bal'amī/Zotenberg, 4:421.

23. *Ibid.;* cf. Tab., 3:345; and Azdī, *Mawṣil,* pp. 200–201.

24. Ya'qūbī, *Historiae,* 2:457–58.

25. Tab., 3:338, 351.

26. Ya'qūbī, *Historiae,* 2:457.

27. Elias, *Chronographie,* p. 110.

28. Gardīzī, *Zayn,* p. 124.

29. Ya'qūbī, *Historiae,* 2:465.

30. Tab., 3:371; IA, 5:610; and Ibn al-Jawzī, *Muntaẓam,* 8:76a–b.

31. Tab., 3:371; IA, 6:44–45; Ya'qūbī, *Historiae,* 2:476; *Fragmenta,* p. 271; *Ḥabīb al-siyar,* 2:221; and Sibṭ/Topkapi, 7:262b–263a.

32. For a fascinating discussion between al-Mahdī and his advisors concerning their problems in Khurasan, see Ibn 'Abd Rabbih, *'Iqd,* 1:191–212.

33. Yūsuf's revolt is amply documented, though the various accounts tend to be brief and repetitive. See Tab., 3:470–71; IA, 6:43; Ibn Kathīr, 10:131; Ibn Khaldūn, *'Ibar,* 3:360; Kutubī, *'Uyūn,* 6:67a; Sibṭ/Topkapi, 8:1b–2a; Ibn al-Jawzī, *Muntaẓam,* 7:106a; Isfahānī, *Aghānī,* 6:47; Ibn 'Abd Rabbih, *'Iqd,* 6:213; Ya'qūbī, *Historiae,* 2:478–79; *idem, Pays,* p. 131; Jahshiyārī, *Wuzarā',* p. 278; Khalīfa, *Ta'rīkh,* p. 459; Bar Hebraeus, *Mukhtaṣar,* p. 176; 'Aynī, *'Iqd,* 8:26a; Maqdisī, *Bad',* 6:98; *Annales,* f. 29b; and Gardīzī, *Zayn,* pp. 126–27. For secondary studies, see T. K. Kadyrova, "K izacheniya kharaktera vosstaniya Yusufa al-Barma," in *Obshchestvennye Nauki u Uzbekistane* (Tashkent, 1964), 1:46–56; Ḥaqīqat, *Nahḍathā,* p. 266; Sadighi, *Mouvements,* pp. 174–75; Barthold, Turkestan, p. 198; S. Moscati, "Studi storici sul califatti di al-Mahdī," *Orientalia* 14(1945):331–32.

34. Moscati, "al-Mahdī," p. 331.

35. Ya'qūbī, *Historiae,* 2:478; cf. Gardīzī, *Zayn,* p. 126. His association with Thaqīf might arouse suspicion that his revolt was a reaction to the appointment of Mu'ādh b. Muslim, a *mawlā* of Rabī'a, over Khurasan (see Ya'qūbī/Wiet, *Pays,* p. 131).

36. IA, 6:43; Ibn Khaldūn, *'Ibar,* 3:360; and Gardīzī, *Zayn,* p. 126.

37. Maqdisī, *Bad',* 6:98.

38. Isfahānī, *Aghānī,* 6:47; and Ibn 'Abd Rabbih, *'Iqd,* 4:213.

39. These details are pieced together from Tab., 3:470–71; IA, 6:43; Ya'qūbī, *Historiae,* 2:478–79; and Ibn Khaldūn, *'Ibar,* 3:360. Khalīfa, *Ta'rīkh,* p. 459, gives the commander's name as Sa'īd b. Salm.

40. Tab., 3:471; Sibṭ/Topkapi, 8:2a; and Kutubī, *'Uyūn,* 6:67a. Ṭabarī and Kutubī note that many of Yūsuf's companions (*aṣḥāb*) were brought to trial along with him.

41. IA, 6:43; Ibn Khaldūn, *'Ibar,* 3:360; and Ya'qūbī/Wiet, *Pays,* p. 131. Their description might be strengthened if we read al-Barm as meaning "the discontent," though this need not imply any sectarian significance.

42. Jahshiyārī, *Wuzarā',* p. 278.

43. Maqdisī, *Bad',* 6:98.

44. Ya'qūbī, *Historiae,* 2:478.

45. Tab., 3:470; IA, 6:43; Sibṭ/Topkapi, 8:106a; *Annales,* f. 29b; Kutubī, 'Uyūn, 6:67a.

46. Gardīzī, *Zayn,* p. 127; cf. Tab., 3:517; IA, 6:73; Ḥamza, *Ta'rīkh,* p. 164; Ibn Ḥazm, *Jamharat,* p. 204; and Ibn Qutayba, *Ma'ārif,* p. 413. The disturbances may have been related to his new coinage; see Barthold, *Turkestan,* p. 205. In any event, the uproar over taxation was so severe that al-Mahdī was forced to convene a special assembly to discuss the situation; the proceedings are preserved in Ibn 'Abd Rabbih, *'Iqd,* 1:191–212.

47. Gardīzī, *Zayn,* p. 127.

48. Ya'qūbī, *Historiae,* 2:488.

49. Gardīzī, *Zayn,* p. 129; Fasawī, *Ta'rīkh,* f. 18b; and Narshakhī/Frye, *Bukhara,* pp. 35–37. On the controversial coinage of Ghiṭrīfī *dirhams*, see also Sam'ānī, *Ansāb,* f. 410a; H. Sauvaire, *Materiaux pour servir a l'histoire de la*

numismatique Musulmane (Paris, 1882), s. v. Ghiṭrīfī; Mehmet Ağa Oğlu, "An Observation on the Alloy of the Ghiṭrīfī Coins," *American Numismatic Society, Museum Notes* 1(1945):101–104; and R. N. Frye, *Notes on the Early Coinage of Transoxiana* (New York, 1949), pp. 41–49.

50. Tab., 3:631–37; IA, 6:145; Ya'qūbī, *Historiae,* 2:492; Ibn Khaldūn, *'Ibar,* 3:467–68; Ibn Taghrībirdī, *Nujūm,* 2:92; *Tārīkh-i alfī,* f. 263b; and Sibṭ/Topkapi, 8:75b. See also Sourdel, *Vizirat,* pp. 145–47.

51. Dīnawarī, *Akhbār,* p. 390.

52. For a representative selection of material on 'Alī, see Tab., 3:648–49, 702, 713–24; IA, 6:150–51, 163, 203–5; *Fragmenta,* pp. 311–15, 322–25; Ibn al-Jawzī, *Muntaẓam,* 9:47a ff.; Ya'qūbī, *Historiae,* 2:510; *idem, Pays,* pp. 133–34; Ḥamza, *Ta'rīkh,* p. 165; Dīnawarī, *Akhbār,* pp. 396–98 (one of the few relatively uncritical accounts); 'Awfī/Ramaḍānī, *Javāmi',* pp. 61–62; Jahshiyārī, *Wuzarā',* p. 228; Bal'amī/Zotenberg, 4:460, 465, 470; and Gardīzī, *Zayn,* pp. 131–32 (surprisingly favorable to 'Alī).

53. For a few classic examples, see 'Awfī, *Javāmi',* f. 207b; and Bayhaqī, *Tārīkh,* pp. 536–37, 541–43.

54. Tab., 3:648–49; IA, 6:163; Bal'amī/Zotenberg, 4:460; Ibn al-Jawzī, *Muntaẓam,* 9:47a; etc.

55. Sources: Tab., 3:649–51; IA, 6:164, 166, 168, 174; Bal'amī/Zotenberg, 4:460; Ibn Khaldūn, *'Ibar,* 3:469–70; Azdī, *Mawṣil,* p. 303; Sibṭ/Topkapi, 8:100b, 103a, 105b; Dhahabī, *Islām,* 5:223b; *idem, Duwal,* p. 85; Ibn Taghrībirdī, *Nujūm,* 2:116, 119; 'Aynī, *'Iqd,* 8:86a; Ibn Kathīr, 10:186–87; Azdī, *Akhbār al-duwal,* f. 111a; Kutubī, *'Uyūn,* 6:170b; Faṣīḥ, *Mujmal-i faṣīḥī,* 1:247; *Annales,* f. 58b; *Tārīkh-i alfī,* f. 265b; Khalīfa, *Ta'rīkh,* p. 493; Maqdisī, *Bad',* 6:103; Ibn al-Jawzī, *Muntaẓam,* 9:47a, 49a, 54b, 57a–b; Ḥāfiẓ-i Abrū, *Geography,* f. 200a.

56. Bal'amī/Zotenberg, 4:460; Ḥāfiẓ-i Abrū, *Geography,* f. 200a.

57. *Tārīkh-i alfī,* f. 265b.

58. Tab., 3:701–4; IA, 6:191; Ibn Khaldūn, *'Ibar,* 3:470; Ibn Taghrībirdī, *Nujūm,* 2:127; Ibn Kathīr, 10:201; Jahshiyārī, *Wuzarā',* p. 228; Bal'amī/Zotenberg, 4:470; Sibṭ/Topkapi, 8:125b–126a; and Kutubī, *'Uyūn,* 7:25b. See also the anecdote in 'Awfī/Ramaḍānī, *Javāmi',* pp. 61–62.

59. Ya'qūbī, *Historiae,* 2:510. R. N. Frye, *The Golden Age of Persia* (London, 1975), p. 188 describes Rāfi' as a Barmakī protege and says they appointed him governor of Transoxiana. This is certainly plausible, and would tend to confirm our thesis, but I have been unable to identify the source for his statement.

For material on Rāfi', see Tab., 3:707–8, 712, 734, 775, 777; IA, 6:203–5, 208–10, 225, 229; *Fragmenta,* pp. 311–15; Kūfī, *Futūḥ,* ff. 256a–b; *Tārīkh-i alfī,* f. 268a; Kutubī, *'Uyūn,* 7:28b–29a; Dīnawarī, *Akhbār,* p. 391; *Fakhrī,* p. 193; 'Awfī/Banū Muṣaffā, *Javāmi',* pp. 316–25; Ibn Khaldūn, *'Ibar,* 3:487–88; *Ḥabīb al-siyar,* 2:244–45; Azdī, *Akhbār al-duwal,* f. 114a; Maqdisī, *Bad',* 6:107; Bar Hebraeus, *Mukhtaṣar,* p. 130; *Annales,* f. 69a; Jahshiyārī, *Wuzarā',* pp. 228, 273–75; Mīrkhwānd, 3:443; Ibn Ḥazm, *Jamharat,* p. 184; Ya'qūbī, *Historiae,* 2:515; *idem, Pays,* pp. 133–34; Ibn al-Jawzī, *Muntaẓam,* 9:95b; Ibn Qutayba, *Ma'ārif,* p. 382; Dhahabī, *Islām,* 5:227b; *idem, Duwal,* pp. 87–88; Narshakhī/Frye, p. 76; *Mujmal,* p. 348; and Faṣīḥ, *Mujmal-i faṣīḥī,* 1:255–57.

60. Bal'amī/Zotenberg, 4:471; cf. sources in n. 59.

61. Tab., 3:707–8; IA, 6:195; Bal'amī/Zotenberg, 4:471–72; *Fragmenta,* p. 311; Ibn Taghrībirdī, *Nujūm,* 2:132; Ibn Khaldūn, *'Ibar,* 3:487; Sibṭ/Topkapi, 8:132a–b; Mīrkhwānd, 3:345; *Tārīkh-i alfī,* f. 268a; and *Ḥabīb al-siyar,* 2:244.

62. *Annales,* f. 69a; Ibn Ḥazm, *Jamharat,* p. 184.

63. Bal'amī/Zotenberg, 4:472.

64. Kūfī, *Futūḥ,* f. 256a.

65. Dīnawarī, *Akhbār,* p. 391.

66. *Mujmal,* p. 348.

67. See Ibn Qutayba, *Ma'ārif,* p. 382; Jahshiyārī, *Wuzarā',* p. 228; Kutubī, *'Uyūn,* 7:28b–29a; and Azdī, *Mawṣil,* p. 311.

68. Tab., 3:712; IA, 6:205; Sibṭ/Topkapi, 8:139a; Khalīfa, *Ta'rīkh,* p. 495; and Azdī, *Mawṣil,* p. 311.

69. Bal'amī/Zotenberg, 4:472.

70. Kūfī, *Futūḥ,* f. 250a; Dīnawarī, *Akhbār,* p. 391.

71. Tab., 3:712, 718; Bal'amī/Zotenberg, 4:472.

72. Tab., 3:713–27; Ya'qūbī, *Historiae,* 2:515; *Fragmenta,* pp. 313–14; and Bal'amī/Zotenberg, 4:473–74. It is typical of the problem of biases in the sources that Bal'amī/Zotenberg, 4:472, says that 'Alī attempted to defend Balkh but was defeated, while Tab., 3:713, indicates he turned tail and ran after his son's death.

73. Tab., 3:733–34, 764; IA, 6:212; Sibṭ/Topkapi, 8:145a; Bal'amī/Zotenberg, 4:476–78; Dhahabī, *Islām,* 5:244a; *idem, Duwal,* p. 82; Ibn Khaldūn, *'Ibar,* 3:488; Ibn Taghrībirdī, *Nujūm,* 2:142; Ibn Kathīr, 10:212; Mas'ūdī, *Prairies,* 6:358; Kutubī, *'Uyūn,* 7:48b–49a; *Fragmenta,* pp. 315–16; and Jahshiyārī, *Wuzarā',* pp. 274–75.

74. Tab., 3:732; IA, 6:208; and Kutubī, *'Uyūn,* 7:50b.

75. IA, 6:209.

76. Ya'qūbī, *Historiae,* 2:528.

77. IA, 6:209 (but 229 contradicts this); Gardīzī, *Zayn,* p. 133 (but cf. p. 71); and Bal'amī/Zotenberg, 4:480.

78. Narshakhī/Frye, *Bukhara,* p. 76.

79. Tab., 3:777; *Fragmenta,* p. 322; IA, 6:229; Azdī, *Mawṣil,* p. 322; Ya'qūbī, *Historiae,* 2:529; Ibn Khaldūn, *'Ibar,* 3:491–92; Ibn Kathīr, 10:224–25; and Khalīfa, *Ta'rīkh,* p. 503. Kūfī, *Futūḥ,* f. 256a, says Hārūn offered Rāfi' a pardon and the governorship of Khurasan, but Rāfi' refused it.

80. The primary sources for this are too extensive to give more than a selected sample: Tab., 3:765–74, 776–94, 795–950; IA, 6:222, 225, 227–35; Dīnawarī, *Akhbār,* pp. 393–400 (noteworthy for its rather favorable account of al-Amīn and 'Alī b. 'Īsā); Ya'qūbī, *Historiae,* 2:529–32; *Mujmal,* pp. 348–52; Kūfī, *Futūḥ,* ff. 261a–265b; Quḍā'ī, *'Uyūn,* f. 93b; Ibn al-Jawzī, *Muntaẓam,* 10:7a–27b; Azdī, *Mawṣil,* pp. 322–30; Ibn Khaldūn, *'Ibar,* 3:493–514; Mas'ūdī, *Prairies,* 6:415–83; Maqdisī, *Bad',* 6:107–9; Michael the Syrian, pp. 26–29; *Fakhrī,* pp. 211–15; Khalīfa, *Ta'rīkh,* pp. 503–6; *Fragmenta,* pp. 320–44; and Gardīzī, *Zayn,* pp. 70–73, 133–34.

For secondary studies and further references, see F. Gabrieli, "La Successione di Hārūn al-Rašid e la guerra fra al-Amīn e al-Ma'mūn," *RSO* 11(1926–8):341–97; S. B. Samadi, "The Struggle Between the Two Brothers al-Amīn and al-Ma'mūn," *Islamic Culture* 32(1958):99–120; Watt, *Formative Period,* pp. 117–19; W. Muir, *The Caliphate* (Edinburgh, 1898; reissued Beirut, 1963), pp. 489–97; and M. Shaban, *Islamic History A. D. 750–1055* (Cambridge, 1976), pp. 37–50 (notable for its emphasis on the political dimensions of the conflict).

81. See Tab., 3:655–62; *Fragmenta,* pp. 303–5; Kūfī, *Futūḥ,* f. 254a–b; IA,

6:173–74; Ya'qūbī, *Historiae,* 2:501–9; Azraqī, *Akhbār makka,* ed. Wüstenfeld (Leipzig, 1858), pp. 161–68; Mas'ūdī, *Prairies,* 6:324–26; Gabrieli, "Successione," p. 344; and Shaban, *Islamic History II,* pp. 39–40.

82. Tab., 3:765–66; *Fragmenta,* pp. 317–18; and IA, 6:222.

83. Ya'qūbī, *Historiae,* 2:529.

84. On these provocations, see Tab., 3:776 sqq., 797 sqq.; Bal'amī/Zotenberg, 4:482–83; IA, 6:227 sqq.; Ya'qūbī, *Historiae,* 2:528–30; Dīnawarī, *Akhbār,* pp. 394–96; Kūfī, *Futūḥ,* f. 261a–b; Gardīzī, *Zayn,* p. 71; Sibṭ/Topkapi, 8:165b–169a; Dhahabī, *Islam,* 5:295b; Azdī, *Mawṣil,* p. 319; and Ibn Qutayba, *Ma'ārif,* p. 384. Note that Ibn Khallikān, 2:470, claims 'Alī was appointed only after al-Ma'mūn had attempted to invade Iraq!

85. Tab., 3:771; Azdī, *Mawṣil,* p. 318. This tradition is, of course, intended to legitimize al-Ma'mūn's assumption of the caliphate.

86. Tab., 3:773–74; Jahshiyārī, *Wuzarā',* pp. 227–29; cf. IA, 6:223–25.

87. Azdī, *Mawṣil,* p. 318; Tab., 3:771–72, 774; IA, 6:225; Bal'amī/Zotenberg, 4:480, 483; Jahshiyārī, *Wuzarā',* p. 279; Gardīzī, *Zayn,* p. 71; see also Sourdel, *Vizirat,* pp. 198–99.

88. Bal'amī/Zotenberg, 4:480; Gardīzī, *Zayn,* p. 71.

89. IA, 6:232; Tab., 3:815–16; and Balādhurī, *Futūḥ,* p. 431.

90. Jahshiyārī, *Wuzarā',* p. 279; Tab., 3:774.

91. Azdī, *Mawṣil,* p. 318; Tab., 3:774; and Jahshiyārī, *Wuzarā',* p. 279. The Persian sources are especially fulsome: See Bal'amī/Zotenberg, 4:480; Bayḍavī, *Niẓām al-tavārīkh,* ed. B. Karīmī (Tehran, 1313/1935), p. 53; Juzjānī, *Ṭabaqāt,* 1:113; and Ibn Isfandiyār/Browne, *Ṭabaristān,* p. 143. This should be contrasted with the caustic appraisal of Maqrīzī, *Nizā',* p. 80.

92. IA, 6:229–30.

93. Tab., 3:222–25; Mas'ūdī, *Prairies,* 6:119–20. On the coinage, see Henri Lavoix, *Catalogue des monnaies musulmanes de la Bibliothèque Nationale* (Paris, 1887), 1:204–6.

94. Tab., 3:798–826 (especially 800, 819, 825); IA, 6:239–45; Ya'qūbī, *Historiae,* 2:530–31; Bal'amī/Zotenberg, 4:484; Dīnawarī, *Akhbār,* p. 397; *Fragmenta,* p. 314, Kūfī, *Futūḥ,* f. 261b; Azdī, *Mawṣil,* pp. 322–23; Ibn al-Jawzī, *Muntaẓam,* 10:7a–b; Ibn Khallikān, 1:650; Ibn Khaldūn, *'Ibar,* 3:496–98; Azdī, *Akhbār al-duwal,* f. 115a–b; Mas'ūdī, *Prairies,* 6:420; Gardīzī, *Zayn,* p. 71; and Ibn Qutayba, *Ma'ārif,* pp. 384–86.

95. Tab., 3:804, 827–32; IA, 6:245–48; Dīnawarī, *Akhbār,* p. 398; *Fragmenta,* p. 324; Ibn Qutayba, *Ma'ārif,* p. 385; Bal'amī/Zotenberg, 4:485–86; Ya'qūbī, *Historiae,* 2:532; Kūfī, *Futūḥ,* f. 262a; Ibn Khaldūn, *'Ibar,* 3:498–99; and Gardīzī, *Zayn,* p. 72.

96. A full appreciation of these events and policies will require a considerable amount of further research. On the *shu'ūbī* problem, cf. I. Goldziher, *Muhammedanische Studien* (Halle, 1889–90), trans. S. Stern, *Muslim Studies* (London, 1967), 1:*passim;* H. A. R. Gibb, "The Social Significance of the Shu'ūbiya," *Studia Orientalia Ioanni Pedersen dicata* (Copenhagen, 1953), pp. 105–14; Ḥ. Mumtaḥin, *Nahḍat-i shu'ūbiyyah* (Tehran, 1354/1976); and Roy Mottahedeh, "The Shu'ūbiyya Controversy and the Social History of the Early Islamic Iran," *IJMES* 7(1976):161–82. The *shu'ūbī* controversy was primarily a literary and a bureaucratic dispute rather than a racial or national one; however, it did have some racial overtones, particularly at a popular level and among such Arab rebels as Naṣr b.

Shabath. On the official promotion of Shi'ism, see Hamdi Sidqi, "The Pro-'Alid Policy of al-Ma'mūn," *Majallat kulliyat al-adab wa'l-'ulūm fī baghdād* 1(1956):96–105; D. Sourdel, "La Politique religieuse du calife 'abbaside al-Ma'mūn," *REI* 30(1962):27–48; and F. Gabrieli, *Al-Ma'mūn e gli 'Alidi* (Leipzig, 1929).

97. Ya'qūbī/Wiet, *Pays,* p. 136 (text, p. 307).

98. On Faḍl and his murder, see Sourdel, *Vizirat,* pp. 196–213; on the significance of the *miḥna,* see W. M. Patton, *Aḥmed ibn Ḥanbal and the Miḥna* (Leiden, 1897); and M. O. Abusaq, *The Politics of the Miḥna* (dissertation; Edinburgh, 1971: publication forthcoming, Leiden).

99. Faṣīḥ, *Mujmal-i faṣīḥī,* 1:325–26.

100. Ya'qūbī, *Historiae,* 2:546.

101. See Tab., 3:1043–44; IA, 6:361 (which implies that this was tantamount to revolt); *Fragmenta,* pp. 360–61; *Aghānī,* 14:37–38; and Bosworth, *Sīstān Under the Arabs,* p. 102.

102. On the appointment, see Tab., 3:1039–44; IA, 6:360–62; Shābushtī, *Diyārāt,* pp. 145–47; Ya'qūbī, *Historiae,* 2:554–55; *idem*/Wiet, *Pays,* pp. 136–37; *Fragmenta,* pp. 360–62; Ibn Abī Ṭāhir, *Baghdād,* pp. 58–67. Sourdel, *Vizirat,* pp. 222–23; and Shaban, *Islamic History 2,* pp. 50–52. For more general accounts of the Ṭāhirids, see Mongi Kaabi, "Les Origines Ṭāhirides dans le *da'wa* 'abbāside," *Arabica* 19(1972):145–64; D. Sourdel, "Les Circonstances de la mort de Ṭāhir ler au Ḥurāsān," *Arabica* 5(1958):66–69; G. Rothstein, "Zu aš-Šābuštī's Bericht über die Tahiriden," in *Orientalische Studien zu Theodor Nöldeke gewidmet* (Giessen, 1906), pp. 155–70; C. E. Bosworth, "The Ṭāhirids and Arabic Culture," *Journal of Semitic Studies* 14(1969):45–79; *idem,* "The Ṭāhirids and Persian Literature," *Iran* 7(1969):103–6; *idem,* "An Early Arabic Mirror for Princes: Ṭāhir Dhu'l-Yamīnain's Epistle to his Son 'Abdallah (296/821)," *Journal of Near Eastern Studies* 29(1970):25–41; and S. Nafīsī, *Tārīkh-i khāndān-i ṭāhirī* (Tehran, 1335/1956).

103. For a rather different assessment of the Ṭāhirid achievement, which emphasizes their enthusiasm for Arabic culture and the correctness of their relationship with the caliphs, see C. E. Bosworth, "The Ṭāhirids," in *Cambridge History of Iran,* 4:90–106.

CHAPTER SIX

Conclusion

Perhaps the most striking aspect of the Abbasid revolt was the sheer magnitude of the movement in Khurasan. Anticipating many modern principles of revolutionary tactics, the period of the *da'wa* offers a classic example of the way to seize power. There was nothing spontaneous or undirected about the Abbasid revolt; it was the product of more than thirty years of meticulous preparation. We have seen that the *imām* and a small cadre of close associates carefully planned the movement's strategy. Training, discipline, and secrecy were the watchwords as they controlled the activities of a number of "cells" scattered throughout Khurasan. Under their direction, professional agitators sought out recruits for the movement and encouraged popular discontent.

The missionaries accomplished this by addressing themselves to local issues, by employing many vague slogans, and by preaching what Lenin might have called "simplified truths." They appeared to collaborate with other insurrectionary organizations in Khurasan, most notably the Zaydīs, but they did not hesitate to sacrifice or to crush these potential rivals whenever it was expedient. The populace perceived the Abbasids as supporters of a number of contradictory causes, but only the innermost circles of the movement knew the real goals (which remain as mysterious to us as to the Abbasids' contemporaries). In this way, the Abbasids maximized support for the revolt in Khurasan. Their great achievement was not so much that they overthrew the Umayyad dynasty (which collapsed almost on its own), but that they were able to exploit and to control so vast a movement at precisely the right moment.

In other words, the Abbasid revolt in Khurasan was just what historians have been most reluctant to call it: a true mass uprising. This is a fact of some importance. The revolt involved or affected virtually the entire province. Many different groups, with many different ideas, participated in it. Many different issues converged when the revolt erupted. This, of course, makes it dangerous to generalize in interpreting the revolt. It has been characterized as a revolt of Iranians against Arabs, of the non-Arab Muslims, of an Arab faction in Merv. It was all of these, and none of them. To appreciate the real significance of the revolt, one should not be misled by a single set of issues or the propaganda of the moment. Rather, one should consider the whole environment of the revolt, and, above all, its consequences.

The most lasting aspect of the revolt was its enormous impact on the social structure of Khurasan. It helped resolve many of the difficulties which had arisen from the disruption of the developing feudal society by the Arab invasion and thus to lay the foundations of a new social order. It is therefore useful to inquire which segments of society benefited from the revolution, and which suffered.

In addition to the ruling Umayyad elite and the "alien" Syrian troops in Khurasan, the chief opponents of the Abbasid revolt were the members of the Iranian *haute noblesse*. This class had been under attack from the Sassanid monarchy, but the shāhs were less successful in Khurasan than elsewhere in breaking the power of the upper aristocracy. The Arab conquest gave the great nobles a further opportunity to strengthen their positions. It was they who arranged the peace agreements with the Arabs, who cooperated closely with them in governing the province, who supported their campaigns in Central Asia.

When the revolt came, the nobles by and large remained loyal to the Umayyads. The assisted in detecting and punishing the Abbasid missionaries,[1] and later they fought alongside the Umayyads to suppress what they saw as a dangerous popular uprising. Some of them probably fell victim to the jacquerie described in apocalyptic overtones by non-Muslim sources, when "the slaves in Khurasan, set on by Abū Muslim, slew their masters in one night and equipped themselves with their weapons, horses, and money."[2] Others were slain in combat or were perhaps among the "chiefs" of Khurasan massacred at Nahāwand. Those who remained in Khurasan became the targets of Abbasid reprisals: The Bukhār-khudā was murdered and other Central Asian nobles were either killed or replaced by more pliant substitutes. Still others, such as Bunyāt b. Ṭughshāda, lost their lives after joining anti-Abbasid revolts.

There are, of course, a few examples of nobles who accommodated themselves with the Abbasids, but they do not seem to have been particularly trusted: Turār-khudā participated in the campaign against Ustādhsīs, but was kept safely in the rear-guard. In a sense, the Abbasid attack on the Iranian aristocracy was a continuation of Sassanid policy and a prelude to the formation of a more centralized empire. However, it is tempting to speculate that it was also part of an effort to break up the great estates owned by the nobles in order to accommodate well-to-do Arabs who wished to become landowners. On this the sources are silent.

It must be emphasized that these comments do not apply to the *dahāqīn,* or lesser nobility. They owned small landholdings, not great estates, and they generally lived on their land, not as absentee landlords in city palaces. Consequently, their interests were quite different from those of the great nobles and very similar to those of the Arab chiefs who had acquired villages throughout Khurasan. Moreover, the Umayyads generally oppressed the *dahāqīn,* especially Naṣr b. Sayyār, who sought to end the *dahāqīn*'s function as tax collectors. At first, they were more inclined to support rebels like al-Ḥārith b. Surayj than the Abbasids (they were perhaps suspicious about some of the movement's popular aspects), but eventually they joined the Abbasid movement. In the words of one source, they flocked to Islam in the days of Abū Muslim.[3] It is not altogether clear what the Abbasids offered the *dahāqīn,* but it does seem safe to say that the *dahāqīn,* including their Arab counterparts, were a dominant element in the new regime. This group's devotion to local interests, a kind of Khurāsānī patriotism, would, however, present political problems for the Abbasid central government, especially after the death of Abū Muslim.

The Abbasids made a special effort to win the support of the artisan and merchant classes in Khurasan. Members of these classes were among the most conspicuous, in a sense the most "respectable," participants in the Abbasid movement. Apparently, they furnished many key members of the inner circles of the *da'wa.*

This does not mean that the urban classes were somehow the natural allies of the Abbasids. The Abbasids had to win their support and were very much in competition with the Umayyads in doing so. The initial strength of the Abbasids was in the countryside, and in case after case the cities had to be won over by protracted struggle, either through violent action or by persuasive propaganda campaigns. Once the revolt in Khurasan was completed, the Abbasids lavished attention on the cities to promote their development—and to consolidate the support of the urban population. The cities were no longer to be simply military bastions, administrative centers, residences for the rich, or conglomerations of villages. Under Abbasid auspices, the cities became much more complex entities. Abū Muslim, for example, sponsored the construction of markets, mosques, and other public buildings in Merv, Nishapur, and elsewhere. Somewhat paradoxically, then, the victory of the small landholding class in Khurasan was accompanied by the florescence of a great urban civilization, and it is the alliance of these two segments of society in Abbasid times which might serve as the hallmark of the new, "Muslim," society in Khurasan.

Certainly, one of the most important ways in which the Abbasids built up an urban base of support was by appealing to a kind of "religious class" closely associated with the artisans and merchants in the cities. This was always characteristic of their dealings with the urban population. As we have seen, the Abbasids encouraged religious activities and addressed themselves directly to this new "aristocracy of the pious" by sending professional theologians (*mutakallimīn*) into the cities to persuade the citizens that Abbasid rule would somehow be more compatible with the precepts of the Koran and the *sunna* of the Prophet than Umayyad rule. The Umayyads retaliated in kind and benefited by pointing out that the Abbasids tolerated some less than "orthodox" (syncretistic) religious beliefs when dealing with their rural supporters. In the end, the religious leaders supported the Abbasids and, in return, their prestige and power increased enormously.

The rise of this Muslim religious class corresponded with the final collapse of the priestly class which had existed in pre-Islamic Iran. The Mazdakite struggle had greatly discredited the Zoroastrian clergy, and the Arab conquest had further weakened their position. Nor was the Zoroastrian ecclesiastical hierarchy very adept at making use of the syncretistic religious movements: One of our last glimpses of them came as they encouraged the suppression of the Bihāfarīdiyya. Still, it would be interesting to know to what extent the new Muslim religious class had roots among the old Zoroastrian clergy. Unfortunately, the question is unresolved and, given the nature of the evidence, probably unresolvable.

Finally, one must not underestimate the role of the peasants and the poorer classes in the Abbasid movement. Though there is no provable connection between the Mazdakite agitation and the Abbasid *da'wa,* the Khidāsh episode did demonstrate that rural discontent, expressed in the guise of heterodox religious ideas, was still a potent factor in Khurāsānī affairs. The Abbasids recognized this, but some factions within the movement were reluctant openly to exploit the disaffection of the masses. They feared, quite rightly, that this would be counter-productive in that it would antagonize the more important landowning and urban classes the *du'āt* were endeavoring to win over. One of Abū Muslim's greatest accomplishments, and a mark of his genius, was his ability to bring the "slaves," "vagabonds," and other social outcasts into the movement without alienating more conservative partisans and without losing control of the movement as a whole. Despite the problems caused by Bihāfarīd, Abū Khālid, and other renegades, Abū Muslim continued to hold together this coalition throughout his tenure in Khurasan.

After Abū Muslim's murder, the peasants realized that the revolution would never fulfill their utopian dreams. It had brought no apparent amelioration of their condition (except that they may have been freer to leave the land), and in some ways actually inaugurated an era of even greater oppression. Without the shāh or the nobles to balance their interests against those of the small landowners, the peasants were leaderless and helpless. The Abbasids were free to implement their policies of centralization and the advancement of urban civilization at peasant expense; despite the *ghulāt* opposition, they subjugated the remaining traditional peasant communities and consolidated their hold on the countryside.

This lasted at least until the rise of the Ṭāhirids. Ṭāhir b. al-Ḥusayn argued that the cultivators of the soil should be treated with respect and justice, and his successors won a reputation as protectors of the peasantry.[4] Of course, the extent to which this concern for the peasants was actually practiced by the Ṭāhirids is an altogether different question, which we cannot attempt to answer here. For our purposes, the important point is that the peasants who helped bring about the success of the Abbasid revolution profited very little from it, and rural discontent remained a serious problem throughout the early Abbasid period.

There was a strong political dimension to the Abbasid revolt in Khurasan, and political controversy persisted throughout the period after Abū Muslim's death. The Abbasid revolutionaries in Khurasan, concerned with local needs and committed to a degree of regional autonomy, clearly wanted to limit the political power of the caliph and thus the central government. On the other hand, they did not want to destroy the ideal of a united Muslim community, nor to relapse into the anarchy which had plagued the Umayyad administration. Therefore, they emphasized the charismatic nature of the caliphate (especially in religious matters) but used the office of vizir as a check on the caliph and government bureaucracy; they vested considerable power in Abū Muslim as governor of Khurasan; and they established a degree of Khurāsānī control over the affairs of the eastern portion of the empire. However, they had not reckoned on the determination of al-Manṣūr and his supporters in Iraq to create a highly centralized empire headed by an authoritarian caliph.

The balance of power temporarily rested with the central government, but it was steadily eroded by the persistent spirit of Khurāsānī particularism and by the incompetence and corruption of some of the provincial officials. A debate over the relations between the central government and the provinces, especially Khurasan, was carried on at the very center of the empire as well as the periphery, and the controversy finally erupted into violence. The Islamic empire, as conceived by the Abbasids, proved too large, too complex, and too diverse to maintain; ultimately the forces of fragmentation triumphed.

The appearance of the Ṭāhirid dynasty in Khurasan marked the end of the Abbasid dream of a universal empire. In its place arose a loose federation of more or less autonomous Muslim states, and the chief function of the caliph became what the Khurāsānī rebels had originally wanted: legitimization and regulation of the competing feudalistic interests in the provinces.

There is, as we have seen, abundant evidence of the political and social transformations taking place in Khurasan during the Abbasid period. These, however, were only the symptoms of change, and it is much more difficult to demonstrate what underlying forces motivated them. Everything from national pride to religious enthusiasm has been suggested to explain the events of this turbulent period of history. A definitive answer is perhaps impossible, but certainly the economic factors of taxation and fiscal policy are crucial to an understanding of what was happening in Khurasan.

It must be admitted quite frankly that our knowledge about Islamic taxation is still hampered by many difficulties: the inherent inadequacies of the source material, the puzzling and seemingly inconsistent meanings of various technical terms, variations in practices from one locality to another, discrepancies between theory and practice, anachronisms, fluctuations in the value of the currency,[5] and so on. Without pretending to have resolved these problems, we may tentatively distinguish several stages of development in the system of taxation in Khurasan which paralleled the social and political developments.

We may assume for the moment that the Sassanids employed the same system of taxation in Khurasan as in other parts of their empire. Originally this was based on a payment of a fixed portion of the harvest, but Qubādh and Anūshīrvān initiated a series of reforms which placed a cash tax on the land rather than the harvest. The various sources depict this as a great boon for the peasants, and Christensen concurs with this judgment.[6] However, it is obvious that such a system would far more benefit the state, by producing a steady source of revenue, than it would landowners and peasants, who would be adversely affected if there was a poor crop or other fall in income. By establishing this new system, the Sassanid rulers were able to raise enormous sums to finance their various projects. It is difficult to believe that this basic fiscal change, which would have had far-reaching repercussions on the existing social structure, and the almost simultaneous Mazdakite uprising were unconnected.[7]

The internal disorders in Iran which preceded the Arab conquest may have permitted the people of Khurasan to prevent full implementation of the Sassanid tax reforms. In any case, the Arab conquest itself produced a new situation in Khurasan. The Arabs, who were initially rather naive about long-term fiscal policies, first imposed a payment of tribute on the subject peoples. The exact amount of tribute collected is unknown, but it was probably between eight and ten million *dirham*s.[8] Later (the exact time is far from certain), the Arabs began to copy the Sassanid system of land-tax to supplement the revenue from tribute. Professor 'Abd al-'Azīz al-Dūrī estimated that in 110/728 tribute (8,000,000 *dirham*s) made up two-fifths of the total revenue from Khurasan (approximately 20,000,000 *dirhams*).[9]

In all probability, the amount of revenue the Arabs extracted from Khurasan was considerably less than the Sassanids had obtained. Yet, paradoxically, there is no question that there was profound resistance to the Arab/Umayyad system of taxation. The sources give the impression that this was directed not at the amount collected but at how it was collected.

The *dahāqīn* acted as tax agents. They were supposed to take tribute only from non-Muslims, but they were reluctant to release converts from the obligation to pay tribute, since they were responsible for collecting a fixed amount (as opposed to a *per capita* sum). Thus, a situation arose in which Muslim converts, and even some Arabs who had become peasants, had to pay tribute. This is often cited as a major factor in the success of the Abbasid movement, on the grounds that the Umayyads were unwilling to lose the revenue from tribute, while the pietists insisted that the government encourage religious conversion by releasing converts from the duty of paying tribute. Nevertheless, it seems to have been a bogus issue. First, the tribute was only a small portion of the total revenue. Second, even if converts were released from paying tribute, they would then be responsible for almsgiving (*zakāt, ṣadaqa*), which may very well have imposed a heavier tax burden. Finally, the Umayyads repeatedly issued orders to correct these abuses, culminating in Naṣr b. Sayyār's fiscal reform in Khurasan. Far greater disaffection would have resulted from the increased importance of the land-tax as income from tribute declined. It is more likely that Umayyad attempts to survey the land, draw up cadasters, and enforce the land-tax led to dissent than their alleged impiety.

If the Umayyads were not particularly adept at making the change from an economy based on tribute to one based on land-tax, the Abbasids excelled at it. They were quick to claim that they were instituting a system of taxation more in accordance with the requirements of Islam than the Umayyad system. Written accounts of the attempts to reconcile the land-tax with Islamic theory still exist.[10] They emphasize that the land belonged "to God" (i.e., the caliph and the state) and that all, Muslim or not, who enjoyed its usufruct were obligated to pay the *kharāj*.

Although this was justified by a number of *ḥadīth*s, the Abbasids were really the heirs of the Sassanid system. Their dreams of empire and their patronage of urban civilization depended, as had the Sassanids', on the efficient transfer of surplus production into their hands. The land-tax was the chief source of this revenue, and the Abbasids created a corps of professional tax-agents to collect it and forward it directly to the central government. Despite its legitimization by the jurists, this created new sources of discontent, and complaints about Abbasid tax practices rise like a litany from the sources, not only in Khurasan but from all over the empire, from Muslims as well as non-Muslims.

As we have seen, protests in Khurasan over the imposition of new and unjust taxes were quite common. The amount of tax collected was only one of several reasons for this. Such reports as are available indicate that the revenue from Khurasan in the time of Hārūn al-Rashīd was 28,000,000 *dirhams* plus various material goods, somewhat more than had been collected under the Umayyads but not disproportionate to what was being collected in other provinces.[11] But there are factors, beyond the amount, which must be considered:

(1) Virtually all of the Abbasid revenues in Khurasan now came from *kharāj,* tax on land. Hence, it is probable that more people than before were responsible for paying taxes, and certain that discontent persisted among the land-owners and rural population.

(2) These taxes had originally been assessed in a debased coinage, but the Abbasids demanded that the taxes be paid in the best available currency. It will be remembered that two governors of Khurasan minted new coins which had to be used when paying taxes. This was tantamount to an increase in taxation, and it provoked much unrest.

(3) Some Abbasid officials were notoriously corrupt and collected far more than the assessed tax-rate in order to enrich themselves. Even if the claim that ʻAlī b. ʻĪsā amassed a personal fortune in excess of 80,000,000 *dirhams* is exaggerated, it certainly makes the point. It is possible that such abuses were more severe in a remote province like Khurasan than closer to the center.

(4) Finally, and most importantly, revenue from Khurasan flowed freely to Iraq, but there is little evidence that much flowed back to meet local needs. This led to a controversy over the fiscal responsibility of the central government which penetrated to the very highest levels of the administration.

Recently, M. A. Shaban has attempted to depict the Barmakid family as the leading advocates of economic oppression,[12] but the facts are otherwise. As we have seen, the Barmakids stood for moderate taxation and attention to local needs; al-Faḍl's governorship of Khurasan was a model of this, just as that of ʻAlī b. ʻĪsā was an example of the most flagrant abuses. The fall of the Barmakids and subsequent events demonstrated that the Abbasids had opted for an imperial system of taxation, and this brought about the great upheaval in Khurasan at the end of the second century A. H. The Abbasid empire was neither the first nor the last in the Middle East to founder on the shoals of fiscal abuse.

In the economic sphere, as in the political and social, the advent of the Ṭāhirids coincided with fundamental change. The most obvious Ṭāhirid achievement was in keeping revenue from Khurasan in

Khurasan, to use for Khurāsānī needs. True, the Ṭāhirids probably sent some of their income to the caliphs as the price for legitimization of their rule in Khurasan, but there is no reason to accept the common assumption that the Ṭāhirids merely collected the *kharāj* to forward to the central government as previous governors had done. It is quite clear that the Ṭāhirids maintained control over Khurāsānī finances, and Ya'qūbī explicitly states that the Ṭāhirids spent the revenue from Khurasan "as they pleased."[13] Not only did the Ṭāhirids stop the excessive drain of wealth from Khurasan to Iraq, but they received 13,000,000 *dirhams* from Iraq (where the family owned various estates). In short, the political autonomy of the Ṭāhirids was accompanied by economic independence.

There was one negative aspect to the Ṭāhirid tax system. Estimates of their revenues vary from 38,000,000 to 48,000,000 *dirhams*, a dramatic apparent rise over revenue collected under either the Umayyads or the Abbasids. This is not to be completely explained by increased prosperity or by changes in the tax-rate. The Ṭāhirids enjoyed the privilege of collecting taxes from many areas outside Khurasan proper: 10,000,000 *dirhams* from Rayy; 6,776,000 from Sīstān; 2,296,000 from Qūmis, 10,176,800 from Jurjān; 5,000,000 from Kirmañ; perhaps 3,000,000 from Transoxiana.[14] If these figures are correct, the Ṭāhirids must actually have *decreased* taxation in Khurasan. This could very well explain how the Ṭāhirids won their reputation as protectors of the rural population. In a sense, they purchased social tranquility in Khurasan at the expense of adjacent areas. Inevitably, this kind of mini-imperial system involved the Ṭāhirids in protracted military activity, especially in Sīstān, and was thus probably a major factor in the eventual overthrow of the dynasty.

We may conclude by suggesting that, ultimately, the intention of al-Manṣūr and his immediate successors to absorb Khurasan into a large, cosmpolitan, centralized empire proved as impractical as the Umayyad effort to govern that province through a segregated mercenary elite. Regional particularism and rural unrest accompanied an ever-closer association of military and administrative authorities with landed estates, an alliance of urban interests with the local landholding elite (rather than with a centralized monarchy), and the consequent subjugation of the countryside to the city. The thrust of Khurāsānī history was thus towards a greater degree of feudalization, which was expressed in political fragmentation and the appearance of petty dynasties. The early Abbasids, like the Umayyads, fought this tide of history, but al-Ma'mūn and the Ṭāhirids rode it to success.

1. For example, Tab., 3:1503.

2. Wellhausen, *Arab Kingdom,* p. 534 (based on Theophanes, *Chronographia,* p. 654). As we have seen, a number of Muslim and non-Muslim sources hint at such a massacre, but are not as explicit as Theophanes.

3. Abū'l-Qāsim al-Muẓaffar b. 'Alī, known as Ibn Abī Ṭāhir, *al-Mukhtaṣar fī'l-qirānāt,* part of a compendium of manuscripts, British Library, Add. 7473, f. 60a; see V. R. Rosen, review of *Bīrūnī's India, Zapiski Vostochnavo Otdyeleniya Imperatorskevo Russkavo Arkheologischeskavo Obshchestva,* 3(1889):156. Barthold, *Turkestan,* p. 194, suggests that Abū Muslim used the doctrine of *tanāsukh* to win the support of the *dahāqīn,* but this is highly speculative. For some general comments on the role of the *dahāqīn,* see Herbert Mason, "The Role of the Azdite Muhallibid Family in Marw's anti-Umayyad Power Struggle," *Arabica,* 14(1967):191–207.

4. Ṭāhir's famous letter to his son emphasized these points: See Bosworth, "Early Arabic Mirror for Princes," pp. 31, 34–35, 37–38. Many of Ṭāhir's ideas, probably taken from pre-Islamic Persian sources, reappear in later Persian books on statecraft such as those of Niẓām al-Mulk and al-Ghazzālī.

5. For example, the ratio of the *dirham* to the *dīnār* is variously cited at 15:1 to 25:1. One attempt to resolve some of the problems surrounding Islamic taxation in Khurasan that should be noted is 'Abd al-'Azīz al-Dūrī, "Niẓām al-ḍarā'ib fī khurāsān fī ṣadr al-islām," *MMII,* 11(1964):75–87. Unfortunately, whatever detailed information may have been available in the *Kitāb kharāj khurāsān* of Ḥafṣ b. Manṣūr is now lost to us (see Gardīzī, *Zayn,* p. 131; Barthold, *Turkestan,* p. 7).

6. Dīnawarī, *Akhbār,* pp. 71–73; Tab., 1:960–62; and Christensen, *Iran,* p. 366. Cf. Lambton, *Landlord and Peasant,* p. 15; Frye, *Heritage of Persia,* pp. 256–57; and F. Altheim, *Ein Asiatischer Staat* (Wiesbaden, 1954). A somewhat different view is given by Ghirshman, *Iran,* pp. 345–46.

7. The usual interpretation is that the Sassanid tax reforms were designed to defuse the Mazdakite movement, but, it is just as possible that the reforms exacerbated the problem: see Ghirshman, *Iran,* p. 346.

8. This is based on the total of the sums stipulated in the peace agreements recorded by Balādhurī, *Futūḥ,* pp. 403 sqq. It is not known what other revenues were collected during this early period.

9. 'A. Dūrī, "Notes on Taxation in Early Islam," *Journal of the Economic and Social History of the Orient* 17(1974):142.

10. The earliest is Yaḥyā b. Adam (d. 818), *Kitāb al-kharāj,* ed. Aḥmad Shākir (Lahore, 1395/1975) and trans. A. Ben-Shemesh (Leiden, 1958); also, Abū Yūsuf Ya'qūb, *Kitāb al-kharāj,* trans. E. Fagnan, *Le Livre de l'impôt foncier* (Paris, 1921). There are other works, but these two may be considered authentic contemporary documents. Unfortunately, neither devotes any real attention to the situation of the land-tax in Khurasan, and, as noted above, Ḥafṣ b. Manṣūr's work has been lost.

11. There are three basic sources on early Abbasid revenues from Khurasan: Jahshiyārī, *Wuzarā',* pp. 281–88; Ibn Khaldūn/Rosenthal, *al-Muqaddimah,* 1:360; and a note appended to the Rabat manuscript of Khalīfa's *Ta'rīkh,* facsimile reproduction and edition in Ṣāliḥ al-'Alī, "A New Version of the Ibn al-Muṭarrif's List of Revenues in the Early Times of Hārūn al-Rashīd," *Journal of the Economic and*

Social History of the Orient 14(1971):303–10. Spuler, *Iran,* pp. 454–78, summarizes much of the information about taxation in medieval Iran; see also Alfred von Kremer, "Über das Budget der Einnahmen unter der Regierung des Hārūn ar-Rashīd," *Verhandlungen des VII Intern. Orientalisten Congresses* (Vienna, 1887), Sem. section, 1 sqq.

12. Shaban, *Islamic History 2,* pp. 32–39.

13. Ya'qubi/Wiet, *Pays,* p. 138 (text p. 308).

14. These figures are from Ibn Khurradādhbih, *Masālik,* pp. 34–39, and apply to the year 212/827–28. Other material on Ṭāhirid revenues may be found in Tab., 3:1338–39; Qudāma, *Kharāj,* p. 243; and Ya'qūbī/Wiet, *Pays,* p. 138. Maqdisī, *Aḥsan,* p. 340, gives a figure (but no date) which probably applies to the Ṭāhirids.

Bibliography

PRIMARY SOURCES

Abū Dulaf Mis'ar b. Muhalhil. *al-Risāla al-thāniyya*. Edited and translated by V. Minorsky. Cairo, 1955.

Abū'l-Ma'ālī, Muḥammad b. 'Ubayd Allah. *Bayān al-adyān*. Translated by Henri Massé: "L'Exposé des religions." *Revue de l'histoire des religions* 94(1926):17–75.

Abū Nu'aym al-Iṣfahānī. *Dhikr akhbār iṣbahān*. Edited by Sven Dedering: *Geschichte Iṣbahāns*. 2 vols. Leiden, 1931–34.

Abū'l-Qāsim Sa'īd. *Kitāb ṭabaqāt al-umam*. Translated by R. Blachère. Paris, 1935.

Abū Yūsuf Ya'qūb b. Ibrāhīm al-Anṣārī al-Kūfī. *Kitāb al-kharāj*. Translated by E. Fagnan: *Le Livre de l'impôt foncier*. Paris, 1921.

Akhbār al-'abbās wa wuldih. Edited by 'A. al-Dūrī. Beirut, 1972.

'Alī al-Khazrajī, Shams al-Dīn. *al-Kifāya wa'l-i'lām fī man waliya al-yaman*. London: British Library, OR 6941.

'Alī al-Ṭabarī, Abū'l-Ḥasan. *Kitāb al-dīn wa'l-dawla*. Translated by A. Mingana: *The Book of Religion and Empire*. Manchester, 1922.

al-Anbārī, Abū'l-'Abbas 'Abd Allah (?). *Kitāb fīhi uṣūl al-niḥal allatī ikhtalafat fīhā ahl al-ṣalāt*. Bursa: Haraççioğlu Kütüphanesi, #1309. [See also Ess, J. van]

Annales Muslimici A. H. 130–241. London: British Library, Add. 23278. [=Ibn Kathīr?]

al-Ash'arī, Abū'l-Ḥasan 'Alī. *Maqālāt al-islāmiyīn wa ikhtilāf al-muṣallīn*. Edited by M. 'Abd al-Ḥamīd. Cairo, 1969 (two volumes in one).

al-'Aynī, Badr al-Dīn Maḥmūd. *Dawlat banī'l-'abbās wa'l-ṭulūniyīn wa'l-fāṭimiyīn*. Paris: Bibliothèque Nationale, Fonds arabes no. 5761.

———. *'Iqd al-jumān fī ta'rīkh ahl al-zamān*. Istanbul: Topkapisaray Kütüphanesi, Ahmet III no. 2911/b7, a8.

'Awfī, Sadīd al-Dīn Muḥammad. *Javāmi' al-ḥikāyāt va lavāmi' al-rivāyat*. Paris: Bibliothèque Nationale, Fonds persans no. 75.

———. *Javāmi'al-ḥikāyāt*. Edited (lithograph of book 2, parts 11–25) by M. Ramaḍānī. Tehran, 1335/1957.

———. *Javāmi'al-ḥikāyāt*. Edited (book 3, parts 1–25) by Amīr Banū Muṣaffa. Tehran, 1352/1974–1353/1975 (two volumes; continuous pagination).

al-Azdī, ʻAlī b. Ẓāfir. *Akhbār al-duwal al-munqaṭi'a*. London: British Library, OR 3685.

al-Azdī, Yazīd b. Muḥammad. *Ta'rīkh al-mawṣil*. Edited by ʻAlī Ḥabība. Cairo, 1967.

al-Azraqī, Muḥammad b. ʻAbd Allah. *Akhbār makka*. Edited by H. Wüstenfeld. Leipzig, 1858.

Bafqī, Muḥammad Mufīd Mustawfī. *Jāmi'-yi mufīdī* (*Tārīkh-i yazd*). Edited by Iraj Afshār. Tehran, 1342/1964.

al-Baghdādī, ʻAbd al-Qāhir b. Ṭāhir. *Al-Farq bayna'l-firaq*. Edited by M. ʻAbd al-Ḥamīd. Cairo, 1964.

———. *Moslem Schisms and Sects,* part 1. Translated by K. Seelye. New York, 1919.

———. *Moslem Schisms and Sects,* part 2. Translated by A. S. Halkin. Tel Aviv, 1935.

Balādhurī, Aḥmad b. Yaḥyā b. Jābir. *Ansāb al-ashrāf*. Istanbul: Süleymaniye, Reisülküttap 597/8.

———. *Ansāb al-ashrāf,* vol. 2. Edited by M. al-Maḥmūdī. Beirut, 1974. (Section on the ʻAlīds.)

———. *Ansāb al-ashrāf,* vol. IVb. Edited by Max Schloessinger. Jerusalem, 1936.

———. *Ansāb al-ashrāf,* vol. V. Edited by S. D. Goitein. Jersualem, 1936.

———. *Kitāb futūḥ al-buldān*. Edited by M. J. de Goeje. Leiden, 1866.

———. *The Origins of the Islamic State,* part 1. Translated by P. K. Hitti. New York, 1916.

———. *The Origins of the Islamic State,* part 2. Translated by F. C. Murgotten. New York, 1924.

Bal'amī, Abū'l-Faḍl Muḥammad. *Tārīkh* (*Tārīkhnāmah, Tarjumah-yi tārīkh-i ṭabarī*). London: British Library, Add. 23497, Add. 26174, Add. 16814, Add. 7622; Royal Asiatic Society, no. 22; India Office, Ethe 2669, 3315; Istanbul: Aya Sofya, 3049, 3050, 3051; Fātih, 4285; Munich: Bayerischen Staatsbibliothek, Cod. Pers. 253; Tehran: Majlis, 2291; Dānishgāh, Aṣghar Mahdavī Microfilm 1590.

———. *Tārīkh-i ṭabarī* (lithograph). Cawnpore, 1916.

———. *Tarjumah-yi tārīkh-i ṭabarī* (manuscript reproduction). Index by M. Mīnuvī. Tehran, 1344/1966. (Copy of Mashhad: Āstān-i quds, 7481.)

———. *Chronique de Abou-Djafar Mohammed ben Djarir ben-Yezid Tabari*. Translated by H. Zotenberg. 4 vols. Paris, 1867–74.

Balkhī, ʻAbd Allah. *Faḍā'il-i balkh*. Edited by ʻAbd al-Ḥayy Ḥabībī. Tehran, 1350/1972.

Banākitī, Fakhr al-Dīn. *Rawḍat ūlī'l-albāb fī tavārīkh al-akābir va'l-ansāb*. Edited by J. Shi'ār. Tehran, 1348/1970.

Bar Hebraeus (Ibn-ʻIbrī, Abū'l-Faraj). *Mukhtaṣar ta'rīkh al-duwal*. Beirut, 1958.

———. *The Chronography of Bar Hebraeus*. 2 vols. Translated by E. A. Wallis Budge. London, 1932.

Bayḍavī, Nāṣir al-Dīn ʻAbd Allah. *Niẓām al-tavārīkh*. Edited by B. Karīmī. Tehran, 1313/1935.

Bayhaqī, Abū'l-Faḍl Muḥammad. *Tārīkh-i bayhaqī*. Edited by ʻAlī Fayyāḍ. Mashhad, 1350/1971.

al-Bayhaqī, Ibrāhīm b. Muḥammad. *Kitāb al-maḥāsin wa'l-masāwī*. 2 vols. Edited by M. Ibrāhīm. Cairo, 1961.

Bīrūnī, Abū'l-Rayḥān Muḥammad. *Al-Āthār al-bāqiya 'an al-qurūn al-khāliyya*. Translated by E. Sachau: *The Chronology of Ancient Nations*. London, 1879.

al-Dhahabī, Shams al-Dīn Abū 'Abd Allah Muḥammad b. 'Uthmān. *Kitāb duwal al-islām*. Haydarabad, 1364/1945.

———. *Ta'rīkh al-islām*. Istanbul: Topkapisaray Kütüphanesi, Ahmet III no. 2917/4, 5, 6.

al-Dīnawarī, Abū Ḥanīfa Aḥmad b. Da'ūd. *Kitāb al-akhbār al-ṭiwāl*. Edited by A. 'Āmir. Cairo, 1960.

Dionysius of Tell Mahre. *Chronique de Denys de Tell-Mahre*. Edited and translated by J. B. Chabot. Paris, 1895.

Diyarbakrī, Ḥusayn b. Muḥammad. *Ta'rīkh al-khamīs*. 2 vols. Bulaq, 1283/1866.

Elias of Nisibis. *Chronographie de Mar Elie ben Sinaya*. Translated by L. J. Delaporte. Paris, 1909.

Faṣīḥ-i Khwāfī, Aḥmad b. Jalāl al-Dīn. *Mujmal-i faṣīḥī*. 3 vols. Edited by M. Farrūkh. Tehran, 1341/1963.

Fragmenta Historicorum Arabicorum. Edited by M. J. de Goeje. Leiden, 1869–71 (two volumes with continuous pagination; same as *Kitāb al-'uyūn* and Ibn Miskawayh).

Gardīzī, Abū Sa'īd 'Abd al-Ḥajj b. al-Ḍaḥḥāk. *Zayn al-akhbār*. Edited by 'A. Ḥabībī. Tehran, 1347/1969.

al-Ḥamawī, Muḥammad b. 'Alī. *Mukhtaṣar siyar al-awā'il wa'l-mulūk*. Paris: Bibliotheque Nationale, Fonds arabes no. 1507.

Ḥāfiz-i Abrū. *Geography*. London: British Library, OR 1577.

———. *Jughrāfiyā*. Edited by M. Haravī. Tehran, 1349/1970. (All references are to the manuscript rather than the published text.)

———. *Zubdat al-tavārīkh*. Tehran, Majlis 257.

Ḥamza al-Isfahānī. *Ta'rīkh sanī mulūk al-arḍ wa'l-anbiyā'*. Edited by Yūsuf al-Maskūnī. Beirut, 1961.

Hilāl al-Ṣābī. *Rusūm dār al-khilāfa*. Baghdad, 1964.

———. *Tuḥfat al-umarā' aw al-wuzarā'*. Edited by A. Farrāj. Cairo, 1958.

Ḥudūd al-'ālam. Translated by V. Minorsky. London, 1937: reprint, 1970.

Ibn 'Abd Rabbih, Abū 'Umar Aḥmad. *Kitāb al-'iqd al-farīd*. 7 vols. Edited by Aḥmad Amīn, et al. Cairo, 1940–53.

"Ibn Abī Ṭāhir," Abū'l-Qāsim al-Muẓaffar b. 'Alī. *al-Mukhtasar fī'l-qirānāt*. London: British Library, Add. 7473 ff. 59–63.

Ibn Abī Ṭāhir Ṭayfūr, Abū'l-Faḍl. *Baghdād fī ta'rīkh al-khilāfa al-'abbāsiyya*. Baghdad, 1968.

Ibn 'Asākir, Thiqat al-Dīn Abū'l-Qāsim 'Alī. *al-Ta'rīkh al-kabīr*. Damascus, 1909.

Ibn A'tham al-Kūfī. *Kitāb al-futūḥ*. Istanbul: Topkapisaray Kütüphanesi, Ahmet III no. 2956/2. (Edited Haydarabad, 1968–75.)

Ibn al-Athir, 'Izz al-Din. *al-Kāmil*. 14 vols. Edited by C. Tornberg. Reissued Beirut, 1965–67.

Ibn al-Balkhī. *Fārs-nāmah*. Edited by G. LeStrange and R. A. Nicholson. London, 1921 (reprint 1968).

Ibn al-Faqīh, Muḥammad b. Isḥāq. *Kitāb al-buldān*. Edited by M. J. de Goeje. Leyden, 1885.

Ibn Funduq, Abū'l-Ḥasan ʻAlī Bayhaqī. *Tārīkh-i bayhaq*. Edited by A. Bahmanyār. Tehran, 1317/1939 (second edition, 1960).

Ibn Ḥabīb, Muḥammad. *Asmā' al-mughtālīn min al-ashrāf*. Cairo, 1954.

———. *Kitāb al-muḥabbir*. Beirut, 1960.

Ibn Ḥajar al-ʻAsqalānī. *Tahdhīb al-tahdhīb*. 12 vols. Beirut, 1968.

Ibn Ḥawqal, Abū'l-Qāsim. *Kitāb ṣurat al-arḍ*. Translated by J. Kramers and G. Wiet: *Configuration de la terre*. Paris, 1964 (two volumes; continuous pagination).

Ibn Ḥazm, Abū Muḥammad ʻAlī b. Aḥmad al-Andalusī. *Jamharat ansāb al-ʻarab*. Edited by ʻA. Hārūn. Beirut, 1962.

Ibn Ḥazm. *al-Faṣl fi'l-milal wa'l-ahwā' wa'l-niḥal*. 5 vols. Edited by A. Khalīfa, et al. Cairo, 1317/1899–1321/1903 (reprint Baghdad, n. d.).

———. "The Heterodoxies of the Shīʻites in the Presentation of Ibn Ḥazm." Translated by I. Friedlaender. *JAOS* 28(1907):1–80.

Ibn ʻImād, Abū'l-Fallāḥ. *Shadharāt al-dhahab fī akhbār man dhahab*. Cairo, 1350/1931–1351/1933.

Ibn Isfandiyār, Muḥammad b. al-Ḥasan. *Tārīkh-i Ṭabaristān*. Edited by ʻAbbas Iqbāl. Tehran, 1320/1944.

———. *History of Ṭabaristān*. Abridged translation by E. G. Browne. London, 1905.

Ibn al-Jawzī, ʻAbd al-Raḥman b. ʻAlī. *Excerpta Historica*. London: British Library, Add. 5928.

———. *al-Muntaẓam fi ta'rīkh al-mulūk wa'l-umam*. London: British Library, Add. 7320; Istanbul: Topkapisaray Kütüphanesi, Ahmet III no. 2908/8, 9, 10, 11.

———. *Talbīs Iblīs*. Beirut, n. d.

Ibn Kathīr, ʻImād al-Dīn Ismāʻīl. *al-Bidāya wa'l-nihāya*. 14 vols. Cairo, 1932–39.

Ibn Khaldūn, ʻAbd al-Raḥman. *Kitāb al-ʻibar*. 6 vols. Beirut, 1956–59.

———. *The Muqaddima*. 3 vols. Translated by Franz Rosenthal. London, 1967 (second edition).

Ibn Khallikān, Aḥmad. *Wafāyāt al-aʻyān*. Translated by M. de Slane: *Biographical Dictionary*. 4 vols. London, 1842–71.

Ibn Khurradādhbih, Abū'l-Qāsim. *Kitāb al-masālik wa'l-mamālik*. Edited by M. G. de Goeje. Leiden, 1889.

Ibn Miskawayh, Abū ʻAbd Allah Aḥmad. *Kitāb tajārib al-umam wa taʻāqib al-ḥimam*. =*Fragmenta Historicorum Arabicorum*.

Ibn al-Muqaffaʻ. *Āthār ibn al-muqaffaʻ*. Edited by ʻUmar Abū al-Naṣr. Beirut, 1966.

Ibn al-Nadīm, Abū'l-Faraj Muḥammad. *Kitāb al-Fihrist*. Translated by Bayard Dodge: *The Fihrist of al-Nadim*. New York, 1970 (two volumes; continuous pagination).

Ibn Qutayba, Abū Muḥammad ʻAbd Allah b. Muslim. *Adab al-kātib*. Cairo, 1958.

———. *Kitāb al-ʻarab*. In M. Kurd ʻAlī, *Jamharat rasā'il al-ʻarab* (Cairo, 1946), pp. 344–77.

———. *Kitāb al-maʻārif*. Edited by Tharwat ʻUkāsha. Cairo, 1969.

———. *Kitāb 'uyūn al-akhbār*. 4 vols. Cairo, 1964.

(Pseudo-) Ibn Qutayba. *Kitāb al-imāma wa'l-siyāsa*. 2 vols. Edited by Ṭaha al-Zaynī. Cairo, 1967.

Ibn Rustah. *Kitāb al-a'lāq al-nafīsa*. Edited by M. J. de Goeje. Leiden, 1892.

Ibn Sa'd, Abū 'Abd Allah. *Kitāb al-ṭabaqāt al-kabīr*. 9 vols. Beirut, 1957–68.

Ibn Taghrībirdī, Abū'l-Maḥāsin. *al-Nujūm al-zāhira fī mulūk miṣr wa'l-qāhira*. 16 vols. Cairo, 1963–72.

Ibn al-Ṭiqṭaqā, Ṣafī al-Dīn. *Kitāb al-fakhrī*. Translated by C. E. J. Whitting: *Al-Fakhrī*. London, 1947.

al-'Imrānī, Muḥammad b. 'Alī. *al-Inbā' fī ta'rīkh al-khulafā'*. Edited by Qāsim al-Sāmarrā'ī. Leiden, 1973.

al-Iṣfahānī, Abū'l-Faraj 'Alī. *Kitāb al-aghānī*. 21 vols. Cairo, 1969–71.

———. *Maqātil al-ṭālibiyīn*. Edited by A. Ṣaqr. Cairo, 1368/1949.

al-Isfarāyīnī, Abū'l-Muẓaffar. *al-Tabṣīr fī'l-dīn*. Edited by Maḥmūd al-Khaḍīrī. Cairo, 1374/1955.

Isfizārī, Mu'īn al-Dīn Muḥammad. *Rawḍat al-jannāt fī awṣāf madīnat harāt*. Edited M. Kāẓim Iman. Tehran, 1959.

Iṣṭakhrī, Abū Iṣḥāq Ibrāhīm. *al-Masālik wa'l-mamālik*. Edited by M. J. de Goeje. Leiden, 1870.

———. *Masālik va mamālik*. Anonymous Persian translation, edited by Īraj Afshār. Tehran, 1347/1969.

al-Jāḥiẓ, Abū 'Uthmān 'Amr b. Baḥr. *al-Bayān wa'l-tabyīn*. 4 vols. Edited by M. Hārūn. Cairo, 1975.

———. *Kitāb al-buldān*. Edited by S. al'Alī. Baghdad, 1970.

———. *Kitāb al-tāj*. Translated by C. Pellat: *Le Livre de la Couronne*. Paris, 1954.

———. *Rasā'il*. 2 vols. Edited by M. Hārūn. Cairo, 1963–65.

Jāḥiẓ. *Risāla fī banī umayya*. In A. Rifā'ī, *'Aṣr al-ma'mūn* (Cairo, 1927), 3:72–80.

———. *Tria Opuscula Auctore*. Edited G. van Vloten. Leiden, 1903 (reprint, 1968).

al-Jahshiyārī, Abū 'Abd Allah Muḥammad b. 'Abdūs. *Kitāb al-wuzarā' wa'l-kuttāb*. Edited by M. al-Saqqā. Cairo, 1357/1938.

Jūzjānī, Minḥaj al-Dīn. *Ṭabaqāt-i nāṣirī*. 2 vols. Edited by 'A. Ḥabībī. Kabul, 1342/1964.

al-Kalbī, Hishām b. Muḥammad. *Jamharat al-nasab*. London: British Library, Add. 23297.

Kāshānī, Jamāl al-Dīn. *Zubdat al-tavārīkh*. Tehran: Dānishgāh, no. 5210.

Kāshānī, Qāḍī Aḥmad. *Tārīkh-i nagāristān*. Edited by M. Gīlānī. Tehran, 1341/1963.

al-Kātib al-Samarqandī, Muḥammad b. 'Alī. *Kitāb aghrāḍ al-siyāsa fī 'ilm al-riyāsa*. Istanbul: Aya Sofya, no. 3844.

al-Kātib, Aḥmad. *Tārīkh-i jadīd-i yazd*. Yazd, 1317/1939.

Khalīfa b. Khayyāṭ, Abū 'Amr. *Ta'rīkh*. Edited by Akram Ḍiyā al-'Umarī. Najaf, 1386/1967 (two volumes with continuous pagination).

al-Khuzā'ī, Nu'aym b. Ḥammād al-Marwazī. *Kitāb al-fitan*. London: British Library, OR 9449.

Khwāfī, Mullā Majd al-Dīn. *Rawḍat al-khuld* (*Kharistān*). Edited by Maḥmūd Farrūkh. Tehran, 1345/1967.

Khwānd-amīr, Ghayāth al-Dīn. *Ḥabīb al-siyar*. 4 vols. Edited by Dabīr Siyāqī. Tehran 1333/1975 (second edition).

———. *Khulaṣat al-akhbār*. London: British Library. OR 1292.

Khwārizmī, Abū 'Abd Allah Muḥammad. *Mafātīh al-'ulūm*. Edited by G. van Vloten. Leyden, 1895.

Kitāb al-'uyūn wa'l-ḥadā'iq fī akhbār al-ḥaqā'iq. =Fragmenta Historicorum Arabicorum.

al-Kutubī, Fakhr al-Dīn Ibn Shākir. *'Uyūn al-tawārīkh*. Istanbul: Topkapisaray Kütüphanesi, Ahmet III no. 2922/6, 7.

al-Māfarrūkhī, al-Mufaḍḍal b. Sa'd b. al-Ḥusayn. *Kitāb maḥāsin iṣfahān*. Edited by Jalal al-Din Tihrānī. Tehran, 1312/1933.

al-Makīn, Jirjis. *al-Ta'rīkh al-mukhtaṣar*. London: British Library, OR 7564.

al-Maqdisī, Muṭahhar b. Ṭāhir. *Kitāb al-bad' wa'l-ta'rīkh*. Edited and translated by C. Huart: *Le Livre de la creation et de l'histoire*. 6 vols. Paris, 1899–1919.

al-Maqdisī,Shams al-Dīn Abū 'Abd Allah. *Aḥsan al-taqāsim fī ma'rifat al-aqālīm*. Edited by M. J. de Goeje. Leiden, 1906.

al-Maqrīzī, Abū'l-'Abbās Aḥmad b. 'Alī. *al-Mawā'iẓ wa'l-i'tibār fī dhikr al-khiṭaṭ wa'l-āthār*. 2 vols. Bulaq, 1294/1877 (reprint Baghdad, n. d.).

———. *Muntakhab al-tadhkira*. Paris: Bibliotheque Nationale, Fonds arabes, no. 1514.

———. *al-Muqaffa' al-kabīr*. Istanbul: Süleymaniye, Pertev Paşa 496; Paris: Bibliotheque Nationale, Fonds arabes, no. 2144.

———. *al-Nizā' wa'l-takhaṣum fīmā bayna banī umayya wa banī hāshim*. Cairo, 1947.

Mar'ashī, Ẓāhir al-Dīn. *Tārīkh-i ṭabaristān va rūyān va māzandarān*. Edited by M. Tasbīḥī. Tehran, 1966.

Mas'ūdī, Abū'l-Ḥasan 'Alī. *Murūj al-dhahab*. Edited and translated by C. A. Barbier de Meynard and A. J. Pavet de Courteille: *Les Prairies d'or*. 9 vols. Paris, 1861–77.

———. *al-Tanbīh wa'l-ashrāf*. Edited by M. J. de Goeje. Leiden, 1894.

Michael the Syrian. *Chronique*. 4 vols. Edited and translated by J. B. Chabot. Paris, 1904.

Mīrkhwānd, Muḥammad b. Khāvand-shāh. *Rawḍat al-ṣafā fi sīrat al-mulūk va'l-khulafā'*. 10 vols. Edited by 'Abbās Parvīz. Tehran, 1338/1959.

Mujmal al-tavārīkh va'l-qiṣaṣ. Edited by M. Bahār. Tehran, 1318/1940.

al-Muqaddamī, Muḥammad b. Aḥmad. *Kitāb al-ta'rīkh wa asmā' al-muḥaddithīn wa kunāhum*. London: British Library, OR 3619.

Murtaḍā b. Dā'ī, Abū Turāb. *Tabṣirat al-'awām*. Edited by 'Abbās Iqbāl. Tehran, 1313/1934.

Muslim al-Laḥjī. *Ta'rīkh*. Paris Bibliotheque Nationale, Fonds arabes, no. 5982.

Narshakhī, Abū Bakr Muḥammad. *Tārīkh-i bukhārā*. Translated by R. N. Frye: *The History of Bukhara*. Cambridge, Mass., 1954.

Nawbakhtī, Ḥasan b. Mūsā. *Firaq al-shī'a*. Translated by M. J. Mashkūr: "Les sectes sī'ites." *Revue de l'histoire des religions* 143(1958):68–78; 144(1958):67–95; 145(1959):63–78.

Nīsābūrī, Abū 'Abd Allah. *Tārīkh-i nīshāpūr*. Edited by B. Karīmī, Tehran, 1339/1960.

Niẓām al-Mulk. *Siyāsat-nāmah*. Translated by Hubert Darke: *The Book of Government*. London, 1960.

Nubdha min kitāb al-ta'rīkh. Facsimile reproduction by P. A. Gryaznevich: *Arabskii anonim XI veka*. Moscow, 1960.

Qazvīnī, Ḥamd Allah Mustawfī. *Nuzhat al-qulūb*. Translated by G. LeStrange. *The Geographical Part of the Nuzhat al-Qulūb*. London, 1915.

———. *Tārīkh-i guzīdah*. Edited by A. Navā'ī. Tehran, 1339/1961.

al-Quḍā'ī, Abū 'Abd Allah Muḥammad. *Nuzhat al-albāb jāmi' al-tawārīkh wa'l-adab*. London: British Library, Add. 23285.

———. *'Uyūn al-ma'ārif*. Istanbul: Topkapisary Kütüphanesi, Ahmet III no. 2898.

Qudāma b. Ja'far, Abū'l-Faraj. *Nabdh min kitāb al-kharāj*. Edited by M. J. de Goeje. Leiden, 1889. (In the edition of Ibn Khurradādhbih, *al-Masālik*.).

Qummī, Ḥasan b. Muḥammad. *Kitāb-i tārīkh-i qumm*. Tehran, 1353/1934.

Rashīd al-Dīn, Faḍl Allah. *Jāmi' al-tavārīkh*. Istanbul: Topkapisaray Kütüphanesi, Hazine 1654; London: British Library, OR 7628.

al-Rāzī, Abū Ḥātim Aḥmad. *Kitāb al-zīna*. In 'Alī Samarrā'ī. *al-Ghuluw wa'l-firaq al-ghāliyya*. Baghdad, 1972 (pp. 247–312).

Sa'd al-Qummī, b. 'Abd Allah al-Ash'arī. *Kitāb al-maqalāt wa'l-firaq*. Edited by M. J. Mashkūr. Tehran, 1963.

al-Ṣafadī, Khalīl b. Aybak. *Kitāb al-wāfī bi'l-wafāyāt*. Edited by H. Ritter, S. Dedering, et al. Istanbul and Wiesbaden, 1949– (in progress).

al-Sahmī, Abū'l-Qāsim Ḥamza. *Tārīkh-i jurjān*. Haydarabad, 1967.

al-Sam'ānī, 'Abd al-Karīm b. Muḥammad. *Kitāb al-ansāb*. Facsimile reproduction by D. S. Margoliouth. London, 1912. (Copy of MS. London: British Library, Add. 23355. An edition is in progress, Haydarabad, 1962– .)

al-Shābushtī, Abū'l-Ḥasan 'Alī. *Kitāb al-diyārāt*. Edited by Kūrkīs 'Awwād. Baghdad, 1386/1966.

al-Shahrastānī, Muḥammad b. 'Abd al-Karīm. *Kitāb al-milal wa'l-niḥal*. 3 vols. Cairo, 1968.

Ṣibt b. al-Jawzī. *Mir'āt al-zamān*. London: British Library, Add. 23277; Istanbul: Topkapisaray Kütüphanesi, Ahmet III, no. 2907/7, 8, 9.

Ṣuvar al-aqālim. London, India Office, Ethe 708. [this corresponds to *Haft Kishvar*, ed. M. Sutūdah. Tehran, 1353/1975. All references are to the manuscript.]

Suyūtī, Abū'l-Fadl 'Abd al-Raḥman. *Ta'rīkh al-khulafā'*. Cairo, 1964.

———. *History of the Caliphs*. Translated by H. S. Jarrett. Calcutta, 1881 (reprint Amsterdam, 1970).

al-Ṭabarī, Abū Ja'far Muḥammad b. Jarīr. *Ta'rīkh al-rusul wa'l-mulūk*. 3 series. Edited by M. J. de Goeje. Leiden, 1879–1901.

al-Tanūkhī, Abū 'Alī al-Muḥassin. *al-Faraj ba'd al-shidda*. Istanbul: Bayezit Kütüphanesi, no. 5067.

———. *Nishwar al-muḥāḍara*. 8 vols. Edited by 'A. al-Shaljī. Beirut, 1971–73.

———. *The Table-talk of a Mesopotamian Judge*. Translated by D. S. Margoliouth. London, 1922.

Ta'rīkh al-dawla al-'abbāsiyya. Istanbul: Bayezit Kutuphanesi, Veliüddin no. 2360.

Ta'rīkh al-khulafā'. Facsimile reproduction. P. A. Gryaznevich. Moscow, 1967.

Tārīkh-i alfī. London: British Library, Add. 16681.

Tārīkh-i sīstān. Edited by M. Bahār. Tehran, 1935.

al-Tha'ālibī, 'Abd al-Malik al-Naysābūrī. *Ghurar akhbār mulūk al-furs*. Edited and translated by H. Zotenberg. Paris, 1900.

———. *The Laṭā'if al-ma'ārif*. Translated by C. E. Bosworth. Edinburgh, 1968.

———. *Thimār al-qulūb*. Edited by M. Ibrāhīm. Cairo, 1965.

al-Tha'ālibī, al-Ḥusayn b.Muḥammad al-Marghanī (?) *Ghurar al-siyar*. Oxford: Bodleian Library, D'Orville 542.

Yaḥyā b. Adam, Abū Zakariyyā. *Kitāb al-kharāj*. Edited by Aḥmad Shākir. Lahore, 1395/1975.

Yāfi'ī, 'Afīf al-Dīn. *Mir'āt al-janān*. 4 vols. Beirut, 1970.

Ya'qūb b. Sufyān al-Fasawī, Abū Yūsuf. *Kitāb al-ma'rifa wa'l-ta'rīkh*. Istanbul: Topkapisaray Kütüphanesi, Revan Köşk 1554; Süleymaniye, Esad 2391.

al-Ya'qūbī, Aḥmad b. Abī Ya'qūb. *Historiae qui dicitur Ibn Wāḍiḥ*. 2 vols. Edited by T. Houtsma. Leiden, 1883.

———. *Kitāb al-buldān*. Translated by C. Wiet. *Les Pays*. Cairo, 1937.

Yāqūt, Shihāb al-Dīn Ya'qūb b. 'Abd Allah. *Irshād al-arīb (Dictionary of Learned Men)*. 7 vols. Edited by D. S. Margoliouth. Leiden, 1907–27.

———. *Mu'jam al-buldān*. 8 vols. Cairo, 1906.

SELECTED SECONDARY SOURCES

Abbott, Nabia. *Two Queens of Baghdad*. Chicago, 1946.

Abusaq, M. "The Politics of the Miḥna." Dissertation, Edinburgh, 1971.

Adham, 'Alī. *Abū Ja'far al-Manṣūr*. Cairo, 1969.

Aḥmad, M. "Dau nābighah: abū muslim khurāsānī va abū ja'far 'abbāsī." *Armaghān* 19(1318/1939):53–61, 100–6.

al-'Alī, Ṣāliḥ. "A New Version of Ibn al-Muṭarrif's List of Revenues in the Early Times of Hārūn al-Rashīd." *Journal of the Economic and Social History of the Orient 14(1971):303*–10.

———. "Istīṭān al-'arab fī khurāsān." *Majallat kulliyat al-adab wa'l-'ulūm fī baghdād* (1958), pp. 36–83.

Āl Yāsīn, M. Ḥ. *Nafā'is al-makhṭūṭāt*. Baghdad, 1964.

Amedroz, H. F. "On the Meaning of the *laqab* al-Saffāḥ as Applied to the First Abbasid Caliph." *JRAS* (1907), pp. 660–63.

Amīn, Aḥmad. *Fajr al-islām*. Cairo, 1928.

Arendonk, C. van. *Les Débuts de l'Imamate Zaidite*. Translated by J. Ryckmans. Leiden, 1960.

Aubin, E. "Le Chi'isme et la nationalité persane." *RMM* 4(1908):457–91.

Aubin, J. "Elements pour l'étude des agglomerations urbaines dans l'Iran médiéval." In A. H. Hourani and S. M. Stern (eds.) *The Islamic City*. Oxford, 1970. Pp. 65–76.

Azizi, Muhsen. *La Domination arabe et l'épanouissement du sentiment national en Iran*. Paris, 1938.

Bari, Adbul-. "Economic Aspects of the Muslim State During Caliph Hisham (AH 105–125/AD 704–743)." (*sic*) *Islamic Culture* 46(1972):297–305.

Barthold, W. *Turkestan v epokhu mongol'skago nashestviia*. Vol. I: *Teksty*. St. Petersburg, 1900.

———. *Turkestan Down to the Mongol Invasion*. 3rd edition. London, 1968.

Beg., M. A. "The 'Serfs' of Islamic Society Under the Abbasid Regime." *Islamic Culture* 49(1975):107–18.

Belyaev, E. A. *Arabs, Islam and the Arab Caliphate in the Early Middle Ages*. Translated by A. Gourevitch. New York, 1969.

Berchem, M. von. *La Propriété territoriale et l'impôt foncier sous les premiers califs*. Geneva, 1886.

Bigg, M. A. J. "The Social History of the Labouring Classes in Iraq Under the Abbasids, 750–1055." Unpublished dissertation. Cambridge, 1971.

Blochet, Edgar. *Le Messianisme dans l'heterodoxie musulmane*. Paris, 1903.

Bosworth, C. E. "An Early Arabic Mirror for Princes: Ṭāhir Dhū'l-Yamīnain's Epistle to his Son 'Abdallāh." *Journal of Near Eastern Studies (1970)*, pp. 25–41.

———. "The Early Islamic History of Ghūr." *Central Asiatic Journal* 6(1961):116–33.

———. *Sīstān Under the Arabs*. Rome, 1968.

———. "The Ṭāhirids and Arabic Culture." *Journal of Semitic Studies* 14(1969):45–79.

Bouvat, L. "Les Barmecides d'après les historiens arabes et persans." *RMM* 20(1912):1–131.

Brockelmann, Carl. *Geschichte der arabischen Literatur*. Leiden, 1934–39.

Browne, E. G. *A Literary History of Persia*. Cambridge, 1956–59.

Cahen, Claude. "La Changeante portée sociale de quelques doctrines religieuses." In *L'Elaboration de l'Islam*. Paris, 1961.

———. "Fiscalité, propriété, antagonismes sociaux en haute Mésopotamie au temps des premiers 'abbāsides d'après Denys de Tell Mahré." *Arabica* 1(1954):136–52.

———. *Mouvements populaires et autonomisme urbain dans l'Asie musulmane du Môyen Age*. Leiden, 1959.

———. "Points de vue sur la 'Révolution abbaside.' " *Revue Historique* (1963), pp. 295–335.

Christensen, Arthur. *L'Iran sous les Sassanides*. Copenhagen, 1944.

———. *Le Regne du Roi Kawadh I et le communisme mazdakite*. Copenhagen, 1925.

Czegledy, K. "Gardīzī on the History of Central Asia (746–780 AD)." *Acta Orientalia* 27(1973):257–67.

Dennett, D. C. *Conversion and the Poll-tax in Early Islam*. Cambridge, Mass., 1950.

———. "Marwān b. Muḥammad." Unpublished dissertation. Harvard, 1939.

Dietrich, A. "Das Politischen Testament des zweiten 'abbāsiden Kalifen al-Manṣūr." *Islam* 80(1952):133–65.

Donaldson, Dwight. *The Shi'ite Religion*. London, 1933.

Dunlop, D. M. *The History of the Jewish Khazars*. Princeton, 1954.

———. "A New Source of Information on the Battle of Talas or Aṭlakh." *Ural-Altaische Jahrbucher* 36(1964):326–30.

al-Dūrī, 'Abd al-'Azīz. *'Aṣr al-'abbāsī al-awwal*. Baghdad, 1945.

———. *Baḥth fī nash'at 'ilm al-ta'rīkh 'ind al-'arab*. Beirut, 1960.

———. "Niẓām al-ḍarā'ib fī khurāsān fī ṣadr al-islām." *MMII* 11(1964):75–87.

———. "Notes on Taxation in Early Islam." *Journal of the Economic and Social History of the Orient*. 17(1974):136–44.

Esin, E. "Ṭarkhān Nīzak or Ṭarkhān Tīrek?" *JAOS* 97(1977):323–31.

Ess, Josef van. *Frühe mu'tazilitische häresiographie*. Beirut, 1971. [See also under al-Anbārī.]

Fahd, T. *Le Shi'isme Imamite*. Paris, 1970.

Fayyāḍ, A. "Abū Muslim Khurāsānī." *Nashrah-yi farhang-i khurāsān* 2(1338/1959):6–8.

Friedlaender, I. "The Heterodoxies of the Shī'ites in the Presentation of Ibn Ḥazm." *JAOS* 29(1908):1–183.

Frye, R. N. "The Abbasid Conspiracy and Modern Revolutionary Theory." *Indo-Iranica* 5(1952–53):9–14.

———, ed. *The Cambridge History of Iran, vol. 4: The Period from the Arab Invasion to the Saljuqs*. Cambridge, 1975.

———. "Notes on the Early Coinage of Transoxiana." New York, 1949.

———. "The Role of Abū Muslim in the 'Abbāsid Revolt." *Muslim World* 37(1947):28–38.

———. "Die Wiedergeburt Persiens um die Jahrtausandwande." *Islam* 35(1960):42–51.

———. *The Golden Age of Persia*. London, 1975.

———. *The Heritage of Persia*. New York, 1963.

Gabrieli, F. *al-Ma'mūn e gli 'Alidi*. Leipzig, 1929.

———. "La Successione di Hārūn al-Rashīd e la guerra fra al-Amīn e al-Ma'mūn." *RSO* 11(1926–28):341–97.

———. "La Zandaqa au Ier siècle abbaside." In *L'Elaboration de l'Islam*. Paris, 1961.

Ghirshman, R. *Iran*. London, 1954.

al-Ghurābī, 'Alī. *Ta'rīkh al-firaq al-islāmiyya*. Cairo, 1948.

Gibb, H. A. R. *The Arab Conquests in Central Asia*. London, 1923.

———. "The Fiscal Rescript of 'Umar II." *Arabica* 2(1955):1–16.

———. "Government and Islam under the Early 'Abbāsids: the political collapse of Islam." In *L'Elaboration de l'Islam*. Paris, 1961.

———. "The Social Significance of the Shu'ūbīya." In *Studia Orientalia Ionni Pedersen dicata*. Copenhagen, 1953. Pp. 105–14.

Goitein, S. D. *Studies in Islamic History and Institutions*. Leiden, 1966.

Goldziher, Ignaz. "Islamisme et Parsisme." *Revue de l'Histoire des Religions* 43(1901):1–29.

———. *Muslim Studies*. Translated by S. Stern. London, 1967.

Grabar, Oleg. "Umayyad Palace and the Abbasid Revolution." *Studia Islamica* 18(1963):5–18.

Guest, R. "A Coin of Abū Muslim." *JRAS* (1932), pp. 54–56.

Ḥaqīqat, 'Abd al-Rafī'. *Tārīkh-i nahḍathā-yi millī-yi īrān*. Tehran, 1348/1969.

Hasan, S. "A Survey of the Expansion of Islam into Central Asia During the Umayyad Caliphate." *Islamic Culture* 48(1974):177–86.

———. "The Expansion of Islam into Central Asia and the Early Turko-Arab Contacts." *Islamic Culture* 44(1970):1–8.

Hasan, H. "Aspects of Shi'ah History." *Muslim World* 47(1957):271–82.

Herzfeld, E. "Khorasan, Denkmalsgeographische Studien zur Kulturgeschichte des Islam in Iran." *Islam* 11(1921):107–74.

Hill, D. R. *The Termination of Hostilities in the Early Arab Conquests.* London, 1971.

Hinds, G. M. "The Early History of Islamic Schisms in Iraq." Unpublished dissertation. Exeter, 1968.

Hitti, P. K. *History of the Arabs.* 8th edition. New York, 1963.

Hodgson, M. "How Did the Early Shi'a Become Sectarian?" *JAOS* 75(1955):1–13.

———. *The Venture of Islam.* Chicago, 1974.

Housseini, A. M. "The Umayyad Policy in Khorāsān and its Effect on the Formulation of Muslim Thought." *Journal of the University of Peshawar* 4(1955):1–21.

Houtsma, T. "Bihafrid." *WZKM* 3(1889):30–37.

Hughes, Thomas. *A Dictionary of Islam.* London, 1885.

Iqbāl, 'Abbās. *Tārīkh-i īrān as ṣadr-i islām tā istilā'-yi mughul.* Tehran, 1939.

Ivanow, W. "Early Shi'ite Movements." *Journal of the Bombay Branch of the Royal Asiatic Society* 17(1941):1–23.

Jafri, S. "The Early Development of Legitimate Shi'ism." Unpublished dissertation. London, 1966.

Kaabi, Mongi. "Les Origines Ṭāhirides dans le *da'wa* 'abbāside." *Arabica* 19(1972):145–64.

Kadyrova, T. K. "K izacheniya kharaktera vosstaniya Yusufa Barma." In *Obshchestvennye Nauki u Uzbekistani.* Tashkent, 1964. 1:46–50.

Kharbūṭlī, 'Alī. *al-Mahdī al-'abbāsī.* Cairo, 1966.

Klima, O. *Mazdak: Geschichte einer sozialen Bewegung im sassanidischen Persien.* Prague, 1957.

Kremer, Alfred von. *Geschichte der herrschenden Ideen des Islams.* Leipzig, 1868.

———. *Kulturgeschichte des Orients.* Vienna, 1875–77.

———. *Streifzuge auf dem Gehiete des Islam.* Leipzig, 1873.

———. *Über das Budget der Einnahmen unter der Regierung des Hārūn ar-Rashīd.* 7th I. C. O. Vienna, 1887.

———. *Über das Einnahmenbudget des Abbasiden Reiches.* Vienna, 1887.

Kurd, 'Alī, M., ed. *Rasa'il al-bulaghā'.* Cairo, 1374/1954.

Lambton, A. K. S. *Landlord and Peasant in Persia.* 2nd edition. Oxford, 1969.

Laoust, Henri. "Classification des sectes dans le *Farq* d'al-Baghdādī." *REI* 29(1961):19–59.

———. "L'Hérésiographie musulmane sous les Abbasides." *Cahiers de Civilization Medievale* (1967), pp. 157–78.

———. *Les Schismes dans l'Islam.* Paris, 1965.

LeStrange, Guy. *The Lands of the Eastern Caliphate.* London, 1905. (reprint, 1966).

Levy, Reuben. "Persia and the Arabs." In *Legacy of Persia.* Oxford, 1953.

Lewis, Bernard. "The Regnal Titles of the First Abbasid Caliphs." In *Dr. Zakir Husayn Presentation Volume*. New Delhi, 1968. Pp. 13–22.
Lokkegaard, F. *Islamic Taxation in the Classic Period*. Copenhagen, 1950.
Madelung, W. "Bemerkungen zur imamitischen firaq-literatur." *Islam* 43(1967): 483–92.
———. "The Identity of Two Yemenite Historical Manuscripts." *Journal of New Eastern Studies* 32(1973):175–80.
Margoliouth, D. S. *Lectures on Arabic Historians*. Calcutta, 1930.
Marquet, Yves. "Le S̄ī'isme au IXe siècle á travers l'histoire de Ya'qūbī." *Arabica* 19(1972):101–36.
Markwart, J. *A Catalogue of the Provincial Capitals of Ērānshahr*. Edited by G. Messina. Rome, 1931.
Mason, Herbert. "The Role of the Azdite Muhallibid Family in Marw's anti-Umayyad Power Struggle." *Arabica* 14(1967):191–207.
Melikoff, Irene. *Abū Muslim, le "Porte-Hache" du Khorassan*. Paris, 1962.
Moscati, S. "Le Califat d'al-Hadi." *Studia Orientalia* 13(1948):3–28.
———. "Nuovi studi storici sul califatti di al-Mahdī." *Orientalia* 15(1946):155–79.
———. "La Revolta di 'Abd al-Ḡabbār contro il califfo al-Manṣūr." *RRAL* 8(1947):613–15.
———. "Studi storici sul califatti di al-Mahdī." *Orientalia* 14(1945):300–354.
———. "Studi su Abū Muslim." *RRAL* 8(1949–50):323–335, 474–95, part 5, 89–105.
Mottahedeh, Roy. "The Shu'ūbiyya Controversy and the Social History of Early Islamic Iran." *IJMES* 7(1976):161–82.
Nadvi, Syed S. "The Origins of the Barmakids." *Islamic Culture* 6(1932):19–28.
Nafīsī, Sa'īd. *Māh-i nakhshab*. Tehran, 1328/1950.
———. *Tārīkh-i khāndān-i ṭāhirī*. Tehran, 1335/1956.
Nagavī, S. 'Alī. *'Aqā'id-i mazdak*. Tehran, n. d.
Nagel, T. *Untersuchungen zur Entstehung des abbasidischen Kalifates*. Bonn, 1972. Bonn, 1972.
Nizamu'd-Din, M. *Introduction to the Jawāmi'u'l-ḥikāyāt*. London, 1929.
Nöldeke, T. *Sketches From Eastern History*. Translated by J. S. Black. Edinburgh, 1892 (reprint, Beirut, 1963).
Nomani, Farhad. "Notes on the Economic Obligations of Peasants in Iran, 300–1600 A.D." *Iranian Studies* 10(1977):62–83.
———. "The Origin and Development of Feudalism in Iran." *Taḥqīqāt-i iqtiṣādī* 9(1972):5–61.
Nyberg, H. S. *Die Religionem des alten Iran*. Leipzig, 1938.
Obermann, J. "Political Theology in Early Islam." *JAOS* 55(1935):138–63.
Omar, Farouq. *The 'Abbāsid Caliphate 132/750*–170/786. Baghdad, 1969.
———. *al-'Abbāsiyūn al-awā'il*. Baghdad, 1390/1970.
———. *'Abbāsiyyāt: Studies in the History of the Early Abbasids*. Baghdad, 1976.
———. "Politics and the Problem of Succession in the Early Abbasid Caliphate, 132/750–158/775." *Islamic Quarterly* 18(1974):31–43.
———. "The Nature of the Iranian Revolts in the Early Islamic Period." *Islamic Culture* 48(1974):1–9.

———. "The Relations Between the Mu'tazilites and the Abbasids Before al-Ma'mūn." *Sumer* 32(1976):189–94.

Parvīz, 'Abbās. *Az 'arab ta dayālamah.* Tehran, 1339/1961.

Patton, W. M. *Aḥmed b. Hanbal and the Miḥna.* Leiden, 1897.

Pellat, Charles. *The Life and Works of Jahiz.* Berkeley, 1969.

———. "La 'Nābita' de Djāḥiẓ (un document important pour l'histoire politico-religieuse de l'Islam)." *Annales, Institut des Etudes Orientales* 5(1950): 302–25.

Peterson, E. L. *'Alī and Mu'āwiyah in Early Arabic Tradition.* Copenhagen, 1964.

Petrushevskii, I. P. *Islām dar Īrān.* Translated by Karīm Kashāvarz.

———. "K Istorii rabstva v khalifate VII-X vekov." *Narodii Azii i Afriki* (1971(3)), pp. 60–67.

Pigulevskaya, N. et al. *Istoriya Irana s drevneishikh vremen do kontsa XVIII veka.* Translated by Karim Kashāvarz. *Tārīkh-i īrān.* Tehran, 1354/1976.

———. *Les Villes de l'état iranien aux époques parthe et sassanide.* Paris, 1963.

al-Qāḍī, W. "The Development of the Term *Ghulāt* in Muslim Literature With Special Reference to the Kaysāniyya." *Akten VII Kong. Arabistik.* Göttingen, 1974. Pp. 295–319.

Rifā'ī, A. *'Aṣr al-Ma'mūn.* Cairo, 1347/1928.

Ritter, H. "Muhammadanische Häresiographien." *Islam* 18(1929):34–55.

Rosenthal, Franz. *A History of Muslim Historiography.* Leiden, 1968.

Sadighi, G. H. *Les Mouvements religieux iraniens.* Paris,, 1938.

Ṣafwat, A. Z. *Jamharat rasā'il al-'arab.* Cairo, 1937.

Samadi, S. B. "Some Aspects of the Arab-Iranian Culture from the Earliest Times Up to the Fall of Baghdad." *Islamic Culture* 26(1952):32–49.

———. "The Struggle Between the Two Brothers al-Amīn and al-Ma'mūn." *Islamic Culture* 32(1958):99–120.

———. "The Theory of the State and Administration Under the Abbasids." *Islamic Culture* 29(1955):120–50.

Samarrā'ī, 'Abd Allah. *al-Ghuluw wa'l-firaq al-ghāliyya.* Baghdad, 1972.

Sayili, Aydin and Frye, R. N. "Turks in the Middle East Before the Saljuqs." *JAOS* 63(1943):194–207.

Scarcia, G. "Lo Scambio di lettere tra Hārūn al-Rašīd e Ḥamza al-Ḥārigī." *Annali dell'Instituto Universitario Orientale di Napoli* 14(1964):623–45.

Sezgin, Fuat. *Geschichte des Arabischen Schriftums.* Leiden, 1967.

Shaban, M. *The Abbasid Revolution.* Cambridge, 1970.

———. *Islamic History A.D. 750–1055.* Cambridge, 1970.

Sharīf, M. *al-Sirā' bayna'l-'arab wa'l-mawālī.* Cairo, 1954.

Skladenek, Bogdan. "Settlements in Gharchistan During the Early Islamic Period." *Rocznik Orientalistyczny* 34(1971):57–71.

Sourdel, Dominique. "Les Circonstances de la mort de Ṭāhir Ier au Ḫurāsān en 207/828." *Arabica* 5(1958):66–69.

———. "La Politique religieuse du calife 'abbāside al-Ma'mūn." *REI* 30 (1962):27–48.

———. *Le Vizirat 'Abbāside.* Damascus, 1959–60.

Spuler, B. *Iran in Frühislamischer Zeit.* Wiesbaden, 1952.

———, ed. *Wüstenfeld-Mahler'sche Vergleichungs-tabellen.* Wiesbaden, 1961.

Storey, Charles. *Persian Literature: A Bio-Bibliographical Survey*. London, 1927–39.

Thomson, W. "The Sects and Islam." *Muslim World* 39(1949):208–22.

Tskitishvili, Otar. "Two Questions Connected with the Topography of the Oriental City in the Early Middle Ages." *Journal of the Economic and Social History of the Orient* 14(1971):311–20.

Tucker, W. F. "Abū Manṣūr al-'Ijlī and the Manṣūriyya: a study in medieval terrorism." *Islam* 54(1977):66–76.

———. "al-Mughīra b. Sa'īd and the Mughīriyya." *Arabica* 22(1975):35–47.

Vajda, G. "Les Zindiqs en pays d'Islam au début de la periode abbaside." *RSO* 17(1938):173–229.

Vloten, G. van. *De Opkomst der Abbasiden in Chorasan*. Leiden, 1890.

———. *Recherches sur la domination arabe*. Amsterdam, 1894.

Waines, D. "The Third Century Internal Crisis of the Abbasids." *Journal of the Economic and Social History of the Orient*. 20(1977):282–306.

Walker, J. "New Coin Evidence from Sistan." *JRAS* (1935), pp. 115–21.

Watt, W. Montgomery. *The Formative Period of Islamic Thought* Edinburgh, 1973.

———. "The Reappraisal of 'Abbāsid Shī'ism." In *Arabic and Islamic Studies in Honour of H. A. R. Gibb*. London, 1966. Pp. 638–54.

Wellhausen, J. *The Arab Kingdom and its Fall*. Translated by Margaret Weir. Calcutta, 1927 (reprint, Beirut, 1963).

———. *The Religio-Political Factions in Early Islam*. Translated by R. C. Ostle and S. M. Walzer. Amsterdam, 1975.

Wiet, Gaston. "L'Empire neo-Byzantine des Omayyades et l'Empire neo-Sassanide des Abbasides." *Cahiers de l'Histoire Mondiale* 1(1953):63–70.

Yakubovskii, A. Y. "Vosstanie Mukanny: Drizhenie hyudei v belyka odezhdakh." *Sovetskoe Vostokovedenie* 5(1948):35–54.

Yūsufī, G. H. *Abū Muslim, sardār-i khurāsān*. Tehran, 1345/1967.

Zambaur, E. K. M. *Manuel de généalogie et de chronologie pour l'histoire de l'Islam*. Hanover, 1927.

Zarrīnkūb, 'Abd al-Ḥusayn. *Dau Qarn Sukūt*. Tehran, 1344/1965.

———. *Tārīkh-i īrān ba'd az islām*. Tehran, 1343/1964.

Index

Abū'l-Najm 'Imrān b. Ismā'īl: 47, 85, 104
Abū'l-Mughīra: 160
Abū'l-Nu'mān b. Yaḥyā al-Ṭā'ī: 141
Abū'l-Waḍḍāḥ: see 'Īsā b. Shubayl
Abū Mu'ādh al-Faryābī: 166
Abū Muḥammad Ziyād: 36
Abū Mūsā: see 'Īsā b. Ibrāhīm
Abū Muslim, 'Abd al-Raḥman b. Muslim: 25, 39, 40, 41, 42, 43, 45, 46, 47, 48, 49, 50, 51, 52, 53, 54, 55, 56, 57, 58, 73, 74, 75, 76, 77, 78, 79, 80, 81, 82, 83, 84, 85, 86, 87, 89, 90, 91, 92, 93, 100-117, 125, 126, 127, 129, 130, 131, 132, 133, 138, 144, 147, 157, 159, 163, 164, 165, 182, 190, 192, 193, 194
Abū Muslim sects (Abū Muslimiyya, etc.): 129, 130-133
Abū Naṣr: see Mālik b. al-Haytham
Abū Salama, Ḥafṣ b. Sulaymān: 29, 33-34, 40, 41, 46, 81, 82, 107-108
Abū Ṣāliḥ: see Kāmil b. al-Muẓaffar
Abū Sharāḥīl: 52
Abū Turāb: 82
Abū 'Ubayd Allah: 164
Abū 'Ubayda: 127
Ādharbayjān: 41, 102, 147, 180
Ādharūya al-Majūsī: 136
ahl al-bayt: 31
Aḥmad b. Asad: 166
Aḥmad b. Ḥanbal: 181
Aḥmad b. Muḥammad Zamchī: 75-76
Ahwāz: 42, 147
'ajam: passim
al-Ajtham, prefect of Marw al-Rudh: 134
Akhbar al-'abbas: 35-36, 40, 49, 53, 54, 57
al-'Alā' b. Ḥarīth: 48, 51
'Alī b. 'Abd Allah b. al-'Abbās: 27, 28, 37, 101
'Alī b. Abī Ṭālib (caliph/*imām*): 20, 27, 28, 83
'Alī b. 'Īsā b. Māhān: 158, 170, 171, 172, 173, 174, 176, 177, 178, 179, 197
'Alī b. Juday' al-Kirmānī: 56, 57, 58, 79
Ālīn: 50, 52
al-Amīn, Muḥammad (caliph): 165, 174, 175-180
amīr āl muḥammad: 106
'Āmir b. 'Imrān: 140
'Āmir b. Ismā'īl: 40

Balādhurī (historian): 31, 34, 81, 100, 127, 129
Bal'amī (historian): vi, 48, 51, 128, 134, 135, 141, 163, 173
Balāshjird: 56
Balkh: 13, 16, 20, 33, 37, 38, 48, 51, 52, 79, 86-87, 89, 138, 139, 160, 161, 171, 173, 174
Barāz: 132-133, 160
Bardha'a: 41-42
Barkath: 112
Barkūkiyya (sect): 131
Barmakids (see also al-Faḍl b. Yaḥyā, Ja'far b. Yaḥyā, and Khālid b. Barmak): 168, 170, 172, 176, 197
Barthold, W.: 105
Bassām b. Ibrāhīm: 78, 110
Bayhaq: 22
Bayhasiyya (sect): 41
Baylaqān: 41-42
Bihāfarīd: 90-92, 93, 105, 129, 136, 145, 193
Bihāfarīdiyya (sect): 92, 133, 136, 143, 192
Bīnah: 19
Bishr al-Sa'dī: 51
Bishr b. Anīf al-Yarbū'ī: 56
Bisṭām b. Layth al-Taghlabī: 41
Bloch, Marc: 18
Bukayr b. Māhān: 29, 30, 31, 32, 33, 36, 38, 39, 40, 41, 49
Bukhara: 57, 87, 88, 89, 106, 111-112, 139, 140, 141, 142, 143, 166, 168, 174, 175
Bukhār-khudā (see also Tughshada, Bunyat b. Tughshada, and Qutayba b. Tughshada): 44, 45, 106, 190
Būnjikath: 141
Bunyāt b. Tughshāda: 146, 190
Būshanj (Pūshang, etc.): 16, 101, 134, 166
Buway': 49
Buzurgmihr: 101, 102

Central Asia: 14, 73, 86, 89, 132, 138, 139, 140, 144, 145, 173
China: 13, 89, 90

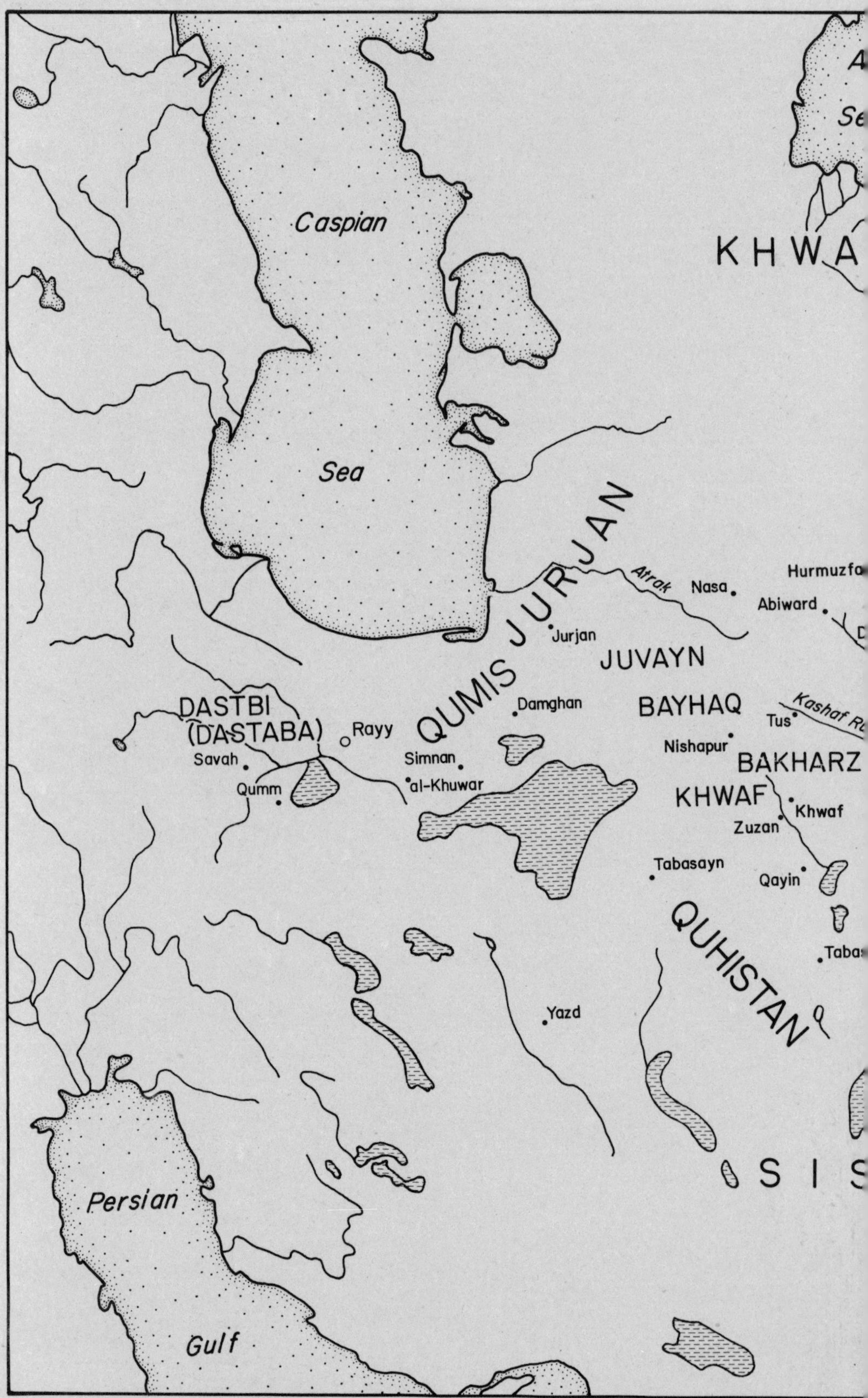

Caspian
Sea
Persian
Gulf
KHWA
JURJAN
Atrak
Nasa
Hurmuzfa
Abiward
Jurjan
JUVAYN
QUMIS
Damghan
BAYHAQ
Kashaf R
Tus
Nishapur
BAKHARZ
DASTBI
(DASTABA)
Rayy
Savah
Qumm
Simnan
al-Khuwar
KHWAF
Khwaf
Zuzan
Tabasayn
Qayin
QUHISTAN
Yazd
SIS